Daughter of a Revolutionary

Daughter of a Revolutionary

Natalie Herzen and the Bakunin-Nechayev Circle

Edited with an Introduction by

MICHAEL CONFINO

Translated by Hilary Sternberg
and Lydia Bott

LIBRARY PRESS
LaSalle Illinois 61301
1973

First published in the United States
of America in 1974 by
Library Press, LaSalle, Illinois

Printed in Great Britain
by Watmoughs Limited
Bradford and London

International Standard Book Number: 0-912050-15-2
Library of Congress Catalog Card Number: 73-86555

Summary of Contents*

*A detailed Table of Contents appears in the back at pages 413-6

Illustrations   between pages 208 and 209

Preface

THIS VOLUME presents a collection of documents by or about Natalie Herzen, eldest daughter of Alexander Herzen, and the events in her life and among Russian *émigrés* in Western Europe in the 1860s and 1870s. An important part of the documents included in this volume is published for the first time. A Note on Sources at the end of the volume gives in detail the references of the texts presented.

The documents have been translated into English by Hilary Sternberg, except for the two letters of Michael Bakunin (items 84 and 85) which have been translated by Lydia Bott. Footnotes and comments are mine, except when otherwise indicated.

It is a great pleasure to acknowledge the help extended to me by the Département des Manuscrits at the Bibliothèque Nationale in Paris, where all the unpublished documents are to be found, and by the Widener Library at Harvard University in Cambridge, Mass. The original work on the Bakunin-Nechayev affair was done while I was a Fellow at the Russian Research Center at Harvard University in 1966, and resulted in several articles and publications of documents in the *Cahiers du Monde russe et soviétique*. I should like to express my gratitude to the Center for its friendly hospitality and support, and to the *Cahiers* for their kind permission to reprint here some of these documents.

I also wish to thank and convey my appreciation to those who have helped me in many different ways during the course of this study: Mme Tatiana Bakounine-Ossorguine, Miss Eva Duvdevani, Miss Dorrit Landes, Mr Jerome Singer, and my good friends and colleagues Professor Richard Pipes, Professor Edward Shils and Professor Walter Grab.

MICHAEL CONFINO
Jerusalem—Tel Aviv
August 1973

Introduction

THIS IS A STORY told by its participants: in letters, diaries, pamphlets, and memoirs. In presenting it here, the historian took mainly the role of a story-teller, this very old form of his craft, and, even more, that of an archivist who, through good luck, discovered new sources, then pieced them together to let them tell, bit by bit, their own tale.

This story has one central character and two partly over-lapping sets of events. The central character, who gives unity and continuity to the story and events, is Natalie (Tata) Herzen, eldest daughter of the brilliant Russian publicist, memoirist, and radical thinker, Alexander Herzen. She partici-pated in this drama of events, and left in her letters (published here for the first time in any language) and in her diary a direct, lucid, and sometimes moving testimony. These letters cover about twenty years of her life—from 1860, when she was a young girl of sixteen, through the late 1870s—and these years are also the chronological framework of the story. Around this main character appear, besides Tata's father, well-known figures from the Western political and intellectual scene, as well as from the liberal and radical emigration: Garibaldi, Mazzini, Henri de Rochefort, Charles Bradlaugh, Turgenev, Mme Viardot, Liszt, Vyrubov, Gabriel Monod, Malwida von Meysenbug, Ogarev, Bakunin, Nechayev, Lopatin, Karl Marx, along with less known personalities such as Valeriano Tassinari, Herzen's cook in London, and Babette, a housemaid in Nice.

As I have suggested, there are two main episodes—and existential dimensions—in which the *dramatis personae* appear and act. The first is provided by Herzen's family circle, the relations within it (particularly between father and daughter), and its connections with society and the different milieus,

9

Daughter of a Revolutionary

Western and Russian, which the Herzens happened to meet in their peregrinations. This is essentially the complex and pathetic problem of *émigré* life, built upon the necessity to secure some sort of immediate stability, and upon the hope that it is bound to be transitory and short-lived. It is, too, the problem of bringing up children in one culture (or cultures)— French, English, German, Italian—while expecting them to remain attached to yet another—the Russian—and to live one day in its midst; and till then, desiring intensely to prevent the estrangement of these children from that distant fatherland, its mother-tongue and the "spirit" of its people. Finally, it is the problem of men who subscribe to radical ideas about the world and society, while being reluctant to apply them in their family affairs and relations. Alexander Herzen's problem was how to combine his aristocratic paternalistic bent with his radical views and progressive ideas. As a result, Tata Herzen's personal problem became whom to marry and when, and how to combine her intimate feelings with her father's opinions on the matter. In the end she never married.

The second episode pertains to the life of Natalie Herzen as well as to the history of the Russian revolutionary and Western socialist movements. Its course and plot are woven within the singular collusion of the old anarchist Michael Bakunin and the young revolutionist Sergey Nechayev. Besides the ideological and psychological aspects of this alliance, which will be sketched below, this is also the story of a young and wealthy woman, brought up in an aristocratic family as an over-protected child, bred in radical ideas, who suddenly confronted "revolution", if not as it really was, at least as Nechayev thought it really should be—a revolution requiring the use of violence, murder (including liquidation, "when necessary", of "brothers in revolution"), deceit, blackmail, and robbery. This brand of radicalism, which has not lost a bit of its relevance one hundred years later, was rather different from the one that Tata used to admire in her father. In this adventure and in the happenings known as "*l'affaire* Nechayev", Tata's role and her background are linked again, and the testimony she left to posterity provides many a clue to this *affaire*.

10

Let me now turn in more detail to each of these two episodes.

I

Exile and Émigré Life

The opening period need only be summarized here. The 1860s were for Alexander Herzen a time of ceaseless quest for some sort of stability in his family life, residence, and public activity. Paradoxically, as time went by, he moved more and more often from one place to another, while the length of his stop-overs became shorter. Herzen longed for Paris when he stayed in Geneva, and when he visited Nice he considered settling in Brussels. Around 1866–7, after twenty years spent in emigration, which he came to regard as one of the greatest mistakes in his life,[1] Herzen already had lost all hope of ever seeing Russia again, and he believed less and less in his ability to influence the course of events in his homeland. Following his painful failure on the issue of the Polish uprising in 1863, *The Bell (Kolokol)*, his personal periodical, never regained its previous fame and wide audience. Autocracy appeared more entrenched than ever, and more resistant to change than Herzen had believed. As his hopes in reforms carried out by an enlightened Tsar faded away, so Herzen's liberal sympathizers turned away from him, publicly declaring that he was a dangerous revolutionary whose "bloody banner" provoked their "indignation and disgust".[2] At the same time, the political groups within the young generation of Russian radicals began to consider him as too moderate, as a liberalizing *grand seigneur* stuffed with money, "a restless old man who had lost his wits", "an interesting fossilized bone", and finally as "a dead man". In a pamphlet published in 1867, A. Serno-Solovevich wrote to him:

> Yes, the young generation has understood you. Having understood you, it has turned away from you in disgust. . . You are a poet, a painter, an artist, a story-teller, a novelist—anything you please, but *not* a political leader and still less a political thinker, the founder of a school and a doctrine.[3]

In this "polarization" of sorts, between a stubborn autocracy and a hardening radicalism, Herzen felt more estranged and rejected by the men of the "young emigration". This was for him a kind of second exile. The first began when he left Russia in 1847. He now found himself outside the milieu that for many years had admired him, and had served him abroad as a substitute for Russia.

Twice exiled, then, with no disciples, Herzen transferred to his children some of his lost hopes and unfulfilled ambitions. He strove not only to give them a broad humanistic education, but also to make them genuine Russians who one day would bring back to Russia his name and his fame. In this respect, as time went on, Alexander (his eldest son) and Olga appeared as complete failures. The late 1860s saw Herzen's attempts to "save" Tata as his only heir and as the last one who could save his moral and intellectual legacy from oblivion.

But the hardships were immense, not only because of the fluctuating paths of Herzen's *émigré*-life, but also because of the peculiar set-up of his family relationships. He never recovered entirely (at least, so he believed) from the death of his wife, Natalie, which occurred so soon after the unfortunate Herwegh affair, and her attempt to beget a "triangle" of "love and friendship". He himself created now such a "triangle"; and he began to live with the wife of his lifelong friend, Nathalie Tuchkova-Ogareva, who gave him three children: Elizaveta (Liza), born 4 September 1858 and who was to commit suicide in 1875 at the age of seventeen; and the twins Alexey and Elena, called Lelya-boy and Lelya-girl, born in 1861, and who died of diphtheria in 1864.

But the "triangle" as such was not the main source of delicate and ambiguous situations. These stemmed chiefly from the psychological make-up of Tuchkova-Ogareva: a passionate and unsatisfied woman, impulsive and immoderate, lacking the gift of happiness and morbidly eager for self-humiliation, jealous and capricious and self-pitying. The care for the twins put an unbearable strain on her in spite of her love for children; their death exacerbated all her traits of character. More than that, she never succeeded in winning the affection of Olga, Herzen's second daughter, while easily obtaining the contemptuous dislike of Malwida von Meysenbug, Olga's governess, herself a frustrated and touchy person with whom she was at daggers drawn. This fact made it practically impossible to bring together the whole family, and completely estranged Olga from her father and from everything Russian, including the language. Thus, thanks to Tuchkova-Ogareva, the relatively simple "triangle" (simple, mainly because of the sweet and innocuous Ogarev) became a strained and broken "hexagon", involving also Liza, Tata, Malwida and Olga, and even occasional outsiders.

This was the "pattern of coordinates" into which Tata's life in the 1860s was set. Under the affectionate and watchful (although often distant) eye of her father she studied, read, and tried lessons in painting and music—all in all, the current "good education" of aristocratic or upper-middle-class girls. She travelled, as *les voyages forment la jeunesse*, sometimes with her father, more often with other members of the family, and (once) even alone. She tried unsuccessfully to find a *modus vivendi* for the complex "hexagon" of her father's relations with Tuchkova-Ogareva, his children and hers, and Malwida von Meysenbug, and to put an end to the endless *chassé-croisé* of all of them travelling in all directions. Here and there she met people, most of them casually and for a short time—encounters with no follow-up, never to be rewarded by lasting bonds. Her only friend, or at least confidante, seems to have been Maria (Masha) Reichel, *née* Ern; but Tata almost never stayed for long in Berne, where Masha lived. The only place she really liked was Florence and her brother's milieu of young intellectuals; but Herzen disliked the city and visited it only briefly. The divergent attitudes and feelings of Tata and Herzen towards Florence may have had one and the same source: Florence and Sasha's circle of young scientists offered a human milieu where one could integrate, feel a sense of belonging, take roots. This is what Tata was longing for—and that is what Herzen feared. For one possible outcome might well have been cultural assimilation—and social and geographical rootlessness was the price of avoiding it. Herzen paid this price and never put down *new* roots anywhere; he felt morally entitled to require it from his children too. But Herzen had once had roots and found substitutes for them; his children had neither. Moreover, for Herzen, emigration and exile were the result of a deliberate choice (at least at the outset); his children found it a biological and geographical *fait accompli*. In making this choice, Herzen acted as a Russian aristocrat prompted by his deep convictions and radical ideas. Existentially, the motivation was essential for perpetuating the attitude. Herzen was driven therefore to instil in his children Russian aristocratic attitudes and radical views—enough to make them reject autocracy, but not too much to lead them to a rejection of Russia herself.

Tata hoped that settling in Dante's city might bring to an end her being a *fuoruscita*. She seems to have been indifferent to the negative undertones which her father found in "assimilation". In a way she may have wished it. At one point, she began thinking of love and marriage; but on this matter, too, she immediately felt that her father had quite clear-cut opinions, and also expectations that she would comply with them. On a similar matter, and in Florence, while Herzen was (as usual) far away, there occurred the first dramatic episode narrated in detail in Tata's papers.

The *"Affaire Penisi"*

A painful, sentimental accident, this episode seriously affected Natalie's health and emotional balance, and also proved an ordeal for Herzen, to whom fate in the past had not been kind on matters of personal and family relations. It left a sad imprint on the last months of his life that made him say: "The story with Penisi was for me a most bitter blow and it strengthened my outlook's scepticism which was quite strong anyway. I do not consider anything anymore as certain. . ."[4] Thus, a relationship which otherwise might have been a minor incident, the *"affaire* Penisi" became by its consequences a trying event for Tata, then aged twenty-five.

The incident itself may be sketched in a few words. Penisi was a blind, twenty-seven-year-old Sicilian nobleman, with some talent for music and languages, who made Italian translations of some of Alexander Herzen's writings. He met Natalie in April 1869 in Florence where she was visiting, fell in love, courted her and proposed to marry her. Rebuked, he had (or simulated) a nervous depression, pondered committing suicide and, in any case, managed to bring that to Natalie's knowledge by the intermediary of Doctor E. Levier, a friend of his and of the Herzens. Although impressed and worried by the news, Natalie did not yield in spite of some hesitations. Disappointed, Penisi adopted another strategy and apparently threatened to kill Tata and members of her family, especially Sasha. Did he also spread the rumour in Florence that she was his mistress in order to compromise her? It seems so, according to several allusions scattered in Herzen's letters. [5]

This is where the consequences of this incident, which were almost a tragedy for Tata and her father, begin. Distressed by Penisi's threats (and eventually by the rumours), Tata had a genuine nervous depression, along with hallucinations, paranoic manifestations, fears that people were coming at night to kill Sasha, and periods of complete prostration interrupted by violent bursts of tears. Informed on 28 October of Tata's health condition, Herzen left Paris the next day and arrived in Florence three days later. He took care of Natalie with boundless devotion and certainly contributed more than anyone else to her relatively rapid recovery. On 18 November, although not entirely in good health, Natalie could leave Florence with Herzen who was impatient to take her away from this city which, in his words, he "did not like in the past, and hated now". [6]

For Alexander Herzen—who at that time nourished the hope "not to have to suffer new ordeals", and believed that "life, tired by so many obstacles, will proceed on its way more quietly"[7]—Natalie's adventure revived bitter memories of the wound he suffered seventeen years earlier from his wife's affair with Herwegh. Memories which Tata involuntarily stressed by saying: "I too have found my Herwegh."[8] Coming to life again, this pain that had broken Herzen's heart occurred at a difficult moment in his family life. He no longer hoped to re-create a link with Olga, by then completely estranged from his intellectual concerns and from everything Russian, and entirely under the influence and authority of Malwida von Meysenbug.[9] Not long before, he was deeply disappointed by the spirit of independence of his son Alexander who married without waiting for his father's advice and consent; he was even more disappointed by Sasha's choice which was leading him, in Herzen's eyes, to "a stupid and pointless ruin", because of the female Sasha married, a young Italian girl of modest social origin whom Herzen considered a plebeian "without wealth, without culture, and without education", a woman who did not know anything "beyond the primitive popular life", and who made through this marriage "a leap—unfortunately too hasty—from that sort of life to a nearly seigniorial one".[10]

Thus, Sasha and Olga were "lost"—the former by way of a deplorable *mésalliance*; the latter in the hands of the woman whom Bakunin called "the mad Pomeranian and Wagnero-Germanizing virgin", and whom Herzen considered sick of "hymenomania" with regard to his daughter.[11] These two children "lost", there remained Tata, who, in her father's eyes, best understood his aspirations and had le *"génie" russe*; hence Herzen's confidence in her, added to a particular fondness stemming from the "psychological similarities" which he found between Tata and her mother Natalie.[12] The *"affaire Penisi,"* thus, struck the child whom Herzen loved most and in whom he set his hopes towards the end of his life.

If we keep this in mind, Herzen's attitude upon his arrival in Florence should not come as a surprise. After being told the circumstances of the incident, he accused not only Penisi, but also everybody connected in some way with the story, including Sasha and Malwida, whom he believed guilty of negligence, inconsideration and lack of understanding of the coming tragedy. As for Teresina (Sasha's wife), her *sang-froid* seemed to him dictated, at least in part, by "the legitimate war of the plebeian against the privileged".[13] He was also convinced that only his personal intervention had saved Tata who, otherwise, would have become mad in the clinical sense of the word.[14] Herzen's opinion on that point cannot, of course, be verified; on other points, however, Tata's diary and correspondence give more reliable information.

But first of all: did she love Penisi? The answer Tata gave to herself during the several weeks preceding the crisis was: "I don't know", or, as she said to the young Sicilian, *"un petit peu"*. Anyhow, when the latter expressed his feelings, Tata leaned towards using gentle means: firstly, out of consideration for a cripple; secondly, in order to avoid scandal or misfortune; and thirdly, as she wrote to her father, in order to give herself time for reflection before coming to any decision.[15] On that subject she wrote to him in her letter of 2 October 1869:

> My poor, dear Papasha, don't be alarmed and exaggerate; after all I have promised nothing and am in no way tied. Why do you want to write to everyone about it? It will only cause a sensation. Neither Sasha nor Meysenbug knows anything; I have not spoken to anyone, and however tormented I have felt, I have been outwardly calm... When I told P[enisi] that I *must* go to Paris (that was after I had received your last letter but one, so do not say that I was acting contrary to your advice), and that I was promising nothing, he saw that I wanted to end it all, and so began begging and pleading, trying to persuade me, and reproaching me; how I bore it without giving way I do not know; he was ill again. I thought that it was all over and I wanted to leave Florence at once... Dear Papasha, there is nothing that can be done *immediately* or *before* my departure without causing a sensation...[16]

Then, after explaining that one cannot treat a cripple as one does other people, Tata goes on:

> Let me finish this little by little; *I promise you* I shall not tie myself down in any way. I assure you that this is the best thing, Papasha. Please don't write to anyone, it will only result in a scandal; and if you still wish me to end the affair immediately, write again and I will obey your desire; but think seriously if it would not be better to act cautiously and gradually; to my mind it is decidedly better; what are you afraid of? I will not make any promises to him except to write and send him translations as he has requested. With anyone else one would have to take abrupt action, but with him one cannot, really one cannot... Write to me again, and I promise you I will obey your wishes.[17]

Herzen, who since his son's marriage feared that "Tata too may make a foolish *coup d'état*",[18] vigorously opposed this "cautious and gradual" solution, apprehending that it might be misunderstood by Penisi, appear as a commitment, and cause an irreversible course leading Tata to marry him. This contingency seemed odious to Herzen. As he wrote later on: "The thought that Tata, this pure and intelligent being, could become the wife of a monster, the thought of a love without sight, of a future shaped by long years of sedentary life—this thought didn't let me sleep."[19] Herzen insisted, therefore, in his letters, that Tata put an end to these relations and leave Florence at once. Tata decided to comply. Remembering her father's sorrow provoked by the "fatal misfortune" of Sasha's "disobedient marriage",[20] she wanted to spare him these emotions, stiffened her attitude towards Penisi, and announced her departure for Paris. We know the rest.

One last detail should be added to the sequence of events preceding Tata's nervous breakdown. On 6 October 1869 Tata wrote to her father:

> Dear Papasha, I don't understand your letter to Malwida;[21] what is it you really want? Is it too difficult for you to arrange for us to live in Paris, or too costly, or do you think that Malwida's consent is too *contre-coeur*?
>
> If your only difficulty is in finding a flat, we can wait a little longer and then stay with Aga for a while, in Geneva, that is. But if life in Paris really is too expensive for you, then name another place. And do not think that you have to do anything to "save" me, as you say. When I thought that I had ended it all with P[enisi] I felt dreadfully sorry for him, and also I was so afraid that he would decide to do something foolish, that I was quite upset, but at the same time I felt liberated and was glad that I had ended it, so do not fear for *me*, I will treat him more and more coolly, which is easier to do by letter, of course; but I would not like you to be hasty on my account, take a flat which is too dear or unsatisfactory, and then have cause for regret. So I *implore* you once more not to think that I need *saving*, not to make a hurried decision because of me. But when everything is ready we will come to you.[22]

This was Tata's last letter to Herzen. On 12 October, writing to Tuchkova-Ogareva, whom Herzen had kept informed of the story, Tata stressed again that she "ended the whole thing" with Penisi, and that Herzen could stop worrying. She adds how much she regrets this stupid incident which now prevents the family from reuniting and settling down in Florence. She deplores that this compels them to choose Paris, which "does not suit our requirements and our means". Finally she begs Nathalie to convince Herzen that, in spite of everything, they can settle down in Florence: "Please let's try it, Nathalie dear. Have a serious talk with Papasha. Perhaps Penisi will go away, perhaps he will behave so quietly and sensibly that I will not have to go away."[23]

Herzen's answer to these two letters of Tata, of 6 and 12 October, is rather disconcerting, and most surprising is his lack of responsiveness to Tata's distress and to the problems tormenting her.[24] As for Tata, one may assume that if she chose, at that point, to dissimulate from her father the real state of things (which led him later to believe that she lied and behaved hypocritically),[25] this was mainly done in order to quiet and spare him the considerable expenses entailed in renting—for her sake—a flat in Paris, which seems to have greatly disturbed Herzen.[26] Perhaps he should not have then insisted so much on that aspect of the matter.

As to the other—romantic—aspect, this was not the first time that Herzen intervened so decisively in Tata's intimate relations and eventual matrimonial projects. She had had in the past several suitors: V. F. Luginin, Prince A. N. Meshchersky, Hugo Schiff. None of them pleased Herzen nor was approved by him, and he let it be known clearly to Tata who, consequently, refrained from cultivating any serious link in order not to annoy him. In this respect her feeling was apparently right, for it seems that Herzen had quite a strong aversion for the very idea that his daughters might marry one day; on that account Ogarev reproached Herzen about being jealous of his daughters, and Maria Reichel earnestly asked him whether he really "preferred that [Tata] should remain a spinster".[27]

But there was another feature, too, complicating Tata's relations with men who expressed their affection and desire to marry her. Tata consistently doubted the sincerity of their feelings, and suspected them of being merely interested in her wealth. She never knew for sure whether they loved the young woman for her own merits or were they attracted to the rich heiress.[28] This attitude was also noticeable in Tata's relations with Nechayev, whom she met a few months later. For, whether or not he put it on when declaring to be in love with her,[29] Tata's reaction was the same as in such cases in the past: she suspected him of seeking to get hold of her money, enlarged in the meantime with her share of the inheritance upon Herzen's death on 21 January 1870.[30] For once she was probably not wrong.

This last theme leads to the second episode of the story, where—switching from love to revolution—a new kind of experience awaited Tata, an experience stemming from the vicissitudes of the meeting, collaboration, and confrontation of two such odd personalities and restless revolutionists as Michael Bakunin and Sergey Nechayev.

II

A short time after the *affaire* Penisi and the death of her father, Natalie Herzen became involved, together with Bakunin, Ogarev and a few other Russian *émigrés*, in one of the most singular episodes in the annals of the Russian revolutionary movement, known as *"l'affaire* Nechayev". Its background dates back to March 1869, when a young man, Sergey Nechayev, aged twenty-two, fresh from Russia, irrupted in the life of the old anarchist Michael Bakunin, whose thoughts and activities were engaged at the time in the international socialist movement rather than in Russian affairs. There ensued a political, revolutionary and organizational collaboration oriented towards Russia. After their first encounter, Bakunin wrote this about Nechayev in April 1869:

> At present I am engrossed in Russian affairs. Our youth, theoretically and in practice the most revolutionary in the world, is in great ferment. . . I have here with me now one of those young fanatics who know no doubts, who fear nothing, who realize that many of them will perish at the hands of the government but who nevertheless have decided that they will not relent until the people rise. They are magnificent, these young fanatics. Believers without God and heroes without phrases![31]

Soon thereafter, Nechayev left Switzerland and went back to Russia to continue the establishment of his organization, the

Narodnaya Rasprava (People's Vengeance). He took part in the student movement in Moscow, and along with four other members of his group murdered the student I. Ivanov, another member of the group, under the pretext that he was a *provocateur*. Having thus provoked a wave of arrests, he escaped from Russia and reappeared in Switzerland in January 1870.

Bakunin was impatiently waiting for him. Nechayev was more interested in Tata. He tried through various means— persuasion, pressures, declarations of love—to induce her to lend her name, give her money and dedicate her person to the "cause". He mainly succeeded to raise in her the suspicion that he was a *provocateur*.[32] At that time Bakunin was no longer saying that "they were magnificent, these young fanatics", but was severely criticizing the doings of his young "hero" towards his own comrades, including Bakunin himself. He defended his anarchist principles against all kind of "communism" and "authoritarianism", and denounced such tendencies as he discovered in Nechayev. He rejected the *Nechayevshchina* which he called "Machiavellism", "Jesuitism", and "police system", unacceptable as permanent methods of organizing a revolutionary party and carrying on political action. This was said in a letter addressed to Nechayev himself, dated 2 June 1870, which is an essential item of this dossier.[33] Shortly thereafter, Bakunin would decide to put an end to his relations with Nechayev. *"L'affaire* Nechayev", though, was just beginning.

This *affaire* was fated to have a significance quite out of proportion to the stature of the man whose name it bears. It left a lasting imprint on the lives of its participants as well as on the Russian and international revolutionary movements. It drew Natalie Herzen away for the rest of her life from any kind of underground activity and radical ideas. It inflicted on Bakunin a sense of painful failure which marked the beginning of his personal eclipse in the European socialist movement, and—curiously enough—preceded the days of his greatest influence on the Russian populists. It provided Marx with a far-fetched pretext for the expulsion of Bakunin from the First International, and gave Dostoevsky a source of inspiration for his novel, *The Possessed*. Finally, it brought forward, for the first time in the typology of revolutionary action, a case of violence within violence, or, as Albert Camus put it, "violence done to one's brothers". Moreover, it uncovered one of the inner mechanisms which transforms violence into "violence for the sake of violence". (In this respect, *"l'affaire* Nechayev" has not lost a bit of its topicality in our own agitated days of the Japanese *Rengō Sekigun* and the German Baader-Meinhof *Bande.*)

The *affaire* has an odd descent; it also had some curious ingredients.

Bakunin's Young Russia

Perhaps the most curious ingredient, and one that contributed much to turn this episode into an *affaire*, was, as Professor Franco Venturi has put it, "the complex and obscure history of the connection between Bakunin and Nechayev".[34] A "complex and obscure" connection, indeed, which has puzzled contemporaries and historians alike. For one may wonder how an old and experienced revolutionary, possessing wide culture and remarkable intellect, could have fallen under the influence of, and been almost completely mesmerized by, a young man who displayed great skills for mystification and had an enormous energy, but no political experience, a very average intellect and a mediocre general culture. Bakunin, nevertheless, was fond of Nechayev. In his own words: "I loved you deeply and still love you, Nechayev. I firmly, too firmly, believed in you . . ." and he stressed further, ". . . how deeply, how passionately, how tenderly I loved you and believed in you!"[35] A romantic by mental make-up and education, Bakunin, for all his weaknesses and excesses, remained a sentimentalist in his personal relationships; he never lost the capacity to love people, to become attached to them, and to participate sincerely in the vicissitudes of their lives. Nechayev, as Bakunin was to experience to his own detriment, loved revolution and nothing but revolution: that is, as he understood it. This included the fact, detected too late by Bakunin, that Nechayev not only identified himself with the revolutionary cause, but identified the revolutionary cause with himself. It implied, finally, the banning of notions such as honesty, truth, human dignity and the like from the methods of revolutionary action. With Nechayev, "bringing this logic to the bitter end . . . revolution [was] going to be explicitly separated from love and friendship".[36] In a sense, Nechayev had all the faults of Bakunin and none of his qualities.

Thus, the relations between them were based from the first on this essential difference. They lasted as long as it took Bakunin to discover that the ties of friendship which he believed to exist between him and Nechayev did not exist at all. For Nechayev they were non-existent by definition and by "revolutionary consciousness", but also because of his psychological make-up; for, obviously, some of his theoretical positions were chiefly rationalizations of his own limitations, his incapacity to communicate with people, and a hatred accumulated throughout his deprived childhood and adolescence, hostilities which now impregnated his "revolutionary" activity.

To be sure, this does not explain everything in the relations between the two men. Certainly, Bakunin wanted also to use Nechayev for the Russian section of his *Alliance Internationale*. There were, too, as shall be shown, ideological differences between them. Above all, Bakunin seems to have been fascinated by Nechayev's intransigence, his extremist deductions and mystifying silences. His lack of scruples seemed to Bakunin an expression of strength, and his simplistic and primitive reasoning appeared as a primary virtue and almost a folkloric revelation. But Bakunin was neither the first revolutionary nor the last to mistake lack of education for a token of loyalty, and to take roughness as a proof of sincerity. This may be an insufficient explanation as to why Bakunin did love Nechayev; but there were other reasons too: part of them stemmed from Bakunin's character, others from that of Nechayev.

Let us follow Bakunin's testimony in his letter to Nechayev. ". . . I said to myself and to Ogarev that we were both old and unlikely to meet another man more dedicated and more able than you. That is why, if we want to be allied with the Russian cause, we must be allied with you and with no one else."[37]

This turned out to be a mistake, but at the twilight of one's life, while so much remained to be done for the revolution and Russia's liberation, were there many choices left? Nechayev had another invaluable attribute.

> It might be said [Bakunin writes to him] that I have been separated from Russia for *thirty years.* . . . I do not know the real youth in whom I believe, this classless class, this hopeless phalanx of the people's revolution about whom I have written several times and only now gradually begin to learn. . . Thus, before I met you, the real Russian revolutionary youth remained for me *terra incognita.*[38]

Thus, Bakunin thought he rediscovered in Nechayev a genuine Russia—young, revolutionary, generous, and loyal. This appeared to be a new anchor in reality and a sort of "second youth" for Bakunin himself, after years of exile from his native country, and already tired by the "dirty intrigues" of Marx, Moses Hess and Utin, and this "judeo-teutonic" clique that made him feel more and more Germanophobe and anti-semitic.[39] By contrast, Nechayev came as a welcome change and as a ray of hope.

What a bitter disappointment for Bakunin to discover, later on, that Nechayev, the personification of an imaginary Russia, was a crook and a liar, a blackmailer and a tyrant. And what an even greater disappointment to find out that this young man, coming from the people and supposed to carry the instincts of the spontaneous and libertarian revolution, was a "central-ist" and an "authoritarian", that he was striving—like the "Germanic communists"—towards a "revolution from above"; in a word, that he had the major vice which Bakunin attributed to Jews, who (he said) "hate the fury of the masses, and are not anarchists at all".[40]

It was a disappointment as intense as the one-sided, "deep, tender, and passionate" love that Bakunin had had for Nechayev.

Action as the Greatest Good

Even in the days of his painful disillusion, Bakunin did not lose an elemental trust in Nechayev and in his revolutionary future.

This trust was based on another trait of Nechayev which Bakunin clearly acknowledged and which also provides a key for understanding the personalities of the two men.

Shortly after he knew beyond any reasonable doubt, and to his great shame and humiliation,[41] the methods and dealings of his young hero, Bakunin wrote the following to Ogarev, Natalie Herzen, Ozerov and S. Serebrennikov:

> Friends, judging by the letters I have received from various quarters, it seems to me that your council has begun to take too unfavourable a view of our friend the Baron [Nechayev]. I use the word friend, not ironically, but in all seriousness, because I, at least, have not ceased to regard him as the most valuable man amongst us all to the Russian cause, and the purest, or, to use Serebrennikov's expression, the most *saintly* person in the sense of his total dedication to the cause and his utter self-denial, and further, as one endowed with an energy, constancy of will and tireless industry the like of which we have never encountered before. I do not think that any one of you would go as far with his criticism as to deny that he possesses these qualities; it is impossible to deny them, for they stare one in the face. The Baron, then, is a jewel, and one doesn't throw out jewels.[42]

Following this *entrée en matière*, Bakunin pointed out that Nechayev was a man passionately and entirely dedicated to the "cause". He had faults, no doubt, but it was always so in "the stronger and more passionate natures". Moreover, virtuous men who have no faults are usually nonentities. Nechayev had all the qualities as well as all the failings of a fanatic. He had adopted a "false system of Jesuitical devices and lies", but he did not choose this system either by egoism, nor by vanity, ambition, thirst for glory, covetousness, or hunger for power. None of these vices developed in Nechayev; they were stifled by a supreme passion, the passion for revolution or liberation of the people and the hatred for everything that oppresses it. Apart from that, Nechayev was an extremely intelligent, fervently sincere, upright and profoundly earnest man. His utter self-abnegation and total disregard for himself revealed "his profound, highly courageous and virginally pure integrity". Finally, being not an egoist or an intriguer, Nechayev was "a deeply loving man who becomes passionately attached to people, and is ready to give away everything to his friends".

In a word, he was a "man filled with love", who had "a tender heart".

Over and above that, Nechayev's greatest quality was that *he acted*. This distinguished him from so many others, would-be revolutionaries and dabbling dilettantes who were content to wag their tongues, scratch on paper and play at revolution. Nechayev, with extraordinary energy, was translating his words into deeds and his intentions into facts. He represented the advancing revolution and truly worked for the realization of the people's aspirations, which—alas!—till then, were only the subject of sterile debates. Nechayev was a *man of action* and therein lay his greatness.

It is not necessary to analyse at length this characterization of Nechayev, to dissect Bakunin's impressions, and point out his errors of judgement in drawing this astonishing and, at times, bewildering portrait. The most striking example is obviously Bakunin's belief that Nechayev was "a man filled with love". In fact, most of the testimonies left by people who knew Nechayev prove the contrary. They clearly indicate that his cardinal fault (which also bred several others) was a mixture of hatred and contempt. "Intense hatred" was, according to Vera Zasulich, Nechayev's main trait; and "this hatred was directed not only against the government and the exploiters, but against society as a whole and against educated society . . . against the rich and the poor, against conservatives, liberals, and radicals", and even against the young men and women he tried to enrol, and for whom he had nothing but disdain. "These children of that hated society, linked to it by innumerable bonds . . . and striving towards love rather than hatred, could not be for him but *tools or means*, and definitely not comrades or disciples."[43] On love Nechayev had a very personal view, which he once revealed to P. Uspensky, his closest collaborator in the People's Vengeance: "To love the people is to lead them to the *mitraille* [the grape-shot]."

On the other hand, Nechayev's major quality, according to all testimonies, was his indomitable energy. "Nechayev possessed an energy which astounded everybody who knew him," asserted A. Kuznetsov at his trial.[44] "In forty years of life, I've never met an energy of that kind," marvelled Ivan Pryzhov, author of a *History of Taverns in Russia*, who attributed this energy to Nechayev's social origin: "That's what become the children of the people when they obtain a bit of favourable conditions."[45] This dominant trait of Nechayev suggests an important aspect of his psychological make-up; and it was clearly perceived by an officer of the Secret Police who noted that Nechayev was a revolutionary not by conviction but rather by temperament (and Nechayev admitted to seeing himself in this way, not without a certain amount of satisfaction).[46]

It appears that Nechayev, driven by a hatred that admitted no postponement, had rationalized this dominant and consuming quality of energy, and had not only adopted it as a line of conduct, but made of it "a principle": the principle of immediate action and of the primacy of the deed. Probably this feeling of necessity for immediate action led him to reject the need and usefulness of theory, including revolutionary theory, a standpoint which would itself later become a theory *sui generis*. It was the "theory of action here and now", leading to the idea of "revolution now or never", and implying that the greatest enemies of the "cause" are immobility and truce (and, consequently, any preparatory work aiming at long-range objectives, too), that all action, regardless of its forms, direction, and the means used, is to be preferred. Nechayev appears to have acted on the hypothesis that the ways of any and all action *as such* inevitably led to the desired aim. This was the essential ingredient of what Professor Venturi has called "Nechayev's revolutionary impatience".[47] It is also through this mental bent that Nechayev found his way to what is termed Russian Jacobinism and Blanquism; in a sense he staked out its first landmark.[48] For, actually, Nechayev's "theory of action here and now" (which is not identical with "propaganda by the deed") was only one step away from Tkachev who was indefatigably sounding the tocsin [*Nebat* (Tocsin) was the name of the paper], and who, to the question "When should the revolution be started?", was invariably replying "*Now*, or perhaps very soon, *never*."[49]

This aspect of Nechayev's thoughts and feelings may be found in his writings too.

> He who initiates himself in the revolutionary cause through books will never be anything but a revolutionary sluggard. An idea able to serve the people's revolution can only be worked out in revolutionary action, and must be the result of a series of practical trials and manifestations, all having one and the same unswerving aim—merciless destruction by any means. Everything that does not follow this course we regard as alien and hostile. We will not let ourselves be seduced by any of the revolutionary phrase-mongering practised nowadays so lavishly by doctrinaire champions of paper revolution. We have lost all faith in the word; for us the word is of significance only when the deed is sensed behind it and follows immediately upon it.[50]

That is why Nechayev also declared that "books do not educate, they put to sleep", an opinion reported with amazement by his followers, and with indignation by his adversaries. That is also why Nechayev disliked any kind of discussion and debate. Having invited a group of students to a meeting with the aim to enrol them in his organization, Nechayev was asked to explain its goals and principles. His answer was that "the days of the theoretical examination of the questions were over, and there was no more room for discussions." In the student movement Nechayev set himself against general meetings *(skhodki)* gathering numerous participants for, he argued, "these meetings are useless, since they always provoke discussions, and discussions are harmful." Even in his own society, the *Narodnaya Rasprava* in Moscow, Nechayev declined "to state its aims to the members", and explained this behaviour to Alexey Kuznetsov, a close collaborator, by saying that "if one now states the aims, this will inevitably give rise to discussions regarding the means to be used for achieving them; these discussions will degenerate into wrangles, which will have a harmful influence on the general course of action."[51] Thus, what Nechayev was requiring from these students amounted to total submission and unconditional participation in "action", the aims of which were unknown to them, and had to remain unknown until they were achieved.

A final detail, revealing that what really interested Nechayev was action *per se*, is to be found in his attitude towards the student protest movement in 1868–9. He energetically participated in it although he considered its objectives utterly vain, naive, and even harmful. As Vera Zasulich recalls,

> at their closed meetings, the *nechayevtsy* asserted that, by demonstrations [the students] will certainly not achieve either the right to assembly or the setting up of mutual aid funds; moreover, there was no need of that whatsoever, for this would only corrupt the students by improving their situation.[52]

One explanation of this position was offered by a student participant, G. P. Enisherlov: "Nechayev was one of those who wanted to take advantage of the student movement for their own aims."[53] To be sure, on the one hand, Nechayev did act with this objective in mind, and he applied (as one of the first, perhaps, in revolutionary annals) a system of infiltration and *noyautage* in order to use groups and movements by imparting to them "from within" a direction which is not theirs and serves the goals of others. On the other hand, a revolutionist by temperament, Nechayev was also an artist *sui generis* in this field, and although opposed to all theory, he practised the theory of *action for action's sake*. Consequently, he did participate in the student movement although he himself was not a student and felt nothing but deep contempt for the goals of this movement. It is in this sense that his attitude may be understood when he declared:

> We no longer need useless propaganda which does not state precisely the time and place of realization of the revolution's aims. Moreover, it thwarts us and we shall oppose it with all our strength. . . We want the only subject of concern now to be the action, so that minds do not get confused with vain babbling words. All the babblers who do not want to understand that, we'll stop their mouths by force.[54]

Hatred, energy, action: these were the essential formative elements of Nechayev's attitudes. They represented, no doubt, only one aspect of his personality and "policies", but this was precisely the main one that attracted Bakunin and commanded his respect for Nechayev. "Believers without God, and heroes without phrases," was Bakunin's formulation—in fact, believers in action, who did not ask themselves where it was leading to;[55] and not heroes but activists who "did not believe in words any more", but only in facts, and only in those that can be "seen and felt". In Nechayev, Bakunin has been attracted primarily by the active man of energy, as he

> dedicates himself and gives himself utterly [to the cause], while the others dabble in dilettante fashion; he wears workman's overalls, the others white gloves; he acts while the others wag their tongues; he is, the others are not.[56]

To Descartes' *Cogito ergo sum*, Bakunin's rejoinder was "He acts, therefore he is."

But Bakunin was too clever and experienced to overlook that the activism and the "theory of action" were precisely the major cause of Nechayev's famous system—otherwise criticized by Bakunin—of "Jesuitism", Machiavellism, blackmail, lies, and "violence to one's brothers". Bakunin did see the link between activism "now or never" and the "system", and he offers an interesting explanation which he may well have heard from Nechayev himself. "Everything [in Nechayev]," says Bakunin, "is subordinated to a ruling passion, the passion for destroying the existing order of things; consequently his first thought was of necessity to create an organization or a collective power capable of carrying out this great work of destruction—to hatch a conspiracy."[57] But at the very moment he tried to carry out this task, Nechayev realized that the Russian youth had no revolutionary passion and will-power, that their "inclination is more to argument than to action", that they were placid and represented "a corrupt and inane herd of jabbering doctrinaires", that, finally, they indulgently contemplated their own depravities. This was Bakunin's explanation of the well-known fact that Nechayev did not succeed in attracting many followers from among the students, while their leaders were his staunchest adversaries. Having detected this marasmic apathy, and having tried (according to Bakunin) "honestly but vainly all honourable means—propaganda of principles [and] passionate persuasion", Nechayev came "naturally" to the following thought:

> Our youth is too corrupt and flaccid to be trusted to form an organiz-ation by force of persuasion alone; but since an organization is

essential, and since our young people are incapable of uniting and unwilling to unite freely, they must be united involuntarily and un- awares, and in order that this organization half-founded on coercion and deceit should not crumble, they must be confounded and com- promised to such an extent that it becomes impossible for them to withdraw.[58]

That was, then, Nechayev's first and original contribution to revolutionary organizing. Bakunin adds: "This is the first natural step towards the Jesuit system; it is a desperate step." But, under what seemed to be the circumstances, Nechayev "could see no other way out. He had either to abandon the cause entirely or adopt the Jesuit system. Abandon the cause he could not, and so he adopted the system. . ."[59] It was in- deed only the first step. The next derived from "the immensity of the state's power which had to be destroyed" and from the very attitude of the people about to be liberated. "He saw with despair," says Bakunin, "the historical backwardness, the apathy, the inarticulateness, the infinite patience and the sluggishness of our Orthodox people, who could, if they realized and so desired, sink this entire ship of state with one wave of their mighty hand, but who appear still to be sleeping the sleep of the dead. . . Such was his vision of Russian reality. How was he to topple it?"[60]

Thus, the people who, according to Nechayev's previsions and Bakunin's hopes, were due to rise on 19 February 1870, and the peasants, constant bearer of the revolutionary flame— all were sunk in apathy, and manifested nothing but lack of motion and endless patience. Nechayev's task, and the problem he decided to solve within this doubly "cursed Russian reality", were therefore: to stir revolt in the people who, at that time, did not want to; and to do it by means of an organization raised in a group, the youth and the students, who refused to follow him. Facing this "vacuum" that sur- rounded him, and driven by his hatred and devouring energy, Nechayev made a step farther, transformed his "theory of action" into theory of "action for action's sake", and adopted the system of action known by the name of *nechayevshchina.*

The Nechayevshchina and Its Catechism

Succintly described, the *nechayevshchina* represented a combination of attitudes and tactical devices based on Nechayev's "hypothesis that morality does not exist",[61] and postulating that all means and actions which could speed the movement towards revolution were acceptable, desirable and to be recommended. These means and actions included not only the struggle against the autocratic government, the class enemy and its allies—the army, the bureaucracy, the scholars ("learned philistines and lackeys of the government")—but also against the other revolutionary organizations which, although opposed to the autocracy, refused to submit to the "true revolutionary party" (that is, Nechayev's). Finally, these same means, which could include violence, deceit, mystification, robbery (called "expropriation"), blackmail, and possibly murder, might (and even should) also be used towards the members of the "true revolutionary party", the comrades and fellow-revolutionists. As Camus noted, "Nechayev's originality thus lies in justifying the violence done to one's brothers."[62] In his own words (which, in view of the matter discussed, are not lacking in elegance), "the merciless logic of the true workers for the cause should not reject any means contributing to the success of this cause, and so much more when they can save it and prevent its fall."[63] That was, then, as Camus added, "the political cynicism which will never cease to weigh on the revolutionary movement and which Nechayev himself has so provocatively illustrated. . ."[64] As for Bakunin, although often described as the chief formulator and organizer of this system, it appears that he deserved on that score neither the merit nor the shame. He makes his position clear, and while admitting that "external use" of these means "is frequently necessary . . . in the fight against organized despotism", he rejects using them "*within* the organization".[65] This position was one of principle and not a belated insight acquired after discovering that he himself was a victim of Nechayev's system.

Similarly, Bakunin's role in the authorship of the notorious

Catechism of the Revolutionist—this famous compendium of Nechayevism—requires reconsideration in view of the new documents discovered recently. The *Catechism* has often been attributed to Bakunin (alone or with Nechayev's participation).[66] However, it is worth pointing out that there was not and still is no *direct* evidence whatsoever to support this view. The available sources do not provide reliable testimony on this point, but only vague opinions, very often contradictory; some emanated from political enemies of Bakunin, others were given with explicit reservations. As a consequence, historians who have shared this view and have to have recourse to guesswork based on some sort of circumstantial inference. Thus, for instance, E. H. Carr writes: "The *Revolutionary Catechism* is a typical specimen of one of Bakunin's favourite forms of composition."[67] Yet, in view of the prevailing forms of composition of Bakunin's writings, this statement is inaccurate; more than that, the argument as such has little weight in view of the fact that this *form of composition* was quite widespread in nineteenth-century Europe, in socialist, liberal, radical, national and other groups and movements, and likewise in Russia, from the Decembrists (one of whom had written a *Catechism*) to the *Narodnaya Volya*. A political anthology of this period would show clearly that not only statutes, programmes, and resolutions, but also numerous other writings were presented in this same "form of composition", which offers the advantages of clarity and concision. Finally, had it been substantiated (which was not the case) that this form of composition had in fact been suggested by Bakunin, it would still remain to be shown that he also participated in composing the content of the *Catechism*.

Actually, this was not the case. An analysis of the text, content, and fundamental ideas of the *Catechism* leads to the conclusion that it was conceived by a group of revolutionists who called themselves "Committee of the Russian Revolutionary Party". Its members were P. Tkachev, S. Nechayev, Z. Ralli, the brothers I. and E. Ametistov, Siryakov, L. Nikiforov, V. Orlov, G. Enisherlov, and others. This Committee was created in Russia in February 1869, that is *before*

Nechayev's first visit to Switzerland and his meeting with Bakunin. The *Catechism* was discussed almost point by point at meetings of the group,[68] and it bears striking similarities to its *Programme of Revolutionary Actions* (which includes an explicit reference to "the catechism . . . obligatory for all the members"), drawn up either by Tkachev and Nechayev, or by Nechayev alone.[69] Likewise, both the *Catechism* and the *Programme* have numerous common ideas and expressions with an earlier article of Tkachev, written in 1868 and published this same year under the title "The Men of the Future and the Heroes of the Bourgeoisie".[70] These explicit textual and ideological analogies (and, at times, plain borrowings) between these writings and the *Catechism* allow one to conclude that the latter was conceived and set down within this group, at that time, by Nechayev, possibly in collaboration with Tkachev, and certainly under his influence. Finally, this conclusion is strengthened by a number of additional facts, the first direct evidence we possess.

In his letter to Nechayev of June 1870, Bakunin sets forth the story of their relations and reminds him:

> . . . you were appearing before me as if you were an envoy of an existing and fairly powerful organization. Thus, it seemed to you, you put yourself into a position to present your conditions as emanating from great power, while you actually appeared before me as a person who was in the process of collecting strength. You should have talked to me as an equal, person to person, and submit to my [approval] your programme and [plan] of actions.
>
> But this did not enter into your calculations. You were too fanatically devoted to your plan and your programme to subject them to criticism by anyone.[71]

The "plan" and "programme" Bakunin is referring to appear to have been the *Programme of Revolutionary Actions* and the plan of Nechayev's tactics and organization, already incorporated at that time in the *Catechism*, which he quite probably brought with him from Russia. For that reason, and because it was Nechayev's contribution to their association, Bakunin also writes in another context: "Do you remember how cross you were when I called you an *Abrek*, and your Catechism a catechism of *Abreks*? . . ."[72] Your Catechism! Nechayev certainly remembered. He not only knew as well as Bakunin, and both of them better than anyone else, who the author was of the *Catechism*; but he also recalled that Bakunin, far from being its author, was taken aback by its main ideas and rejected them as "an absurdity, an impossibility, a total negation of nature, man and society".[73] This is, in the present state of the sources, fairly conclusive evidence, I believe, on the controversial question of the *Catechism's* authorship.

Ideology, Money, and Psychology

The clash of opinions and the reasons that led to the break between Bakunin and Nechayev did not bear only upon the *nechayevshchina* and the *Catechism*. There were also ideological differences, and some discord on financial matters too.

Until the spring of 1870 Bakunin appears to have believed that Nechayev shared the main ideas of his populist-anarchist creed. Nechayev certainly gave him good reasons to believe so. But, although scattered anarchist elements do appear in the few writings he left, Nechayev, at bottom, was not an anarchist. As far as an ideological trend can be detected, he was much nearer to Blanquism, to Jacobinism, and to the authoritarian, centralistic Marxian brand of communism. This *pot-pourri* should not surprise. For, at times, Nechayev changed his tune to that of a moderate, a liberal, and even a conservative, and, on that account, he has been sometimes described as an "opportunist" and a "demagogue".[74] In view of that, one may wonder, indeed, whether Nechayev could find his way through the intricacies and nuances of Russian radical politics and ideas. Did he believe in some ideology, or in some—even loosely defined—set of principles? Was he driven by sheer hatred alone? Did he strive towards anything else but "naked" revolution (which, in his version, manifested itself much more as an intense desire to spread confusion and disorder, than to organize a rebellion)?

Anyhow, Nechayev clearly displays, in this respect too, a consistent lack of principles. It could be that he believed that all the "nuances" were nonsense, and therefore a "true revolutionary" might say whatever he wanted, whatever suited the moment, whatever seemed useful. Be that as it may, he ultimately arrived at a position in the realm of ideas, symmetrical to the one he held in matters of "revolutionary tactics", namely that *everything is permitted*. Thus, in order to take advantage of Bakunin in his revolutionary schemes, Nechayev may have deceived him and made him believe that he shared his anarchist programme. It took Bakunin some time before he began to doubt the reality and seriousness of this ideological affinity. But, once having reached this point, he didn't put off warning Nechayev that the absence of a common political programme "would oblige [him] to break off all *intimate political relations* with you, if your convictions and your, or your friends', departure from it were completely final".[75] Bakunin may have been a fool, but he also had some deep convictions, sharing—for better or worse—the notorious *principialnost* of the Russian intelligentsia.

He was fooled, too, in his financial dealings with Nechayev. Thanks to Bakunin and Ogarev, Nechayev had obtained (first from Herzen, then from his heirs) the major part of the so-called Bakhmetev fund.[76] Nobody involved in the "transaction" expected him to be grateful. Bakunin expected him at least to sign a receipt to the effect that he received the money. Nechayev had no intention of so doing. Bakunin became insistent when Nikolay Utin, and other followers of Marx in Switzerland, began spreading rumours about his use or misuse of this money. Bakunin wanted to clear himself in advance, for he feared—and rightly so—that Marx could use this affair against him in the International. Nechayev never submitted a receipt.[77] Bakunin never received anything but pennies from this fund. However, he had previously asked to be granted a regular remuneration in order to be rid of financial worries and devote himself entirely to "the cause". But at the time of his bitter "explanations" with Nechayev, he did not raise this demand again, he simply tried to explain why he had raised it in the past. And this explanation goes revealingly beyond the financial side of the matter.

"All my life," Bakunin writes to Nechayev, "I have struggled with poverty, and every time I managed to undertake and do something more or less useful [for the cause], I had to do it not with my own, but with other people's money. . . You also know how untrue and ignoble are the rumours about my personal luxury, about my attempts to make a fortune at the expense of others. . ." Yet, curiously enough, Bakunin doesn't only feel the need to explain, but also to justify.

> It is clear that in order to devote myself fully to the service of the cause, I must have the means to live. I am getting old. Eight years of imprisonment have led to a chronic illness and my impaired health demands certain care and certain conditions so that I can usefully serve the cause. I have also a wife and children whom I cannot condemn to death by starvation. I try to reduce expenses to the minimum, but still I cannot exist without a certain monthly sum. Where can I get this sum if I give all my labour to the common cause?

That is what an old revolutionary felt compelled to say to the young Nechayev; an old revolutionary who, moreover, thought it necessary to recall that he had devoted all his life "to the liberation of others".[78]

But the day came when the old revolutionary seemed soft and mellow compared to the young Nechayev, so hard and tough. Nechayev required total abnegation, and for him all these pecuniary affairs (chit-chat about "monthly sums" and "means to live") were irrelevant trivialities, alien to the action to be carried on, and revealed only on Bakunin's part a grievous alienation from the real spirit which suffuses revolutionary activity. Beyond the financial problem (certainly not a trifle), here is another dimension of the relations between the two men. Bakunin was no longer the model of the type required by the *Catechism of the Revolutionist*. Age, ailments, family obligations were setting up limitations and dependencies. Others who were younger and stronger began to fancy themselves as "lost men", without name, having destroyed their bonds with society, family, and all obligations towards the "bourgeois world" and its "tottering civilization". Bakunin didn't quite see himself among them: it amounted to a sad withdrawal. There stood Nechayev, young and vigorous, having "broken" the social links which he never had, and "given up" the family ties he never created—looking with scorn at that "old ruin", Bakunin, who talked of care, wife and children, monthly stipends and the like—and all the while everything remained to be done for "the liberation of the people", and nothing would move forward without a total forgetfulness of self.

Nechayev, no doubt, felt this way. Perhaps he also said so, or at least hinted it, since Bakunin writes to him: "I clearly saw and felt that you were far from having full confidence in me, and in many respects attempted to use me as a means to immediate aims which were unknown to me."[79] Thus, for Nechayev, Bakunin was not a true comrade, a "real revolutionary", but one of those people of the fourth or fifth category, who should be used unawares and manipulated, who represented "a capital" which the real revolutionary should spend "economically", but without compunctions.[80]

It was an awkward and tragic *finale* for the great revolutionary venture of a lifetime. Awkward, for Bakunin was fully aware of it; tragic (if not unusual) as the personal fate of an old militant, rejected finally by the young whom, all his life, he had been calling to join him.

Natalie, the Epilogue, and After

These were the actors, the plots and counter-plots which Natalie Herzen found in Geneva at the beginning of 1870. She met Nechayev there for the first time during her brief visit to Ogarev after the death of her father. Nechayev quickly gained a considerable influence over her, which proved great enough to convince her to settle in Geneva and take part in his group's activity for "the cause". To achieve this, he used not only his personal magnetism and roughness, but arguments intended to have an effect on the feelings of a conscience-stricken aristocrat: the sufferings of the people, the immensity of work to be done, her "parasitism" and "aimless" existence, the "emptiness" of life in her milieu.[81] Up to a certain point he succeeded remarkably, probably because he consciously manipulated some general ideas about Russia's present and future which Natalie had heard from her father and to which she was not insensitive. This success is all the more striking, because Natalie knew, from the first, that Nechayev had committed murder, although at that time she believed that the man killed was an *agent provocateur*.[82]

Nechayev's success began to fade when he managed to awake Natalie's latent suspicion that he had an eye on her money. It came to an end the moment he spoke of love. In personal relations with Natalie, to touch on these two themes at once represented the grossest psychological blunder. Although he was himself not a very acute connoisseur of the human psyche, Bakunin rightly reproached Nechayev for his "ignorance of the social conditions, customs, morals, ideas and usual feelings of the so-called educated world", and he warned him: "You do not know as yet how to acquire influence and power within it, which is bound to lead you to inevitable blunders every time the needs of the cause bring you in contact with it. . ."[83] With Tata, too, Nechayev failed. But perhaps not even a much more skilled and experienced man could overcome her deep suspicion of these two delicate subjects: love and money.

The later aspect of their relations need not be detailed here. Natalie's diary and her correspondence with Nechayev give a rich and fairly accurate picture of the events. She began to have an inkling of what Nechayev really was on about, perhaps a little earlier than Bakunin. Both of them owed much to German Lopatin, who uncovered the whole truth about Nechayev's dealings and true personality.[84] Bakunin still wavered for several weeks in his attitude towards Nechayev. Even after his harsh letter of 2 June 1870, he kept up the hope that Nechayev might repent, accept an anarchist programme, and at long last act sincerely. At that point, Natalie Herzen appears to have been less naive than the old revolutionist. She writes to him in mid-June:

> How can you still envisage the possibility of working with [Nechayev] after all that has passed between you, after all that you say yourself in your letter to him? On what will you base your trust? And if you have none, how will you work with him? How do you know that, even if

> Nechayev accepts your conditions and goes as far as to put his accept-
> ance in writing (using his real name or some invented one)—[how do
> you know] that he will not secretly be tricking you precisely as he has
> been doing ever since you have known each other? For myself that
> would be absolutely impossible.[85]

Not so for Bakunin, not yet. At the end of June, he still warned
Natalie (whom he considered, otherwise, "a truly honest and
truthful person")[86] not to betray them and commit "a
treachery against [her] conscience and honour", and, more
specifically, not to disclose things she knew or heard about
persons to his political enemies (and particularly N. Utin).
And he went on:

> I implore you not to say or do anything that might damage Barsov
> [Nechayev] and the work he is accomplishing, perhaps not always in the
> correct manner—but always with boundless dedication and self-
> forgetfulness. Whatever his errors, he remains nevertheless, in my opinion
> and, I hope, in yours, the finest and, where the cause is concerned
> though not where people are concerned, the most honourable of us
> all.[87]

A vain hope, for Natalie did not change her mind about
Nechayev and about collaborating with him. Consequently,
she did not participate in the discussions with him which
began a few days later, but only recorded in her Diary (on
7 July 1870): "It appears that all is indeed over between
Bakunin, Ogarev, and Nechayev. The latter, too, is here in
Geneva once again. Apparently they have had terrible arguments in recent days."[88]

Of course, Natalie was quite right in asking Bakunin how
he could ever work again with Nechayev; but her appre-
hensions were pointless. For Bakunin's risky hopes and
hazardous plans were based on another error of judgement,
namely that Nechayev would accept the *pax Bakuniniana* he
was offered. He had no such intention. Actually, at their last
meeting in early July, he pretended to do so only in order to
take advantage of Bakunin's friends (viz. Mroczkowski and
Talandier) in Paris and London which were his next stops;
but so did Bakunin too, who pretended to believe him only in
order to gain time and warn them to beware of Nechayev. At
that moment, Bakunin already knew that Nechayev had stolen

letters from him and his friends, including Natalie. No other way to recover them occurred to him but to enjoin Mroczkowski: "It would be splendid of you, and you would be doing our sacred, common cause an enormous service, if you were to succeed in stealing from Nechayev all the papers he stole, and all his own papers. But I am afraid you may have become quite rusty and lost all of your former agility. . ."[89] Quite so, for not only did Mroczkowski not succeed in this revolutionary assignment, but—so far as we know—did not even try. Nevertheless, Nechayev comprehended that Bakunin had learned something from him, this time had played his own game, and had beaten him. He was quick to react. His last letter to Bakunin and Ogarev is a rare specimen of shocked knavery:

> Why, when we parted and you kissed me like Judases [Nechayev writes] did you not tell me you were going to write to your acquaintances? Your last letter to Talandier, and the warning to Guillaume about the danger of participating in a cause of which you have always been the theoretical instigators, are acts of the most dishonourable and despicable kind, committed out of petty spite. With total disregard of common sense and the interests of the cause, you are bent on wallowing in the mire—well, then, wallow! Farewell.[90]

Nechayev was caught by the Swiss police in August 1872 upon information delivered by an *agent provocateur* of the Third Section. He was extradited to the Russian authorities as a common criminal, stood trial in January 1873, and died, a tough and stubborn prisoner, in 1882 in the Peter and Paul Fortress in St Petersburg.

Bakunin went back to revolutionary business as usual, in France, in Italy, and wherever the opportunity arose. In spite of Nechayev's harsh words in his last letter—in spite of Bakunin's feeling that "no one has done [him], and deliberately done [him], so much harm as [Nechayev]"— despite all that, Bakunin not only felt "dreadfully sorry for him" upon his arrest, but also kept a fundamental trust that that man had the stuff heroes are made of and a sort of greatness all his own.[91] Once again Bakunin was mistaken. He was, after all, a naive, sentimental and generous man: three sins

that contemporaries (and sometimes historians too) rarely
forgive, and which rivals often exploited. Till his last boisterous
days he remained a poor and prodigal son of the Russian
nobility and the European revolutionary movement, died in
Berne in 1876, and was entered in the official deaths-record as
Michel Bakounine, rentier.

Natalie Herzen lost sight of all her old circle of associates
and their preoccupations. She did exactly what she once wrote
to Bakunin:

> Although [Nechayev] never hypnotized me, as you seem to think, he
> did something worse: he poisoned and paralysed me by developing in
> me a mistrust so great that it will be a long time before I manage to rid
> myself of it.
>
> Now I cannot and do not wish to participate in any Russian affairs
> whatsoever. Call me a sceptic, Mikhail Alexandrovich, perhaps you are
> right; [but] on this occasion my scepticism has saved me from God
> knows what toils and troubles.[92]

Actually, Natalie went even further: never again did she
participate in Russian affairs. Yet, in her heart, she always
kept a kind of special memory of those days. First, there were
the simple recollections of these episodes and of her thrilling
association with those dangerous bombsters; then, the recollections of past recollections which, as time went on and
attitudes changed, served to overlook certain events or to re-
cast them in tranquillity. It was these recollections of recollections that gradually made many things seem strange, or
so very different from what they had really been. Nevertheless
they had happened. But not exactly as Natalie Herzen, now a
living monument of Russian history and a respectable Swiss
citizen, believed they had. And not as she related them again,
for the last time, in her *Reminiscences*,[93] written in 1931, only
five years before she died, in Lausanne, an aged Russian lady
who had known such odd people in her youth, and who was
the daughter of a great and famous rebel.

MICHAEL CONFINO

I

RUSSIAN ARISTOCRATS AS PROFESSIONAL EXILES

"I have no idea where we shall take off to, Papasha seems to be trying to arrange for the two of us to stay together. We shall live somewhere in Vevey, Montreux, Lugano, the South of France, Mesopotamia, or maybe China. But I feel uneasy; I am afraid I shall become unsociable. In any event I shall go and visit Olga and Sasha in Florence from time to time. I have a lot of acquaintances there. . ."

NATALIE HERZEN TO MARIA REICHEL

Geneva, Chateau de la Boissière
21 December 1865

1. *Natalie Herzen Comes of Age*

1. *Natalie Herzen to Maria Reichel*

21 OCTOBER 1860

Eagle's Nest
Bournemouth
Hampshire

DEAR MASHA!

See what came of Sasha's plans—he didn't manage to arrange things his own way after all. I am staying in England and in boring London for the whole of the winter and perhaps the spring too. Olga is going to Paris with Mlle Meysenbug for four or five months, and since I cannot live alone with Papa and Ogarev there will be an English girl living with us—the one Papa wrote about and I told you that she was unusually intelligent and cultured, Miss Reeve.[1] I cannot tell in advance if living with her will be pleasant; I have never spoken to her. But she is the *steife* English type. Firstly, she is far from young, she must be about forty; her nose is pointed, very pointed, and she has tiny wee eyes, and spectacles too; moreover, she always dresses in the most ridiculous fashion. But I must not make fun of her. I hope that the winter with her will not be spent in vain.

On the subject of Olga. I wanted to tell you, it's true she is still a naughty child; that's nothing to worry about. But since my arrival she has begun behaving far more sensibly with me, she doesn't tease me or get on my nerves. On the contrary, our short separation, and the fact of my coming back in a long dress, has had such an effect upon her that *sie hat viel mehr Respect* for me than for Mary or even Mlle Meysenbug; she tells the latter to her face that she will not obey her, but she is very amiable with me. She is a very odd child too. She plays on the beach here every day, just nearby, not far from our house, and there she has got to know a girl of her own age; they are always discussing religion. The girl, who is English, has of course had a totally religious upbringing and tells Olga that she knows "God is a ghost" and that it is very wicked to work on Sundays; and now Olga has a passion for asking constantly—ironically, of course—if it is true that "God is spirit", and always lifts her gaze to the heavens and then lowers it to the floor in such a manner that one simply has to laugh. Then she takes her leave of us, saying "Oh Mary, how loudly you are laughing; today is Sunday, one mustn't laugh." Yesterday she summoned us over into the corner with an extra-serious air, showed us a spider and said: "There, that spider's working on a Sunday, *es ist eine Sünde*." She is taking lessons in Russian with me, and is really doing amazingly well. She is as small and thin as ever, and extremely pretty; I'll try and get a picture of her to send to you so that you can have just some idea of her. *A propos de portraits*, Papa has done a splendid portrait of himself with Ogarev, a small picture, like ours, that is, the picture of myself and Sasha; and Sasha too has done two more different ones, but much better than the Dresden ones.

Guess what! Katerina, the housemaid who tore my dress, has gone quite mad; just imagine, she is saying that everybody knows about her, the whole world is up in arms against her, and she is afraid to go out of the house.

How is my little Sashenok?[2] Give him a big kiss for me and show him my picture from time to time so that he doesn't forget me too soon. Is he still a good pupil? What is he reading? Has Ernst started talking? And how is little Adolf? Still the same little darling?

Thank you for the letter from Dusha; might I ask you to send on the note I have enclosed when you write to Russia? How unfortunate that aunt L.'s health is so poor—and consumption too! How sorry I feel for her, the poor thing.

Well, did you get tickets for the "Schiller lottery"? Don't bother to send the numbers, divide them as you please, let us not quarrel over them. I really have no idea what to send you, sending a parcel is a most difficult business. Did I promise you? It seems so! I know: I left in Dresden, that is, at your house, two pairs of brown boots—take them, at any rate they're better than the yellow satin slippers. Do you remember? I was joking. But I really do not know what to send you.

And now goodbye, I kiss you and all of yours.

Your TATA

What of Zebeki? Give him my regards. Amalia and Christel *viele Grüsse*. Papa has left already, he is now looking for a house in London. So write to us at Alpha Road again.

Mlle Meysenbug sends you her regards.

2. *Natalie Herzen to Maria Reichel*

18 SEPTEMBER 1862

Tower Cottage
Shanklin
Isle of Wight

FORGIVE ME, my dear, kind Masha, for taking so long to reply to you. The instant I received your first letter I settled down to answer, but I was interrupted and kept putting it off from day to day. Since then the Levitskys[3] have been here, and I have been to visit Nathalie at Cowes and returned to London; and now I am on the Isle of Wight, at Shanklin, a most delightful place not far from Ventnor. The famous painter Gallait is here with his family—a wife and two daughters, one of whom, Amélie, is my age and the other, Marie, Olga's age. Olga and Meysenbug have been staying with them as guests for some time.

Mme Gallait and Mlle Meysenbug are friends. We, that is, Sasha and myself, have been invited too, but we only came here two weeks ago and have taken a small flat for ourselves to live in, but we bathe with the Gallaits.

We all bathe together, go swimming, jump off the boat into the sea, and go riding, but of course we devote most of our time to drawing. They have invited me to go and stay with them for a month or two in Brussels before my trip to Italy—I am at this very moment dreadfully impatient to receive an answer from Papa. Will he allow me to go or not? It would be very useful for me, of that there can be no doubt, but I am very much afraid that Papa will not allow it.

They are awfully rich, I've heard they have a house like a palace in Brussels and another in Paris.

25 SEPTEMBER

Once again I can get on with this letter, but now I know. Papa has given his permission and I am leaving for Brussels in a week's time (at the moment I am in London again), and you just cannot imagine how happy I am. I was annoyed to find Miss Biller had left while I was away—when will there be another opportunity to send you the little briefcase?

I am spending all my time at the moment packing and tidying up. It has been decided that I am only going to Brussels for one month. Now we still have to settle the question of Italy—if Papa lets me go; I shall not be returning to London, and then he will move from Orsett House, and in case that happens all my things have to be put in order, and that demands a great deal of time and energy, as you will appreciate; if, though, he refuses to let me go, I shall be coming back to London.

7 OCTOBER

Would you believe it, my dear Masha? I am in Brussels, yes, and in that palace about which I have heard so much, and I am so happy. Everyone is so kind, Amélie is such a dear, and Mme Gallait is like a mother to me. We arrived the day before yesterday. I shall be here until 1 November, but what will happen after then the Lord only knows.

I believe you have moved, and I do not know your new address, but I hope this letter will reach you all the same. Write to me soon, dear, good Masha, I kiss you and the children affectionately.

Your TATA HERZEN

How is poor Reich[el's] health?

My address is: Mme Gallait
No 72 rue des Palais
Bruxelles

3. *Nikolay Ogarev to Natalie Herzen*

9 OCTOBER [1862]. NIGHT   [*London*]

MY DEAR TATA,

I wanted to write you a long letter, but I scarcely have time. I shall put everything I can into one page. I am extremely happy with your letters. They are sweet and open-hearted. I divine from them a sincerely loving nature that is childishly pure and far deeper than might seem at first glance. They say you have been brought up on reading and observation of the artistic world; but that you do little work yourself. I am sure that work will come all in good time. Given again the profound effect of the Roman landscape and Roman art—and the influence of *Gallait*, you will begin doing a lot of work. *Osez— c'est tout dans les révolutions,* said Mirabeau. *Osez*—that is all you are lacking in your art. You work little, because of your timidity. I understand this instinctively and therefore I say to you: *osez!* You see, I want you to be an artist, both because there is perhaps no *better,* finer and happier thing, and because it develops a person's understanding and heart to such a degree that he suddenly becomes a kind of focal point for all those near to him. And I am convinced that you will be the focal point for all the members of our families, old ones and young ones. Whether you marry soon or not does not matter: we old folks will find rest in you and the young ones will find a maternal wing. Do understand this situation. But you will understand all its grace, because you can be an artist. And therefore you will be an artist. There, I have said all I have to say. So then, I kiss you.

4. *Natalie Herzen to Alexander Herzen*

2 FEBRUARY 1863   [*Rome*]

I MUST begin with a most entertaining anecdote, Papasha dear; the day before yesterday, that is, on Sunday, we were at Dell'Ongaro's[4] again, myself and Olga this time, because he

49

D

had been most insistent that we should come. We entered, and guess who we saw: the fair-haired Russian who travelled with us in the stage-coach from Nice to Genoa. Dell'Ongaro at once led him up to me and introduced him as a compatriot of mine: *Monsieur Semenev—Mlle Herzen.* I said to him that I had apparently already had the honour of seeing him, and so forth. He recognized me and simply would not believe that I was Russian, and the daughter of *the* Herzen-Iskander, until I addressed him in Russian. He is a writer—of what, I know not; I think he has written a great deal in French, and he looks very stupid. Friken[5] knows his uncle and says that the whole family belongs to the "anti-*Bell*" party—how he came to be at Dell'Ongaro's, God knows.

Dell'Ongaro has latterly stepped into Friken's shoes and been our *cicerone.* He took us to the Church of the *Annunziata* where we saw the splendid frescoes of *Andrea del Sarto*—he has presented me with a large self-portrait and copied out a mass of poetry, both published and unpublished. What a fine portrait he has of Garibaldi! We simply must buy it—it is a real *capo d'opera*, and he, that is, Dell'Ongaro, has promised to sit for me, he reminds me of Tassinari'[6] as I think I have already told you, but he is worse. He is interested in my drawing too and encourages me. No, Papasha, I have no doubts as to my talent—that would be difficult after Gallait and Ussi and so many other people have said and continue to say that I have a great deal of aptitude and am not lacking in zeal, of course, and consequently I am doing as much work as possible. Ussi was very pleased again with me yesterday. I hope, Papasha dear, that you will not regret having let me go to Italy! We have disobeyed you in one respect, Papasha, but it could not be helped, I mean, we have set aside a day, Wednesday evenings, that is, for receiving guests, because both we and our visitors felt ill at ease. They are all very unpretentious, and we have got to know their wives. Mme Ghé[7] and her sister are very agreeable, simple ladies, not at all *à la Tepliakova*. On the contrary, they understand perfectly that if they come unexpectedly they will either disturb our reading or studying, or find that we are not at home, and what is the point of their exerting themselves in vain? Mme Zabella is a Swiss lady, and very sweet; we have visited her once but she has not been here yet. And when all is said and done, we *can* spare one evening a week, especially as I can continue my drawing in their presence; they are all interested in my work; I show it all to them and they make criticisms.

Concerning the memorial stone: I will talk to [Mr] Zabella tomorrow; he has already done one big stone for the same cemetery, for some Russian lady—don't think I've forgotten, I haven't, but I did not know how to broach the subject—it seemed so awkward to me. Although Friken does not read well and stammers, we are making progress with the reading, and have finished Sismondi's book. Yesterday evening we read the tale of the *Masaniello* uprising, a short but very interesting story —I do not know who the author is.

5. *Natalie Herzen to Nikolay Ogarev, Alexander Herzen and Nathalie Tuchkova-Ogareva*

8 APRIL 1863
Via San Basilio
Piazza Barberini
Roma

I CONGRATULATE you, Aga, Papasha, in short, all of you, upon the anniversary of your *arrival* in London—how many years ago was it? Seven, unless I am mistaken—and the anniversary of an event we celebrated two years ago, the liberation of the serfs.[8] What plans we were all making then. Tchorzewski was already thinking of packing, and Papasha said that in six months time we should be in Russia—and what came of it all!

Today we were at the Villa Albano, which now belongs to some count or other, but was built in the eighteenth century by Cardinal Albani—there are quantities of old statues and paintings—Winckelmann had some part in the building of the villa and the general design, there is an enormous bust of him in the garden. But, tired as we still were from the previous day, Papasha's birthday, we did not pay much attention to the *curiosities*. It was a wonderful day, the sun was almost too hot,

and we were tempted most of all by the idea of *dolce far niente*
and lolling on the grass. We shall try to get more tickets and
spend some more time there before our departure, because we
missed many fine things.

Although I have inquired several times, I still have not
received any reply: just write and tell me in a little more detail
how your domestic affairs are working out. And what you
intend to do: will you stay at Orsett House or go into the
country? How did you "enjoy"[9] the sea, what did you do, and
how much time did you spend there? I don't know a thing.
Write also and tell me about the children and what they are up
to, tell me how Liza discusses politics and what she thinks of
Langiewicz.[10] We were greatly amused by Osip Ivanovich's[11]
anecdote—where is he now? And tell me about the little ones
Lelya-boy and Lelya-girl; I think that now is the time to go
and see Francis the photographer. I remember his saying that
in three months' time he would have a new *establishment for
babies*.

About ourselves—you probably know already—I am in
"seventh heaven" because of being in Rome. And how right
Papasha was. For the first few days this *manque* of almost all
domestic comforts was unpleasant, but one grows oblivious to
everything; there's no time to be thinking of such petty things—
and how time does fly. We have been in Rome for two weeks
now already, and what a mass of things we still have to see. Of
course, I have no time here to be drawing heads—whenever we
are somewhere in amongst the ruins I do sketches—we come
home in the evening terribly tired, of course, about eight o'clock,
after dinner (we dine in restaurants)—Malwida and Olga go to
bed almost at once, M[alwida] still feels unwell, somehow, you
know, she has to be very careful—I stay up a little making
notes and reading various books on Rome, about what we saw
during the day.

Olga has become very friendly with Friken—they are
inseparable and call each other "Paolo e Francesca". Olga puts
on simply hilarious tragic sketches and pantomimes.

11 APRIL 1863

Why no letters from you for so long—the last one I received

in Rome, that is, the only one I have received here, was sent on 24 March. Has one perhaps gone astray?

Yesterday was a very full day. We began with the Palazzo Doria, amazingly rich!—quantities of portraits, by the finest artists—Holbein, Leonardo da Vinci, Raphael, Titian, and so forth; and the number of people I have met here! Everyone must be expecting something extraordinary—I shall run across one of your people at any moment, really. The day before yesterday at the Palais des Césars, which is quite covered with earth, we watched them clearing it, throwing out lamps, fragments of tankards, pieces of mosaic—the effect is a strange one; little by little they are uncovering rooms, the remains of frescoes on the walls, mosaic on the floor. The French are really applying themselves to this work, one has to grant them that; they do get things moving, unlike the Italians. At the Thermae of Caracalla we saw how the Italians work—in the first place, there were no overseers; half a dozen emaciated beggars, starved to death, were lolling on the ground and taking half an hour to dig up a single blade of grass with a kind of fish-hook. God knows whom they employ—the first beggars they come across in the streets—old Jews with terrible faces; it is annoying, and one cannot but be angered to see that nothing is moving at all—that's what the Pope is doing. Two years ago the French bought a part of Mt Palatin, under which the wonderful palaces of the Caesars lie buried. Friken was here two years ago and says it is completely unrecognizable now, so much has been done. Well, while I was strolling about there, I met an acquaintance of mine, Miss Buchley as she was formerly; she introduced me there and then to her husband—she married him two weeks or so ago. I don't think you know her, she is a friend of poor Johanna. Also, I've several times run into the Greek girl-students of Boehm and Spartalli, and various girls I had known in England.

You cannot imagine, Nathalie, what a garden we were in yesterday—a famous one, the Villa Borghese. First, the actual villa is so abundant in statues—no paintings—then, the garden: it is not like ordinary gardens hereabouts which are laid out on the French model, like Versailles and so forth; even the Pope has not enough taste to get a decent garden for himself. At the Palais du Quirinal, his summer residence, all the trees are spoiled—clipped and styled as though by the French court hairdresser. The garden of the Villa Borghese, by contrast, is a real old rambling park with huge trees, lanes, and fountains, but all of them concealed or tree-lined—simply beautiful. There are swarms of foreign tourists spoiling the whole effect as usual, particularly large numbers of English and Germans— I didn't expect to see so many Germans, I thought they were too poor and *ekonomisch* to travel.

Well, goodbye. I kiss and embrace you affectionately, the children too.

Your TATA H.

Mr Friken sends you his regards.

6. *Natalie Herzen to Nikolay Ogarev*

17 APRIL 1863   *Rome*

I CANNOT tell you how overjoyed I was to receive your letter, my dear, kind Aga. I sympathize so much with everything you say and describe to me that I keep on reading it over—I am very, very grateful to you for it and I kiss you affectionately. We too have taken such a liking to Rome that we cannot bring ourselves to say farewell to it so soon (I don't know if Papasha will be very pleased). We want to stay here for the month of May so as to get to know the city really well and visit all the places you did. So you were at the Villa Borghese too, and liked it—but how could one fail to like it! Such beauty, especially the park with its enormous trees—but Monte Pincio must have changed since you were there, surely—the views of Rome from it will always be wonderfully fine; maybe the actual garden is nice too, but if so, only very early in the morning, otherwise there are so many foreigners and French soldiers and priests there it's simply awful; and the garden itself is so artificial— the park at the Villa Borghese is so much better, don't you think?

We have seen the well by the Porta di Ripetta too—Mikhail Petrovich Botkin[12] lives in that part of town—we were his guests the other day—but when we passed the well I didn't know then that you had lived there. I shall go again. We have not yet been to the top of Monte Mario, but shall certainly do so—so far the best view we have had of Rome and a part of the Campagna has been from San Pietro in Montorio—did you go there? By the Pauline fountain. The Corso will probably, almost certainly, be better in a few weeks' time, but all the same it will not be what it was in your day—for the same reason, to my mind, why everything else is being spoiled—the foreigners and the French. There are so many of these soldiers that they just don't know what to do with themselves; wherever you look you continually see wide red breeches and white gaiters.

Today we were on Monte Aventino—what a view of the town there is from it!—you can see the whole of Rome—but the weather was bad, the sky grey and overcast—we could even see rain in the distance. Of course, it had a charm of its own, but I prefer a bright, clear, hot day. The view of San Pietro is good from here too, with the key of the big garden door in the lock— everybody must know it, our coachman pointed it out to us. Indeed, San Pietro is visible on its own, standing out in the distance—in the foreground there is a dark avenue [of trees]— San Pietro, of course, is better seen from a distance than close by. And I love the Castel Sant'Angelo also. There is a very good view of it from the monastery where T. Tasso was a monk and where he died—Sant'Onofrio on Mont Janicule; but so far my favourite view, as I have said already, is the one from San Pietro in Montorio; from there more than anywhere else one can see the vast and melancholy Campagna, which comes to resemble even a sea if one half-closes one's eyes in order to make the line of the horizon even straighter. And then the Forum . . . yes, there is an amazing power in the remains of those temples, graves, palaces and all the splendours of the past. Of course, it frequently attracts one more than real life itself, as you say, and most probably because one has a liking— not for "fear", it cannot be called a sensation of *fear*—but what else can one call it? I don't know. The thought that so much was lived through in that place. As I have already written to Sasha, a great deal is spoiled for me by my terrible memory and my absentmindedness, that is to say, my poor knowledge of history.

We also went to the Temple of Vesta at the Bocca della Verità—what a shame they have restored the roof so badly with those rough, red bricks. In olden times the roof was probably like the roof of the Pantheon—that's yet another wonderful temple, with its majestic portico! We shall certainly go to Albano as soon as the lease of our apartment here expires, so as not to waste money by paying for two apartments; we shall go into the hills for a few days to visit all those places— Albano, Tivoli, Frascati, etc. I'll send you something from Albano without fail—can you recall any favourite view or spot? Tell me, and I will find it and do a sketch for you. The lease of our apartment expires on Thursday, 23 April.

We've been to Santa Maria Maggiore too, and to St Jean du Latran. The other day we were there again, with Gregorovius,[13] who pointed out and explained everything to us. The most interesting things there were copies of various frescoes discovered in the catacombs, and ancient sarcophagi of the first Christians; the Roman type of head was still characteristic at that time, and you find for the most part that Christ is represented as a slender, beautiful, beardless youth, his face oval but fairly full, with long curly hair, and dressed in the Roman toga. When you look at some Byzantine Christ afterwards it sends a shiver down your spine—how frightful!—and this type goes on until Masaccio—he was the first to depict Christ in the way that is still used nowadays—in his Florence fresco. But where did Michelangelo get the model for his Christ in the Sistine Chapel?

Today we plan to visit the catacombs—that should be very interesting! Oh, why does Papasha write that he's coming— goodbye Italy, goodbye Rome, blue sky, etc.—the thought is unbearable. No, Papasha, come, but come and stay for ever— no, that's silly; it's impossible, of course, but do leave us a little more time; just think what a mass of things we still have to see and learn. Everything here lives and breathes art so

intensely, it will surely be all right, even disregarding the fact
that during the whole of our time in Florence I was only three
times obliged to lie down with a headache; and here in Rome
it has not happened once, I have not even felt the onset, despite
our going round the galleries and different places. At night I
am nearly always with you—oh, if only my dreams were to
come true! Just today I dreamed that you all came to see us,
and arrived so unexpectedly—and the lounge of Orsett House
was in Italy—but I awoke, and that was the end. Do you by
any chance remember the Villa Doria, Aga? We were there
yesterday. The park is *even finer* than the Villa Borghese. What
views there are from it: from one side you can see San Pietro
with Monte Mario to its left, in the distance the hills; from the
other side of the garden the view is of the Campagna; the
foreground is covered with trees, but to the left one can see
part of a range of hills and the tip of Monte Cavo, on whose
summit there is a monastery; one sees the hills getting gradually
smaller and smaller, and the beginning of the endless Campagna. How can one fail to fall in love with it! ...

7. *Natalie Herzen to Alexander Herzen*

SATURDAY, 16 MAY 1863   *41 Via Porta Pinciana*
                                                              Roma

WHY NO letters from you for so long, Papasha my dear? Has one
of them perhaps gone astray? The last one, written on 2 May,
I received on 7. Since then I have become acquainted with the
Grant Duffs,[14] who love and respect you a great deal. They
returned a few days ago from Naples and at once sent word to
us that they wanted very much to make our acquaintance; we
betook ourselves there and were received very kindly and I was
immediately invited to take a ride with them to Tivoli. The old
lady told me how she had heard such a lot about you for so
long, and then at last you came for dinner and she "had the
happiness" to sit next to you; she says "he is certainly the most
amiable, clever, interesting, etc. man I ever met with".[15] Her

daughter says the same; I don't know if you remember her—rather thin with an exceedingly English face, but a clever and very charming woman. She seems to have taken a liking to me. It is a pity they did not stay here—her husband is a Swiss doctor and they live in Zurich all the time. And the mother is going directly to London and will pay you a visit—so please, receive her well and make a fuss of her.

We had a very jolly time at Tivoli. Gregorovius was with us and was exceedingly amiable with the daughter, that is Mme Obrist. The next day she came to see us again to go out for a drive, but we were not at home, we were in various Russian studios with Botkin—he had asked us to come because they were all *"Kolokolisty"* [supporters of *The Bell*], for the most part very poor. One of them had even been a serf, and this serf paints groups of children on mirrors, very charmingly; he is now completing his fourth mirror, for one of the grand princesses. But the best of the Russian painters we saw was in my view Bronnikov; if I am not mistaken, he too was a serf or a domestic; he paints mostly pictures of scenes from Ancient Roman history.

I have still not received *The Bell* and I fear I shall continue not to receive it. It is a great shame and very vexing—so much for *liberté* here—what does Malwida write to you? They do not allow any of your books through, nor *Punch*. So Mr Friken has to open all our cases in Florence and take out all your writings—such a nuisance!

Relations between Rome and Florence are almost non-existent and they refuse absolutely to send unstamped letters. But we can arrange to get *The Bell* in this way: send it to someone in Florence, Vieusseux, for instance, *sous bande*, and then let him send it to Rome in a letter. In this manner they will pass it. You could try sending it from England in a letter if that is [not] too expensive. What do you think? Did you know that old Vieusseux has died?[16] They say it is a great loss for Florence; his Saturday gatherings were most interesting. His nephews will not be able to fill his place in this respect, but they will carry on the bookseller's business. Some people are saying that Langiewicz has fled, that he gave his word to remain in the city and not take flight if they granted him his freedom—he was freed, and he fled. Others say that is not true and that he tried to escape from the prison but was retaken. But it seems there will not be any war.

Yesterday we visited the cupola of St Peter's—only from here does one appreciate the height of the church. Olga and I even clambered up to the dome—Malwida had not enough strength (it was excellent exercise for the thigh muscles)—and we were well rewarded, for we saw the place where the late Tsar Nicholas I had written with his own hand that he had been here and prayed for Russia. But how terrible the heat is now, simply dreadful. We were a little late returning, that is, we came home at midday—I am surprised we did not suffer from sunstroke. I do not advise you, Papasha, to come while it is still so hot, you would not be able to endure it. Settle instead for Sorrento or Capri, or Naples. The Grant Duffs have just been there and say we must visit it without fail, but in summer one has to arrange one's day wisely and then one will not suffer from the heat; that is, rise at four, or *even three* if possible (you will probably like that) and work or take the air before the heat sets in, then sleep during the heat, and in the evening, when it is cooler again, walk or work—it sounds splendid!

Now I have recommenced teaching Olga, she has not been studying of late. She has made a good start, and her other teachers are very well satisfied. Mlle Bongiorno (or something [. . .])[17] is pleased with her piano-playing, sig[nori]na Flegnaso is happy with her progress *nella lingua italiana*, and she is being altogether tricksy and amusing.

Signorina Flegnaso is coming at any moment. I don't know if we shall have dinner after her, and after dinner . . . the model will be *Stella*,[18] and so I must finish.

I kiss you all heartily, and again

Your TATA

We have also been to visit that famous Italian who shows cameos at all the exhibitions; he really has some amazingly beautiful trinkets, you would certainly have liked them; they are all so artistically done, simply like miniature sculptures. And also thanks to Mme Mae Grant Duff, I met Lehmann at their house, on the eve of their departure. You must have heard of him, a very fine German artist, he paints nothing but Italians and Italian girls and Italy; his wife is a young and extremely rich Scottish lady, a friend of Mme Grant Duff's daughter. He is fairly old; he at once offered me his services if he could be useful to me in any way, invited me to look in and see his atelier, and so forth.

8. *Natalie Herzen to Maria Reichel*

THURSDAY, 29 OCTOBER 1863
                                    Casa Bernato
                                    Bagni di Lucca

WE ARE already in Florence, 6 November.

So much time has passed since I wrote to you, my dear kind Masha, that I have been quite unable to bring myself to begin this letter, and now I blush as I take up my pen—but news is so slow coming to and from London and takes so long. I would like to hear something from you again and tell you one or two things myself. If you had at least scolded me for my slothfulness—but no, you made absolutely no allusion to it in your last letter, and then you stopped writing altogether—that was a severe punishment for me, but I deserved it.

But I say again, I have thought of you often, nevertheless, and now Sasha has advised me to send you all my unfinished letters as proof—one from the time when I was still in London and the others from Nice and Florence. But I am ashamed of them—they are stale and out-of-date—and I will just tell you about Nice, I expect you will enjoy that. You must know by now that our plans and hopes have been realized, that we have been in Italy for a long time now and that I have seen Nice once more (your last letter to me was sent to our London address).

Almost ever since the day we left Nice I had been longing to visit it again and see once more the places where I used to play with Kolya[19] or where I was accustomed to go with Mama, or simply see the town—so often had I dreamed of it and tried to recall every little incident and place that in fact I remembered a great deal, all those things that impress themselves on the memory of a child, those trifles that grown-ups, *i.e.* adults, do not notice. Just as you told me that you remembered your brother's hat blowing off and landing in the water. It was you who told me that, was it not?

So then you can imagine how my heart beat as we drew near to Nice; unfortunately it was night and I could not recognize anything. But the town seemed to me much larger than I had expected, and indeed there has been a great deal built since my first time there, and much has changed. Our last house there, the Maison Douïs, has been enlarged, another floor added, and the garden ruined—they are going to run a railway line through it. But the top end and the entrance are untouched, and the lime trees too—beneath which (I remember it so clearly) Olga and I used to sit and wait for you. . .

The Maison Sue is exactly as it was, even my own special little garden. It has been left untouched since I was there, and the gardener Jean and Claudine his wife are still living there; they recognized us at once and their delight and concern were so touching when they asked about everything and everyone. How different from the English! In England, a servant would never greet his master or show any concern for him—with the exception, perhaps, of domestics who have spent twenty or thirty years in the same household—and even after a period of separation he would not dare to be the first to hold out his hand and "shake hands". And here was "Claudine" embracing me on the spot and covering me with kisses, and obviously with such sincere joy and without the slightest thought that I might be displeased and take offence, as any English girl might think. Our cook Rocca, whom you probably remember, and his wife and daughter, treated us like their own children—how else would they? They have aged, of course, all of them; their daughter, who is my age, has already married and is the mother of two boys. They are good people; they live near the cemetery and all this time they have looked after the flowers on Mama's grave, written to us once or twice a year and sent us a flower.

I visited the grave, and Lord! how vividly I recalled the last days, that final day, the morning when Papa told me and I was taken in to kiss her, and the funeral, and our departure. I recognized the spot in the graveyard at once by the trees (there is still no inscription but now Papa wants to commission a memorial stone); they have grown a deal, but I remembered the location itself, in the left-hand corner. Hers was the only grave there at that time, now there are many of them, and many are Russian.

But I must tell you too what we are doing at the moment, so I have to go on with the journey. We arrived at Florence on 24 December, that is, the eve of my birthday, which I spent in a very dismal fashion despite my being in Italy. The day was a dismal and rainy one, and our hotel rooms so gloomy and *"unheimisch"*. But that soon passed, and a new life began, [new] occupations and [new] surroundings, and although we lived a very secluded life we could not fail to make the acquaintance of a few people. Professor Ussi came regularly to give me advice and correct my sketches, and sent me models. We soon became proficient in the Italian language, and so three months soon passed by. But something else happened during that time—I lost a friend and comrade, that dear, sweet girl Johanna Kinkel,[20] about whom I used to write to you. And the sad news came so unexpectedly, only a few days after her last letter to me, that I could not believe my eyes. The poor girl was only seventeen—too young to die—and so intelligent and full of promise.

She had written to me in her last letter that she had been ill (there had been a fierce epidemic of scarlet fever in London at the time, and Liza Ogareva had been sick too), but that she had quite recovered and was going out walking—and it was that unfortunate walk that was the end of her. She went out into the fresh air too soon, and a few days later, in February, she died in a coma. . .

So here I am again without a friend of my own age. What plans we used to dream up together, how we wondered what would happen to us in ten years', twenty years' time, how we resolved to try and be together always—and never once did the thought occur to us that one of us might die, although there had been many instances in both our families. How fortunate are those who believe in the immortality of the soul—I envy them at times. Why should they mourn? They know that their friends and relatives are not lost to them and that they will soon see them again and be happy for ever and ever. And so poor Johanna was buried next to her mother, who was also called Johanna and died a terrible death three years before her daughter—you probably know the tale.

At the end of March we went to Rome thinking to spend a month there, but stayed more than three.

I loved Rome very much. Partly because of memories—not my own, of course—but I found I already knew many places from Papasha's and Nathalie's stories. What a gay life you led then! And the city itself is so rich that one could spend a whole year, or even more, and still not know it properly. Papasha, who has been occupied solely and exclusively with politics, especially of late, cannot understand how one can possibly live there—and of course, it would be impossible for him. Censorship is very strict, there are hardly any journals and consequently even less news. But we don't find such things so essential and we had a very good time indeed there.

At the beginning of July the heat became intolerable. Everyone went away, and we decided to follow suit, and went to Naples, where we also spent about three months, not in Naples itself but nearby, a month at Vico Equense near Sorrento, five weeks on the isle of Capri, where we saw the famous blue Grotto, then back to Naples to await the arrival of Papasha.

He came on 28 Sept[ember], bringing Sasha with him for a surprise. You can imagine how overjoyed we were. I had not spent so long away, you see, ever since Paris. I was glad for Papasha too, [glad] that he would have some rest and distraction—at least for a little while—but he has grown more and more accustomed to his free and solitary life in England and nothing abroad is to his taste. He was extremely displeased with Naples. Indeed, the Neapolitans, and their lives, are so dreadfully *empty*, the town itself such a humdrum place (of course I am not talking of the wonderful views, or the museum,

63

which is splendidly rich), and one cannot travel outside the town, for the danger of brigands is greater than ever. Papasha did want to see Florence but, afraid of meeting some acquaintance there, he decided to spend a little time with us in peace and quiet, and so we went to Pisa, and then to here, Bagni di Lucca, and the day after tomorrow we leave for Florence for two weeks.

On 22 November or thereabouts we shall part again. Papasha and Sasha will go to London, and we will go to Rome, so please write to me there at the *poste restante*. Are you tired of me, dear Masha? There is so much else I would like to say but I will leave it for another time.

Forgive me for my long silence and write and tell me how you are keeping and what news there is of auntie L[. . .]. Papasha and all of us send our best regards.

Your TATA HERZEN

Has Mme Tepliakova been to see you and has she given you the briefcase and the little album which I sent for my Sasha?

In Alexander Herzen's handwriting

9 November. Here we are in this dreadful wilderness and about to come back to the mists of London; we send you all our sincerest regards.

PÈRE ET FILS

9. *Natalie Herzen to Sasha Herzen*

1 AUGUST 1864 [*Bournemouth*]

FROM THE moment we arrived in Bournemouth, dear kind Pan has been running from one end of London to the other again, from Fulham to Hampstead, from H[ampstead] to Richmond, from R[ichmond] to Primrose Hill, finding us magnificent houses. A house in Fulham, for instance, of immense size, with innumerable rooms, a big garden, a kitchen-garden (the products of which could be sold—*profit tout clair*—*in winter*) *and a field* where we could keep *hens and a cow*!! And what's more, it's almost next door to that "great wit", our friend Prince Petr Dolgorukov.[21] Papa was dreaming of this house even before Garibaldi's visit, but then the whole idea was suddenly dropped, like a *pot au lait*; Gueneau de Mussy[22] declared the house was damp and unhealthy. However, Pan was ready with another proposition—on Maida Hill, right beside the canal, by the bridge that you cross to go to *Kinkel's*; a large house with a garden, built after the American fashion, that is, as described in *Paris en Amérique*; there is a bath in every bedroom, with hot and cold water etc.—in short, yes, an ideal home. We only await the signing of the lease, but instead of it, an entirely different document is being signed, quite unlike the lease for a house. And about time too!!!

Ogarev and Nathalie add that they, that is, Nathalie, has agreed and decided that at the end of October 1864 she will go to . . . ?? Away from England; but Ogarev, who is to join them, will go in March 1865.

What wonderful sights, one cannot believe one's own eyes, and, oddly enough, I feel sad at having to say farewell in earnest to England.

What do you say to that? At the end of October we are going to Rome; Papa will go with us as far as Switzerland to find a boarding-school for Olga! I kiss you affectionately.

Your TATA

I'm expecting Katya to arrive; she promised to come up from Wales for a few days; Amélie sent me a long letter, to which I am just about to reply. They lead a fine life, though not greatly engaged in intellectual pursuits.

10. Natalie Herzen to Maria Reichel

24 AUGUST 1864   *Bryanston House*
                                                Bournemouth
                                                Hampshire

WE ARE in Bournemouth again, Masha dear, that charming place where we spent the autumn four years ago, after my trip to Dresden. We are having a fine time here—at least, *I* am, although I feel sad every now and then.

I have learned a great deal about the past—[Papasha's] "Past"²³—and I have come to treasure Papasha's love for us more and more of late. I feel we are becoming closer to each other. He has grown more affectionate, though he regards me as a "grown-up", not a child. We spend more time together and often go for walks, just the two of us. Consequently our parting is becoming more difficult, more painful, but I cannot work at home. Of course, I can't say it has been a complete waste of time, I have been reading, playing the piano and developing my mind in other ways. But everything distracts me—the children, the conversation—and I cannot concentrate sufficiently on my painting. I feel I must spend the winter at least in a place where none of these interests intrude, [I must] be in an artistic milieu.

Here in England, you see, we do not know a single artist; and, distances being what they are in London, it is so difficult to do anything; we can only bring ourselves to pay a visit to an art gallery once a year. So it is very likely that we (that is, Mlle Meysenbug, Olga and myself) will winter once again in Rome. We hesitated at first for fear that this solitary life was doing Olga more harm than good. She is as intelligent as always, but scatter-brained and a dreadful child still, I mean, uncultured, *très enfant* and an *enfant terrible*, especially when the three of us are together, because she is aware of Malwida's blind adoration, which quite often makes her speak unfairly, and insists on having everything her own way, refuses to listen to me, and with her passion for teasing (inherited from Papasha) she has driven me at times to curse Italy, Rome and our *trinité*, but I have been unable to do anything about it.

31 AUGUST

I had begun this letter before my note of yesterday. I wanted to write a little more to you but Papasha was in a hurry and so I added a few words to his letter.

Don't imagine, though, that Olga's pranks are so dreadful, after all, it is most often the fault of the adults and not the children. Perhaps it is a fortunate thing that she is still such an *enfant*; she hates learning and cannot sit still at all for a moment. Her chief pleasure is climbing trees, dressed in boy's clothes; like me, she is very partial to horse-riding, and we often ride out together. Her features are clearly altering, and she is growing more and more like Sasha. She can be very graceful *when she wants*, and very sweet and funny and comical. She has a talented nature but she is terribly difficult to cope with. I have taken Liza somewhat in hand and have been trying to play the role of mother. She has been sleeping in my room, and I dress and undress her, and I give her lessons, which has afforded and still affords me great pleasure, because she is a clever child and eager to learn with me. I must admit I have not been torment- ing her with dry subjects, I simply tell her anything I know, draw maps for her and read to her. All Ogarev's children are clever.[24] The twins are awfully funny. You cannot imagine two more contrasted natures, both physically and mentally. Firstly, to Nathalie's great shame I discovered that they speak only English—they understand a little Russian but cannot speak a word of it. Since they are both *Lelya*, they are called Lelya-boy and Lelya-girl to distinguish them. The girl is bigger, stronger, and more lively; she rushes about noisily and gives us no peace, and has poor Nathalie under her thumb; she is dark-skinned and much more like a boy than her brother, who is very quiet and serious and always plays by himself, the little *misanthrope*. His hair is nearly white; but they are very attached to one another, although Papa says that when they are grown up and living together she'll say to him: "We're twins, we were born together, so you pay my debts!"

It is terrible and vexing to see how such dear children can be spoiled by blind love, or foolish love, I don't know how to describe it. Nathalie spoils them in the same way that Malwida spoils Olga, and although their characters are so different, Malwida being perpetually calm and patient while Nathalie is impatient and quick-tempered, love makes both of them act wrongly and the effect on their children's upbringing is identical in both cases.

But I am probably boring you with all these details, Masha dear; you cannot be as interested as I am in them. For myself they worry me tremendously, because, however much I may love those two women, there is always something that prevents us becoming really sincere, close friends.

Farewell, I embrace you warmly and beg you once again not to be angry and think that I do not love you any more, when the reason for my not having written is my laziness.

Your TATA HERZEN

We are alone now in this big empty house. It is dreadfully dismal and the weather is rainy too. Papasha and Ogarev are already in London at *Tunstall House, Maida Hill.*

My warm greetings to Reichel, and I kiss the children, especially my Sasha. Is there any news from Russia?

Have you heard anything of Mariechen? She should have returned by now.

You will probably get a letter from me on my name-day; write me a few words or just think of us, and I will drink to your health.

11. *Natalie Herzen to Alexander Herzen*

22 MARCH 1865   *136 Via Felice*
                                                        Roma

FORGIVE ME, my dear kind Papasha, indeed I feel I have been dreadfully absentminded of late. But don't be angry, don't think I am forgetting you or thinking of you less often; no, I often see you in my dreams and when I awake I feel so vexed and grieved at not being able to hug and kiss you and everybody in reality. Mme Schwabe[25] is partly to blame for my absentmindedness. I have never seen a woman like her; she is liable at any moment to make anybody she pleases sit down at the desk and write, copy or read, or give them heaps of errands and suchlike.

I am sending you my photograph, taken here in Rome. Many people think that I am very like Napoleon I, but that's nothing new; new, though, is the fact that Mimi Oppenheim contrived it. What is your opinion? Everyone here likes it very much.

How odd, Papasha, that a few hours before receiving your letter I had been writing and complaining that we had no Russian acquaintances now, that we had found ourselves in a circle of Germans and had become stuck there. So it seems we share the same view. I too am vexed. But one thing I will say to you—I doubt if these are any better than the others. At Mme Schwabe's we have met many English girls, and they are all leading such an empty life, you simply cannot imagine. Mornings and afternoons spent in visits and more visits, and in the evenings dances and parties, all of them in their own circle: today *chez* Mrs So-and-so, tomorrow Mrs What-have-you, the next day at Lady —'s, the whole season exactly like London.

The Russians I am unable to judge, since I know absolutely no one except Mlle Kapnist, who has spent so much time away from town this winter that I have seen her only two or three times, and then only glimpsed her for a minute or two. She is very often to be seen in the Italian circle, which is easy for her since her brother serves in the Embassy. She goes to the balls at Doria's, Borghese's, and all the ministers'. The other Russians probably lead the same sort of life. What have we in common with them, and what would be the point of making their acquaintance?

It would be interesting to go to a ball at one of the palaces here to see the effect—those magnificent, vast chambers with their paintings. But all this is not for us. One has to have fine clothes, carriages, and so forth. The Germans do everything *gemütlich* and simply, but we have little in common with them either. I am seeing hardly anyone at the moment except the Oppenheims. The daughter is very sweet, lively and amusing, utterly German by nature.

Gregorovius visits us frequently and we give him English lessons, that is, we make him read Macaulay's essays about the India of Lord Clive. He in his turn brings me various books to read. I have just finished Calderon's tragedy *Das Leben ist ein Traum*. Do you know it? It all takes place in Poland. A Polish king brings up his son in the wilds, in a remote castle in a

69

forest, because he has learned from the stars that the son will be a tyrant and a villain. Gregorovius advises me to read two or three more things by Calderon, and then some of the ancient Greek poets.

What makes you write so about Olga? Malwida says she never wrote to you that the lessons were going well; she says that *the lessons themselves* and the teachers are good ones, but Olga is still so absentminded that she drives one to despair, the more so since it is evidently not a matter of *mauvaise volonté*: she is willing but unable. I have just written to Nathalie to say that she, *i.e.* Olga, now has a very sweet girl-friend who is having a very good effect upon her nerves, Theophania, the fifteen-year-old daughter of the gentleman who was asking after you. But the things Olga does at school! Even the serious Theophania cannot control herself during lessons and sometimes wets herself with laughing. Now there are four of them, Olga, Ersinia, Ginevra and Theophania; all [the others] are far ahead of Olga despite the fact that the Italian girls have never studied in French before. I am very glad to hear that Aga is recovering; where can I write to him?

I kiss you, Papasha, my friend
Your TATA H.

12. *Natalie Herzen to Maria Reichel*

21 DECEMBER 1865
Château Boissière
Route de Chêne
Genève

YOU HAVE not had any direct news from us for ages, Masha dear, and I should like to know how you are and what you are up to, so I shall do without lengthy preambles and give you some idea, though I fear a distant one, of everything. First, imagine you have come to Geneva, and have been riding for ten minutes on the *Tramway* (American omnibuses on rails); the conductor rings the bell and the driver comes to a halt outside some big gates. "*La Grande Boissière, Madame.*" You go in at the gates and up a long avenue fenced on both sides. Then suddenly you see some more gates to your right, and an enormous, grey, two-storied house; not the usual, fashionable quadrangular box that one sees nowadays, but slightly [more] decorative; with a door in the centre, under a big colonnade, and above this colonnade another, or rather a long terrace ornamented with architrave, which gives it the appearance of a Greek temple. Like all who come here for the first time, you would make for the large central door which is always locked in winter.

But let us assume that for some special reason it is open, and you open the glass [inner] door and step into a large, square room with a terribly slippery stone floor, apparently deserted, cold and comfortless. To the right and above the stove Napoleon stands in an alcove, arms folded, wearing his three-cornered hat, and glaring at the bust of Granovsky in the left-hand corner. This is the summer dining-room. What are you to do? There are three doors, one to the right, one to the left, and one in front of you. And everywhere silence. But suddenly you hear the cacophonous barking of dogs, and it is easy to tell that the noise is coming from the right. You knock, and barking is the only reply. You open the door and in an instant Mme Linda (Olga's dog) and her puppies are all over you. Evidently you have made a mistake, for this is a bedroom—also abandoned and chilly (formerly Sasha's). You close the door thinking, "I'll try the one in front of me." You knock: silence. You enter —it is a huge drawing-room. In every corner there are statues poised on their pedestals, and in the centre, large tables with a few books lying on them; there is a pianoforte, but it is cold here too and feels uninhabited. There are two windows, and a glass door leading into the garden, with a view of the vast garden and the mountains. There are doors to the right and left—what are you going to do? Once again you take the right, open it and—what is this? Pitch blackness! All the shutters are closed, but thanks to the light streaming in through the door as you enter you see an apparently endless hall about fifty-four feet in length. Here too there are alcoves accommodating Venuses, Cupids, and Bacchuses . . . and chandeliers hang from the ceiling. You close the door again and begin to think that you have come to the wrong place, that this house is antediluvian, abandoned. You go through the left-hand door, and there too you find no one. The wallpaper is a fantasy of imaginary tropical plants reminding one of the dining-room at the Villa Livia, which belonged to the wife of Augustus, at the Prima Porta near Rome, except that there the artist had evidently studied nature rather more carefully—well, it can't be helped, art has progressed. Here, however, there hang other works of art: first an allegorical painting showing limpid figures flying, bearing a Bell, while above them shines a Star, and below . . . [——][26] There are various copies, heads of Rembrandt, Galileo, "Bella di Tiziano". So you discover after all that you are in Herzen's house, and in the dining-room.

You go out, though, and find a passage, and a staircase. You mount it and open a door to your right, and there you see a kitchen, also unused. The doors are numbered, just like in a *hôtel*. You open one and step inside, and there is a table, chairs, a cupboard, a settee; everything is tidy and in its place. Two windows open onto a large balcony—but no one is there. You step into the next room; it is bigger than the first, with two windows and a glass door giving onto a balcony; sparsely furnished, but there is a bed, which means it must be a bedroom—also uninhabited. You enter the third room, the windows of which also look out over the balcony; this room too has a bed, and is also evidently uninhabited. Had you not lost your patience, and continued instead along the same side of the corridor, you would have seen two more rooms, making in all five uninhabited rooms on one side. But you have grown weary of this; you come out into the passage and go into a room on the other side. Here you are aware of a pleasant warmth in the air. The furniture is prettier and in the centre of the room there is a big round table with books, papers, journals, flowers, pencils and such like on it. There are shelves of books, and on the mantelpiece a bust of Pushkin and an Etruscan vase. . . A little table standing by the window is also piled with books and papers, and a microscope; there is an easel in one corner with an unfinished portrait of "Iskander", rags, paint-boxes and brushes. To the right are two small steps into a bedroom; to the left a door leading into a minute boudoir with a small table and a vase of flowers, a tiny sofa, a bench and a diminutive apology for a harmonium. . . Yes, this is Tata's winter hide-away. At last you have discovered where I am. Here is where I spend my whole day.

What do I do? I have become a "schoolgirl"[27] again, although I shall soon be of age, you know. Most of the morning of course, I spend drawing. Recently I did a portrait of Papasha, a small-scale profile—I usually manage to get a good likeness. At the moment I am about to embark upon a big, "serious" portrait of our neighbour, Mme Kasatkina,[28] in oils, of course. Thanks to Mme Lion,[29] who has persuaded me to take singing lessons, I am now occupied with that too. Sometimes, fre-quently, even, my voice strays and changes *ad libitum* from soprano to contralto. I often catch cold, you see, and after one very severe chill my voice really did change. Of course, I do not dare to sing in front of anyone. I am learning for purely egoistical, family reasons—I give Papasha, Ogarev and myself pleasure, and for the rest I care nothing. Were it not for the terrible effort it would cost me, I might perhaps try it, but then the pleasure would become a torment for me. It is natural that in my almost monastic solitude I cannot rid myself of my "prim, embarrassed shyness". Apart from this I am visited regularly by a Pole who tells me all kinds of wondrous things about the natural sciences. It is awfully interesting. And then I read and write a little and chat with Papasha, and before you can blink an eyelid it's time to hop into bed. . .

So you see I am still all by myself. Olga and Mlle Meysenbug and Sasha are in Florence. Mlle M[eysenbug] could not endure the climate here, to which even my iron constitution was forced to yield, and then, too, perhaps Olga can be made to settle down to her studies there. Knowing her character and the routine in our household, you can understand that it has been almost impossible here. Nathalie has still not come to her senses, and never will—her life is over. Last year's misfortune destroyed her completely.[30] It is her awareness of her duty to Liza that sustains her, otherwise she would long since have ceased to live. The poor woman tortures herself, and that is worse than anything. Instead of trying to forget or at least to distract herself, she surrounds herself with all the children's things, and their cots, and never goes to bed. Somehow she eats and gets sleep, no matter how—she is indifferent to everything, and waits impatiently for death. I feel dreadfully sorry for her, but there is nothing I can do to help. Fearing the severe winter and the *bise*, she too has gone away, with Liza; they are in Montreux. We frequently visit them by turns. It was there that I caught a cold, but I did do some good work; I mean, I arranged Liza's studies. It is a shame to leave such a clever, lively child with nothing to occupy her. And futhermore, unlike us, she is an excellent pupil and loves to learn. As for ourselves, we are developing our minds so late in life that it would not be worth the trouble for such a short time.

My correspondence too has declined considerably. Paulina Levitskaya is now in Russia, Mimi Oppenheim, a most charming and lively girl with whom I made friends in Rome, has followed the example of all my other close girl-friends and died. In England I have left nobody behind. There is only Katya and my "old friends" like you, my dear Masha. Apropos of that, Sasha receives whole volumes, with illustrations and all sorts of rubbish, called "The Little Bell". He really is a good lad despite the fact that he is my brother; I am very fond of him. I cannot get on with the Genevan girls—what have I in common with them? I should only be dragged into their society life and visiting round.

There are lots of Russians here but for the most part they cannot or do not wish to become acquainted with us, while the *émigré* community—like all other such—if it consists of only ten people will form as many (or more) factions. The chief foes, the Montagues and Capulets of Geneva, are the "Boissièreites" and the so-called "Lyudmilovtsy", led by Herzen and Mme Shelgunova.[31] And the Russian youth of today are so strange, the women as well as the men. You must have encountered some of these Nihilists at sometime or other and know some of them. It is a stupid name, but that is what they call themselves. This absence of any "forms", to the point of gracelessness, startles us "backward" people. . .

So then, I am living a life of the most egoistical kind. The only good I am doing is perhaps that my presence gives Papasha pleasure.

He is still as lively and cheerful as ever and seems pleased with me, and so I am happy too. Poor Ogarev is growing weaker and his health is bad, but he has not changed either—still a gentle, kind, affectionate old bear. What will become of us after the lease of our flat has expired I don't know. We shall not, in any case, stay here. Papasha is used to large towns and naturally has grown weary of all the gossip here. And the house is no good to us any more; indeed, it stands almost empty. I have no idea where we shall take off to. Papasha seems to be trying to arrange for the two of us to stay together. We shall live somewhere in Vevey, Montreux, Lugano, the South of France, Mesopotamia, or maybe China. But I feel uneasy; I am afraid I shall become unsociable. In any event I shall go and visit Olga and Sasha in Florence from time to time. I have a lot of acquaintances there.

Now tell me about yourself and your family—how is Sasha? Is he still difficult to cope with? What of Ernest and the stranger? How is your health, and Reichel's? I thank you and kiss you for the postcard, although the photograph is a bad one and I cannot recognize anything on it.

Did you follow the affair of the "fires" and the accusations made against Papasha?[32] Do you see how all our former friends are dropping away? Turgenev, though, sent his regards again a few days ago, and a message to say that he hoped their relationship would continue as before. I don't know why, but I was overjoyed. It is sad, after all, to see people who were once friendly and intimate becoming gradually estranged from one another; and then, you must admit, he is an agreeable person despite all those dreadful caprices of his. And what of Annenkov?[33] And Botkin? I met Annenkov in Paris about eighteen months ago. His attitude to me was the same as ever—that of an old friend, but since then I have not heard a word from him. As for Botkin, Papasha recently met him quite unexpectedly in Montreux. Papa went up to him and he became all flustered and mumbled something or other. The next day they merely bowed to each other. Well, I take my leave of you and wish you all the best for the new year, and embrace you. Write to me, please.

Your TATA H.

13. *Natalie Herzen to Sasha Herzen*

15 MAY 1866   *7 Quai Mont Blanc*
Genève

MY DEAR SANDRO-SPECOLINO,

At last we have received a few words from you. There is no need for me to write and tell you how glad I am just to think you will soon be coming.

It[34] would be awfully nice! If you don't mean to be peevish and difficult we might arrange a jolly little uncomfortable hole for your dear bonity here! It would be good for your pocket too. Do, doooo come.

But now, how, where, when, for how long?? Do answer quickly. As to Berthe, you know how heavily my solitude weighs upon me, I long to have a companion and friend. I like Berthe already, for your sake and thanks to the portraits you give of her character—if they be thine my affection can only increase after personal acquaintance. It is true I'll feel my "Zeroness" by the side of her, I am rather afraid of it. Confess it is anything but agreeble [*sic*]. But I hope she will be kind to me, so I will profit of her company—give her my warmest, kindest regards if she still shines upon the "City of Flowers". So we will soon see [?], welcome Phoebus, we require you here—it is so cold, that I have caught a cold and must stay indoors. And so let thy dear head be kissed by thy own sister's ruby lips and forget not to give the compliments to Schiff and Co., Levier et Berduschek. You might well send me the *photographes of both*. B. owes me one, promised at her [?] goods [?]. N.B. *Letat'* ["to fly", in Russian] is spelt with an *e*. I wish you would do the same for my [mistakes].

76

14. *Natalie Herzen to Maria Reichel*

26 MAY 1866   *No. 7 Quai Mont Blanc*
                                               Genève

I CANNOT tell you how grieved I was to read your letter, my
dear Masha. Grieved, conscience-stricken, annoyed and
ashamed to be living at Boissière in such comfort while you are
cramped, uncomfortable and ill-housed! What would I not
have given to change places with you at that moment! To fly
to your side and offer what help I could—to look after the
children! When will you ever be at peace, when will you ever
manage to take a rest?

You have perpetual worries, perpetual troubles; first the
children fall sick and then Reichel. I meant to write to you
from Boissière, the moment I got your letter, with a proposal
and an invitation to come and stay with us. I would have
tried to pamper you a little. You would have loved to be in
the big garden, and sit on the velvety grass under the old
trees. But the time came for us to give up the house and we
said farewell to it and exchanged it for a small flat in the town,
where Papasha and I have made our new home, just the two
of us together. Ogarev is in the mountains taking an ice cure,
and with some success.

There isn't a single inch to spare here; even our faithful Pan
Tchorzewski has had to rent a tiny room for himself in the
neighbourhood. Two bedrooms, a drawing-room and a dining-
room—just right for the servants' quarters—that's all we have.
But what a view! Over the lake to Mont Blanc, and wonderfully fine and peaceful of an evening, with innumerable lights
reflected in the lake. And I am often left quite alone here (as
I am now), when Papasha goes away for a few days to see
Nathalie and Lizochka in Lausanne. But this is nothing new
for me. The days pass so quickly and without my noticing,
especially when the weather is bad. I sit here on my own and
study and suddenly it's evening; but if it's fine outside I am
vexed that there is no one for me to go out with (when Papa
is away).

But I spent five weeks going out and having a fine time in

77

Montreux. Having bade farewell to Boissière I went to Nathalie's intending to stay with them for a week, but remained for more than a month. We lived in the Hôtel des Alpes Veytaux, in the vicinity of Chillon, a little way beyond Montreux.

Our *co-pensionnaires*, for the most part English, were very courteous to me; and furthermore, a relative of Nathalie's arrived and we went skating on the lake, walking and climbing together; in a word, I had a splendid time. Please don't make a romance out of it. A girl has only to mention a person of masculine gender and it becomes a *fait accompli*, a ready-made romance, everything is obvious to everyone and everybody knows everything, when there is nothing to it! Nathalie's relative is almost as unhappy as she herself—he recently lost his wife, whom he passionately loved, and his daughter—her mother died after giving birth to her.

I read a strange sentence in your letter to Papasha, Masha my dear. You ask him, apparently in horror and amazement: "Are you really training her to be an old maid?" referring to myself. You might think what I am about to say to you rather odd, but it is true that family life holds no particular attraction for me.

Statistics have proved here in Switzerland that the majority of girls get married at the age of fifteen, between the ages of sixteen and eighteen, and even more frequently after the age of twenty-five. It is probably the same in other countries too, and it is very natural. Until she is eighteen a girl may still dream, *se faire de belles illusions,* may throw herself into the arms of the first man she meets and bind herself for the rest of her life without considering what she is doing, and even so that is more likely to happen here, and in France, and in Europe as a whole, than in the Russia of today where, thanks to that much-maligned nihilism, girls develop intellectually and try to be independent at a much earlier age. Of course, there are the giddy ones even amongst them. But there is another reason for that—boastfulness or bravado, to prove they are "emancipated". After the age of eighteen a girl begins to reason, *on devient plus difficile.* For myself this early period passed off very calmly and peaceably—now I have reached the *difficile* stage, and I must confess, my dear Masha, I don't know whether it's because I see too few people or whether I am hard to satisfy, but I have not yet come across a man whom I have liked in every respect—and I am not talking about his appearance, which to my mind is, if not utterly immaterial, then still one of the least important considerations. But perhaps I am cold by nature—however unpleasant I find the thought, I have to admit that it must be so. . .

It is unpleasant to refuse, but what can one do when one feels that it is never the *right person*. Just this last summer I had to refuse someone.[35] And I myself was vexed and grieved by it. He was a young Russian, so good and clever and serious, and was studying the natural sciences (in my opinion an *important quality*). Papa had taken a great liking to him. But he simply wasn't what I was looking for. He was almost too practical-minded; or, how should I express it, I am not seeking after idealism (may God forbid, we leave that to the Germans, *n'en déplaise à Reichel*), but, for example, it was clear that the arts did not exist for him, despite all his desire to understand and appreciate them—it all smacked of utilitarianism, and offended me. Next winter I shall be going once more to Italy, and this time again to Florence. We are expecting Sasha. He wants to see Ogarev, who is unable to travel. He will stay here a while and then we shall go together to Florence to visit Olga and Malwida. I shall remain there, but Papa will return and live in the little apartment with Ogarev. It is quite possible that first Papasha and I will go on a short excursion to *"Como"* to pay a call on Garibaldi. The headquarters of the volunteers will be there.

So Europe will soon be once again flowing with blood. This terrible war! Many people here desire it and are waiting impatiently for it to begin.[36] But the more I hear and think about the whole of this business of war, the more I am disgusted, repelled and frightened by it. Man becomes worse than a wild beast and millions of people kill each other, for the most part ignorant of their aim and unthinking of the consequences and of the sufferings of their near and dear ones after every death, every wound. Read the next issue of *The Bell* and you will see how good life is in Russia too at the moment. Reading about those *horrors* really makes one's hair stand on end. That wretched Karakozov, he certainly did Russia a good turn by his shot.[37] There is no end to the arrests—all our acquaintances have been arrested and are in the hands of Muravev,[38] and that's as good as saying they are being tortured. Karakozov is a fanatic, that's clear, and there was no conspiracy there; but the opportunity to "clean up Russia" was too good to miss.

And look how they're tackling the job—the student Belgin was arrested and ordered to implicate Nikolay Utin in the affair—a young *émigré* who has been living perfectly peaceably and quietly here. Belgin refused to lie, so they treated him to a whipping. He preferred death to *falsehood* and hanged himself one night. You will find out from *The Bell* what they are doing to Karakozov. I believe even *that* will be printed too. What has become of Stankevich and Dusha? Where are they?

I embrace and kiss you heartily, my dear Masha, and all your family. What is my Shushka up to? Does he still intend to go to America, or has his "fiery, mettlesome blood" grown cooler?

Your TATA HERZEN

15. *Natalie Herzen to Alexander Herzen*

26 NOVEMBER 1866   *41 Via S. Monaca*
                                    Firenze

IT LOOKS as if they will never give you any peace, Papasha dear. More nasty business with the Poles—what is it this time?[39] And I did not expect it of Serno-Solovevich; you really must break off all relations with him after this. The whole thing must be founded on some sort of misunderstanding. But do explain in more detail what it is. You will soon have been two years in Geneva, and not a month has gone by without some unpleasantness or other, first the "Lyudmilovtsy", then Kasatkin, then Dolgorukov, then the printing press. . . And the worst of it all is that the end is nowhere in sight. Come to us quickly and have a rest here. What makes you write to Malwida that it would not be a rest for you? Nonsense—you can be sure that we shall arrange everything properly for you and be "good girls" ourselves. Come quickly and forget about silly Geneva and its malicious gossip.

We have been in a state of dreadful agitation these last few days. Many of the professors who are not engaged in the [teaching of the] natural sciences but more in political economy and, in particular, the economy of the Italian government have been complaining loudly of late that foreign professors are having to be appointed and paid to educate Italian youth—young professors, while they labour in humble obscurity for the "good of mankind" and the natural sciences in general. This, of course, applied above all to Schiff. And so one fine morning Schiff was invited to see the Minister of Education, who offered him the chair of Professor of Physiology at Naples. Schiff asked for a few days' grace to consider the offer. Imagine the mess that would have resulted from it—the Schiffs would have left in December, Sasha would have been stranded here with absolutely no purpose, or would have gone to Naples, and we should be left here without our best friends. And so the whole of our circle was dreadfully alarmed for all of the week. Fortunately, though, Schiff turned down the offer and instead wants to stay and improve the educational establishment here. We are assured for another year, the "skiffs" are near at hand and we shall not drown...

The public lectures are beginning just now; tomorrow we are going to hear Professor Villari on the history of Florence. From next week there will be popular Sunday lectures in Specolo.

Farewell—when should we make your room ready for you, for what date?

I kiss Nathalie and Lizochka; I have written to them and Ogarev; have they received my letters? My regards to Pan.

Your TATA

I am getting to know some young girls. The two I like best are Berthe Sommier and a half-Italian, half-English girl, Alice Sonino, but we do not see each other often.

F

Everyone sends you kisses, that is, M[alwida], S[asha] and Olga.

16. *Natalie Herzen to Alexander Herzen*

6 DECEMBER 1866   *41 Via Santa Monaca*
                                                                  Firenze

DID OLGA frighten you? How I laughed when I read her letter. I wonder if you will like our way of life or not; unfortunately our circle will be losing its chief members by the time you arrive. At the moment it is all as Olga described it *(for external description look page 4th)*.[40]

1) Schiff—on physiology
2) Blaserna—on physics
3) Berduschek—on architecture; he has only lectured once
4) Monod—on literature and history; but he too has only read one lecture
5) Levier—on botany
6) Sasha on physiology, No. 2.

So far there has been no connection between these *conversations*, and all the people concerned with the natural sciences come in for by far the most questions. Blaserna talks more than anyone; knowing that he will soon be going away, everybody wants to make the most of his presence. On Sunday he gave a public lecture at Specolo on the earth's magnetism. The public was exceedingly pleased. There is a popular lecture every Sunday, and, besides that, twice-weekly instruction in various subjects, so that every day there is something to listen to. I will try to go to all these lectures. Emile Vogt[41] is here and came yesterday to hear poor Levier's *début*. Levier is so shy that he was as afraid of giving his lecture to our circle as anyone else would be of reading a public lecture. But everything went well in spite of his continually blushing and saying *"Oh! Mon Dieu, je m'embrouille . . ."* Now I am impatiently awaiting Sasha's *début*; he explains things very well when we are alone. But I can see that the very thought that the same people will be gathering in order to *listen* to him is a little frightening. I think you will like

Monod best of all; he really is very sweet in spite of Malwida's rapturous descriptions (I say *in spite of*, because descriptions like that usually spoil one's impression).

He has read an awful lot, one cannot name anything without his saying *"Oh, je connais cela!"* He is far more serious than the rest, more abstract, and incapable of making a joke; though he did today tell us a most amusing anecdote (he visits Malwida on two mornings a week for German language lessons). He told us how he arrived in Pisa one evening last year and wanted to go to the theatre and see what it was like. He set off in search of it and finally caught sight of a large, magnificently illuminated building (he is very absentminded, always lost in theories and forgetting *present reality*). He went in and was struck by the fact that there was no one on the ground floor and even the tickets were being sold on the first floor. He mounted the huge staircase and entered a brilliantly lit hall, the doors to which were open *à deux battants*, and saw a throng of people, the ladies in *décolletés*, the gentlemen in tails (Monod was wearing his travelling-suit). Suddenly a gentleman came up to him and very courteously requested him to leave his coat and come in. Monod was dumbfounded and only then realized that he had made a terrible mistake and wandered into a private house where there was a ball or an evening reception.

WEDNESDAY

Papasha, although you do not explain why you can only come for ten days now, it is clear that it would be better to wait, but you *simply must* come for the New Year and my birthday. Really, you must arrange that. And now farewell, I have a terrible headache.

The picture of [?] in *Punch* is indeed dreadfully vile.

1) Schiff.   *Height:* of small stature, always wears suit, fur-coat.
  Head: rounded, masses of grey and black hair covering almost the whole of his face.

2) Blaserna.   *Height:* if anything smaller than Schiff, plump, always wears suit even on the coldest of days, frock coat. Very fair, Jewish type. Voice diminutive, quiet, attractive. Expression extremely good-natured, loves laughing. Italian simplicity and *sans-gêne*.

83

    3) Berduschek. *Height:* equal to that of Blaserna standing on Schiff's shoulders. Ultra-fair, ultra-German type, ultra-unattractive hands reminding me of lizard's claws, ultra-unhealthy look, ultra-sparse beard, an ultra-fastidious creature, ultra-tiresome . . . but a very nice man.

    4) Monod.   *Height:* tall.
                    Head: pure French . . .

I cannot go on, my head aches too much, but let me just set your mind at rest about the Mondays of which Olga wrote. So far hardly anybody has been except Friken and the Muravevs, but you yourself will understand that it is far better to arrange a definite day and say "we are in from 2 to 5", and not to receive anyone else for the remainder of the week.

Where are you going? I cannot make head or tail [of your movements]. Liza and Nathalie wrote that Nice was too expensive and most probably nothing would come of that idea.

Concerning the linen: Tchorzewski knows that only *the items marked "nouveaux"* or *"nouvelles"* in his book are to be included, because the rest is jumble; we have taken one tablecloth, twelve napkins and twelve towels, that is all.

17. Natalie Herzen to Nikolay Ogarev

[18 APRIL 1867]   *[Florence]*

I SHALL commence with the most important event, my dear Aga. Yesterday evening we were at Garibaldi's! On the previous day Mme Mario[42] had met Olga and said to her: "Garibaldi is here. If you wish to see him, come tomorrow evening—*we'll be alone with a few gentlemen.*"[43] Well, to say the least, I was expecting it all to turn out very badly; after all, there are crowds of people waiting to see him everywhere. We went, and as we drove up to the house we could see a mass of carriages; and [inside the house] upstairs, the arrangement was exceedingly stupid. In the first room there sat Garibaldi, wearing a rather too original costume—just as he appears on the most recent photographs—Papasha saw them here. Some sort of embroidered velvet cap, and a brightly-coloured greatcoat over a red shirt—so there he sat, surrounded by the ladies, who were gazing at him and saying nothing; a dreadfully stupid arrangement—the men were all in another room. However, when we entered, and Mme Mario said that we were Herzen's daughters, he was exceedingly amiable and courteous [to us]. I took a seat near him and he at once began questioning me about Papa, asked me to convey his best regards to him, and inquired also: *"Où est donc Alexandre?"* Poor Sasha, though, was in bed with the most terrible headache and nausea. But he will be going to visit him now.

What a splendid head Garibaldi has, and such a calm, kind expression. I am very sorry that I cannot see him in peace, but still, I am content [merely] to have seen him. . .

18. *Alexander Herzen to Natalie Herzen*

FRIDAY, 7 JUNE 1867   [*Geneva*]

DEAR TATA,

I am very pleased with your letter and kiss you for it with all my heart. That you are right about Liza there can be no doubt. But the main thing that is essential is for you to exert influence upon Nat[halie]. I will be absolutely open with you and tell you that the evil in her nature flows from two sources: jealousy and lack of restraint. She can love people and do goodness-knows-what to them out of jealousy. If I had not clearly seen that her principal emotion was her affection for me (in whatever form it was expressed), many things would have been otherwise. If you can overcome her to such an extent that you are able to influence Liza, that will be a great achievement. But I hardly think you need to stay there now; perhaps it would be better for you to return in winter if N[athalie] is really expecting.

Incidentally, you say she is *embarrassingly* expectant. I think that we who talk so much about a new outlook are just as old as the people who don't talk. Ogarev stands head and shoulders above us all, and he says, most sensibly of all, that it is too late— and silly—to hide it. (Don't parade and don't hide.) I want to be absolutely frank with you. When Ogarev noticed Nathalie's intense love for me, he had hardly had occasion to say a word about it when she told him everything—and *only then* did she tell me. It was a pure and courageous act. Ogarev was infinitely noble, as always, and since he for his part no longer felt any particular passion, he said he would freely give Nathalie to me and remain her brother.

All the evil came not from that, but from her extravagant licence and lack of restraint. Her caprices alienated Ogarev, her caprices alienated you, and the dreadful calamity in Paris—it all flowed from the same source. But there was Liza, the great link between us, and I understood what was my duty to her, its harsh as well as its gentle side.

Our move from Boissière drew a new line. Ogarev moved to Lancy, and our whole life scattered into pieces like a broken string of beads. If only someone had managed to gather them all up. . . *You* must be the one to manage.

Treasure this letter. It is my confession.

I shall not write to Luginin now; I am still waiting for a reply from him. Let him go to Russia—it looks now as though he will be pardoned . . . then he can come again with his question. Do you think you will accept his proposal then? Ogarev believes he is very jealous—why, I don't know.

Farewell. I kiss you as my dearest friend. Why not go to Genoa for the winter? I am free now from 1 July until 1 December.

Let me tell you that you have the right to go whenever you wish. It is time you arranged a meeting with Olga and told her everything.   Farewell

Keep this letter a secret.

19. *Natalie Herzen to Alexander Herzen*

12 JUNE 1867   *87 Promenade des Anglais*
Nice

MY DEAR PAPASHA, you did not understand what I was referring to in my last letter but one when I wrote that Nathalie's position would be awkward. I meant to say that it would be awkward for her to remain here *alone,* and from that point of view I understood her desire to go to Russia. But it seems that once again Nathalie has seen *the error of her ways* and is talking less of Russia now.

You say the time has come to live openly. Of course, it is a dreadful pity that that was not done right from the start, but it's no use regretting the past. How can the long silence be explained? Perhaps Ogarev is right, and I would agree with him, were it not for Olga and Liza. It's too soon to tell them, Papasha, believe me. And this is more important, in my view, with respect to Olga, than to Liza. It would almost be better to tell Liza now, better that she should get accustomed to the truth while she is still a child, while her mind is occupied with her little friends, games and pranks and she has no time to brood on it. I think that the later one leaves it, the worse, or else it should be left until her mind and thoughts have reached maturity. Perhaps I am mistaken. What do you think? I should not like to tell Olga now for anything.

Nathalie has been very kind to me so far, and her whole character seems to have grown a little gentler, except with Liza. Of course, she is difficult to cope with, but who is to blame, *whose* fault is it? I cannot tell you how it pains me to see her, that is, Liza, answering affectionate, patient requests or re-marks with grimaces or sneers or the remark that *"Ça m'est bien égal ce que tu dis. Crois-tu que cela me fasse quelque chose?"*

Not only is she losing all her childish graces, but her very soul is being maimed. There are times when I just do not know what to do.

Thank you for *Blocus,*[44] we are all reading the novel together. On my own, and with Nathalie, I am reading George Sand's *Horace*. I find his character a little exaggerated, almost a caricature.

We heard about the shooting long ago, of course, and knew that it must have important consequences.[45] The *émigrés*, however, have declared that they have nothing in common with this Pole, but his character, it appears, is no worse than Karakozov's. What will they do to him? There was a *spectacle* here on the subject, as there have been all over France. And the entrance to *our garden* was adorned with two banners rejoicing at Alexander Nikolaevich's escape!! But whatever would have happened if he had hit the target? The young man was not thinking of the future—all he wanted was his revenge.

Papasha, you write that you are a "strange man" for living so much by memories. Well, then I am a "strange girl" because I understand this so well and sympathize with you.

I am continually meeting old acquaintances. The other day I was stopped on the street by Julie; she had recognized Nathalie and guessed that I was *little Tata that used to be.* Imagine, I recognized her at once. Her odd nose, the *disposition of her teeth* and her long-haired wart, everything had remained distinct in my memory, and I was overjoyed at meeting her!

I kiss you heartily
Your TATA

20. *Natalie Herzen to Maria Reichel*

THURSDAY, 19 DECEMBER 1867

No. 9 Piazza San Felice
Palazzo Guidi
Firenze

PAPASHA HAS gone, and, as always after his departure, everything seems so quiet and empty. This visit left us, and all our entourage, with even more agreeable an impression than all his previous visits. He was in such good, bright spirits, and as young and gay as ever. It's sad, vexing and stupid that we are continually bidding each other farewell. It's time I grew accustomed to it—we have been travelling for so long now—but I cannot. As I say goodbye I catch myself thinking involuntarily: "Perhaps this is for ever, God knows what may happen . . ." As for Ogarev, it is more than a year now since I last saw him. I spent all the summer in Nice with Nathalie and Lizochka; I went there for three or four weeks but stayed five months.

You cannot imagine, my dear Masha, how attached I am to that corner of the globe, and with what pleasure I recognized the places, the faces and the views—I remember it all so vividly. Five years or so ago we stopped there for the day *en passant*. But this time I inspected all the sights and sought out everyone. Just imagine, all our servants are still there. They recognized Papasha on the street, stopped him and asked about us, and it was clear that they were still very attached to us. One of them has a shop, and another a little tavern, and Adelheida (you remember, grandmother's maidservant, the one who was on the steamer at the time of the accident?)[46] has a café and an enormous hotel, the Hôtel du Luxembourg— one of the largest in Nice, and that's saying something. (Nice has changed very much and is now an extremely wealthy and "fashionable" town.) She remembers you and Reichel very well and sends her regards. Rocca's family are so attached to us, it makes one feel ashamed. You remember the young girl called Marianna who used to bath me in the old days—her old mother had one wooden hut (for dressing and undressing) —well, now she's become rich and has not one hut but twenty pavilions by the name of *"Grand établissement de bains de mer Mme Georges"*. I went to visit her at first without realizing that she was the same old woman, and when I talked to her husband it turned out that we were old friends, and that they remember us all perfectly well.

I spent the whole of those five months in extremely quiet and solitary fashion. Nathalie is unsociable and unwilling to become acquainted with anyone, and there is no society in Nice, particularly in the summer, when everybody flees from the heat. But my aim in going to Nice was to take charge of Liza for a while, and to effect a change in Nathalie's monotonous way of life, and therefore I had no interest in meeting people or getting to know society. I love children very much, love taking charge of them and teaching them—I have written to you more than once and told you how I love Liza and how much pleasure I should derive even from taking her education upon myself. But now I see that in the circumstances that is definitely impossible. She is an uncommonly clever and quick-witted child, but very spoilt and so quite unmanageable in her mother's presence.

Olga has changed a great deal for the better; she is very sweet, especially with me, and always nimble and lively. She makes everyone laugh, little rogue that she is—and such a cunning one!—and she is so well-behaved, nothing upsets or alarms her. We are living very quietly, have no social life, but content ourselves with our own intimate little circle. Like last year, we all visit the Schiffs on Thursdays, and on Mondays they all come and see us, and each of them takes a turn at delivering a lecture. The natural sciences, of course, play a very prominent part.

On Wednesday evenings I visit Mme Laussot, a most remarkable, intelligent and energetic woman who occupies herself most intently with music and is trying to awaken the interest of the Italians in serious German music by organizing choirs and *Singvereine*. At the moment I am singing with the contraltos. We are giving a concert tomorrow, at which the violinist Wilhelmi—you may have heard of him—will be playing. We spend our other evenings sitting quietly at home; Malwida's eyes are very bad, so I read to her and Olga.

I re-read Chernyshevsky's novel in Nice—you are absolutely right, there are many strange, ridiculous and unnatural things in it, but how much sense it makes! I am not surprised that it has had such an enormous influence on the youth of Russia. I have had occasion to meet some of these Nihilists and Nihilistki [as the girls are called.—Tr.] (although it is a silly word, and they themselves find it difficult to explain why they call themselves so—of late it has become an offensive word in Russia, because everything bad is attributed to them). Their careless disregard or scorn for outward forms does them a great deal of harm, but many of their ideas are sensible ones. Well, goodbye, my best wishes to yourself and all of you for the new year, and I embrace you heartily.

Your TATA

Give our regards to Fontano and the Lion family. Would Reichel be so good as to give my greetings to my old friend Bakunin when he sees him in Vevey? Ogarev wrote and told me a meeting was being arranged.

21. *Natalie Herzen to Alexander Herzen*

SUNDAY, 22 MARCH 1868   *No. 9 Piazza S. Felice*
                                                              Firenze

MY DEAR PAPASHA, what are you writing to Sasha? Please tell
me. All about Teresina, I suppose? But what do you want him
to do now? What do you want? He doesn't show me your
letters and only refers to them by way of allusions, but I can
see that they cause him great distress. It would be best not to
mention the subject any more, really. Please, don't think that
he has asked me to write; I haven't even told him I am writing
to you about it.

You are probably forming a totally wrong idea of our
attitude to Teresina. Nobody stops to ask themselves whether
she is his fiancée or not. Those who have guessed say nothing
about it, and we all treat her in exactly the same way—that is,
as a dear child, a friend of Olga's and a pupil of mine. Her
visits to us are so few and far between, and moreover there is
nothing to attract attention in her behaviour with Sasha.
What do you expect of him? He is happy, she is sweet and
high-spirited and a good student, doing well in everything. He
believes in her love and in [their] future happiness.

I cannot say I am as sure, but his mind will not be changed.
And then anyway, how can one know in advance? Everyone
has his own idea of happiness. He is dreaming now of perfect
solitude and peaceful family life in isolation. I think that is a
great pity, because I believe that society has a good effect upon
him and enlivens him. But the deed is done now; what is the
use of distressing him with these arguments? He cannot possibly withdraw—indeed, he does not wish to—and this is clear
and natural when he believes in his love for her. And so I beg
you earnestly, my dear, good Papasha, not to speak any more
of it, not to torment him; let him live happily *after his own
fashion.* Why should we grudge him this if he really is happy?
What harm can it do us? You cannot say in all seriousness that
a man ought to get married sooner or later to provide a *home*
for his sisters. Teresina's character has many good points, and
I have not so far noticed any grave defects. And one certainly

cannot ascribe the fact that our life is more monotonous now than it was last year to her and her relationship with Sasha. That could not possibly have affected it in any way. The only thing that has affected it has been the considerable decrease in the size of our circle and Malwida's and Mme Schiff's continual ill-health.

And so I beg you once more not to offend Sasha. Write to me and ask me about anything you like, but leave him in peace, Papasha dear. The fact of his not wanting to go away in summer at exactly the time when we will also be away is natural. How could he go off and leave Teresina again in a household, in a society to which she no longer belongs; for her interests now are utterly different. Everyone will be going away in the summer and even her beloved music lessons will stop, and the people around her are coarse-natured. It would be bad indeed of Sasha to leave her on her own this summer.

The day before yesterday there was a big concert here in the Sala Filarmonica. It was arranged by Mme Laussot. The whole thing was a great success. Les Chérubins, that is the members of our "Cherubini" society, have made tremendous progress since the last occasion, thanks to the singular energy of Mme Laussot. A marvellous woman; even Panovka,[47] who was *en cérémonies* with her, could not restrain himself and rose to pay her various compliments; and is still repeating continually: *"cette femme a du génie, cette femme a du génie!"*

This was our programme—show it to Ogarev:

1) Ouverture avec Choeur de O. Niccolai, arrangée pour deux pianos. Berthe Sommier played one of the pianos.
2) Choeur de Pélerins, "Ave Maria", Arcadelt.
3) L'Étoile du Soir, air du "Tannhaüser", Wagner.
4) Mottetto "Iste Dies", pour choeur, Cherubini.

Quite by chance Cherubini's eldest daughter, an old woman of ninety, happened to be staying in Florence to break a journey. She was invited, of course, a special armchair was brought to the concert hall for her, and after the *Mottetto* Mme Laussot presented her with an enormous bouquet in memory of her father.

5) La Jeune Religieuse, Schubert.

6) *Allegro, Adagio e Scherzo,* Bronsart.
7) *Quatuor* de l'opéra "Fidelio", Beethoven.
8) *Ballades* du pays de Galles, chantées par Miss Wynne.
9) *Mottetto* "Giammai, O Signor, ti lascero" pour choeur, Bach.

It all went very well. Olga presented Mme Laussot with a large bouquet, very charmingly. The musical season is really getting into full swing here now and there are no end of concerts. Moreover, Salvini is here; I have already seen him several times. I did not take to him at all in *Hamlet*; his terribly passionate interpretation does not seem to me to suit the northern type or the character of Hamlet. But the money, the money! I am surprised that I can afford to pay for everything myself. I buy my own clothes (true, I haven't needed any special outfits, ball-gowns or evening-dresses, that is), I see to Teresina's wardrobe and myself pay for various entertainments, such as concerts, theatres, riding, and so on. And how I keep house! I economize like a real Necker. Of course, the accounts are in better order now than they were before my ministry, and when anything doesn't *add up right,* I make up the difference out of my own pocket.

I have finished Mignet; it was rather like reading a dictionary, but well done. We have finished the first volume of Quinet too. But in spite of the fact that the second volume is far longer, Meshchersky is already saying that after that we ought to read Tocqueville also; and he is only staying for two more weeks.

I have also read a few chapters of *Histoire d'un paysan*[48]. *Il y a des longueurs* occasionally, but it is very fine all the same, like a folk tale, and there are some shocking scenes of poverty and its consequences, for instance, when he tells of the mother rejoicing that her son has drawn a lucky ticket at the time of *conscription.* Not because it releases him from the military life, but because she can sell it on the spot for nine *louis d'or* and not die of starvation. But for all that, she loved her son terribly and suffered. The son [. . .][49] he squandered it all on the very first night. Have you read the story or not?

We are awaiting the continuation of your "Day"; the beginning made us laugh a good deal. I can just see you barricading yourself in every morning now, and then Pan coming in for breakfast and complaining of indigestion! You are always so high-spirited, Papasha my dear! I embrace and kiss you with all my heart and kiss Aga too.

Your TATA H.

I press Pan's hand. Which photograph did he finally choose for himself?

What makes you tell Sasha to wait and not read us the reply to Dr Krupov[50] until he has received all of it, and then write to me and ask why I haven't read it? None of us has read it yet; Sasha has given it to Penisi, who has not yet returned it.

Everybody sends you their best regards, and Olga sends a kiss.

22. *Natalie Herzen to Alexander Herzen*

1 APRIL 1868   *No. 9 Piazza San Felice*
Firenze

CONGRATULATIONS, PAPASHA dear, on your birthday. We drank your health yesterday in a tiny trattoria in a charming little place two stations from Florence on the line to Rome. The Russians here had been planning to hold a *pick-nick* for ages and to invite me. Yesterday it was all organized. There were ten of us, two Ghé's, two Myasoedovs (husband and wife, that is), both the Kamensky brothers, Mlle Ushakova, a Nihilist (close-cropped and exceedingly droll and gay), Zabela, Meshchersky, and myself.

This Mlle Ushakova is a most original Russian phenomenon. A young girl of twenty-three or twenty-four, she has already been travelling around Europe—Italy, Switzerland, Spain— for three or four years now, entirely alone. Now she wants to return to Russia for a short time and go from there to Egypt, and all alone, without even a maid. She is very wealthy, of course, so she finds everything easy and convenient to do, but it appears she is not particularly interested in anything, but is simply having a good time. But don't be afraid there might be any closeness between us, Papasha. I became acquainted with her only yesterday, and it is very unlikely I shall see her again, because she is going away in a few days. Apparently the Utins in Geneva know her well. She made a very disagreeable impression on me, too *ausgelassen*, like a spoilt child, though not a coquette. But if she and Katya were to get together, what foolish things they would do!

One does meet some odd characters in Russian society. Myasoedov, for instance—such an eccentric, rather in the style of Bazarov. I became acquainted with him also at the *pick-nick*, but I hardly know him. But just imagine; they (that is, he and his wife) live in separate apartments despite the fact that they love and respect one another greatly; address each other in the polite form and call each other Grigory Grigorevich and Elizaveta N[. . .]vna, with such formality—and they do all this for the sake of various principles. For instance, he refused to drink Ushakova's health, saying, "What matter of mine is her health? She is no use to me and doesn't interest me. But everything in life is done out of egoism. Maybe I'll drink to women in general." And Ghé was true to character; made philosophical remarks the whole time and lay on the grass talking utter nonsense just like some prophet or other, surrounded by all of us. He always treats me so respectfully that I feel simply ashamed. He asks me for my opinion in every argument and he knows very well that I hardly ever agree with him.

They *are* amusing people. Zabela was very jolly too—he has had an unexpected stroke of good fortune in the shape of a small legacy, enough to live on comfortably and not to have to worry constantly about a crust of bread for his children; he is going shortly to Russia to put his affairs in order and after that, apparently, he dreams of America.

That Levier's affairs are going well you probably already know through Sasha. The night before last he only got an hour's sleep. And with whom did he pass the night? Dear old Prince Petr Vladimirovich Dolgoruky, who apparently suffers from asthma and has returned to Florence for Easter Sunday—there is probably no Russian church in Naples.

2 APRIL

I have received your letter and Sasha's regards. I am sorry for you; there you are complaining of the cold and the *bise*, while the weather here is simply marvellous, so warm that when I was out walking yesterday I had to take off my light coat. All of us, that is Malwida, Olga, Teresina, Meshchersky and myself, went to the Villa Montier and were baked by the sun.

How we laughed when we read how you spend your day, Papasha my dear. But it really is the best way of giving us a vivid notion of your way of life. Even in our monotonous life there do occur the most amusing episodes. Usually it is the cooks who play the most comic roles. You already know what our old Rosa looks like, her old face as wrinkled as a baked apple. As I always order the dinners now, my faithful Rosa presents herself punctually at seven o'clock every morning, opens the door—oh so quietly!—and every time is surprised to find me with my eyes already open, and exclaims *"ah! la mia lepre non dorme più, il mio serpino ha gli occhi aperti e pure è tornata tardi dal teatro ieri, dorme, dorme, poverina."* This is repeated every single day. After the introduction, that is after this preamble, we get down to business and discuss how lunch can best and most cheaply be arranged. I tell her I have had a wager with Sasha, that he is always laughing at me and saying that I understand nothing of accounts, and I want to prove to him that everything will be perfect order in my hands, and so I promise to give her a present at the end of the month if we manage to arrange everything economically, and she sets about the task with the utmost seriousness. As soon as she goes away I get dressed as quickly as I can, and often even come running into the drawing-room without having completed my toilet, simply to escape the sooner from my uncongenial room—it's so big, bare and cold, the window faces north and the light is dismal and grey, while the drawing-room is so cheerful even in the early morning; the sun lights it up so prettily. The others are usually still in their bedrooms, so I have a peaceful and most agreeable half hour in which to do some reading before coffee. *And I enjoy it very much.*[51]

With the coffee comes every imaginable kind of hustle and

bustle. In the first place, we have to hurry with the coffee because Bakoshka comes early. Then the accounts have to be drawn up as speedily as possible and the money given to Rosa, the seamstress told what to do so she doesn't sit idle, the dirty linen counted with Adelasia, or the clean linen which has just been delivered; various other bills usually arrive unexpectedly —*legnajo, latajo, calamajo, Bizzari, Gilli*,[52] etc. etc. When all that is done I once again seek out a quiet corner in the sun in order to sit down in peace, and that is not nearly as easy as it seems. I would like to stay in the drawing-room, because it's nice and warm, but Olga plays the pianoforte there and I can't read with that. If I go and sit in Malwida's room she at once begins talking about something or other and I cannot get on with my reading. I cannot go to Olga's room either because Adelasia is just then cleaning it; so one might sing *"Das Wandern ist der Tata Lust, das Wandern"*,[53] till the end of Bakoshka's lesson, that is until ten o'clock. After that all is quiet until lunch at twelve o'clock; though occasionally someone rings and delivers a note, and Adelasia says *"una riposta, subito"*. It's a note from Meshchersky asking if we are disposed to go out for a drive to Fiesole, Certosa, Pisa, Livorno; Malwida usually replies: *"Ach nein, das ist doch nichts für mich, mein Kopf ist schwer,*[54] *und ich bin ganz erkältet, für Olga ist es auch nichts—sie wird sich erkälten."* So, depending on whether it is the day of Teresina's lesson or not, I agree to or postpone the drive.

But as for the way Malwida looks after Olga's health, why, she is almost worse than Nathalie with Liza. I marvel at Olga's patience. Sometimes when I am dressing my hair in Olga's room I see Malwida come in response to the slightest movement from Olga and tell her: "I think you were speaking too loudly. Take care of your voice, you'll probably be coughing now. And mind you put on a jacket when you go down the corridor." During walks she does not allow her to run and jump around. She stops on the staircase when Olga tries to run up a little more quickly [than she should], and she will never agree to let her go on a *pick-nick* anywhere with me. What I find most unpleasant of all are the scenes which have become

G

an almost daily occurrence, involving the pianoforte; because this sort of thing breeds such a passion for possessions. She has everything under lock and key—the pianoforte, the room—and to procure the key takes a whole hour's strenuous effort, and cunning, and begging. But I've decided not to mention the subject any more. It will pass with time, and at the moment leads only to unpleasant exchanges. Malwida gets angry.

As soon as I began reading Tocqueville I said that it was a book for the general reader, but I could not read it on my own. So far I understand everything and find it interesting. Leviatansky[55] too I read with great interest, although I was sad to see that there is no dedication. I have not seen Schiff since then and do not know his opinion. The title page says *Ière variation*—does that mean there will be more articles to follow? How did the affair of the Geneva workers end? Farewell, then—I kiss you warmly—think of us on Monday.

Your TATA H.

Meshchersky has just arrived and sends you his regards.

23. *Natalie Herzen to Alexander Herzen*

18 APRIL 1868   *No. 9 Piazza S. Felice*
                                                      Firenze

JUST IMAGINE, Papasha dear, we received your letter from Marseilles only yesterday. I would have answered at once, but yesterday was a busy day and I spent most of it with a charming Russian family, the Voronins. It appears that Mr Voronin is a rather outstanding botanist, engaged in the study of microscopic fungi and cryptogams; he has written a great deal, according to Schiff, who saw him simply in his capacity as doctor. Schiff invited them immediately for that evening, and I met them at his house.

His wife is young, yet clever, quiet and extremely likeable as far as I can judge after so brief an acquaintance. She was very glad to make our acquaintance, as she had been wanting to meet us somehow. They spend almost all their time in

Petersburg; she was there at the time of the Chernyshevsky business,[56] and the Karakozov affair. She has had something to do with the organization of schools, and teaching. They are friends of Suslova's,[57] because Bogdanova, a friend and comrade of Suslova (they were at university together), married Mme Voronina's brother, a gentleman by the name of Bokov, who has since died. They told us that they had heard so much about us and seen so many pictures that they felt they had known us for ages. Not surprisingly; they know Petrusha and the Levitskys very well, and Blagosvetlov[58] too. And we have various other mutual acquaintances. During the winter they were in Nice, at the Villa Fay, and glimpsed you several times from afar. There is another person with them, a young girl, Mme Voronina's sister, who devotes much time to studying music, attends the conservatoire in Petersburg, and is very distressed that Rubinstein has gone away.

Unfortunately all these Russians are here only *en passant.* Myasoedova and Ushakova, of whom I have already written, have left already. The Voronins are going tomorrow [. . .]. There is no point in saying any more about Sasha; we can only wait patiently and see, and who knows, perhaps everything will turn out better than we expect.

You write, "happier is the man who lives a little more by reason and a little less by passions." Can one say that such a man is happier? *More tranquil,* yes. *Qui ne risque rien, ne perd rien, mais ne gagne rien non plus!* Do you really think, Papasha dear, that this tranquillity can be called happiness? Leviatansky himself recalls the quotation: *"Si la raison dominait le monde il ne se passerait rien."* If only you could hear what Ghé is continually saying to me: "Why are you always sitting at home, Natalya Alexandrovna, peering at frogs or reading books? It's all very commendable, but one can do that in one's old age. In one's youth one ought to be enjoying oneself. When will you ever learn about life? You must *live* while you are young."

I am also learning little by little that everywhere, absolutely everywhere, people love to gossip—it is incomprehensible— about anything and everything; and as far as we are concerned it is simply laughable. I think I have written to you of it already. People to whom we are complete strangers, people who have never set eyes on us—what can it matter to them, what interest can they possibly have? First they say that Sasha wanted to marry Katya[59] even when he was in Rome—he never saw her in Rome. Then, that Olga is a Catholic and myself an aristocrat, and they add "not surprising—the father's an aristocrat too." They say I am proud, that I talk to everyone *de haut en bas,* go to balls frequently and in general keep the company of marquises and barons exclusively—they have probably heard about the ball at Baron Sonino's, the only one I have been to in Florence. At first I was very angry at all this, but then I could not help seeing the funny side, and now I pay no attention. Of course I received the necklace, and like it very much indeed; once again I thank you and send you a kiss.

Utin and his sister Mme Stasiulevich came back a few days ago, but have not yet been to see us. Did you see Mazade's article in the *Revue des Deux Mondes?*[60] Monod has sent Olga Langel's book *Problèmes de l'âme*—do you know it?

Papasha, why do you attach so much importance to dancing? I agree that it is nice to know how to dance, and useful for persons who are awkward and graceless; but I don't see anything important about it. I find it disagreeable when Olga says she doesn't like dancing, because everyone sees it as an affectation; for a character as gay and frolicsome as hers it is unnatural and indeed even a kind of coquetry. Were hers an earnest and intense nature, she might perhaps have reached the reasoned conclusion that dancing is stupid, and taken a serious decision not to dance. But of course it is merely a prank. But please don't mention any more about it in your letters to Malwida. She will once again say that I have been gossiping; but do answer me in detail.

Farewell, Teresina has arrived, I embrace you and kiss you heartily,

Your TATA

I kiss Nathalie and Lizochka. You will soon receive a parcel addressed to Nathalie; please give it to Katya. It is the mosaics she asked for. A relative of Voronin's will be bringing them; his nephew, I think; I don't know him.

24. *Alexander Herzen to Natalie Herzen*

SATURDAY, 23 MAY [1868]   [*Nice*]

YOU BELIEVE, Tata, that my letters, or my latest letter, contain no questions—and you are very much mistaken. They deal (like yours) with *life's questions*—and those are far more important than questions of whether to go to S. Terenza or Prangins. You have understood much—but a great deal is still vague. For instance, when I talk of educating oneself for an education, you ask what one should devote one's attention to, and which books. Devote yourself to softening and tempering your character, and as for the books—read what you like.

As regards painting—that is a matter for your own conscience—it seems to me that with more practice you could do some fine work—you have proved that, if only by your little pencil sketches. Not to develop one's talent when there is no external hindrance is a sin. But *"S'il ne sent point du ciel l'influence secrète"*, as Boileau used to say, one must take up something else. Workshops, if you like, schools, cooperative societies, something which does not hinder one's own education in the slightest. I have even had an idea on that score— perhaps we should meet at the end of June; there is quite a bit to learn in France, in Alsace.

Ogarev's theory on the subject of Sasha and his marriage is utterly useless: it is not at all the same whether it is Akulina or Teresina. Any marriage can lead to disaster, but one which is based not only on passion alone but also on equality of development, on a common religion, on mutual *respect*, one which takes into account the provision of a crust of bread for oneselves and one's children, that marriage has better prospects, rationally speaking. Ogarev's theory is useless too because, as you observed, it offers no substitute. Individuals are liable to rebel against objectionable institutions and try to destroy them or put [something] in their place—but not as an exception *for themselves*, but comme *règle générale* for everyone. Luther refuted priestly celibacy as an absurdity and could

101

therefore marry with a clear conscience. It doesn't work vice versa. Until historical forms are replaced by others, people of necessity (not even logically) live under them. I am convinced that the present distribution of wealth with the monopoly of real estate and capital gives [me] a *more than* fair annuity, and I shall not say a word when it drops for me as for other people. But if I were to take it into my head (which is exactly what the Bazarovites in Geneva wanted) to give them, for instance, four of the five per cent, I should be left half-destitute and would deprive myself of my weapon and the possibility of fighting during the struggle.

There's a whole heap of questions for you to ponder over. I shall never say to you (except in some extreme situation): *go and get married*. But I shall certainly not say: *do not* marry, in a case where aspiration and circumstances, heart and mind, are in accord.

It is a pity you are not here. Nice is at her most beautiful, and Liza revels in the epithet of *la petite Tata*. The weather is hot, but *"ein sanfter Wind vom blauen Himmel weht"*[61] and it *smells*[62] of lemon-blossom. A wonderful place; it is a shame to leave it. If only it were possible to fix up something in these parts just for the four of us—Nathalie, you, Liza and myself—first. But even that is too Epicurean—we must live where there is *most for us to do*, and whether in Klin or Spezia circumstances will decide.

That is my humble philosophy.[63]

I am sending Olga some rather felicitous verses by Hugo addressed to the Pope.[64] And for all of you, the news-sheet *Liberté*, with the Senate meeting, which I beg you to read. I have enclosed with it a *plaisanterie atroce* from *Figaro*.

Tell Sasha to send the first volume of Schiff's physiology,[65] when it comes out, to this address:

France
Mr le Dr Bernacki
Cannes (Alp[es] Marit[imes]).

If you need anything after the 29th you can address [letters] to Lyon—*poste rest[ante]* or to Tchorzewski. We are renting the house from 1 [June] and travelling on 2 June at three o'clock.

Shchenkovich, Solovevich and the other Psevichi[66] answered me on Mieroslavski's behalf with various insolences.[67]

What about your flat—I seem to remember that the lease was to expire towards 1 June?

25. *Nikolay Ogarev to Natalie Herzen*

SATURDAY, 11 JUNE [1868][68]   [*Geneva*]

HOW LONG it is since I wrote to you, my dear Tata! I do not know where you are, I can't find your last letter to me; I must have sent it to Sasha with a manuscript or used it as a bookmark, so goodness knows what has become of it. All this time I have been working for *The Bell* and wasting away for nobody. I have fairly tired myself, so that even now I am still not fit for very much. Sometimes I feel I have had enough of it all. I am not entirely happy even with my leg, not that it's anything in particular; but I have become so tired that working is difficult. The day before yesterday I had a visit from Mlle Portugal and her friend; both of them are mistresses at the Kindergarten. They are terribly keen to have Toots for the holiday (one month). What do you think? I'll let him go, but will he really learn any more there than with us? Write at once.

What else is there to say to you?

> Bright dawn starts peeping in the window,
> And walking, on the wall I see
> Galileo's honoured image,
> Given by your own hand to me.
>   Which vividly to mind recalls,
> With the approach of morning light,
> The measured toil of lucid science
> And memories of Tata bright. . .

And with that I say farewell.

I am waiting for news of your pater, I haven't known where he is for three days now. Perhaps you are in Berne? I am sending everything to Tch[orzewski]—the letters, your aria and a positivist philosophy.

I have written to Herz[en]. Your letters are not being given to Henry[69]—perhaps because there are none; but I have heard that they are not allowed into anybody's hands except by your own order.

Give my regards to the Reichels. What wouldn't I give to see them!

26. *Natalie Herzen to Alexander Herzen*

9 NOVEMBER 1868

Hôtel des Catalans
(the street is unnecessary,
we are on the cliffs)
Marseille

No, NOTHING has been done yet. We have not spoken with Liza; all is quiet and calm. But the mistral is still raging outside. I have never seen anything like it. I pity the ships!

I have thought a great deal, Papasha dear, about that plan, that *dream* of yours to "let Liza know that she is your daughter but she need not change her name".

But that would be putting her in a false position, she would always be having to explain—or tell a lie. Perhaps one could do it if she were grown up, but is it a good thing to put a child in an *ambiguous* position? I do not think she will *suffer* from it, and I cannot possibly accept the comparison between her position and the disagreeable, distressing, ambiguous position in which Nathalie finds herself (a comparison made by Nathalie).

What do we have to do with people who have not managed to shake off their various prejudices? And Liza in particular? It will be many years yet before she "grows up" and forms her own circle of sympathetic friends. And so I do not believe that she will suffer. But who knows, might it not be harmful to accustom a child to deviousness and deceit—for what else is one to call it? Because she will have to call her father "uncle" and her uncle "father", will she not? I am not so sure; it is impossible to foresee the consequences. It seems to me that an attitude of frankness would be the best. We could write to Olga even now when we have finally made up our minds. But I should prefer to leave her in peace until the spring or summer; in a word, until she leaves Florence. She is very absentminded as it is, and if we were to tell her now, it would distract her even more and divert her from her studies. However *unimportant* they might be (her studies), it would be better for her to spend a few more months reading quietly and playing. At the moment she does not have to explain anything to anybody. Let us say that we meet in Zurich, and everything will be accomplished before her arrival. She will be surrounded by *new* people, and there will be no occasion for her to have to provide answers or explanations. It will all be done before she arrives. But there will be plenty of time for us to talk it over; the first thing is to reach a definite decision.

You say that it (that is, the change of name) is all immaterial, and I agree with you, because I do not see *what* we can have in common with people who have not succeeded in ridding themselves of their prejudices. Nathalie thinks differently, and because her ambiguous position worries her I think it must be ended; and I fervently hope that after that has been done her character will become just a little more harmonious. In any case there will be no more of these conversations, and that will be a great step forward.

I embrace and kiss you and Aga. Heavens, *how* am I to answer your questions about my art, my singing, my painting? *How* can I console you? How can I cultivate a *passion* in myself when it is not inborn? I don't feel like singing, and when I spend hours at my drawing I am aware of a kind of emptiness, an isolation, which frightens me and leaves me somehow in a state of dissatisfaction. Why? I have no idea. I never feel like this when I am reading. I got along very well in Vichy; I found books, articles, everything interesting. I would very much like to try and write something, but I do not know enough yet. I get along well almost anywhere with interesting books. Please do not be annoyed with me, dear Papasha, but instead, tell me what to do about it.

Your TATA H.

27. *Nikolay Ogarev to Natalie Herzen*

To TATA

At three o'clock—pitch blackness. Then thunder and lightning, hurting the eyes and making the windows shake. A downpour. Then a thin blue streak begins to glow in the West, over the Jura, and Salève is occasionally discernible. How beautiful it is!

That was only an introduction. Yesterday I received your letter, my dear Tata—and now I do believe you are improving fast and that now you will not only be able to read, but will even want to. So ever since morning I have been intending to write to you, and thinking continually, I must write something that will not make tedious reading—and I was still thinking when it became so dark in the middle of the day that it was simply impossible to write. And now I can write again, and somehow since the storm I feel more cheerful myself.

I had wanted to amuse you and write a whole comic story for you, that is, a memoir of my entire day (including, of course, selected episodes from various days all amalgamated into one day).[70] But somehow I can't get going on it—I'll put it aside for a while, but I'm not abandoning the idea, I find it a very interesting one. And also I'm afraid that something gloomy might just creep into the comedy; and you're better off without such nuances at the moment.

I have delivered your messages, that is, one to Tchorzewski, who cannot find the book you mention. I am sure I do not have it, or I would remember; I am not totally lacking in memory, but it does have ways of its own which I find very interesting to observe. I sent your other message to Mme Czerniecka by post.

What else can I say to you this time? These last days I have been feeling somehow unwell and feverish, even my leg has been troublesome. Probably everything will improve after the storm has cleared.

How could you have imagined that I did not want to come to you? Really! But it's good that you were able to manage without [my] travelling, because the journey would anyway have been very difficult.

All my family send you their kind regards and remember you with the greatest sympathy. Toots sends you a hare. I am sorry it has been sitting in my pocket for so long, I very nearly forgot about it. At the moment I am intensively occupied with a rather abstruse article. I kiss you, and Liza and Natha[lie] and *addio* for the time being.

Your PAPA AGA

I keep meaning to write to Sasha and Olga and I keep being lazy. I don't wish to write *bonjour*-farewell; and to write what I [really] wish would be an impossible task.

28. *Natalie Herzen:*

A PHOTOGRAPH (FROM THE ORIGINAL)[71]

(1)

Before coffee. A bedroom on the top floor of the house

Tata and Babetta[72] *finish making Nathalie's bed and go bounding down the staircase, heading in the direction of Herzen-Iskander's bedroom. . . . He is seated at a large writing-desk wearing a knitted jacket the colour of* café-au-lait. *. . . His dishevelled hair indicates that he has not yet attended to his toilet.*

TATA *(hugging and kissing him).* Good morning, Papasha. *(Jokingly)* How is your lordship rested?
ISKANDER. Not too badly . . . good morning. But you come earlier and earlier every day . . . *(Looks at his watch.)* Allright . . . allright . . .
TATA *(glances at his book over Iskander's shoulder).* So, Vater Unser, you're still at work on your "Doctor"?[73] *(Begins to make his bed with Babetta.)*
ISKANDER. Yes . . . Yes . . . *(twirls the tip of his beard, and chews at it).* It's come out very well . . . you'll see . . . I'll read it to you later . . . *(smiles complacently).* The speech of that *père* Amante—ha-ha-ha what a name! *père* Am-marante! Mar-

vellous! That ought to be translated now . . . Drive those damned French mad . . . and Vyrubov[74] too, for that matter . . .

BABETTE. Oh! Oh! . . . voilà quelque *soze* qui a sauté . . .

TATA. Qu'est-ce qu'il y a?—Ah, non, ce sont des graines de tabac!

BABETTE. Madame Rocca, il m'a dit comme cela, qu'il aimerait beaucoup voir une puce dans le mic . . . mic . . . *(becomes confused and blushes)* dans la *macine* en bas . . .

TATA. Dans le microscope—dites: mi-cros-cope . . . *(Babette becomes even more confused and refuses to repeat the word)*. Avec grand plaisir je lui montrerai à elle et à vous. *(Turning to Iskander)* She interrupted you—you were about to say. . . .

ISKANDER. Nothing, nothing, but . . . I'll give you one or two things to copy out later . . . *(Sound of singing and footsteps in the garden.)* Aha, here's the post. . . .

Tata finishes making the bed slowly, waiting for the arrival of old Madame Rocca,[75] who should bring [certain] letters. The old lady enters with the journal Temps.

MADAME ROCCA. Bonjour Mr et Mlle . . . ah! *(Points to the bed.)* Je vous attrape, méchante! *(Wags her finger threateningly.)* Non, vraiment, vous êtes trop bonne. . . .

TATA *(handing the journal to Iskander)*. Rien que le journal? There you are! Bonjour, Madame Rocca, vous n'avez pas à me gronder, les lits me regardent—allez tricoter. . . . *(Takes her gently by the shoulder, turns her round and good-humouredly escorts her out into the lounge.)*

ISKANDER *(tears off the wrapper and opens the paper)*. Our correspondence cannot be called a lively one . . . Ogarev is not writing—as if purposely—he knows I await his reply impatiently . . . Confounded casualness. . . .

TATA. And there's been nothing from Florence for ages either. Maintenant mon lit à moi, Babette, venez.

Exeunt

(11)

The dining-room

Iskander pours himself some coffee. Nathalie stands cutting the bread.

Natalie Herzen: A Photograph

Liza is conversing loudly with the dog through the window-pane. Tata kisses Iskander and Nathalie, then walks up to Liza.

TATA. Good morning.

LIZA *(presenting her cheek)*. I've seen you already.

TATA. Well, never mind—what of it? C'est le bonjour de la salle à manger. . . .

Nathalie catches a spoon with her mantilla. (Iskander frowns abruptly.) Tata rubs her hands with cold. Liza starts to sing at the top of her voice . . . The wretched Iskander knits his brow, scowls, waves his hands in the air like wings . . . and says in a despairing voice:

[ISKANDER]. Calm down . . . calm down now . . . spare me . . . I'm an old man. . . .

TATA. Stop scowling, Papa . . . How cold it is! ! !

Liza sits down at the table wearing her hat and still singing.

TATA *(to herself)*. Is she really never going to stop? She might at least remove her hat . . . I'd drop her a hint, but I'm afraid she might be insolent and Papa might hear. I'll try and tell her in a whisper . . . *(Whispers to Liza)* Don't sing, Liza, and take off your hat before you have to be told to. . . .

(Liza looks at her with round eyes, shrugs her shoulders and continues to sing, without removing her hat. . . .)

There's another lesson for me . . . I'll never say anything. . . . Nathalie notices nothing . . . it's painful and vexing—but what can I do?

HERZEN. Dis-*gusting* climate . . . No-o *(wags his finger)*, you'll see. . . .

NATHALIE. Liza, stop that singing—I can't hear a thing—and take off your hat.

ISKANDER. Calm down . . . calm down *(waves his hands)* . . . No, one can live only in the North. These southern winters—all prejudice. . . .

NATHALIE. Let's go to Russia . . . The Satins. . . .[76]

ISKANDER *(gazing intently at Nathalie)*. What, is that a hint or a joke?

NATHALIE. A joke . . . a joke . . . Of course you are right, here we can't even get any heat.

ISKANDER. No, I warn you *(taps his finger on the table)*, be assured that we saw the most brilliant season last year at Nice.

Now even the costumes are worse on the Promenade des Anglais
—everything is cheap and trashy. They'll see, the fools. . . .
LIZA *(interrupting him impatiently)*. Mais donnez-moi donc du
café, maman.
NATHALIE. What sort of a voice is that?
LIZA. But when you don't give me anything. . . .
ISKANDER *(frowning; his hands, which had been holding the paper,
fall on to his knees in despair)*. Now Liza, if you love me just a
tiny bit, then sit quietly at table . . . You know perfectly well
that you'll be given everything—just ask politely and *(loses his
patience)* don't give me those insolent, round eyes . . . Take off
your hat. . . .
LIZA *(through clenched teeth)*. Vieux ty-rrran. . . .
ISKANDER. You come in, and we want to talk, have a quiet
chat, but no, you invariably have to spoil everything. *(Crimples
the paper in his annoyance. Sits morosely . . . Finally Liza is ashamed,
removes her hat—and suddenly resolves to make up.)*
LIZA. But no, uncle darling . . . you're a nice man, uncle . . .
Let's talk about interesting things . . . there. . . .
ISKANDER. You know that I'm always willing to talk with you
. . . to explain things to you . . . but this insolence of yours. . . .
LIZA *(gets up, goes over to Iskander, strokes his beard and cheeks)*. My
darling uncle. *(Kisses him and collects up left-over breadcrumbs.)*
Will you let me—for the cat?
ISKANDER. Take them, take them, but in future be more careful.
LIZA. Merci, [uncle] dear! I'm going to the cat.
TATA *(to herself)*. How charming she can be when she wants to.
Her insolence, her spoilt nature—that is her only fault, but it
spoils everything. Nothing you can do will stop her. She stops
herself only when she has driven you to despair—Ksevna,[77]
pass me the butter, please.
NATHALIE. Here you are, Ksandrovna.[78] I'll give you the
"Devonshire cream" too. It's wonderful—so thick today—
just look. *(Serves Liza.)*
TATA *(with a sidelong glance at Iskander, thinks*: "Will the business
with the cream be repeated today or not? If it does, I'll certainly note it down. . . ." *Passes the plate to Nathalie, smiling;
half whispers)*. That'll do, Nathalie, that'll do, merci. . . .

LIZA *(stands up and shouts).* Ma-a-ma, you're treating yourself badly, you've given us too much cream—you've left none for yourself!

ISKANDER *(suddenly drops his hands once again, letting fall the newspaper which had almost completely hidden him. With an expression of despair, shrugs his shoulders, and speaks in a voice which suddenly passes from descant to deep bass. In a bass voice)*: Nathalie, spare me! *(In the same breath passing to a rather shrill descant)* Do you really find pleasure in tormenting me . . . with such trifles. . . .

NATHALIE *(reproachfully).* For goodness' sake, c'est ridicule, I'm going to take some, I'm going to, it's ludicrous [to quarrel] over cream. . . .

Herzen picks up the saucer of cream in one hand, while his other remains in the air waving the spoon.

ISKANDER. But that's not the point . . . Oh, my God! Yes, maybe it really is old age . . . My nerves are growing weak . . . I hate this self-sacrificing attitude—the cream's for everybody —take some yourself too, like the rest of us *(in a descant)*— surely *that* trivi. . . .

NATHALIE. That's enough, Herzen, really, my head's splitting already as it is . . . But you're not to serve yourself *(quickly)*, no, please, give me the saucer . . . *(covering her cup with her hands)*— on the plate, I don't like it in the cup, you'll spoil the coffee. *(But then Iskander, who had been awaiting a suitable opportunity, managed to pour a whole spoonful of cream into Nathalie's cup. Tata and Liza cry "Bravo!" With a contented smile Herzen falls back heavily in his armchair and, sipping his coffee, continues to read the journal.)*

TATA (how is it they don't both get sick and tired of this [game]? It is at once painful and ridiculous . . .). Why aren't you reading us out anything, Papasha?

ISKANDER. There's no news. *(Pauses.)* That swine Emile Girardin. Yes, I loathe France more and more with every day. Vyrubov can say what he likes, but it's nonsense. There's one man in the country who understands anything—and he's a rogue.

NATHALIE *(stands and puts sugar-bowl in cupboard).* Why, what's the matter?

ISKANDER *(waving his hands)*. Calm down, calm down, stop rushing around, there's no hurry . . . It's a long story, all about the Belgian railway—take it later and read for yourself . . . There's a long panegyric on Lamartine—scoundrels and fools, the lot of 'em . . . *(crumples his napkin as if making a snowball, flings it down onto the table, goes over to the window. Stands there looking foppish).*

(Tata takes up her work; Liza collects the remains of the bread and puts on her hat; Nathalie sits on the sofa, sewing [. . .] The old gardener passes by the window, hunched, in a warm, knitted, pointed cap. He is pushing a cartful of wet linen.)

ISKANDER. There's Ivan Alexeevich going about his business.

TATA *(goes over to the window)*. Yes, from a distance there is a likeness, but close to, this one's expression is far kindlier than Ivan Alexeevich's—judging by the portraits of him.

Silence.

ISKANDER *(opening the door)*. I'm off . . . I'll try and get a bit of work done. . . .

All disperse

2. *Love in Florence, 1869*

29. *Natalie Herzen to Alexander Herzen*

EVENING, 26 APRIL 1869   *Casa Fumi*
presso alla Porta Romana
Firenze

HEAVENS, HOW many times I have had to say hello, and relate and re-relate all I have done and where I have been since leaving Florence last year!

The journey was magnificent (as you know already from the telegram I sent from Livorno). Not the slightest trace of motion, and I did not feel the least bit sick. I was up on deck the whole time, gazing at the distant coastline or reading. After the *table d'hôte* a venerable-looking old Italian gentleman came up to me and began conversing and asking me all kinds of questions, and could not get over his amazement when he discovered that I was travelling quite by myself. He kept raising his hands in surprise and repeating that he was entirely at my service: *"Ma mi comanda, ma la prego, mi comanda."* I assured him that I did not need anything. He brought me a cup of coffee, which I refused. Then, suddenly, he asked me: *"La sua casa fa il commercio?"* Upon which I gave him some faint indication of who my Paternoster was, and my brother. He then began showering me with compliments and said that if I or any of my family were ever in Catania, in Sicily, we were to visit him without fail and even stay with him. It was all very amusing.

As we sailed into port at Genoa I caught sight of Pan Tchorzewski's anxious gaze even from a distance. We went off to dine at the Café della Concordia and resolved to make the journey by night—it was as bright as daylight. Nobody was ill; only poor Pan distinguished himself during the last quarter of an hour before Livorno.

113

H

No-one in Florence was expecting my arrival on Sunday. I met Olga on the staircase and she gave such a shriek that Malwida came rushing up in a fright, thinking she had tripped and hurt herself, or something of the sort. Sasha and Teresina were out, and cried out with surprise when I opened the door to them. But I was welcomed very warmly and kindly by everyone. Unfortunately I had a headache and therefore could not take dinner; I had to lie down.

We had seen no one, but the news of my arrival had spread, and that evening we had a visit from the [entire] *Casa Schiff*, Levier and two or three other acquaintances.

Sasha's flat is exceedingly fine, with an enormous staircase, well-lighted. The rooms are spacious, with large windows, and the furniture is good, but there is still a great deal lacking.

For the rest, of course, I cannot judge as yet. But I can see that Sasha is happy and very content with Teresina. She is very industrious. Everyone is overjoyed at my arrival, especially Olga. She is as playful, as frolicsome and as entertaining as ever, and has lots of friends here; the girls are much older than she. Malwida is very affectionate with me and recalls our correspondence about Genoa with some distress, expressing her regret that our letters were, or had been, so dreadfully unclear, that it had been impossible to understand them. She had been astonished to learn from my last letter that we (that is, you and I) would not be together at all this summer.

Olga would like to come and visit you in Genoa, but frankly, in my opinion, it would serve no purpose other than to afford you the pleasure of seeing one another. I have not spoken seriously with her yet; I shall probably arrange to dine three times a week here with Sasha and three times with Olga.

Pan appears to be more enamoured of Florence than of anything he has seen so far.

Olga is very pleased with the perfume, the dress, the casket and the other things. Malwida finds your present *zuuuu reizend*. Sasha and Teresina simply adore my *robe de chambre* and the foulard I bought.

Hugo Schiff has become a dandy. Penisi paid me personally a surprise visit today. At present he is translating Turgenev's

Smoke. Malwida's memoirs are on sale here for the price of 6 francs but even so they are selling well.

However, I must say farewell; I am tired. Give Mme Rocca my best wishes; and I embrace and kiss yourself, Babette, Nathalie and Liza. Remember, Liza, you *promised* to write to me in *English* too. The story of how the children appeared, "Muna", is keeping us all amused and making us laugh here. What are they doing? Do you remember all their names?

Once again, my dear Papasha, I kiss you warmly, kiss you from the bottom of my heart; write soon and tell me lots of things, everything.

Your TATA H.

Olga thanks you for the 50 francs but I am keeping them here for the time being, otherwise they would all be spent on frivolities; she agrees.

30. *Natalie Herzen to Alexander Herzen*

14 MAY [1869]

Casa Fumi
Florence

IT WAS terrible to read in your last letter from Geneva that "you were glad I was getting to trust you more." I always have trusted you *personally*, Papasha dear, and I assure you that I will never take any important step without talking it over with you and seeking your advice. Whatever the relationship be between a young girl and a young man, be it simply the most innocent friendship, people will not leave them in peace. They begin chaffing and making allusions (with words or looks); and so I prefer to say nothing at all and especially not to mention anything in Nathalie's presence. With her I never feel at ease. Whenever I talk to any man, in spite of all she says about simple relationships between men and women, I cannot recall an occasion when I have talked to anybody for more than two minutes without Nathalie making derisive remarks or equivocal allusions (but please do not mention this to her). Perhaps she is not aware of how much this has become a habit with her, because she simply denies everything when I call her attention to it and tell her how disagreeable it is for me. In that respect I feel so nice and free here with Sasha and never have occasion to blush so foolishly and senselessly.

Do not worry about Hugo Schiff; and I am very glad you believe in my good sense in this matter. I do show him that there is no hope, but he comes frequently nevertheless and is very fond of spending hours in conversation and discussion with me. He has expressed a wish to come and read with me too, but so far I have been discouraging him. He is very much altered in manners since you saw him last. He dresses stylishly and even wears a *tall hat*; he came to Mme Laussot's evening party, whether on account of my being there or not I do not know. On the subject of his character you may be right—but then again you may not. We have had occasion to talk of jealousy, from which, by his own account, he does not suffer. His character is wonderfully pure and noble, and, moreover, he is very clever and interesting; that is why I feel sorry for him.[1]

31. *Natalie Herzen to Alexander Herzen*

25 MAY 1869   *Casa Fumi*
                                              fuori di Porta Romana
                                                        Florence

MY DEAR, kind Papasha, you seem dissatisfied with my last letter and say that I did not really answer your question. What am I to say to you? For the moment I know only one thing, and that is, that Meshchersky and myself are on very good and friendly terms. There was a time, when he was in Florence a year ago, when he felt such a strong attachment to me that he found it very difficult to go away, and sometimes he spoke of the future, saying that he wished most earnestly to come and see us from time to time; and he would certainly have come to Prangins had his financial circumstances not prevented him. They prevent him, as it happens, from doing many things. I must confess for my own part that I find him one of the most attractive personalities I have ever known; I like and respect him very much and have great faith in his advice.

He is compelled to return to Russia, where his domestic affairs are in dreadful disorder, and, most important, he wishes to apply himself to some sort of activity. He would very much like to see me before his departure but here again he does not know if his funds are sufficient. He is a very fine and serious man.

Farewell for the time being. I embrace you and kiss you with all my heart.

Your TATA

I kiss Ogarev and Toots, and press Pan Tchorzewski's hand.

Regarding what you wrote about Teresina, "preserve her from the bourgeoisie"—I have noticed nothing so far; she treats the servants very properly. Why do you cite Mme Vogt as an example? Make your questions more precise so that I can answer more precisely. . . In what respect do you think that Paris would be useful for Olga? She cannot follow lectures yet.

32. *Natalie Herzen to Alexander Herzen*

17 JUNE 1869

115 Villino della Torre
Via dei Serragli
Florence

DEAR PAPASHA,

Olga read your letters in our presence.[2] Malwida was dreadfully agitated, fearing the [possible] effect on Olga; I confess that I, too, waited impatiently for the consequences. But to our great surprise Olga read to the end with supreme calm, and then handed the letter to Malwida and told me that she had long suspected it, adding: "How can it change anything? I have always loved Liza anyway and looked upon her as my younger sister." She assures us, though, that she has never asked anybody and never made any allusions to the fact. From the calmness with which she took it all it was obvious that she had grown accustomed to the idea, and that she found everything perfectly natural except that it had not been divulged to everyone right from the very beginning.

117

But none of this will alter characters, so I see no more reason than before to hope for harmonious existence together.

How will you tell Liza? Perhaps it would be best if she too were left gradually to guess. And what has Nathalie decided for herself: does she still wish to change her name or not?

We are getting our *Égalité*.[3] I read about the shocking consequences of the arrests made after the strike of workers at Pfefer's and Pukk's. If it is all true, it is an outrage; and in Belgium even worse things have happened, I mean the behaviour of the soldiers at a certain station [during] the strike of *des puddlers*. They wounded and slaughtered innocent passengers who had no part in the proceedings, and threatened the women and children, and so on.

We are reading the papers; but what will come of all this hue and cry in Paris? I can see no serious intention so far; it seems to be only *gamins* doing the shooting.[4]

I was very interested to read your letters, or rather your polemic with Bakunin.[5] What is the use of his activity if these gangs of workers are the only result? They will all be fired. And even if they didn't fire them, what does he mean by *"destroying things"*? To what purpose?

Malwida is very keen to leave Florence on 1 July, but she doesn't know where she is going; first she talks of a little place near Genoa, then of Riva on Lake Garda. She is continually complaining of a perpetual heaviness and pain in the head, and hopes that the change of air will help. After that she wants to take the waters, but she still doesn't know and hasn't quite made up her mind. She and Olga both assert that after Kreuznach Olga did not suffer from migraine for three months.

Sasha, Teresina and Volodya[6] are in good health. Volodya is being fed entirely on the bottle now; he is a little darling, but rather thin.

I embrace you all. Olga will write tomorrow, meanwhile we kiss you with all our heart.

Your TATA H.

Have you had a letter from Penisi? Send me *Mazurka* and *Interrupted Tales*.[7] Give Tchorzewski and Czerniecki my best regards, and Blagosvetlov too.

33. *Natalie Herzen to Alexander Herzen*

8 July [1869]   *Antignano*
                                                 presso Livorno

Look where we have ended up, Papasha, my dear. I wanted
to write—that is, to send this letter from Florence—but
Malwida could not make up her mind until the last minute,
and also I had such a violent migraine that I could not write.
Malwida chose this spot because Panovka wishes to remain a
few weeks longer in Livorno. Perhaps Olga will go on with her
lessons if the sea air somehow increases her capital! She wants
to dreadfully.

The air here is magnificent and exquisitely fresh, and the sea
is splendid, but that is all. The landscape is ugly, barren and
formless, so it is very unlikely that we shall decide to stay here.
We are accommodated right by the sea in the remains of an old
fortress. There are no more than four bedrooms in all, and an
inscription over the door in huge letters: *Albergo dell'Antica
Fortezza*.

Farewell for now. I am going with Malwida and Olga to
survey the neighbourhood and see if we can find some beautiful
and shady nook—even the most miniscule spot. Write to Sasha's
address.

I embrace and kiss you, Nathalie and Liza with all my heart.
                                                 Your Tata H.

I recently wrote to Masha and sent her children some views
of Florence, via Mme Schiff. She left on 3 July, is now in Berne
and will remain there for one month.

I wrote to you myself about Penisi and told you I was
giving him lessons in writing. He is exaggerating, of course,
hot-blooded Sicilian that he is. Unconsciously, perhaps, because he almost always seems to think that everything I do is
done well.

I have read [Goncharov's] *The Precipice*.[8] I kept hoping I
would find something interesting, but there was absolutely
nothing; it is utter nonsense.

34. *Alexander Herzen to Sasha Herzen*

SATURDAY, 31 JULY 1869 [Brussels]

I AM undertaking to write to you so soon because I want to explain to you once more my views on the problem of Tata, which it appears I broached most opportunely. First of all, I would not be against any marriage—it was Tata who was against Luginin. I had nothing against Meshchersky. Schiff I have everything against, despite the fact that he may be a remarkably learned man.

Why all my most legitimate desires and dreams burst one after another like soap bubbles I do not understand, but it is so. I have a job to do that must be continued after my death. From my place of exile I have created a name for you by virtue of which you would be received with open arms in a country where, despite all its trivialities and its sombre sides, there is a future simmering of colossal dimensions. And then, while others are trading, working, and seeking after a dowry, I am pointing to the capital that lies in the clutches of the Russian government.[9]

You were the first to leave—you went your own way, you made a success of it, and you are content. Olga is a foreigner, thanks to Meysenbug. On Tata I had pinned my highest hopes—she has our tastes, *notre génie* (in the sense of *génie de la langue,* as they say)—she has been altogether closer to me, and I shall regard her loss as one of the heaviest blows [I have experienced]. Yes, dear Sasha, do not be amazed that I use the word *loss.* In our foreign circle I am a foreigner, a perpetual outsider. What can I do? We have become so tightly-knit that it is not only the ultra-socialists in Europe who regard us as outsiders. And the Schiffs, in addition, are an odd, eccentric lot—you once compared Maurice with Ogarev, but you are mistaken. Maurice Schiff may have far more serious qualities and talents than Ogarev—but he does not have that aesthetic, mellow nature of his. All the misfortunes of Ogarev and his whole life stem from wine—he has drunk himself to ruin, but even the remnants are impressive.

And now what kind of a future lies in store for Tata—in that circle? . . .

In short, "let this cup pass from me." Keep this letter—if it would be appropriate then show it to her. I shall write to her— if my fears grow even greater. If all this is not so, then write to me at once—I shall read your letter with tears of joy. If it is too late for advice, I shall retire even further into myself, for all my fifty-seven years and my old age.

These are painful times. Ogarev and I disagree in many things . . . even on the subject of Toots. The terrible business of Bakunin is having a powerful effect on him.[10]

I am just reading *Aus den Memoiren eines russischen Dekabristen.* Baron Rozen, who was in Siberia, wrote it, and it's interesting— I'll send it to Olga.

35. *Natalie Herzen: Diary*

26 JULY 1869   *Antignano, All'Antica*
                                                              Fortezza

WHAT A difficult situation I am in! What am I to do, to whom can I turn for advice? I have hardly ceased to worry on poor Hugo's[11] account, and now I have to worry even more about Penisi. He has not got Hugo's firm but mild nature; there is southern blood racing within him. Goodness knows, he might really go out of his mind, or something even worse may happen!

But as far as I remember, I have absolutely nothing to re- proach myself with! He has always been exceedingly amiable towards me, but I took all his remarks for foolish compliments. How could I believe, last year for instance, that he really was sorry that I was leaving Florence? It never occurred to me that he was in earnest, and I thought privately: "Why is he wasting so many words, and all to no purpose? Oh well, he'll give vent to his feelings six or seven times, and that's all. We've only seen him for one season, what can it matter to him whether we are here or not?"

When I returned at the end of April this year I was a little surprised to see him present himself at once, the very next day, and say how glad he was that I had come back. Smiling derisively to myself at this, as I did in response to all his courtesies and flattering remarks, I was convinced that it was all the kind of Italian verbiage that the majority of Italians feel they must employ in conversation with ladies. Sometimes I even stopped him in the midst of a speech, saying to him jokingly: there goes the Italian in you again!

He had already long since asked me to occupy myself with him a little. On the first occasion more than two years ago, he had asked me, only half-seriously, to give him lessons in the English language (which I promised, in jest, to do). But from time to time he would either remind me of my promise or else ask if I would agree to give him lessons in German or Russian.

30 JULY [1869]

Visitors, incessantly; who would have expected that, here in Antignano? Nevertheless, it is hard for me to go on like this: I have scarcely the time. And one cannot refuse when someone has journeyed three or four hours or more to see us. Our situation is worse than in the town: a guest is sure to remain the whole day.

And so, although Penisi had asked me to occupy myself a little with him, and although I would in fact have liked to comply with his request, feeling a kind of pity for him as I did, I nevertheless kept temporizing and inventing different pretexts, for various rumours had been spread abroad. Everyone told me: be careful in every possible respect; and Malwida was so truly frightened by them that she was even afraid of admitting him too often into the house. This year I have been more independent, living at Sasha's, and guests have been able to come without fearing to disturb Malwida's sleep. One evening Penisi asked me yet again to teach him, this time writing. I wanted to be useful to him in at least some way; I knew he was often melancholy and sad. In a word, I agreed, glad to be able to do something for him. I was interested by his exercises. He prepared many and various [strokes and letters], and at the end he added a few lines in the form of a letter, with different sorts of courtesies, which too I again took to be mere verbiage, and accepted with a smile, repeating that it was "[just like an] Italian. . . ." So many evil aspersions had been cast on him that I was utterly at a loss to know whether I should believe him or not, but for the most part I did not believe him.

Finally, one evening, he handed me a long letter and begged me to read it in his presence. I asked him to [have the courtesy to][12] permit me to read it alone, at my leisure, but he refused to agree, and I was obliged to read it in front of him.

1 AUGUST [1869]

It was easy to guess the contents, but nonetheless I was very surprised, because I had not imagined that he had already been in love with me for over six months. He told me in this letter how he had suffered when I had begun to treat him so coolly after the Katya affair,[13] and how he had suffered when I had become friendly with Meshchersky, when I had gone away, when I had fallen ill and, lastly, when he heard, soon after my illness, that I was to be married.

I found it dreadfully painful to read this letter—I did not know what to do. Because of my customary mistrust, particularly with regard to him, after all the scandalous gossip, I simply did not believe what he said and wrote to me, at least, I did not believe a good half of it. Part of me felt sorry for him, but suddenly I would be stricken with doubt: was it not all a game? He needed a wife, I had turned up at the right moment, so there he was concocting various stories to convince me that he was passionately enamoured of me. Or was he thinking of our fortune? These questions, and my doubt as a whole, tormented me dreadfully. But I could see he was suffering, and could not believe that it was *all* play-acting. I paused in the middle of reading the letter, wanting to say something. From my air of composure it was obvious to him that my only answer could be a negative one; and therefore he gave me no time to utter a word but began begging me not to reply.

"For God's sake do not answer, I know your answer, spare me, no, no, I implore you not to answer!"

There was so much suffering and despair in his tone that I

thought again that it was possible that it was all true. At the
end of his letter too he had asked me not to reply if my answer
was a negative one. In consequence of which, my silence was
an answer in itself. At that moment somebody came in, and
we went on with the lesson: but he managed to implore me to
être bonne, as they say, not to repulse him, to let him come and
see me as in the past. I promised that I would not alter [my
attitude], and said that if he wished to hear Mr Orey's recital
the next day he could come to us at the Villino della Torre.
He did not come. I did not see him for two days. I learned that
he had been to Sasha's and was in such a state that Sasha
could comprehend nothing and thought he had lost his mind.
On the third day I went to Casa Fumi; Volodya was sick, and
Levier was visiting him several times a day. On this occasion
he came up to me and said he must speak with me alone. I, of
course, was surprised and alarmed—I thought perhaps it concerned Volodya—but at the same time, I had a vague presentiment that he might be going to discuss Penisi. And
indeed, with an earnest and anxious air, and apologizing for his
indiscretion, he asked me if anything had happened between
myself and Penisi in the last few days.

"Why do you ask that?"

"Please excuse me, you know I never interfere in other
people's business, but seeing Penisi in such a terrible state I
considered it my duty as a friend to come and question you,
hoping to discover the causes and to see if there was any way of
helping him."

"Can it be that he really is ill? If only you knew how he
surprised me the other day. Has he not told you anything
himself?"

"No, nothing at first, but I guessed—and it was not difficult
to guess—that he was not indifferent to you. Sometimes I even
teased him with my allusions, but he always protested and
assured me that it was all nonsense, that I was imagining it,
and broke off the conversation."

"The evening before last, he gave me a long letter and
forced me to read it in his presence, it was when you came in
during our lesson, remember?"

"Yes. That night, just after that letter, I was up late working. I saw that there was still a candle burning in his room. It was already three o'clock, I rushed over to him; he had been sorting out papers. Many of them he had burned, the rest he placed in a pile; then he stopped and sat silently and in such grim despair that I began to be worried in earnest. He did not hear my questions, or did not wish to reply, but kept repeating as though to himself: 'is it possible to be so mistaken?' "

"Good Heavens, though, what does it mean? Levier, I assure you that I have never deceived him, that is encouraged him, either by words, gestures or allusions. And think for yourself, you know that after everything I heard about him, after the affair with Katya, there was a time when I felt almost a repugnance to him and I was dreadfully cold towards him. But can one fail to feel sorry for him in his unhappy situation?"

"I assure you that all that is malicious gossip and he is not to blame for the Katya affair."

"Yes, well I was myself unsure which of them was to blame, and gradually overcame my feeling and reverted to my former courteousness and amiability with him. And I agreed to give him the lessons because I really did pity him. You had no time [. . .];[14] and then I did not seriously suspect that he was not indifferent towards me, and I was pleased to be useful to him."

"It seems, though, that he did have some slight hope."

"That is impossible, Levier! I am not to blame at all for it: for pity's sake, I refused him everything—he asked me to go for walks with him, then to go riding, or to give him lessons—and [the reason I refused was] to prevent other people talking about it, rather than for his sake, for I did not for one moment suspect that his feelings towards me were serious. I became tired of all his compliments and clichés, I took them for Italian prating, and often interrupted him and laughed at him. Good Heavens, if I had suspected for one minute that part of it was the truth, I would never have tormented him. For God's sake, tell me frankly—are you sure that it is all true, that there is no trace of play-acting? I am so accustomed to doubt and mistrust people, especially him."

"Come now, how can it be a joke? I have sat with him for two nights. I was afraid to leave his bedside; God knows what was the matter with him. I have seen nothing like it in all my born days, and if we do not calm him, the affair may end badly. Tell me, is there no hope for him? I did not know how to calm him at night. I started assuring him that he must be mistaken, and promised to ask you personally."

"How can I answer you? You know now that I cannot promise him anything whatsoever, knowing that I feel nothing for him and do not see any possibilities [for the future]."

Levier: "How shall I begin to tell him? Be kind to him at least, as you have been until now. He implores you not to repulse him."

Myself: "But I was not thinking of repulsing him, and I will be all the more indulgent and prudent now that I know, and am coming to believe, that his sentiments are serious. Let him keep coming as before."

Naturally, this conversation was dreadfully agitating for me. I was so distressed to think that he had suffered so much, he who was so gloomy and wretched as it was. I was so annoyed at myself for the frivolous way I had taken and only half-listened to what he had said to me at those times. I imagined his sufferings and could scarcely restrain my tears. I continued to be in this agonized state for a few days more, until Levier told me that he simply had to offer a faint glimmer of hope to Penisi in order to help him recover.

Levier: "Otherwise I don't know what will become of him. He has relinquished all his affairs; yesterday he missed a very important conference at the Ministry. You understand, it can't go on like this."

Myself: "What am I to tell him, what can I promise him without deceiving him?"

Levier: "He is sick; one must treat him like a sick child. The slightest sign of sympathy from you will revive him, and that is essential. What is killing him is the absence of any hope, the consciousness that whatever he says or does, nothing will change."

Myself: "But how can I help him?"

Levier: "Tell him, for instance, that although you feel nothing now, perhaps when you become better acquainted, in a year or two, or three, or even four—time means absolutely nothing to him—perhaps then, many things will have changed. Or if you like, tell him that you will speak with him about it in a year's time."

Myself: "Now the second I might be able to say. But tell me frankly, don't you think it will pass of its own accord?"

Levier: "*De tout autre j'aurais dit oui, mais de lui, comme je le connais—non,*" answered Levier after a silence. Then he added: "But what has caused and causes you to have such a bad opinion of him? I assure you it is [nothing but] gossip; it distresses me to see that you believe it. I want you to get to know him *as he really is* and not as he is represented. That is too unfair."

36. *Natalie Herzen to Alexander Herzen*

24 SEPTEMBER 1869

Casa Fumi
fuori di Porta Romana
Firenze

TO PAPASHA,

But I wasn't asking you for money, Papasha, dear, I only wanted to know to whom you had given the extra for me—Sasha or Malwida. I don't need anything for the time being; if I spend all I have on the journey I will tell you in Paris and ask you to give me some for clothes. Don't worry for the moment about Olga; she went to Munich with a passable wardrobe. There are various things she will have to do in Paris, and she will need long dresses. One cannot live cheaply in Paris—the apartment alone will cost heaven-knows-what.

The story of the Wagner opera was simply delightful—pure comedy![15] Everyone turned up, not only Malwida but Turgenev, Mme Viardot, and Liszt. They say that ten or fifteen thousand foreigners gathered in Munich.

I am sorry I wasn't with you in Holland. I only know Rembrandt's *portraits*, they are superb; but I have seen none of his paintings. I too find Rubens a little rich for my taste, and Teresina agrees with us—and she has an unerring eye.

How can you say that Liza loves Olga and Sasha, Papasha dear? It is only words; how can she know? It is an easy thing to say without having lived together.

Now about P[enisi]. Once, when he was again in a terrible state, he begged me in desperation to tell him the truth and say if I felt the slightest love for him. I told him the truth, replying *"un petit peu"*. Let me go away and live a while in Paris before I come to any decision. Find a flat and write and tell me when I am to come.

I embrace you, dear good Papasha, and kiss you with all my heart.

Your TATA H.

P[enisi] is staying here.

I don't know what has become of the second volume of the French edition of *My Past and Thoughts*; I will ask Olga when she returns. The Italian translation is due to appear by March. P[enisi] asks if he can translate the fourth volume *before* its publication in French—from the proofs, for instance?

Olga has written to you *Poste restante, Paris*; ask if there are any letters for you.

Sasha is at the medical congress from morning till evening. He is going to have to argue with a so-called important person, Doctor Baccelli from Rome.

37. *Natalie Herzen to Alexander Herzen*

2 OCTOBER 1869   [*Florence*]

MY POOR, dear Papasha, don't be alarmed and exaggerate. After all, I have promised nothing and am in no way tied. Why do you want to write to everyone about it? It will only cause a sensation. Neither Sasha nor Meysenbug knows anything; I have not spoken to anyone, and however tormented I have felt I have been outwardly calm. In Antignano only Olga might have noticed that I was not really calm and cheerful, because we shared the same room. Sasha was either in Specolo or busy with the congress; he left before morning coffee and would sometimes return exhausted in the evening. When I told P[enisi] that I *must* go to Paris,[16] and that I was promising nothing, he saw that I wanted to end it all, and so began begging and pleading, trying to persuade me, and reproaching me. How I bore it without giving way I do not know; he was ill again. I thought that it was all over and I wanted to leave Florence at once. I thought of Delesalo, where Malwida was, but as luck would have it I received a letter from her in which she said that she was thinking of returning any day now. For several days I stayed at home in a state of confusion. Sasha asked what was the matter with me, and I said I was unwell and had a migraine. And then on the evening of the third day, the day of his lesson, P[enisi] appeared once again quite unexpectedly (the previous day I had received a pathetic letter from him, but had not replied). He began begging my forgiveness for his letter, which had been written in a moment of despair, *"et maintenant je n'en pouvais plus, je devais vous revoir."*

Dear Papasha, there is nothing that can be done *immediately* or *before* my departure without causing a sensation,[17] and that would be more painful for him.

Everything is easier from a distance, and perhaps he will not give up his occupations or think of leaving for Sicily. He will become gradually calmer, and that really is better, Papasha dear, both better and more humane. Really, one cannot treat him like one does other people; he is a sick man. Let me finish this little by little. *I promise you* I shall not tie myself down in any way. I assure you that that is the best thing, Papasha. Please don't write to anyone, it will only result in a scandal; and if you still wish me to end the affair immediately, write again and I will obey your desire. But think seriously if it would not be better to act cautiously and gradually. To my mind it is decidedly better; what are you afraid of? I will not make any promises to him except to write and send him translations as he has requested. With anyone else one would have to take abrupt action, but with him one cannot, really one cannot. I think he is already a little calmer. He knows his letter had an extremely bad effect on me and that since that time I have treated him more coldly. Farewell. Write to me again, and I promise you I will obey your wishes. I embrace you and kiss you from the bottom of my heart.

Your TATA

Do not blame Levier—in what way is he to blame except for having advised me to say "let's talk it over in a year's time." But even then he added, "of course, you must not bind yourself in any way." There was no *intrigue* at all there; Tchorzewski has invented it all! Levier was doing his best to help me, and you must not blame him for anything.

Tessié[18] and his wife have arrived. They left their cards on Friday and came to visit us on Saturday evening; they were extremely amiable. I thought about your advice; but they came here *quasi*-secretly and today, Sunday, they are leaving early in the morning. In a week's time they will be in Paris. He was very jovial, criticized all my photographs and said he would take some himself in Paris.

Masha's children thank you for the money. Poor Egor Ivanovich, what a sad end!

Did you get my telegram? And the French edition of *My Past and Thoughts?* I wrote to Tchorzewski about it.

38. *Natalie Herzen to Alexander Herzen*

WEDNESDAY, 6 OCTOBER 1869

Casa Fumi
fuori di Porta Romana
Florence

DEAR PAPASHA,

I don't understand your letter to Malwida. What is it you really want? Is it too difficult for you to arrange for us to live in Paris, or too costly, or do you think that Malwida's consent is too *contre-coeur?*

If your only difficulty is in finding a flat, we can wait a little longer and then stay with Aga for a while, in Geneva that is. But if life in Paris really is too expensive for you, then name another place. And do not think you have to do anything to "save" me, as you say. When I thought that I had ended it all with P[enisi] I felt dreadfully sorry for him, and also I was so afraid that he would decide to do something foolish that I was quite upset. But at the same time I felt liberated and was glad that I had ended it, so do not fear for *me*. I will treat him more and more coolly, which is easier to do by letter, of course. But I would not like you to be hasty for fear on my account, take a flat which is too dear or unsatisfactory, and then have cause for regret. So I *implore* you once more not to think that I need *saving*, not to make a hurried decision because of me. But when everything is ready we will come to you. What is the point of trying to persuade Malwida to put it off now? I have a very severe cold and have been unwell for several days; my head still feels a little heavy but it's nothing.

Farewell, I embrace you, N[athalie] and Liza and kiss you with all my heart.

Your TATA

I wrote to Tchorzewski about the French version of *My Past and Thoughts*. He answered that you had removed that volume from my drawer with your own hands and taken it with you to Paris. It's the only one I have.

Teresina kisses you all and is proud that Sasha is playing an important part. She is interested in his quarrels with Baccelli at the congress. There was an announcement in one journal that the opening of the new Specolo was attended by *"l'egregio Prof. Alex. Herzen colla sua signora"*. I was suffering from a migraine on that day and did not go with him.

39. *Natalie Herzen to Nathalie Tuchkova-Ogareva*

12 OCTOBER 1869

Casa Fumi
fuori Porta Romana
Firenze

"We await your final order!"

DEAR NATHALIE,

You ask how it is that we have suddenly all decided to come to you. The fact is that the decision was not made at all

131

suddenly. Perhaps it seemed so to you at a distance, but actually we were talking about it constantly even *before* our departure for Antignano, and in Antignano itself. I could see that Olga not only had no objection, but wanted to come to you; and that it was only the effect of the northern climate on Malwida's health that was holding her back. I began reinforcing Olga's desire and persuading Malwida. I don't know how we shall arrange our life there. But in my view it is essential that we come together and do all we can to ensure that everyone is as happy as possible and everything goes harmoniously. I have been continually saying this. Incidentally, Malwida agrees with me; naturally she wants Papasha to settle somewhere permanently. To satisfy Papasha and Malwida I made every effort to persuade you to move a little south. Seeing that nothing would come of that, that Papasha would not be able to bring himself to live in Italy even for a trial period, and that he found the north so agreeable, I began working in the other direction, that is, persuading Malwida to go to you. I sent on Papasha's letters to Olga, adding always that in my opinion it was our duty to come to you immediately and that I would come in any case. Then Olga made up her mind and wrote to you, and that is why you thought it all so sudden, Nathalie dear; but in fact it has all been going on for months, even years.

Yesterday I had it out with Penisi, and ended the whole thing. What he intends to do I don't know, because he left hastily and dreadfully agitated. But be assured that *it is all over* and poor Papasha is to stop worrying completely. Perhaps he will simply decide to remain a friend, as a reasonable man, like Hugo Schiff. I very much doubt that he will decide to commit any "foolishness"—by foolishness, of course, I mean what he said to me about committing suicide. I knew (although he himself never said anything about it to me) that he always carried poison on him. Although I did not entirely believe him, there were nevertheless moments when it seemed to me that his Sicilian blood was capable of anything, and I was terribly afraid.

Nathalie, wouldn't it be better to choose some other place for our reunion than Paris? What's to be done? Everybody has shown *bonne volonté*, but that doesn't increase our income. Clearly life in Paris would be impossible with our means, so why not try the *south*—do you want to? Let's try Italy, and when we receive [the money from] our estate in Russia we can settle in Paris then. Ah, were it not for this stupid affair with P[enisi] I would beg and persuade you with all my might to try Florence. The villas are simply delightful, and moreover they are just completing a huge new promenade round the whole town, knocking down walls to enlarge the capital. I can understand that Papasha cannot be entirely happy with life here, that's clear, but what can we do if Paris does not suit our requirements and our means? Florence and Naples are better than Nice, of course, aren't they? But Turin and Milan are awful. Please let's try it, Nathalie dear. Have a serious talk with Papasha. Perhaps Penisi will go away. Perhaps he will behave so quietly and sensibly that I will not have to go away. But if Papasha is very desirous of spending the winter in Paris in spite of life there being so dear, tell him we are quite willing and only waiting for the signal from him. If it's impossible for everybody, I will come by myself to you, and please don't think I am put off by the "false position"; I had not even thought about it. I embrace and kiss you all heartily.

Your TATA H.

13 OCTOBER 1869

(Malwida's 53rd birthday)

Papasha asked about Meshchersky. I had had no news for a long time, because I missed my chance, that is, I did not answer him for ages. He went away from Alexandersbad and I did not know where to write to, and was sure that he must be in Russia already. But Sasha received a dispatch from him in Hamburg, asking where I was; we replied that for the moment we were here. I shall probably get a letter from him soon.

40. Alexander Herzen to Nikolay Ogarev

3 NOVEMBER [1869]   *H[ôte]l New York*
                                                    Lungarno
                                                    Florence

I WROTE to you yesterday in a kind of haze—today I will give you a more detailed account. Yes, my old old friend, this bolt from the blue in the autumnal calm has shattered me also. Imagine Tata, her expression so meek, her eyes turned upon me filled with love, and comprehending nothing. Penisi terrified her, and she is constantly seeing murderers who will cut my throat, Sasha's and even Schiff's. She is perfectly quiet now and obeys her *garde-malade* like an animal. She listens to Schiff and most of all to me. She loves me passionately. Schiff has given orders for her to be put to bed at six o'clock. Yesterday she lay in her bed and cried bitterly, then took my hand, pressed it to her lips and remained thus for a quarter of an hour. To move her now is out of the question. It might drive her to a frenzy. Schiff is waiting for a certain critical time to begin intensive treatment; he advises complete rest and then, after about two weeks, that we should go somewhere—anywhere, as long as it is to a town where there is a well-known psychiatrist; Milan, for instance, where Biffi lives, the director of a lunatic asylum.

Let me tell you exactly how her madness began. She had been distracted and immeasurably distressed by the slanderous rumours that blind monster had spread abroad—and was terror-stricken by his threats. One day some man or other knifed a girl outside her window and the girl fell, bleeding profusely. Tata saw the police carry her away. That evening they went to Schiff's. Sasha was delayed for some reason in the street, and Tata went up alone. When Sasha arrived he found her lying unconscious on the sofa. Schiff and Professor Blaserna were bathing her forehead with cold water. Tata had thought that Sasha had been murdered—and from that moment she has not regained her senses—it was on about 20 or 21 October. At first they all thought that a hallucination of this kind would pass, but by the 24th it was just the reverse. Tata wanted to throw herself from the balcony—Sasha managed to restrain her by force—and since then she has been under constant surveillance day and night. At night the creole woman (a midwife friend of Osip Ivanovich's)[19] looks after her, and during the day we all take it in turns. She is absolutely quiet . . . spends long, long moments in thought and asks me: "I don't seem to understand anything, do I?" She took up her pen and wrote to N[athalie]: "Don't believe that I am insane."

Sasha is badly shaken. He dismissed Levier immediately. That fool is all repentance now, but his interference was the most criminal thing. I have not seen him and do not wish to do so.

Schiff says that during this stage of the illness he does not recommend that Olga and Liza be exposed to the influence of the patient. At the moment she is at Sasha's (his flat is a nice one). Nathalie and Liza will probably arrive the day after tomorrow and stay at a hotel for the time being. Use Sasha's address [to write].

We shall have to summon up all our strength and wait to see how it will all end.

I thank Tchorzewski—but why is he coming? Absolutely nothing is needed now except ourselves and patience.

[In the handwriting of Sasha Herzen]

My dear, kind Aga! Don't be angry with me—you see, I didn't know myself at first what it was all about, and the awful thought never entered my head. Everything I wrote to you was perfectly true—only two or three days afterwards— for we all thought that it was an irritation that would soon pass. Remember, I knew *nothing* of the whole story, and Tata has only recently told me. Schiff thinks it will be possible to travel in about ten days, and she will then make a speedy recovery.

I embrace you heartily
SASHA

41. Alexander Herzen to Nathalie Tuchkova-Ogareva and Liza Herzen

3 NOVEMBER [1869]   *H[ôte]l New York*
                                                     Florence

I HAVE finally pulled myself together sufficiently to be able to write coherently. Tata's condition is awful. She is quiet now, but constantly under the influence of terror and fear, and she understands nothing. She obeys me and Madame Raymond—the latter like a persecuted animal. She has asked me two or three times whether it is true that Lelya-boy and Lelya-girl are alive in Nice, and that Madame Georges rescued them from the sea, and if it is true that Madame Georges is Louisa Ivanovna.[20] On one occasion she tried to jump from the terrace and Sasha managed to restrain her by force. In fact she has shown clearly, leaving aside Schiff's opinion, that our departing now is out of the question. I took her for a drive in the carriage with Olga and Meysenbug, out in the country. At first everything went well, but suddenly she asked where we were going and tried simultaneously to seize the coachman by his jacket with the aim of stopping him—Meysenbug and I held her hands, smiling and making jokes. It is all so painful that I can only just restrain my tears in her presence.

She is passionately attached to me and simply says in front of everybody: "Send them away—I want to be with you." In the carriage she suddenly said to Olga and Meysenbug: "It's time you got out—or else I'll get out with Papa. I'll be his sunshade for him."

I was quite wrong to blame Sasha. He dismissed Levier at once. Schiff is treating her in earnest and does have some influence over her. He says that he had noticed a morbid distractedness about her ever since her arrival from Nice. He is waiting for a certain critical period to see what will happen and then he wants to commence treatment by galvanic currents. He absolutely refuses to let her be moved and says that a journey might frighten her into a frenzy. He does not recommend any diversion now but complete peace. If things improve, he advises us to go away from Florence but only to a town with a well-known psychiatrist. In Italy therefore he would choose Milan. This strict medical supervision will have to be maintained for a long time—months.

Meysen[bug] has only just now recovered. Sasha says that during the first few days she was so affected that she looked like a madwoman herself. So we do not expect her to be of any real help to the patient. And later Schiff did in fact say that *at the moment* if Tata lived in too close proximity with Olga and Liza it might prove a considerable strain on the nerves of both. See her they can and should, but to spend whole days with her is inadvisable. On the whole he is of the opinion that it would be better to isolate her with Raymond. . . And anyway she is only too willing to stay in her room. Schiff has ordered her to be put to bed at six o'clock in the evening—and yesterday she let herself be undressed like a child, lay down in bed and started to cry bitterly. Her expression is one of total meekness especially when she looks at me. Lying in bed she took my hand, pressed it to her lips and held it thus for a quarter of an hour—then she whispered once again: "Take me away. . . They'll kill you and Sasha here. . ."

Penisi turned out an utter scoundrel. He spread malicious gossip about Tata and informed her of the fact. Tata said sadly: "So I found my Herw[egh] too. . ."[21]

Another detail—when she began raving and was in continual terror of meeting assassins. Some man or other had thrust a knife into a girl outside her window; the girl fell in a pool of blood and the police took her away in a dead faint. Later Tata went to Schiff's with Sasha. Sasha stopped [to talk] to someone. . . She went on up alone and when Sasha came up he found her on the sofa, with Schiff applying cold water to her; and ever since that turn, her mind has been in a swoon. She thought that some men bribed by Penisi had cut Sasha's throat. She gets up and listens ten times a night. Mme Raymond orders her back to bed at once—and she goes.

That is all for the moment.

Clearly you ought to come here. The courtesy and efficiency on the railways are amazing. The carriage is changed once at Alessandri *(cambio di vettura)*—the coaches are large. Best of all is to leave Genoa at 6.20 p.m.—you will arrive at exactly 8 (there is a short rest-stop). Sasha and I will be waiting at the landing-stage. Should you decide to come, telegraph the details to Sasha's address; it is sufficient to write to "Casa Fumi, Porta Romana, Firenze". For the time being you should stay here at the Hôtel New York Lungarno.

DEAR LIZA,

Do your packing and pack Mummy, and come here. Tata is very ill and will not be able to drive out for ten days or maybe even more. Mummy will tell you. I am very sad—we all are. Come and cheer us up. There is no reason for Olga to come now. They have a small flat—but very charming—but Sasha's is splendid. We will stay together at the Hôtel New York Lungarno (where I now am). The big room has just been taken, but if you telegraph I will arrange everything. Tell Mummy to have the hotel messenger go with her to the station and change some money into Italian notes, because French ones are not accepted on the railway.

We await your telegram.

[In the handwriting of Sasha Herzen]
DEAR LIZA,

We are expecting you to come too to our poor Tata. She often speaks of you and asks about you. Kiss Mummy for her note to me and tell her I will do everything in my power and that we are all counting on her help also—we need her very much.

I kiss you
SASHA

42. Alexander Herzen to Nikolay Ogarev

4 NOV[EMBER 1869]   *H[ôte]l New York*
[Florence]

N.B. My third letter from Florence. Have you had them all?
MY ARRIVAL has had a powerful and good effect. All yesterday

Tata was quieter and less anxious. She even answered several questions correctly. Schiff is satisfied, but he is waiting to see if she continues thus for the next few days. Travelling is still impossible now—the noise of the train, the strange faces and the immediate danger of her throwing herself out of the carriage all make it inconceivable. Today Biffi—who is regarded as one of the most astute psychiatrists—will be coming with Schiff to see her. Como is to Milan what Richmond is to London, and we shall probably move there. In the meantime Schiff advises us to take a flat here for a month, somewhere quiet out of town. He doesn't want Olga and Liza to spend too much time too often with her, remarking that the youngsters' nerves wouldn't stand up to the experience.

Sasha is to blame—if one can blame a person for slow-wittedness—only inasmuch as he *noticed nothing* until after 20 October. And Malwida probably thought it was *all over and done with*. When he suddenly decided to take her to Paris (on the day when that girl was knifed in the street) Tata said most emphatically that she wouldn't go anywhere in the world with anyone—except me.

Tata deceived Sasha, Malwida, and everyone, apart from Olga, by her extraordinary guile. Olga, clearly more intelligent than the grown-ups, was resolved to write to me much earlier, but Tata dissuaded her from doing so by saying (quite truthfully) that she was writing to me herself.

When Penisi saw there was no hope he wrote Tata and Sasha the most insolent letters containing threats. Tata at once said to Sasha: "He's a Herwegh", but, deeply injured and humiliated, she became quite distracted. Penisi assured her that he had some hired assassins who were under his thumb since he knew of all their villainous deeds and could ruin them (which may well have been true)—and her fear for Sasha and Hugo Schiff (who had behaved splendidly) made her completely crazed. She is better now—but the slightest noise can undo everything. Levier, that ass and blackguard, took fright and rushed off to Penisi and told him he was a villain. Then he stopped visiting even Sasha—which was marvellous. Then Penisi began bombarding Sasha with anonymous menacing letters containing abuse, threatening public disclosure and so on (indeed, Herwegh's methods exactly).

Pass on some of all this to Tchorzewski—he deserves to hear it by virtue of his love for us all. . .

Don't forget.

Incidentally, I quit Paris in such haste that I left Bakunin's manuscript with Aristide Rey;[22] I shall write to him. I hope Bakunin will forgive me when he learns the reason.

N[athalie] and Liza will probably arrive tomorrow.

Could you find out something for me just in case: would Robin[23] agree to go to Como for four or five months and give lessons to Liza and Olga? Living separately but giving lessons daily. *E[xempli] gr[atia]*, for about 250–300 francs per month.

Next, the moral. Well, there you have freedom in female education for you. There you have lack of authority, anarchy, and so on and so on . . . Look back *sine ira et studio*. Try ruthlessly to remember everything from Mar[ia] Lv[ovna] and the deceased Nat[alie] to Park House and Teddington . . . and tell me what the source is of all our blows and misfortunes. It is a man's drunkenness and debauchery and a woman's immaturity, which, uncontrolled by any martingale, lashes out and strikes down everything in its path.

It is infinitely tedious—I cannot even read. What's more, I caught a chill all over on the Corniche and crossing the Apennines.

I think that we ought all the same to go back to Paris afterwards. There is nowhere with a better *Anregung* for work.

When you send your telegram you can economize on three words—instead of: "Dr Herzen, Casa Fumi *fuori di* Porta Romana", write: "Herzen, Casa Fumi-Porta Romana".

Farewell

"Shpekin"? Can you really have forgotten about our dear good old postmaster Shpekin who used to open Khlestakov's letters? Well, I wrote to you that I could write more from Paris were it not for Shpekin. Understand?

43. *Alexander Herzen to Nikolay Ogarev*

Now I will say a few words at my leisure on the subject of your intention to write to Qu[adrio][24]—what can he do? Precisely what he and Osip Ivanovich did with Herwegh, that is, nothing. Words won't make a man like him blush, and blindness saves him from deeds. On a closer examination, especially of the pile of letters, I [now] believe that he really was enamoured of her and tried to persuade her first with threats of suicide and then—when that failed—by threatening to cause a scandal, spread gossip and take revenge. That is the way these vile-natured persons usually act.

Notice that it is an exact repetition of the Herwegh affair. They have a logic of their own. Platonic weapons are no punishment for them. All he has to do is move from Florence to Venice or Naples and there's an end to the whole thing, but he won't even do that. I even stopped Sasha from taking certain *démarches*. The disgraceful behaviour of *Levier* is far more easily excused—and he has gone off his own head with remorse and with finding himself in a position where his closest friends repulse him. He went to Penisi and told him to his face that he was a "vile hypocrite"; Penisi probably laughed and called him a "vile idiot".

I look upon life coolly and passively, Ogarev. How can one choose upon whom to take one's revenge when *all* are guilty? Think rather on this: why is it that the melodramatic Leo Leonis, the Horaces, and the inveterate scoundrels exert the most powerful influence over the finest women, not only in novels but in real life itself? And by the way, you and all female-Nechayevs, give up these *abortive* liberations—in history one can forestall events—but if you do, then cease to feel sympathy for the victims, sympathy for the individual. Yes indeed, neither Pugachev nor Marat felt any sympathy for them. What rubbish you (and I) were preaching about total freedom not only of choice but of change too—especially before you slid into familism like [a picture] into a frame. Look now at the ruins all around you. (And don't go and quote the opposite extremes to me—I know them.) Even this latest affair would never have happened if Sasha had bided his time (which he promised me he would). Everything that happened with Penisi could not have taken place in any house where there was a serious-minded woman. *Teresina* is a sweet little bundle of mischief and of course is less aware than Mary of what are the limits and bounds—Tata could have no confidence in her; and she was insulted by Sasha's inattentiveness (all of which I predicted in my letters to you). Meysenbug's idealistic and narrow-minded self-righteousness, her moral blindness and her faith in her own genius, made falsehood and dissimulation easy. Tata resolved to tell Sasha the truth when she became cut off, when she became frightened, seeing that the concessions and the game of indulgent pandering had developed into a menacing monster. She told Penisi repeatedly that she had not decided on anything, that she would wait another year or two and then give her answer, and that she was not indifferent to his suffering and his love. My letters made her change her mind. Penisi, seeing preparations being made to go to Paris, demanded a direct answer, and she refused. The would-be suicide turned out to be a cold-blooded butcher and villain.

Well, and if I had not written letters and summoned her to Paris (and Tata was deliberately delaying her departure) she would now be Penisi's wife, and he would precisely thus have revealed his vile nature. Levier was even pressing him to get it all over with in Antignano. She would have been acting *freely*— at twenty-four one does, I think, know what one is doing. . . But H. Schiff quite truthfully says: "Better to die, of course, than to be the wife of that scoundrel."

I am a harsh and merciless judge. Saving the righteous is no problem, but saving the wrongdoer by love, without reproaches and [. . .],[25] is another matter. I shall do it, but my conscience, my judgement and my ideas I will not change. I have never hesitated to draw conclusions and speak truths in either the general or the particular. So there you have the whole story once again. How can one take one's vengeance?

Incidentally, we must rescue Olga—how can we trust Meysenbug after what has happened, and what faith can we have in Sasha? By the grace of God and by the prayers of the Holy Fathers I shall do so. The time has at last come for me too to pay off old debts.

[Tata] is improving all the time but travel would still terrify her, and so I will name no day.

SUNDAY, 14 NOVEMBER

Today she is even better—the absolute quiet has done a great deal, and perhaps we shall be able to go as far as Spezia towards the weekend. It is *three weeks* today since the illness manifested itself properly; her fainting fit at Schiff's was on 23 October, a Saturday. I cannot say that it has been a waste of time.

Sasha brought me a closely written notebook—Levier's justification. I read it—he has been made an utter fool of, but even this notebook casts a big shadow over the mystery. I am beginning to think that Schiff senior is right in saying that even as early as August or September her mental faculties were not all in order and that she was acting under the influence of morbid nightmares.

Liza is well and cheerful and living with Olga.

Farewell

I am doing absolutely nothing, I don't want to do anything and I am not reading anything—hence my long letters.

44. *Alexander Herzen to Sasha Herzen*

29 NOV[EMBER 18]69   *Genoa*

MY DEAR SASHA,

Meysenbug and Olga have arrived. Meysenbug's flighty character makes her more maniable than she thinks; she is well—also more than she thinks. But I found Olga delicate—I believe she has worms and the medicines have emaciated her. I shall attend particularly to this in Paris.

Concerning Berd[uschek]—and this is between ourselves—it is really only a guess of mine, because *people were saying it* perhaps before I arrived. Let the matter rest. I wish neither to forgive nor to punish Levier—but I do not wish to know him, as I would not wish to keep a dog that might prey upon Voldyrchik in my home.

Tata sees eveything in a sombre light. It is clear that she is decidedly attracted to Meshchersky, so why has she been making things so complicated? He ought to write her a letter. All in all, it is essential to keep in contact with him. Write to him cautiously without signing. Apparently he has written to Olga. Tata is afraid to write—I can pass on a note from her via you. Think it all over and write to me at once in Nice—*poste restante*.

I have been badly shaken by this affair. It was as bad as the shipwreck of Louisa Ivanovna, the whole year [18]52,[26] and the moments when I held Lelya under the surgeon's knife. I was utterly unprepared for this blow—indeed, I was about to settle down to some work in Paris. I don't know how soon I shall be able to pull myself together. But at the moment I am incapable of occupying myself with anything, my mind is ageing, and then there are these cursed boils on my hands making me suffer stupidly and hinting at a recurrence of my diabetes. I take a very mournful view of the future—everything seems to be *wandernde Gestalten* and *dissolving views*.[27]

Why is it—*caro mio*—that you do not understand that you are not to blame in a positive sense, as is Meysenbug, but negatively, and profoundly. It is bad enough that you could be by her side and know nothing, but *worse still* that Tata *did not wish* to speak to you, and she *had no need*. And one thing is clear to me—the bond of intimacy there was between you before 1868 has withered away. I said as much to Ogarev on the occasion of your arrival in Geneva, and I said so later in Prangins. Delve into your soul, and instead of finding excuses take a critical look at yourself. To be frank with you, I doubt whether Teresina was too fond of, or at all close to, Tata and Olga (I assure you, neither of them has said a word to me) . . . She was so content with her *salto mortale* upwards that she had no interest in becoming intimate with your sisters. Their natures are a little more complex. How else is one to explain the fact that she could sit with them in a room evening after evening and know nothing? Believe me, I have an instinctive feeling—and I am an impartial judge—but a painfully harsh one. You have become estranged from Tata, not in your way of life or your habits of communication, but *in spirit*. You have not been concerned for her, you have not *felt* for her—a result of familism, naturally. Teresina's coolness I understand less well; perhaps we have here a small part of the just war waged by the plebeian against the privileged—but if so, then why is she more of a grand lady than we are? For God's sake, do not think that I say this because of her blunderings or her rudeness to Nathalie. I mean something more serious and broader. I was referring to the total lack of educated humaneness amongst the plebs—and that can be glossed over—but the lack of warmth with regard to your family cannot be glossed over. . .

I have just read Meshchersky's letter to Olga. Poor Tata. . . How foolishly she has acted. He should come to Paris and have a talk with me—that is the only salvation I can envisage.

Tell Mme Walter that Granovsky writes only that he found relaxation and cultured company in her house in Vienna. That all the celebrities of the times used to frequent it, and that she had two unusually intelligent daughters.[28] I am afraid to send the book—Ogarev wants to write about it.

12 O'CLOCK

I received your Postcript to Turgenev's letter. A month in prison is nothing—you should not deny yourself the pleasure of a caning if necessary for such a trifle.[29]

N.B. Olga has just confirmed to me that Berduschek has been telling all and sundry what I wrote. She says she has heard it from a dozen people. There are your friends for you. Olga was talking about it to some Greek woman. Clearly Berduschek has spread it all around—there's another blackguard for you—tell Hugo Schiff. Fine friends you have!—he used to visit you too! Anyway Olga has told you about that. Yes, I have rescued them from a cesspool—and they will not fall into it as long as I am alive—nor will I either.

It makes my flesh creep!

K

Are Tata's 200 francs included in your "send 140 francs" or are they separate? Write and tell me, and then I will send it all together in January.

Buy Schiff a garden chair and a table for the New Year.

We sail for Nice today if possible.

Farewell

Give my regards to Teresina and kiss Voldyrchik.

4 O'CLOCK

I read your letter to Tata and I am very happy with it. Remember Meshchersky. That is vital. Write to him yourself. Olga has written to him. I cannot decide whether to go by sea.

45. *Natalie Herzen to Nikolay Ogarev*

7 DECEMBER 1869   [*Nice*]

YESTERDAY WAS your birthday, my dear kind Aga. I thought of you and wanted to write to you, but I could not—my head was not behaving well. You cannot imagine what confusion there is in my brain at times. I see, I realize that life is so short, that one should make use of every minute, *do* something for others, for one's near and dear ones at least, but there is always something that prevents me. What is it? Probably the fact that I keep playing a game, keep thinking (it's rather like a *jeu de patience*), recollecting everything that I have heard—your arguments, the arguments at the Schiffs, and so on. It's so hard for me, everything is incoherent, much is muddled, and I want to put it all in order—I'm searching for a conclusion. It is a kind of madness, I can see that since my illness. Imagine that I had lost myself; I was seeking myself in all the ages, throughout all the centuries, in all the elements—in short, I was everything in the world, starting from gases and ether, I was fire, water, light, granite, chaos, all kinds of religions. . . I know little about historical fact—but all the same I saw a great deal, and dreadfully vividly. It was extremely interesting, and I do not regret being ill. There were times when I suffered greatly, first for the others; they tortured all of them, and then set upon myself; and the countless times they killed me!—and guillotined me, and hanged me, and shot me, carved me to pieces and poisoned me. I felt it all; that is what it means to have an imagination—a sick one. . . I took myself to be the personification of all phenomena—electricity, phosphorescence, autopsy, harmony, stupidity, everything good and evil—and it all came out as a pot-pourri—and I was a coward of the first order. *Je suis l'univers personnifié*—such was my conclusion. And indeed, every man is a little world unto himself and understands the world after his own fashion. Sometimes I kept hearing: *"Nichts ist drinnen, nichts ist draussen, dann was innen das ist aussen!"*[30] And everything grew dark, I thought that the end of the world had come, everything vanished, the globe and the solar system and all history with it. And far, far in the distance there was a tiny star—a new world was beginning. I wanted to rescue everyone and take them there with me. But it's impossible to tell the whole story, and then, I do not wish to think about it any more. Farewell, I hug and kiss you affectionately, and love you.

Your TATA-KASHA H.

46. *Natalie Herzen to Nikolay Ogarev*

22 DECEMBER 1869

No. 8 Rue Rovigo
Paris

YOU SAY there is much that is unclear in my letter from Nice. That is very probable, my dear kind Aga. I am aware myself that I still become easily confused and unwittingly mingle fact with dreams—especially when I am making an effort to recollect more clearly which is which.

But now I am feeling very well indeed. The only odd thing is that I am left with a kind of involuntary tearfulness which I am utterly unable to control; at times it frightens me a little, I imagine I am suffering from a softening of the brain. . . That would be horrible. But how am I to explain to myself the fact that I am exactly like an old woman?—I find the sound of a few voices in conversation so disagreeable that I am ready to run God-knows-where; while in the mornings I simply *cannot* bear it, the blood rushes to my head, I feel dizzy and I have to cry. It vexes me so, particularly for Papa's sake—he seems not to believe that I cannot help myself. It pains me to grieve him, and I do not know what to do. . .

Now I should like to creep into a little nook and read a few classics. I have no clear idea of any literature. It is all in separate fragments in my head, because my development progressed in a terribly jerky fashion, now to the right, now to the left.

How is Pan Tchorzewski? I press his hand; you know he was my doctor in Lyons.

I embrace you and kiss you warmly, over and over— yourself and Toots.

Merry Christmas and Happy New Year, to Mary and Henry.[31] I greet you and Pan doctor on the occasion of my birthday and the New Year. . .

TATA H.

27 [DECEMBER]

See how long this letter has remained undispatched. Since then I have received your note, and a letter from Tchorzewski, and my birthday is past—but poor Papasha is still running around looking for a house. Snow is falling, the weather is cold—but I shall nevertheless go out for a walk—I am told to do so, since it will put my brain cells in order. I dearly wished to come and see you in Geneva when we were in Lyons, but upon reflection I decided to postpone [the journey] until my head is perfectly clear.

Once more—my regards to Pan, and I kiss you.
Write to: 172 Rue [de] Rivoli.

PART II

RUSSIAN EXILES AS PROFESSIONAL REVOLUTIONARIES

"At present I am engrossed in Russian affairs. Our youth, theoretically and in practice the most revolutionary in the world, is in great ferment . . . I have here with me now one of these young fanatics who know no doubts, who fear nothing and who realize that many of them will perish at the hands of the government but who nevertheless have decided that they will not relent until the people rise. They are magnificent, these young fanatics. Believers without God and heroes without phrases."

MICHAEL BAKUNIN TO J. GUILLAUME

(13 April 1869)

3. On Heroes Without Phrases

47. *Michael Bakunin to Nikolay Ogarev (and others)*[1]

12 JANUARY 1870 [*Locarno*]

MY DEAR ONES,

When I received your note I so jumped for joy that I nearly smashed the ceiling with my old head. Happily, the ceiling is very high. There, that is the effect of the good news:[2] I almost put in an unnecessary comma in honour of Pogodin's pupil.[3] For my part, I *simply must* see Boy [Nechayev]. But I certainly cannot come myself. In the first place, as you well know, I am absolutely penniless—Ogarev knows the reasons why—I can hardly make ends meet. And in the second place, even if I had the money I would not be free to absent myself from home at the present time; I am in hourly expectation of an event also [well] known to Ogarev.[4] So then, I will expect our Boy, or rather, our boisterous [Boy],[5] here. At my place he will find a roof, a bed, a table and a room, and also the deepest secrecy. He should come—by whatever means—under a false name, a Polish one, for instance. I am in the middle of nowhere here, everyone is devoted to me and nobody will be uneasy or say anything. No rumours or scandals ever get out of here to anywhere. In this manner I have already been visited by Frenchmen, Italians, and Spaniards, and no one has paid any attention to them. Well then, I await our dear boisterous boy.

And tell Czerniecki that Antosya[6] has given Mochnatski's History to Mroczkowski to read, and she will ask him to return it without fail, but that will take a little time.

Incidentally, I hope you have ordered Czerniecki seriously to stop some of the printed things. You noticed, I suppose, that Mr Utin made no more nor less than a thinly disguised denunciation of us. That is O[zer]ov's impression and it is correct.

Farewell, I await Boy.

Your M. B[AKUNIN]

48. *Natalie Herzen to Maria Reichel*

23 JANUARY 1870

Pavillon Rohan
172 rue Rivoli
Paris

WHERE SHALL I begin, my dear Masha? Perhaps you have already learned from the newspapers. Papasha is no more. He died on Friday 21 at three o'clock in the morning. I have lost the thing that was dearest to me in the whole world. He did not know himself how greatly I loved him, how tormented I was by anything that grieved him. How I forced myself to be cheerful so that he might think I was happy.

I embrace all of you and kiss you affectionately.

TATA HERZEN

We are all here except poor Ogarev. Sasha was too late and only saw the body. Where we shall go, and when, I don't know. Write to me here.

49. *Michael Bakunin to Nikolay Ogarev*

23 JANUARY [1870]

[*Locarno*]

OGAREV! Is it really true? Has he really died? It seems so. Your dreadful telegram can have no other meaning, and with your letter which I received yesterday it can have no other meaning. You poor thing! Poor Natalies, both of them! Poor Liza! My friend, words fail me in the face of such misfortunes. No, there is one thing I can say: we shall die in action. If you can, write to me—just a line.

Your old, and now your only [old] friend M. B[AKUNIN]

50. *Michael Bakunin to Nikolay Ogarev*

5 FEBRUARY 1870   [*Locarno*]

MY DEAR AGA,

Your telegram is obscure. *Venez de suite*—urgently; *affaires commerciales* allow postponement. But I would still leave at once if that were possible. For various reasons I cannot set out earlier than next Wednesday, the ninth, that is. But most importantly, I shall be in no condition to set out until you find a way to send me the 350 francs I need in order not to leave Antosya and the children in debt and with no means of subsistence. Where you will get them from I don't know. But do realize that I am chained and fettered, and that in the circumstances it is impossible for me to move. I await a detailed letter from you which I hope will explain your telegram.

Your M. B[AKUNIN]

51. *Michael Bakunin to Nikolay Ogarev*

8 FEBRUARY 1870   [*Locarno*]

MY DEAR OLD FRIEND,

I have been slow in answering your last letter because our Boy has quite turned my head with his work. Today at his request and immediately upon receipt of his letter I wrote a hasty article on the police services being rendered by foreign governments to the Russian government in its search for alleged brigands, robbers, and note-forgers. You will have to revise and alter this article in general terms and send it via Perron to Robin,[7] who will do his best to have it included.

But a single article is not enough. The present state of things in Russia, and especially the position of Russian *émigrés* in Europe, makes it our duty to do our very best, without wasting any time, to overcome public opinion in Europe. Otherwise we shall all very likely be extradited to the Russian government as thieves and brigands. Remember that we do not rank very highly in the opinion of the bourgeois public, for whom we, as socialists, are suspect and odious. If we keep silent any longer this public will willingly believe that we really are brigands, counterfeiters, and thieves; and it will be as easy as pie for the foreign governments to extradite us. The silence of Russian *émigré* circles in the Obolenskaya[8] affair was a great mistake, the blame for which, however, falls squarely on that little worrying Jew Utin. We must not repeat that mistake. Therefore I am suggesting the following to you: that [we] formally set up a bureau for the continuous dissemination of news from Russia, and when [we] need publicly to dispute official and semi-official slander, [we send it] to all the foreign journals: French, German, Italian, and Spanish. Best of all would be to issue a weekly lithographed leaflet and send it to the editors of all the more important journals, asking for nothing in exchange other than those journals be sent regularly to us free of charge. For that it will be essential, of course, that Boy arrange a regular correspondence from the Committee in Russia, better than the one he promised to arrange for *The Bell* and never did. But even if there is a shortage of correspondence a reading of the Russian papers and the various bits of nonsense put out by government agents in foreign journals will be sufficient to squeeze out a leaflet of this kind every week. I am convinced that something like this can be managed without great expense —any expenses must, of course, be paid from the fund[9]—if the will is there, serious and constant. I am convinced that we *must* do this.

I advise you to set up this bureau in the following manner— executive members: Ogarev, Zhukovsky, his wife, the dear Adya (who will be a precious, intelligent and active helper, and silent as the grave), and Perron. I don't know if you have reached an understanding with him, my friends; if not, you have done a very silly thing. He deserves your complete trust, and, if you avoid antagonizing him, will be of enormous assistance to us in all respects. Ask him for his advice. He is as silent and as sure as the grave. Corresponding members: Alexander Alexandrovich Herzen and myself. My friends, get this organized. I repeat once more, we *must*, simply because we are Russians, we are duty bound to do it and we can do it easily if we have not lost the capacity to will. So, hold a meeting, decide [what is to be] the spirit, the programme, the style and the material terms of the leaflet, and do not disperse until you have settled the business sufficiently for it to become a business. Besides that, we shall from time to time have to correspond in our own names with French, and sometimes with other, journals. You have read my letter on Herzen to the *Marseillaise*. Boy writes that you are pleased with it. I shall continue if the *Marseillaise* prints my first letter, which I firmly hope it will. I have asked Perron to read to you another article which I have sent via him and Robin to *Rappel* in reply to some Prince Vyazemsky who dared to write to the paper and say that the death penalty had been abolished long ago in Russia. Vyazemsky will reply, of course. I'll thrash him a second time. But in order to do so I need two things.

First, that you, my old friend, with the help of Zhukovsky, copy out for me, from the latest code of laws now in force, all the articles relating to the use of the death penalty for such and such crimes, with the most punctilious precision. And second, that you all remember as many facts as you can concerning the execution of muzhiks by court-martial for insubordination and alleged insurrection during the present reign, beginning with Anton Petrov, citing the name of the province, district, village and all the circumstances in as much detail as you can, with the date, month and year. I have forgotten all these details; even in the case of Anton Petrov I cannot recall the village. I only know that it was in the Kazan province, and that his executioner was Apraksin, an Adjutant-General, I think.[10] In a word, as many facts as possible, detailed and circumstantial, as many as you can, with a list of names of the executioners and their victims. And I need all of this as quickly as possible, because Vyazemsky is sure to reply and, having begun the polemic, I must bring it to a victorious close.

And I shall know no rest until that time, and none of you is to lie down to sleep until we have driven all these foul scribblers about Russia and the Russians out of the best journals of Europe. But to do that I require yet another donation from the fund, more precisely 35 francs, 15 of which I ask you to give to Perron immediately, who will dispatch them together with the attached letter of mine to Robin in Paris. When you read my letter to Robin and the enclosed letter to Reclus you will learn why. And the 20 francs are to be sent to me. With the help of some acquaintances here I am subscribing to *Rappel* and the *Marseillaise*. 32 francs for three months—I shall be paying twenty and they 12. After I have read them I will send you all the interesting bits, and, if you wish, I will send the whole issues. You are to take out a subscription to *Réveil* in the same way and send it to me when you have read it. *Réveil* is read and respected by the entire democratic, non-socialist public of Europe. It has the same character as the *National* did in its day, only its scope is wider. It is our enemy, but for our Russian purposes we must gain control of it without fail—and I intend to do that through Elisée Reclus, but if Alexander Alexandrovich knows of another way, he should indicate it and help us.

Alexander Alexandrovich writes German like a native. Tell him, while he is in Geneva, to write a few little articles like the one which I sent you today, concerning police persecution, and have Boy and Zhuk take them to old Becker,[11] without, of course, saying who wrote them. They will of course manage to make use of him in the matter—and Becker is acquainted with everyone in Geneva who corresponds with German and Swiss journals. Get Herzen to write an article, in English too, and send it off to some Englishman he knows, or to Tabardin, for example, but an Englishman would be preferable, or, if all else fails, tell him to dispatch it to me and I will send it to my friend Stepney.[12]

But you must not sleep, my friends. You must fight, for the filthy Petersburg police wants to bury us.

I will send back the foul Russian cuttings from *Golos* tomorrow or the day after. Keep on sending me everything relating to Herzen and to our cause.

Farewell, my old friend—and do not waste any time—reply, and we shall get on with doing the most important thing.

Your M.B.

Embrace Natalya Alexandrovna and Alexander Alexandrovich for me, their old friend.

52. *Sergey Nechayev to Natalie Herzen*[13]

12 FEBRUARY 1870   *Geneva*

AFTER YOUR departure he [Ogarev] went on a spree and has been unconscious now for three days. I have to go away for a short time, and there is no one to look after affairs in my place. My head is spinning. I am certainly leaving today in any case. Make haste, in the name of all that is sacred! . . . To us you are now indispensable and inestimably valuable.

I press your hand warmly, warmly . . . Goodbye.

                                                               LAENDLEY[14]

P.S. I hope you have written already and that I will find your letter upon my arrival in Neuch[âtel]. I have learned that all the editors have been arrested.[15] Is it true? . . . Until I receive definite news from you I cannot send anything. So write.

53. *Natalie Herzen to Sergey Nechayev*

12 FEBRUARY 1870   *[Paris]*

IT HAS almost been settled that we shall not remain in Paris, but there are many things to attend to, and I do not know *when* it will be possible to leave. Many people are saying that as far as publishing and translating are concerned it would be better to remain here. All our acquaintances are clamouring that we should not leave, and there is frequent cause for argument.

No one realizes why I wish to go on ahead, and it is hardly likely that they will allow me to do so. I have difficulty even in carrying out your commissions, because I never can get out on my own. I am expected to look after my sister, take her for walks, see to her leisure occupations—and all this the more so after our move.

Nor is it easy for me to compose and dispatch letters unobserved; someone continually comes in and asks me "Where to, who to?"

My brother is leaving on Friday with my father's coffin. Perhaps they might agree to let me go with the maid: I cannot promise yet, you will know more by my next letter.

One commission I carried out today; tomorrow I shall endeavour to deliver the letter I brought.

REGINALD WILSON

The weather is terrible; I am tormented by severe headaches and prevented from doing what I would wish.

13 FEBRUARY

I have just received your letter. I will do what I can, but you must realize that if I act too hastily, *everybody* is sure to guess. My brother, certainly, suspects already. It was he who brought me your letter today, and he pressed me. I find it horribly difficult to tell a lie, I blush at once. However, he will keep it to himself.

The editors have almost all been arrested but the journal is coming out; send all the necessaries as quickly as you can.

It appears that they have been harassing Polyakov[16] a great deal of late.

Goodbye

54. *Natalie Herzen to Sergey Nechayev*

13 FEBRUARY 1870   [*Paris*]

I INTENDED today to deliver [your] letter of recommendation; I set off for the rue Racine, and discovered that the gentleman with whom I was to have spoken had already been gone a long time; he had left for Odessa about six months ago.

Whether that is the truth or not I do not know.

Is my old friend really behaving in such a debauched fashion? Truly I do not know whether to believe everything you write or not. In any case, I shall leave as soon as possible.

The ladies here are all unwell; the house is a veritable hospital, and I have been running from one bed to another. Do write quickly [and tell me] what to do with the letter, and what you want to know.

I shall obtain the names and addresses in a day or two.

Be in good health, and strong.

REGINALD WILSON

55. *Natalie Herzen to Sergey Nechayev*

17 FEBRUARY 1870   [*Paris*]

I DID not tell my brother *anything*. He brought the letter, asked
who had sent it, and wished to read it. I refused; he guessed
who the sender was and put a few questions to me; I replied
with a mixture of answers and invention. It all seems suspicious
to him, particularly the fact of my wishing to go alone. They
tell me it is folly, capriciousness, that I have wasted a great deal
[of money] as it is and now I want to abandon a room which
has already been paid for—that my duty here is to be of
assistance, while *there* there is nothing I can do. Perhaps it can
be arranged more easily after my brother's departure. I shall try
to leave on Monday evening—but I cannot promise for sure—
there can be no question of my setting off any earlier.

I shall most probably never see you again—to my sorrow.
After I left you I read a part of what you had given me: it
would have been better if we could have talked a little longer.

It is hard not to trust you as an individual. But knowing that
you work like a *Jesuit*, I shall naturally never know when you
are telling me the truth. It is all the same to you, but I find it
somewhat unpleasant. Be assured, though, that I will carry out
all your commissions as precisely as possible.

I press your hand and hope that despite all we shall meet
somewhere, and so I say—until we meet again.

REGINALD WILSON

If you are not too pressed, and so can write [and tell me]
where and *how* you are (even when you have no commissions),
I shall be most grateful to you.

56. *Natalie Herzen to Sergey Nechayev*

SUNDAY, 20 FEBRUARY 1870   [*Paris*]

How YOU could find the slightest trace of "indifferentism" in
my last note I really do not understand. I foresaw and warned
you that there would be considerable obstacles. If I could act

openly it would be a different matter, although even then there would be a hard struggle, because they would *all* try to restrain and dissuade me. *Everyone* here regards your activities as some kind of madness. Upon receiving your first letter I wished to go at once; my brother prevented me, saying there were *various papers* I had to sign. All these intolerable comedies came to an end only on Thursday—I had put my signature twenty or thirty times. When the whole thing was over, I announced my desire to leave on Monday. This caused such a commotion—it was simply horrible—and if I had not promised *not to leave* without the others, I think we would all have fallen to quarrelling. And did you really think that it was so easy to abandon everything at a moment's notice! To hear reproaches from all sides. Furthermore, one of my friends told me that "this senseless desire to go is proof positive that I have *not yet recovered*"! Indeed, if this restless, well-nigh feverish state, in which I have been ever since my return, continues, I shall very likely start to ramble again!

Everything I said to you was spoken in all sincerity. How could you, how can you still think that it was all *mere words*?

These ephemeral obstacles, as you call them, are not in the least ephemeral for myself—they are a *terrible torment*.

You were surprised by my vacillation. When trust is formed too hastily, it is never *lasting*—or rarely so. Moreover, I am very mistrustful by nature. I must acquaint myself much more closely with the Cause, and see much more clearly by what means you wish to achieve your aims, before I can have *absolute* trust.

I do indeed display a certain lack of independence, an indecisiveness, a timidity—I myself can see it, and will strive with all my might to change it all.

I will bring the letters and tell you a great deal. My people believe that the old friend [Bakunin] has invited me, and that *he* will give me no peace—they curse him roundly and say that he knows it is less than a month since I am recovered, and he will be the ruin of me.

"You cannot reason clearly or act judiciously—just as before; therefore we cannot and must not let you go alone." That is what they tell me. And you must admit, you have indeed not given me very much time in which to think all this over properly.

My brother had left; at this very moment he will be lowering the coffin. But of course you will have no patience for that; you will probably say that it is sentimentalism to be thinking still of Papa.

I cannot *possibly* come on my own without quarrelling with all of them, and that is something I do not wish to and cannot do. I have done everything that it was in my power to do. *I shall leave on Tuesday* with the others, that is, with my younger sister and her mother.[17] Please do not wait if it is inconvenient for you: tell the old man to say what you need.

You will never understand how *difficult* it has been for me to achieve what I have achieved. You are a lone wolf, and in your opinion all this is prejudice; that is why I have written so little to you and spared you the details.

Until we meet—if that is possible. I press your hand.

REGINALD WILSON

I am trying to have everything ready for Monday, but it's unlikely the others will manage it.

57. *Michael Bakunin to Nikolay Ogarev*

21 FEBRUARY 1870   [*Locarno*]

MY DEAR OLD FRIEND AGA,

Thank you for not being angry with me. I shall love and respect you doubly for it.

Here is a letter for the Natalies.[18] Give it to Boy to read.

It can't be helped my old friend, *we must move to Zurich*. I positively cannot settle in Geneva. You know that yourself, and you understand it. But apart from that, to carry out our enterprise in Geneva now is *absolutely impossible*. We must go to Zurich, or if not Zurich, then Lugano.

You say that your finances are in a bad state. I find it hard to believe that your economic condition could have deteriorated in the hands of Alexander Alexandrovich. I hope also, firmly hope, that both the Natalies will agree to move to Zurich, the younger one at any rate. And why should Mme Meysenbug— your Great-German Jeanne d'Arc—and Olga not move there too—I shan't tease her—we have all grown a little wiser in our old age and have learned to put up with each other. But most important—the Russian cause demands that we unite, therefore we *must* unite. And since that is impossible in Geneva, unite in Zurich or Lugano.

My business seems to be working out well in agreement with Boy and Company.[19] I stated bluntly the terms on which I could give myself over *completely* to the cause. I overcame my false modesty and said everything I had to say. They would be foolish not to agree to them, and *powerless* and *impotent* if they failed to find a way to fulfil all the terms necessary for the cause. We really have acted like idealists so far, according to our inner aspirations, and rarely using pious propaganda. He who wishes to accomplish great things must be very clever and very daring. *Nous devons devenir des hommes d'affaires*—and not let ourselves become bound and condemned to impotence by our own helplessness and impecuniousness—we must find the wherewithal. Otherwise we might as well send in our resignation and take the vows. So then, to Zurich, my old friend. He who is not a child or a blond-headed idealist must desire all means which lead to the end.

Alea jacta est.

Your M. B[AKUNIN]

You write that you are getting the *Marseillaise* and *Rappel*. How is it you haven't grasped that you must send them *immediately* after you have read them, *regularly*, every day. I don't need *Rappel*—we have it here—but the *Marseillaise* is essential. If you want me to return them to you, write and say so, and I will send them promptly.

Action!

Congratulations on Milyutin's impending retirement and his replacement by Prince Vasilchikov in the War Office. It's a good thing for us!

58. Michael Bakunin to Natalie Herzen and Nathalie Tuchkova-Ogareva

21 FEBRUARY 1870
Locarno

TO BOTH THE NATALIES,

I did not want to write to you during those first days, because words cannot assuage a grief such as yours. And anyway, I now no longer have the absurd intention of trying to console you. I wish merely to press your hands as a friend, and indicate, if you will permit me, as an old man who has been connected with you for some ten years now, indicate a way for you to find not consolation but satisfaction, and that is, through the cause. We are continually pondering how by our combined efforts we might continue Herzen's work and translate his theory into practice in accordance with the demands of the age and the present state of affairs. Everything that Herzen thought was courageous enough to think—and as a theorist he is unsurpassed—we practical workers, who are humbler, less gifted and of lesser repute, want to do. We want to resurrect *The Bell*, the finest monument we can erect in his memory—*help us*. For the time is past when a line was artificially and forcibly drawn between the rights and vocation of women, and those of men. Your responsibilities are identical with ours.

True, you, the older Nathalie, have a special task—your daughter. But you love Herzen, you have always been associated with his work, both intellectually and emotionally, you have ventured far beyond the close confines of family life— you have an obligation to continue his work, even though it be in new circumstances and forms.

You, my poor Natalie the younger, have no aim in life. Your heart is filled with love, your lucid mind with power. Nature has richly endowed you—yet at the same time you have no ground underfoot and, leading a life of idle dilettantism, you are a disoriented, bewildered creature. "What is there I can do?" you will ask, if you decide to ask and do not lose your temper. Work with us for the Russian cause. Both of you have done enough of this rambling and roaming about the wide world like pallid phantoms. Gather yourselves together. Let us all rally around Ogarev, our old saint and Herzen's best friend, and let each one of us, on the general advice, do what he can, to the best of his ability, for the liberation of the Russian people. Let us not be over-modest, but let us not hold ourselves in excessive esteem either—it is not [our] talents that count, but the cause. Two heads are better than one. We may quarrel occasionally, perhaps even heatedly, but that is no misfortune. We shall have our quarrel, but shall not let dissention part us— we shall reach a peaceable settlement. Herzen was the last Russian to act in *isolation*. The time has now come for *clear thinking* and *collective action*. It is to this collectivity I summon you.

I am trying to persuade Ogarev and have been insisting that he move to Zurich. It will be impossible for me to take up residence in Geneva for various reasons. Moreover, Geneva has now become an absolutely impossible place, *politically speaking*. In Zurich the freedom is *real*. In Zurich there is a university and various professors for Liza: come to Zurich this spring and let us spend the summer there together.[20] See for yourselves, I am acting *à bout portant*, telling you straight what I have in mind; and I shall end this letter with these words: it will be unforgivable, criminal of you, to abandon Ogarev to his melancholy solitude.

Permit me to call myself your old friend.

M. BAKUNIN

59. *Michael Bakunin to Nikolay Ogarev*

22 FEBRUARY 1870   [*Locarno*]

MY DEAR OLD FRIEND,

My thanks to you for your trust. The matter is fairly clear. It appears that *they* do not wish for the revival of *The Bell*, nor for your elder girl[21] to participate in the Russian cause, your cause. From the heights of their well-known wisdom they have decided it is all nonsense, a futile waste of money, and have concluded therefore that the younger Natalie's craving for this cause is an unhealthy exaltation. They do not realize that if she remains any longer in the desert of their aimless, hopeless idleness, she may really lose her mind, and that her health, just as much as her heart, demands that she live with you and help you. You won't lecture her or prevent her from living as she wishes, and for her there will be someone to love and something to do. For myself I have no doubt that if she stays with them she is lost. It is your duty to save her, and in this sacred cause you must show a granite-like firmness and speak with all the authority you command.

But when you make this direct and firm statement of your idea, and, most importantly, of your will the basis of all your discussion and correspondence, you must, I think, at the same time use a certain amount of cunning. Do not put all your propositions to them at once, or you may frighten them, and in that same golden wisdom of theirs, they might declare you too to be in a state of exaltation or even to have taken leave of your senses in your old age. So *at first,* insist only that your elder girl come to you as soon as possible, at once, and tell them that in this way you will be in a position to satisfy yourself by your own observations, and not on the basis of other people's arguments, what it is that impels her: exaltation, or serious desire. Write and say also that if it is indeed exaltation that moves her, then the best way of overcoming and curing it is not to deny but on the contrary to gratify it, all the more so since gratification by this means, that is, by her coming to you, does not in any respect whatsoever compromise her or bind her for the future. To deny it is highly dangerous and *is certainly the surest way of driving her mad.* One does not have to be a profound psychologist to know that any denial merely irritates, nourishes, and aggravates exaltation. On the other hand, if she comes to you, this first, innocent gratification of her desire will calm her, and if she is under the influence of exaltation, it will gradually abate and the transient yearnings that occupy her mind now will be replaced by others. You will not force her to do anything, and they [the family], knowing your profound respect for the freedom of the individual and the infinite delicacy you have shown to the dear elder one, must be assured of that.

Do not mention anything about *The Bell* for the present, but merely demand insistently that the entire fund be paid out. *This is not only your right but your sacred duty* and in the face of this duty all the niceties of relationships are swept aside. In this matter you must display a Roman severity, be a Brutus.

You alone can and must save your elder daughter. Whether she will afterwards be in any state to have retained her eagerness to occupy herself with the Russian cause we shall see later. You will not, of course, coerce or constrain her thoughts or her will in the name of some abstract patriotic cause—that is not in keeping with your character. I believe, and so do you, that she will find a new life for herself in the Russian cause; they believe the opposite. The future will show who is right and who wrong. But first and foremost you must save her. Because there is no doubt in my mind, Ogarev, that *if she stays with them she will go mad.* You must *liberate her from that unreasonable but instinctive* egoism of theirs which lurks before their very eyes in the guise of golden wisdom and common-or-garden bourgeois good sense. Is poor dear Tata really to have no better outlet in life than that of being nanny to Alexander Alexandrovich's children or companion to Natalya Alexeevna, or the friend of that veritable lunatic, that Wagnero-Germanizing Pomeranian Virgin[22] with the consolation of drawing pictures *ins Blaue hinein*?

And so, first of all, without raising any other points about *The Bell* or the Russian cause, have her come and settle at your place. There she will be able to rest her soul and, if necessary, her mind. There, in complete freedom and independent of any alien influences, she will decide freely for herself how she is to live and what she is to do.

You are [to write] and persistently demand that she come to you, and in case they refuse your request, *on the pretext that you too are in an exalted state, or have become insane or feeble-minded,* you must pretend to be a model of good sense and write them *a letter not passionately patriotic* but as reasoned and sceptical as you can. Scepticism for them is wisdom. It was in this wisdom that your friend Herzen died. Incidentally, if you haven't sent my letter off to them yet it might be better not to send it at all.

But if you really want to send it then do so in such a way that Tata will read it first, before Natalya Alexeevna. Otherwise I can say with certainty that Alexeevna will not show it to Alexandrovna, on the pretext that persons in an exalted state should be treated like children. However, do as you see fit and as you wish.

My old friend, did you receive the excerpt from the Paris journal *La Presse* which I sent to you on the 18th? It says that the Russian government is apparently demanding that the Swiss government extradite a certain Nechayev. This is such a critical time now that one has to know if every letter, every line, has reached its destination *intact* or not. I ask you therefore from now onwards to answer every letter immediately if only with a couple of lines: *your letter of such and such date received.* I shall do the same, and to set a good example, I say to you: your letters of 17 and 19 February received, and I dispatched a letter to you on the 21st, that is, yesterday.

Boy wrote to me on the 17th and requested that I reply to Geneva, but today I received another letter sent on the evening of the 19th, from which I conclude that he is not in Geneva yet. Write and tell me what you know.

And send the enclosed letter, if you will, immediately to Perron via Heinrich. Invite him to your place and discuss Russo-Swiss affairs with him. Believe me, Ogarev, and forget your prejudices against him—and take no notice of his cold, antagonistic Genevan façade—beneath that façade there beats an ardent, honest, and steadfast heart. I have tested him for a whole year on *routine matters*. He is especially valuable at the present time and you would be utterly foolish not to speak to him with trust.

Did you read Nechayev's letter in *Progrès* no. 8? He really exists, then, and how odd that it is printed in the very same number in which I express doubt as to his existence. Come on, tell me the truth—do you know him? Whatever the truth of the matter is, that number must without fail be circulated and both my article and his letter reprinted in as many Swiss, German, and French journals as possible. That is the subject of my letter to Perron. He is to call on Becker and arrange the German publicity with him. And you, my dear friend, are to get that number and dispatch it—oh so cunningly and carefully—to the Natalies in Paris, by two methods. One, in a sealed envelope, and the other, inside Russian newspapers wrapped as printed matter; and ask them *immediately* through their acquaintances Reclus, Robin, Rey and others to have the two articles (1) *la Police Suisse* and (2) *Nechayev's letter* reprinted in all the Paris journals they possibly can (*Siècle, Réveil, Démocrate, Rappel, Avenir, National,* etc. etc.).

At the same time, send a copy to Talandier and write to him yourself, begging him fervently in the name of our old friendship to make every effort to have the article and letter reprinted in English journals. Do all this without wasting any time; I for my part am not sleeping.

Here is Talandier's address: Angleterre via Allemagne (this is essential, it would vanish via France),

> Alfred Talandier, Esq.
> g.R.M.C. Terrace—York-Town—Farnborough
> near London

Your M. B[AKUNIN]

60. *Natalie Herzen to Maria Reichel*

1 MARCH 1870

Pension Maguénat
3 Tranchée du Plainpalais
Genève

YOU WILL probably be surprised, my dear Masha, to learn that I am in Geneva again; on this occasion I came with Liza and her mother. We went to be near Ogarev for a while; he is ageing rapidly. We shall live here for a few months, or perhaps settle down for good, depending on the circumstances. In May or June, Olga and Malwida will come and visit us here, and then we shall discuss the matter and decide whether to go to Florence together or not.

Sasha went with Tchorzewski to Nice to accompany the coffin. It was placed next to Mamasha's, but not beneath the same stone, because some of the Russians want to collect money and put up a special monument.

Young Kireevsky read a poem at the cemetery—it is said to have been very good, I haven't seen it. He read it and then vanished immediately, so Sasha was unable to find him and express his thanks. Sasha is now in Florence. How few we are, and how we are scattered about the world!

When the articles of which you wrote appear I will obtain them and send them to you.

I had a rather awkward conversation with Mme Tessié on the eve of my departure, on the subject of Nathalie; she began speaking in a tone I just cannot tolerate. She wanted to show me that it was bad and damaging to my reputation to remain with Nathalie and Liza. I saw that we should never agree on that score, or ever understand one another.

About the letters: I am repeating my request, please copy out everything. I ask this for myself, personally, because not everything relating to the Herwegh affair will be printed, and we, Herzen's children, must know it all, that was his wish.

I embrace you and kiss you warmly, Masha, my dear. We are so close to one another that we shall very likely see each other again soon.

TATA H.

Has Reichel fully recovered?

If you write to Tatyana Petrovna, give her my regards, and Egor Ivanovich too.

About the boy: think it over carefully and tell me if you think it possible to arrange something—*without tiring yourself*, in my opinion that is the main thing, but it is a very serious obstacle, though.

61. Sergey Nechayev to Natalie Herzen

[UNDATED]   [*Geneva*]

YOU MUST come over today, if only in the evening. There have been some dirty tricks here, and they must be cleared up.

P.S. We needed you very much this morning.

62. *Natalie Herzen to Sergey Nechayev*

13 MARCH 1870   [*Geneva*]

UNTIL SUCH time as you give me your *word of honour* that you will
not kiss me, I shall not go to visit O[garev].

And also, it would be better if we did not meet again. I cannot
give myself body and soul to the cause, despite the fact that I
heartily loathe the entire existing order. I have said my last
word—a meeting would lead only to acrimonious exchanges.
So, farewell. I wish you success.

N. HERZEN

63. *Sergey Nechayev to Natalie Herzen*

[UNDATED]   [*Geneva*]

I GAVE you my *word* yesterday, and consequently there are no
reasons for your non-attendance.

Your LAENDLEY

And you gave me your word that you would be here today,
so keep it and that means come after lunch. This you must do
in order to have the right to rely on the word of honour of others.
We await you.

64. *Natalie Herzen to Sergey Nechayev*[23]

17 MARCH 1870   [*Geneva*]

I HAD a presentiment that I would be in no condition to come
today, and indeed, I have such a headache that I shall probably
stay at home all day.

How ironical that it should be today of all days, when I
could have been of greatest help to you—it is most vexing. But
as I do not find this mechanical occupation tiring, I beg you
once more to send to me *here* whatever you wish *(with explanations)*: I will execute and dispatch it.

If only the "stew" would cool down and they would give me a little peace!!

You may leave until tomorrow what is not urgent, since tomorrow I shall almost certainly be at O[garev's].

Farewell "Tigr Medvedevich" [Tiger-Son-of-a-Bear]; pay a little more attention to external forms—it will be more pleasant both for you yourself and for others.

N. HERZEN

You are not to speak in person with our maid: she must not know your face. Camperio might someday take it into his head to question her, and there would be trouble.

"what nonsense you talk."

65. *Natalie Herzen to Sergey Nechayev*

SUNDAY, 20 MARCH 1870   [*Geneva*]

I AM still unwell, and still in bed; I shall not go out this morning. I will see how things are after lunch, and if I feel better I will come and help you. If you will not be at home, leave an explanation of what I am to do.

When I recall our conversations, I can see contradictions in some of your words. Do you remember, for instance, saying once: "But do not confuse that which concerns myself *personally* with *the cause*." But then on several occasions you said something quite different such as: "I am a whole man. What concerns the cause concerns *myself* also; I cannot separate the two. There is only one question. I am talking only about the cause." I must confess that there is something here that is unclear to me. I am of the opinion that these [two] questions must certainly be kept separate. And lest there be any misunderstanding, do not forget that the moment I realized that, as well as the cause, you were asking about *personal relationships* too, I at once replied in the negative, and repeated my reply several times. You tell me that I do not know my own mind. You are a strange man. I ought to know whether or not I love you; well, I am telling you once

171

more—no, I do not. I am very sorry that you have come to feel this sentiment, but I am not in the slightest to blame for that, and I repeat that I had noticed absolutely *nothing* until the moment you spoke directly of it. Some very long letters have just arrived from Italy. Until our meeting.

N. HERZEN

66. Sergey Nechayev to Natalie Herzen

27 MARCH 1870   [*Geneva*]

IF YOU can come especially early tomorrow then do so (about 8–9 o'clock). You must. [Come] quietly and [go] straight into the corner room.

Yours head over heels

Ah, if only you would think more, and more straightforwardly and consistently!

Give free rein to your mind, do not constrain it with comfortable prejudices!

You will soon cease to be tossed by the waves of the tempestuous sea and reach the shore of the promised land if you are more consistent.

Do you know how much pain you cause me? You see, I . . .

67. Natalie Herzen to Sergey Nechayev

28 MARCH 1870   [*Geneva*]

I shall not come and see you until I receive what I mentioned in my letter this morning.

I say this in all seriousness.

And if you do not wish to comply [with my request] then you can send everything to me here with explanations. I will do the writing and copying.

What is this about Aga's eyes?

N. HERZEN

68. Sergey Nechayev to Natalie Herzen

[UNDATED]   [*Geneva*]

I SPEAK with you simply and straightforwardly, and I do not
want to have somehow to speak seriously as well. Stop acting
so capriciously simply because you are being treated as a
valuable person and not a spoilt little miss. After all, I am not
Tchor[zewski].

These whims are beneath you. They are nonsensical. And
you are a woman of sense!

Instead of wasting your brainpower reflecting on proprieties
and improprieties, you ought to meditate on the real essence of
life and not its outward semblance. Or do you want to be a
drawing-room ornament for the rest of your life? Well, do as
you see fit!

There has been some gossip here. Its origin must be elucida-
ted. Come without fail, or I shall come to you myself.

Yours

Oz[erov] has not left because you were not here this morning.
Bring the money for Czerniecki.

69. Natalie Herzen to Sergey Nechayev

31 MARCH 1870   [*Geneva*]

How YOU do pass from one extreme to the other. One day I am
your "most precious creature in existence", the next a "monster"—and why those crude, cruel reproaches?

I know myself that my death would be no loss; two or three
people would mourn for a while, others would be glad—and
that is all. I have told you myself plainly and simply that up till
now I have done nothing—but I am willing to do something.
I *"insult the word love"*. What right have you to say that? "In
order to love, one must know what for." That is quite true.
Have I not said to you that your affection for me is entirely
without foundation?

Why did you fall in love with me before I had done anything?

But it is better not to speak of all this—the storm and the sorrow are not yet passed and gone.

I am very glad that our meeting will not have been in vain; I wish your pamphlet success with all my heart.

I shall be coming tomorrow: prepare what there is to be done.

N. HERZEN

70. *Natalie Herzen to Sergey Nechayev*

31 MARCH 1870 *[Geneva]*

Do NOT place me in such a ridiculous position. You are well aware that I cannot go on visiting Ogarev while you are there. You will not leave me in peace; you do not know how to treat people in a civilized fashion; and there is Aga, continually asking me to come and saying that there is work for me. Do be reasonable, please. Write to me what I asked you. I assure you that for myself, these questions—or rather, this question—*is settled absolutely*. I beg you to torment me no longer and never speak of this matter. And if I cannot be of assistance to you in anything, then say so at once.

N.H.

I really have caught a cold—that evening, coming home (hungry) with Czerniecki. If you fulfil my request I shall come tomorrow.

71. *Natalie Herzen to Sergey Nechayev*[24]

TUESDAY *[Geneva]*

YOU CAN see for yourself that all of what happened yesterday evening and the day before was extremely unpleasant for me. Most annoying of all is that you could suppose that N[athalie's] decision was taken *after* the bad news, *after* what happened chez Aga, etc. The truth is that she had long since found the whole thing *embarrassing and unpleasant*. But I, in my stupidity, or my absentmindedness, had not noticed this, otherwise I would have spoken directly to you and yesterday's scene would not have taken place. I assure you that I am heartily sorry.

You know my decision—therefore you cannot and *must not* torment me further. I have received a letter from B[akunin] for you; I can send it via Z[amperi]ni or otherwise: name some person.

[Did you receive the money?][25] Reply in the same way via Z[amperini].

I will not come and visit you: in the first place, for the various reasons we have spoken of, and secondly, because it would not be good for you—ladies attract attention.

Take care.

Can I give the money to Z[amperini]?

72. *Sergey Nechayev to Natalie Herzen*

[UNDATED]   [*Monthey*]
RECEIVED 27 MAY 1870

I HAVE ended up in the most dreadful hole, and, worst of all, am obliged to stay here more than a week. I foresee the most awful tedium.

Do you realize what pleasure *your* letters will bring me? Do you know how impatiently I await them?

Write, write as soon and as much as possible. Write more directly and openly.

I am just about to write you a long letter which you will receive by post after this note. I hope you will not wait for it but will write earlier. Yes! Here is my address (to be kept a secret)

> chez Mr. Constantin Baraldini
> pour Mr Pierre
> à Monthey.

Have Sereb[rennikov] collect letters from Og[arev], Oz[erov] and the others for me, and take them to you, and you send them on.

Be more decisive and *independent*.

Has Ogarev by any chance got any letters for me? Send them.

N[atalya] A[lexeevna] spoke about you a great deal on the way.[26] I shall write of that later. What is she?

How I should like to write more, and hasten the departing Z[amperi]ni. Until we meet!

Give the message to Ivanov and the bill to Ozerov and the letter to N. A[lexeevna].

73. *Sergey Nechayev to Natalie Herzen*

[UNDATED]   [*Monthey*]
[RECEIVED] 26 MAY 1870

DEAR TATA,

Writing to you is becoming a difficult task, but one that I love. You are well aware *why* I cannot speak with you in roundabout phrases, why I cannot conceal what I think and why I am powerless to restrain the ardour (or, as you express it, the coarseness) that gushes straight from my soul. Nevertheless, in my thoughts about you, my conceptions of you, there is much, so much that is utterly opposed to your milieu, that conflicts with the habits you have not tried to lose or somehow or other shake off. In short, my open, straightforward words with you are frequently intended as a rebuke, a reproach for your indecisiveness, your weakness, your hesitation and those other qualities from which you once promised me you would strive to liberate yourself. That is why you have often found my words disagreeable, but I have nevertheless spoken and will speak them. I know that you will come upon no compliments in this letter either.

During the first days after our meeting you expressed dissatisfaction with your petty life, but you did dimly realize what the reasons were for that pettiness. Life is petty when there is no aim to it, when a person is conscious that his existence is unnecessary to all except people of the same trivial ilk, when a person has so little faith in himself and in his powers that he cannot bring himself to make any decision to take any active step on his own initiative, but waits for fate (that most foolish of notions) sooner or later to give him a push. And sure enough, people like these are jogged along by fate in the guise of papas and mamas and various guardian-angels-custodians such as. . .

As long as a person moves only in such a milieu he feels little discontentment; he is a corpse, and therefore may be tranquil, for bondage and servitude do not offend him. But once he has encountered *other* people, once he has caught a glimpse of independence in someone, he can no longer live the life of *contented ease*, he must either leap boldly out of the mire or, consciously sinking into it, despise himself more and more until his powers of thought finally cease and the person turns into a vegetable.

Until now you have been living an utterly trivial life, without aim and without object. If anyone were to ask you: Why are you living?—you would be unable to give an answer. Remember your letter: "I know that my death would be no loss; two or three people would feel sorry and mourn for a while. . ."

My heart was near breaking when I read that admission of a person's own uselessness. And it was a young, fresh girl writing it, who had not yet made any attempt to live. So whence that despair, [the despair] of a moribund person; that fear of casting off your fetters? Here we have the fruit of your meaningless past life, the fruit of foolish cares and worries which have surrounded you ever since your childhood and so accustomed you to being in swaddling-clothes that even now you feel yourself, as it were, bound [by them].

Yes, if you know that you are useless then *cease* to live as you have lived till now! Make a move! Shake off your cowardice! Look at others with the eyes of a living, feeling person and not the dull gaze of a rich heiress who fears robbery and deceit at every moment. There are many good people—join us, work, and most of all, free yourself from this bondage, this servitude gilded with the tawdry glitter of feigned attachment.

This absence of a life's object has prevented you from developing firm convictions to guide you in your actions.

177

M

Without convictions you have been weak-willed, shy, in-experienced and timorous. You have always avoided conflict and struggle because a struggle without an aim is ridiculous. This is why you have been totally under the influence of your milieu (and it has been a very bad one), and you have never attempted to repulse it. This is why N. Alexeevna—herself already an effete woman—regards you with pity and believes that without her advice you will perish. She told me, by the way: "When I strongly objected to her intention to undertake a second disguise, Tata blushed and became flustered, kissed me and agreed with me. It grieved me to see her so timid and obedient: so little was needed to dissuade her", and so on. I will tell you the rest some other time.

To her you are a positively spineless creature who continually needs nannying (this is also how your brother apparently sees you). It pained and distressed me to hear those semi-contemptuous remarks, ill-concealed by her concern. I almost came to blows over you. Something makes me believe in your power. I have suggested that you come out of hibernation and go with us towards our common aim. I believe in you, believe that you are still fresh and can grow strong and develop in the service of the cause. In my treatment of you I have acted rashly and not altogether wisely. (Do you know why?) I have frequently forgotten your weakness, your lack of independence. I have been abrupt and have frightened you. You have begun to shun me. How painful it has become at times, but still I have not lost my confidence that the truth will prevail. You are in constant fear of deceit, cunning, and intrigue, and you sit idle. I ask you: when is there a greater danger of your falling victim to intrigues —when you follow a definite path with a clear goal before your eyes, scrutinizing every step taken by yourself and your fellow-travellers, or when you are in a position like yours, without any plan for the future, and totally lacking in understanding of life, in love and in commitment?

I would like you to give me your answer after independent reflection and not under the influence of a conversation with anyone else.

Write, please, as soon and as much as you can.

As a result of the recent alarm over the persecutions, the plan for my own personal participation in the cause is undergoing considerable changes. Answer me as plainly as possible, and if the little trust you have in me is still alive, then I would suggest—you know what.

Give the attached note to Ogarev and destroy it.

74. *Natalie Herzen to Sergey Nechayev*[27]

27 MAY 1870   [*Geneva*]

I RECEIVED the letter you sent by post long before that note.

Yesterday Z[amperini] was here, and entertained us with the long, lively and detailed story of his journey, the building, etc.

Well, you have excelled yourself; I did not think you capable of writing letters such as the one you wrote to Natalya Alexeevna. You are capable both of courtesy and flattery— well, it is simply charming.

Regarding your observations: I repeat that many of them are just, and just observations and reproaches do not anger me. It is not your words which anger me, you know that perfectly well; but your outrageous, despotic manner.

Why do you keep on telling me my life is unnecessary to anyone, etc. I have already answered you on that score, so why, then, do you touch. . .[28]

I have so far done nothing for others, but that does not mean that I will never do anything. Only from you—knowing your Jesuitism—could I fear robbery and deceit. This too certainly does not mean that I am "a wealthy heiress who fears robbery and deceit at every moment", *at every step and from everyone*, as you are pleased to express it. It applies only to you and B[akunin]. And anyway, I was not afraid of you; I simply found it [———][29] and disgusting to look at you *at times*, when I took all your actions for different kinds of trickery aimed at obtaining "my kopecks" or treating me exactly as you liked, like a doll.

If Natalya Alexeevna spoke of me pityingly it was because she was affected by her recollections of my illness. But I am sure that she could never have spoken and never did speak of me with contempt or semi-contempt: it may have appeared so to you, but then many things appear [what they are not].

You do not understand our relationship in the slightest. If she sometimes had influence over me, I too influenced her mode of action or her opinions on more than one occasion, and this would have been impossible had she held me in contempt or treated me as a simpleton. Concerning a second disguise, I myself had absolutely no desire to repeat that comedy. I agreed purely because I thought it would be less disagreeable for N. A[lexeevna] than your other proposition; and when I saw that she preferred the latter, I was simply overjoyed that I would not have to go out with you. I did not grow in the least flustered talking to N. A[lexeevna], but set about calming her and saying that I would arrange everything. And so I did, thereby satisfying both her and myself. To you it made no difference. Why are you telling me all this again? You want to injure our relationship, that is, [the relationship] between N. A[lexeevna] and myself. I warn you that neither you nor anybody will succeed. I know her too well, know her faults, but at the same time am able to value her good qualities.

Why did you not defend B[akunin] when she attacked him? You're a fine friend. If she mentions him again and says that he dragged—or wanted to drag—me into your "Carbonarism" too soon after my illness, I shall tell her that it is not he but *you* who are the chief culprit, that you perhaps knew more than any of the others about my condition. Enough of accusing poor B[akunin], there is no sense in inventing or adding to the affair; even silence on your part is bad. N. A[lexeevna] has not the slightest notion that you were far more active in all this than B[akunin].

He is at this moment in Berne, seeing about Nechayev and Serebrennikov; the latter will be coming to see us—to take lessons in the French language. *All* letters should *be given to* Z[amperi]*ni*, not me; it might attract attention. England awaits you impatiently; make haste; the best way is via the Mediterranean. Do not write directly to my address. Give everything to Konstantin. Be in good health.

N. Alexeevna thanks you for your letter (is there so much as a single sincere word in it?) and for your compliments; she will carry out your commissions.

We have received the pamphlet: "A. I. Herzen—a few words from a Russian to Russians". I have not yet read it—it arrived [only] today.

75. *Sergey Nechayev to Natalie Herzen*

FRIDAY, 27 MAY [18]70. MORNING   [*Monthey*]

THERE ARE no letters from you. I expected one yesterday, and expect one today; you will understand how impatiently. It is dreadfully tedious here. The place I am living in is thought of as one of the most beautiful in the country; and indeed here are combined all the so-called beauties of nature. For a poet or artist it is paradise. For me it is torture; however many times I force myself to admire the sunsets and sunrises, the effect is nil. It all seems stupid, meaningless. I am surrounded by mountains, forests, streams, valleys, ravines and other "charms" of nature, which I am unable to delight in and which only bore me to death—and how!

I cannot get *you* out of my head: is she thinking something at this moment? what is in her mind? what will be her answer? I recall all our conversations, and the more I ponder over them the more displeased I am with myself. Yes, I have been too sharp, too abrupt with you. I did indeed frighten you, who had never encountered anything of the kind before. You were surprised and scandalized by many things in me. You are too tender and young a plant, you are only just beginning to bloom. I ought to have treated you carefully, but I acted with open sincerity and unrestrained forwardness. You have been so accustomed to drawing-room artificiality and social constraint in your relationships that you were initially antagonized by the mere fact of my overstepping the bounds of decorum (which you yourself admit in theory are stupid). But now it appears you have become accustomed to me, you already feel less ashamed of speaking freely and do not take offence at displays of deep and reasoned affection. You understand the essence of the question which has such immense significance for myself and for you. You are on the verge of finding the solution to your life's problem. And I believe now more than ever before that you will not remain in hibernation, in child-like dependence, but will rise to the life of freedom and reason. I believe in the truth of my convictions, believe that they will prevail. My confidence in you is so great that I have not wavered even at those moments when (through lack of under-standing, or rashness, or under the influence of your surround-ings) you appeared to hate me, when you were ready to break with me.

I repeat—it would be too weak, too spineless of me to doubt the possibility of your finding a way out of your position of dependence, your aimless vegetable life.

I do not think it necessary to explain my desires, my aspi-rations to see you a *real woman*. The reason for my persistence must be clear to you: I love you.

Write more, write more often, write everything that is in your soul. As soon as I receive your letter I shall write another.

Should S[erebrennik]ov be in need of money, give it to him.

76. *Sergey Nechayev to Natalie Herzen*

MONDAY MORNING, [30 MAY 1870]   [*Monthey*]
RECEIVED 30 MAY 1870

I SENT you three letters and a telegram yesterday—not a word in reply either from you or from any of the Genevans. What has happened? I am lost in conjectures! Can the police be inter-cepting letters? Either something especially important has happened at your end (in which case you ought to notify me as soon as possible) or our famous conspirator Z[amperi]ni has intimidated you and persuaded you to send your letters only through him, and has then put them in his pocket and is

probably waiting for a suitable opportunity. *Am I not clever?*
The latter seems more likely. But look, I told you my address
in my first letter. What are you frightened of? I receive letters
here straight from Germany.

Here in the obscurity of this backwater, without letters, I
am dying of boredom. I shall not be able to stand it for long.
I am already longing to fly to Geneva. And how I crave for
letters from you! How I should like to see you. There is much
I have to say and ask. I shall stay here for another two weeks.
From R[ussia] there is very bad news which determines my
future situation. It is just this that I have to talk to you about,
because it is very important for me and for the cause how you
react to my proposal.

Prepare yourself to come and have a good time here. It is not
as far as Locle.[30] Only six hours' ride from Geneva. Ah, how
glad I should be to see you. Here in the mountains I have a
whole hotel at my disposal. Do come, I implore you as a friend.
But please, without the humiliation of begging permission.
The thought of it distresses and pains me. After all, you have
already proved that you can travel independently without
having to explain your destination.

So then, I have faith in your determination and I await you.

This letter will be delivered to you tomorrow morning
(Tuesday); when you have read it, telegraph me "Je viens ce
soir. *Wilson*" at this address: Mr Baraldini à Monthey, and
leave on the twelve o'clock, that is, the midday train for
Monthey via St Moritz. I shall wait for you tomorrow, *i.e.*
Tuesday, in the evening *près de la gare*. But please say nothing
to anybody.

Incidentally, Z[amperi]ni is to come in a week's time. If you
manage to see him, have a talk with him. Tell him you wish to
go yourself, explain the urgency; collect all the messages from
him and instruct him to keep silent and not even tell N.
Alexeevna (what is she?).

If Z[amperi]ni starts trying to dissuade you, do not listen
to him; tell him "you have to go" and come in spite of him.

Oh, how impatiently I shall be waiting for your telegram!
Ah, what yearning!

For the sake of the "cause", for the sake of everything you hold sacred after your own fashion, do not think that this passionate desire of mine to see you yet again conceals some ulterior motive. I have not known many glad moments in my life; my past has seen few joys. Do not now mar with suspicion the purest, loftiest and most human of feelings. Come to me as an old comrade, as a dear friend with absolute trust. A great deal depends on this conversation with you. If it is clear to you that I am of considerable importance to the cause, then it must be even clearer how much you mean to me. In short, it depends on you whether I am to be ten times stronger or weaker than I am now. Our talk is too important and necessary. Do not make me travel to Geneva when you can come here. I await your telegram and I hope that your soul will be responsive to my plainspoken words.

Bring some cigarettes and the Russian papers if they contain anything of relevance.

77. *Natalie Herzen to Sergey Nechayev*

31 MAY 1870   [*Geneva*]

PLEASE DON'T worry. All four of your letters and two telegrams have arrived. I gave the reply to your first letter to Z[amperini] on Friday evening; it is very odd that you have not received it yet—he must really be sending them only by other people.

I have no intention of coming to visit you, and work for the same cause as yourself I never will. There is absolutely no need for us to see each other. Go to England or America and live there until you are forgotten.

I sincerely wish you to become convinced—and the sooner the better—that to treat people as you do is impossible without arousing their distrust, which easily grows into indignation or loathing, or both.

Your things are here—what am I to do with them?

If you are going to make constant use of my address it might attract attention—so much the worse for you. The other method is slower, but surer.

Did you receive my letter of 27 May?
If not, Z[amperini] is to blame.

N. HERZEN

I thought it quite unnecessary—and imprudent—to telegraph you.

78. *Natalie Herzen to Sergey Nechayev*[31]

WEDNESDAY (MORNING)[32]   [*Geneva*]

IF I were sure that there really was no-one except myself who could carry out your commissions, and that it was essential that they be carried out, then I would come to you. But I am tired of your long conversations and especially of your dreadful behaviour, and I positively do not wish it to continue in this way. I do not want to participate in any intrigues: therefore, I do not understand what commissions I can carry out. Use *your people* for them. What makes you ask if I have taken fright? What could happen to me? Absolutely nothing: The People's Vengeance[33] alone may desire to punish me or teach me a lesson.

Do send the money to poor B[akunin]—he is probably waiting impatiently.

Understand this too: I ought not to come and see you, *for your own sake*, that is, so that you don't get into hot water again.

Also, remember that you are not to call me *Tata*; I find it unpleasant.

N.H.

After talking to Z[amperi]ni I am once again convinced that I certainly ought not to come and visit you.

Did you know they are promising 5,000 francs to whoever runs you to earth! How repulsive!

Please keep quiet for a few days at least, and take Z[amperi]ni's advice. He will arrange everything when he can. Meanwhile, write to me through him—if it really is necessary.

But the best thing would be for you to go away for a time—really. . .[34]

79. *Sergey Nechayev to Natalie Herzen*

JUNE 1870

WHAT INTRIGUES are *you* writing of, you who are a participant in the foulest of intrigues, the exploitation of millions, you who have fed off the *muzhik* since the day you were born, who have done nothing and refuse to work for a cause. You are reproaching me! Come to your senses, are you writing "gibberish" or is it out of fear that I will show your letters to someone?

Ah, you are a "budding Natalya Alexeevna". If I do not see you today I will come tomorrow and must [see you].

Are you not ashamed to abandon us at the critical moment? Why have you sent money? If it is for me, then let me tell you that I will not accept a kopeck from you. If it is for the fund, then someone else will take it; it has to be done intelligently. Wait three or four days. I don't understand why Z[amperi]ni's seal is on the package, and there is a great deal else I don't understand either. In any event I am returning it to you; it is not my job now. (I don't even know how much there is.)

I *have to* see you. My position is indeed not a very safe one, and so if you have any common sense left you will spare me the necessity of coming to you and will ask Z[amperi]ni immediately to arrange a rendezvous.

Do not expose me to a danger which can be easily eliminated.

80. *Natalie Herzen: Diary*

28 MAY 1870

EARLY IN February I went to Geneva with Tchorzewski. I was tormented by the thought that we would all be settling in Paris and Florence, but Aga would be left all alone, as if we had abandoned him.

One morning, a few days after my arrival, I went to see Ogarev. He was still asleep. I came into the drawing-room. Tchorzewski said to me in a whisper:

"Mr Volkov [Nechayev] is in that room there. Shall I call him in here?"

"Please do," I replied.

I had only a very vague idea of this man, but I had heard one or two things about him, and I was very curious to see him. Tchorzewski opened the dining-room door and showed, or rather invited, in a young man, saying: "Would you like to come in? Natalie Alexandrovna is here too."

The appearance of Volkov made a very strange impression on me: everything about him was original, pure Russian, but it was his dark eyes, peering out every so often from behind his large, dark spectacles, that were especially striking. As he came into the room he muttered "Good morning", thrust his left hand into his pocket and his right hand into the front of his buttoned jacket, and began pacing the room from corner to corner without raising his eyes.

"Have you brought the *Journal de Genève?*" he asked Pan.

"No," replied the latter, offended that Volkov should dare ask him, as though it were his duty to bring the journal every day.

"Well, then, bring it later, we must have a look at it," Volkov continued, paying no attention to Pan, who went away after a few minutes.

We were left alone. Volkov continued to pace the room with lowered head. I stood leaning against the mantelpiece, waiting for him to speak. We passed several minutes in silence. Finally, still with lowered gaze and without looking at me, Volkov asked:

"Will you accompany your father's coffin to Nice?"

"No, my brother will go alone with Tchorzewski. I shall return to my sisters in Paris."

And again—silence. Finally I asked:

"Have you been reading the Russian papers? Is there anything new?"

"Are you really interested in Russian affairs?" he asked, and looked at me for the first time, with only a darting glance from behind his spectacles, and then lowered his eyes once more to the floor.

"How can one fail to be interested, especially of late. Arrests and interrogations have begun again."

"How should I know if you are interested or not—after all, you must have been abroad for a long time now?"

"Yes, a long time. I was one year old when we left,[35] I do not remember anything. But none the less I am interested in everything that is going on there."

With this our first meeting ended. Ogarev appeared, and I began talking to him. Judging by Volkov's laconic questions and answers, and by the curt tone of his arrogant mutterings, exactly like some kind of superior officer, I decided that he considered it a complete waste of time to talk with a *baryshnya* [noble lady], and consequently I made no further overtures to him, and paid no attention to him at all, though I did continue to observe his eccentric behaviour and his outbursts. Two or three days after this I spoke to Ogarev of my intention to go to Berne, and from there to Paris. Volkov was pacing from corner to corner as was his habit, like a bear in a cage.

"Have you mentioned the drawings?" he muttered as he passed Ogarev.

"No, not yet," Ogarev replied slowly, and turned to me, even more slowly, as though preparing to say something.

"What drawings?" I asked in surprise, and, God knows why, the idea flashed through my head that they were going to suggest that I should design or copy a vignette for forging notes.

"It is a long story," Ogarev went on. "I will explain to you later. But you will be gone the day after tomorrow, won't you? How will you do it? Will you have time?"

I had some difficulty in understanding what he meant, I was to draw, first of all, a Russian *muzhik*, but then it appeared that it would be better to draw a group of *muzhiks*. At this point Volkov too began explaining, paying no attention to my remark that all my drawings would be clumsy, unauthentic, and lifeless, because I had never set eyes on a Russian peasant, and I did not know how to draw figures, I only drew heads—which was quite another matter.

"That is immaterial," continued Volkov, "we don't need works of art. The subject and the costumes will be explained to you. You will just do the drawing, and then we'll see if it'll do or not. If it turns out well, you will be doing us a great favour."

At last I understood what they wanted: in the first place, not merely one drawing but a whole series of pictures designed to influence the people, the peasants. Volkov explained the subjects like this:

"In one drawing you will show, for instance, a crowd of *muzhiks*, armed with whatever they can lay hands on, scythes, sticks, and so on. In front, there's a young fellow who's lost his hat. He's straining to rush over to one side, pointing at the soldiers standing there. But he's stopped by a priest who is beating him over the head with his cross. Do you understand?"

"I understand. But the task is a difficult one, it is too much for me. I am very sorry."

"It's no use giving up before you have tried; start with one figure, and then we'll see. For example, a gentleman-landowner, as they used to be—fat, rich, sprawling drunkenly on a couch, and then a landowner as they look nowadays—thin, dressed in rags."

"Now *that* I *could* do."

"Then, if that turns out well, we want you to draw some *muzhiks*; for example, on one page—what the *muzhiks* are doing, and on another—what they ought to be doing."

"And what do you think they ought to be doing?" I asked.

After a moment's silence he replied: "Well, for example, some *muzhiks* steal up to the master's house and set fire to it."

"Mercy on us, what are you thinking of?" I exclaimed. "I would not draw that for anything, even if I could. One shouldn't teach the *muzhiks* to kill or set fire to things. The people are cruel enough when they rise up, they should be restrained, not incited. . ."

An ironic smile appeared on Volkov's face, and, still pacing up and down, he shouted to Ogarev, who was sitting in the dining-room: "Hey, listen what 'they' say here! They refuse to draw, because, you see, it's contrary to their way of thinking to teach *muzhiks* to set fire to things."

Ogarev laughed and said nothing. We argued a little longer. I refused to draw groups, saying that I would try and do single *muzhiks* or figures.

Ogarev insisted that I should come back from Berne a little sooner, and he would explain to me and tell me many more things. Sasha, on the contrary, was eager to leave for Paris, and asked or advised me to stay with Masha as long as possible.

"I hope that you will then find Ogarev on his own. You know what it's like now—one cannot have a real talk with him, there is always someone else there. But did you hear how Zamperini gave himself away yesterday evening? I was very surprised, for such a hardened conspirator. We had hardly greeted each other, when he said to me with a mysterious air, indicating Volkov with a movement of his thumb over his shoulder: 'I have come'—he said—'about this matter, you understand, but I have not yet got . . . , it's not easy; I have already delivered three, and I am trying for the fourth!' I, of course, knew nothing of the matter, but I felt sorry for the old man, I thought how ashamed and annoyed he would be if he realized that he had given away a secret, so I replied, also with a mysterious air: 'Yes, yes, I understand—it's no joke.' Ah, how ridiculous and useless all these carryings-on are! What a pity that the young man is wasting his energy."

"The young man is doubtless very energetic, but his views on everything are one-sided," I remarked.

"Yes," replied Sasha, "but what can you do? From his point of view he is right: without that narrowness one cannot do anything. And if he did dispatch that *agent provocateur*[36] to a better place, you can only praise him for it."

"Of course," I agreed. "How interesting it would be to know what they are really up to over there in Russia. Was there a conspiracy or not?"

I really was very interested. I had already questioned Ogarev several times, and asked him to explain to me what their cause was, why Papasha had separated from them and why he did not believe in them or sympathize with them.

Ogarev: "Papasha had been growing further and further removed, keeping himself apart for a long time, and consequently there was much that he simply did not know. He could not judge the present position of young people in Russia, or what they are doing."

Myself: "Do you believe that they have organized a group which has great influence?"

Ogarev: "Volkov's escape, and the fact that he was freed by his comrades[37]—that alone proves that they are strong. But anyway, even if there were only a few of them, say fifty, twenty, or ten, I would still be with them, because I believe their cause to be a just and sacred one."

I wanted to understand more clearly what exactly this "cause" and this "group" were and so I was impatient to be away from Berne. I stayed there for only two days, and on the third day I returned [to Geneva] and once more began questioning Ogarev.

I was not satisfied by his answers. He gave the impression that he knew a great deal but could not or must not speak, and so I began to question Volkov and even had lengthy conversations with him about the workers in general, the "bourgeois", the exploiters and the "parasites". But I became none the clearer on the subject of the Russian cause. I understood one thing only, and that was that he was preaching the most terrible hypocrisy, with his repeated assertions that "the end justifies the means."

"Mercy on us," I could not help exclaiming, "but that is pure Jesuitism!"

"Yes, of course it is," answered Volkov, "and the Jesuits were most intelligent and ingenious people. There has never existed another society like theirs. One should just take all their rules from beginning to end and act according to them— changing the aim, of course."

This declaration surprised and frightened me. How can one work with such people, I thought. The more Volkov developed the idea of the necessity of such a system, and launched into details such as, for instance, the need for occasional eaves- dropping, opening other people's letters, lying, and so on, the more amazed I grew that Ogarev could agree with this kind of activity. When I questioned him about it, he merely answered:

"There are times when it is necessary to lie."

"But eavesdropping, opening other people's letters, and the rest?"

"But in practice one never has to do that," was his ingenuous reply.

From all the conversations I could draw the conclusion that their aim was good, that they were striving to change the existing order, and that they wanted to begin by overthrowing or destroying the power of the Russian government—but as for the means! . . .

Two days before my departure for Paris, Volkov began to put all manner of questions to me concerning myself personally, and my occupations, and finally asked why I was going to Paris and what I would do there.

"I do not know myself yet," I replied.

"That's bad," he muttered.

"While I am staying with Natalya Alexeevna and Liza I shall be looking after Liza, and helping Natalya Alexeevna copy out and translate Papasha's manuscripts. But what after that, I do not know."

"That's bad. But you say you are looking for something to do and that you would even be prepared to help us."

"Of course, if I can be of any help. But how, what is there to do?"

"There is no end of things to do, all around you. You only have to decide that you seriously want to help, and you will find them, and discover what they are. For instance, even here you could be of so much help to Ogarev."

"In what way exactly?"

"Come here this evening and I will explain. But you really ought to move here to Geneva."

"It is too late now. There will certainly be a flat rented in Paris by now. But still, I will see. If I thought that I would really find something to do here, then of course I would move here."

I went back in the evening although my head ached terribly. Ogarev had been drinking and was playing the piano. Volkov sat down beside me and began in a mysterious whisper to tell me that there existed in Russia a great and powerful secret society, that he was taking the risk of talking to me of it although he was hardly acquainted with me, because I had inspired his trust, and he was relying on me not to speak of it to anyone.

"You know the aim of the society. So now you only have to say if you consider yourself one of us."

"What do you mean? Do I belong to your society? Of course not!"

"That is not what I meant. To put it briefly, do you wish to remain as you are, to live in peace as a fashionable society lady, or do you wish to become one of us, like those strong women you find in Russia nowadays, whom we consider our sisters?"

Myself: "In other words, you are asking me if I wish to belong to your society? I cannot answer that. After all, I know too little about it as yet."

Volkov: "Just make up your mind about one thing: are you closer to the bourgeois parasites who do not wish to change anything, or to us, who wish to transform everything?"

Myself: "To you, of course; that is to say, I sympathize with your aim, but I cannot approve of your means. . ."

Volkov: "That is all I wanted to know. You agree with our aim, and that means you are one of us. But you must prove it in practice, you must work and help us."

Myself: "But if you will allow me, you say that I am one of *you*. I say that I agree with your aim, and I am willing to help, but I wish to know the rules of your society before I can consider myself a member, and what I shall have to do."

"We do not need any rules except silence. In Russia it is a different matter. Over there I would not have decided to talk openly with you so soon. We do not need any signatures or rules—what use are they? A man who does not want to do anything will not do anything even if he has signed, and a man who sincerely wishes to work will work without signing. What is the use of unnecessary formalities?"

"But what are you proposing that I should do?"

"I will explain now. You are aware that over there of late there have been arrests and all kinds of dirty tricks. Also people have started escaping from prisons and fortresses, and when they flee abroad and finally get here they find nothing. They

N

stop in Germany, and there they are handed over again to the Russian government. We must without fail set up some kind of *centre*, here abroad, which would be in touch with all Russians who are scattered outside Russia—so that an escapee would know where to turn and would not come to grief. The Committee of our group thinks that the most convenient place for setting up this centre would be Switzerland, more exactly, in Geneva—even at Ogarev's place, for example, since he is known and respected. But Ogarev is old, and often unwell, or in the condition in which you see him this evening. He simply must have a young, clear-headed person to help him and prompt his memory. It would be best and easiest for you to take charge of that. Without such a person, there will be no end of trouble. I have to go away in a day or two, and I am simply terrified at the idea of leaving him alone. For example, things like this happen: a few days ago a most important telegram arrived with a message that one of 'our men' had fled. That telegram should have been read at once, and a second telegram sent as quickly as possible somewhere else to inform them of what was happening. Well, Ogarev opened it and fell asleep in his chair with the telegram in his hands just as he was about to read it. Fortunately I arrived in time and managed to send off a dispatch to the right place, or God knows how many people would have perished. You can see that we simply must have a *loyal*, clear-headed person who would gradually take over everything. In other words, a person who would receive all the correspondence, answer it promptly, send it on, and such like. If you would take charge of this, you would be doing us a great service. You see, it is a case of human lives being lost over there to no purpose, all because of Ogarev's carelessness.''

The situation as he described it to me was indeed extremely serious. I believed that something really was going on in Russia, that everything was in ferment, that a storm was brewing and that something was being prepared for 19 February 1870.[38] I fell to thinking, weighing up all the circumstances and trying to find a way of arranging my move, after I had in Paris been so firmly *against* moving to Geneva. Moreover, the memory of my illness came back to me, and I was terrified at the thought that

I would have to participate in a secret society. I recalled how I had been tormented by all kinds of conspiracies, visions, etc., during my illness. Volkov cut short my reflections with the question:

"You can see the necessity for coming here, even if only for a short time, a few weeks or two or three months, in a word, while things are so hot over there. You have nothing to do in Paris, whereas here you will be tremendously useful. Make up your mind, and we will find you a room here at Ogarev's place. Or . . . but perhaps you are rather spoilt on account of . . . well, the creature comforts. . . ?"

"Oh no, I am accustomed to anything, and I pay little attention to comfort!"

"So much the better," he continued. "Then we can simply rent a room for you."

"What do you mean? . . . I shall not be coming alone. One of my family will be with me. After all, I have only just recovered, they will not allow me to leave on my own."

"What for? That is quite unnecessary! No, you must arrange it so that you come alone. We should not involve other people in this—they would only be a hindrance. What I have said to you must remain between ourselves. Well, when will you be back in Geneva? Remember that every day is precious. In three or four days?"

Myself: "How can I? It is impossible to arrange everything so soon. In two or three weeks—certainly not before."

Volkov: "No, two weeks at the most, but I hope it will be sooner. Things are already very bad indeed here. Have you decided?"

Myself: "I cannot promise for certain. I will see what has been arranged in Paris and how things are. I shall do what I can."

"No, you must arrange it without fail! You yourself can see and understand how important it is, what terrible consequences can follow from the slightest negligence. I am counting on you. In the meantime I will give you one or two commissions for Paris. Come and see me early tomorrow morning and I will explain to you what you have to do."

The next day he gave me several letters to take for his acquaintances in Paris, and added a letter of recommendation which I was to give to Mr ——, and in which he had written that this gentleman was to carry out all my commissions.

"It would be advisable if you did *not* meet him at your house."

He asked me to write as soon as possible and describe to him in detail what the attitude of my family was to my desire to move. "How will you explain it to them? No one must know yet that you are in touch with us. Please do not speak of it even to Ogarev."

"Well, I can explain it by saying that I wish to stay a while with Ogarev. As it happens, I had already written that, even before our conversations, because I would be truly grieved to leave him on his own. Natalya Alexeevna wrote in reply that she did not mind, and that if we could be useful in any way at all (this was a reference to his habit of drinking too much) then she was willing to move here."

"It would be advisable for you to come alone. You have no need of a nanny. If I am not here, we can arrange a meeting, a rendezvous somewhere along the way. But that can be done by letter."

"That would be difficult to arrange. I hope it will not be necessary."

"I will give you the address in any case, and explain where we could arrange to meet."

Whereupon he named the town of N.[39] and said that a certain Mr ——[40] knew him by the name of *S.*, and that when I arrived I was to say that I had come on behalf of *Narodnaya Rasprava*.

I returned to Paris, carried out the commissions promptly, and almost fell into a *"souricière"* laid in the offices of *La Marseillaise* since I had a commission for the editors there. It was pure chance that I did not fall into the trap. I discovered later that all the editors had been arrested. I wrote to Ogarev at once.

Only a day or two afterwards, I received a letter from Volkov with a lengthy dissertation on "parasitism", and on the fact that for twenty-five years I had been living aimlessly, without benefiting others, and so on. In short—a summary of our conversations and arguments. At the end he asked me to abandon these "ephemeral intimacies" and this "sentimentality", to shake off the continual surveillance and go alone to Geneva.

I replied that to arrange all that was more difficult than he supposed, because the things he called ephemeral and sentimental were in my eyes very important and serious. And that he was incapable of understanding my relationships with other people because he had most certainly been living and working alone for a long time now without caring about others. Ogarev also wrote to me, asking if I would come and help him.

By my second letter I was refusing to go, believing that it would cause too much alarm and distress for my family, who were beginning to suspect something. I added that to move would be unreasonable, since I could not tell lies, and neither my explanations nor my silence would satisfy them. And indeed, the endless conversations and argument with N. A[lexeevna] and with Sasha distressed me terribly. I could see that they feared for my health, and I realized that they had good reason, for I was indeed in a state of terrible agitation. They had noticed that I was receiving letters in an unfamiliar hand, and imagined that these were from Bakunin.

Sasha had completed his business with the lawyer, and I had signed all the necessary papers; Olga too. He had no more matters to attend to in Paris, and moreover, he was in great haste to see Teresina. He and Tchorzewski undertook to accompany the coffin as far as Nice and arrange everything there. On the eve of their departure we had yet another long conversation. Sasha tried to prove to me the absurdity of my desire to go to Geneva, saying that he regarded it as an after-effect of my illness.

"Look, judge for yourself," he said. "In what way can you help Ogarev, since you say it is to help him that you are going? If you think you can influence his drinking habits, that is ridiculous. You will achieve nothing."

Myself: "Aga wrote in his last letter that I could help him with some things, and be useful."

Sasha: "That is nonsense too! You know that at the moment he is incapable of thinking for himself. He is completely under

the influence of those around him. I can well believe that he is
very eager for you to stay with him, but even in asking you to
come, he is under the influence of other people who are simply
after your money. Give up the idea! You will find no work to
do there."

Myself: "I cannot do that. I shall see there what there is to
do, and who is right."

Sasha: "In any case there is no need for you to be in such a
hurry," went on poor Sasha, driven beyond his patience but
trying not to argue too heatedly with me, fearing a possible
recurrence of my illness. "Why do you have to go on ahead?
Wait till the end of the month and think it over properly, and
if you have not changed your mind, go with Natalya. But just
now, let me leave with my mind at rest. Promise me that you
will not go alone. Think how it pains me to go now and leave you
in this strange, unnaturally agitated state."

It grieved me to see how I was distressing him and the others;
I could not bear it and promised that I would not go without
Natalya, and that I would wait until the end of February.

"God be praised," said Sasha, giving a sigh of relief. "But
what an effort it cost to achieve that! It is very late. Let's go
to bed!"

At this point Pan joined in: "We can rely on Natalya
Alexandrovna's word, and we know that. Therefore we know
that *until the end of the month* we can set our minds at rest.
Natalya Alexeevna will certainly not think of leaving before
the first of March."

As soon as Tchorzewski began speaking, I started taking my
leave, kissed Sasha, and went without replying to Tchorzewski's
remark.

A day or two after their departure I received the following
letter from Volkov.[41]

It may be, indeed it is very likely, that everything he said
and wrote to me had had such a violent effect on me because I
was still under the influence of the phantoms of my sick mind.
I could not help seeking a resemblance between my present
circumstances and my hallucinations, and I saw them as some
kind of prophecy. Sasha and Pan left.

I was tremendously agitated by Volkov's letter. The thought even occurred to me that if this situation continued, I would very likely become confused again and fall ill. It was essential to come to a decision, and so I began to pack my things. Natalya noticed everything and grew more and more worried for me. At the same time everyone was afraid to oppose me, and avoided doing so. However, seeing that I was packing, Natalya asked me what I was doing: had I decided to leave, and when? She was not at all pleased by my appearance. Upon learning that I had decided to leave in two days, she said quite calmly that she would be ready too, and that she preferred to waste the money she had paid in advance for my accommodation, rather than let me leave alone. And indeed, two days later we left. Natalya telegraphed to Sasha and Tchorzewski asking them to go directly to Geneva without making a useless detour to Paris. We arrived at Geneva tired, both suffering from head-aches, and in a wretched state. Nevertheless I went to see Aga and find out if there was anything new, and *how exactly* I might help him.

He was overjoyed at our arrival, and said that I could indeed be of great assistance to him, and he would tell me before long what I should do.

Next day he gave me a letter from Bakunin *"to the two Natashas"*,[42] in which Bakunin wrote that he offered his con-dolences to us but that one should not lose heart, especially when one could still be of use to others and when there was work waiting for us as important and sacred as that which was being done in Russia and for Russia. When I had finished reading it, Ogarev asked: "What do you think, what will be Natalya's attitude to this?"

"You know her views," I answered, "and you know that she has no sympathy at all for your activities and believes that no good will come of them. This letter will have no influence whatsoever on her."

"In that case it would be best to give it back to me. Bakunin and I have been having a real correspondence about you. Here, have a look at his last letter—a whole article, and all about you."

Myself: "What can he write about me? He hardly knows me, what is he going on about?"

Aga: "He's heard you were ill. We were speaking of you—I agree with him that you need something to occupy yourself. Well, here you are, and we can find you work to do. Those others, Natalya and Sasha, think that I am ruining you, that work is harmful for you. But I am convinced of the contrary. In that empty, aimless, bourgeois milieu you will most certainly go out of your mind again. I do not want to ruin you—I want to save you. . ."

I was struck by his irritated, intolerant tone. I began defending Natalya and Sasha and trying to prove to him that they had never wanted me to lead an aimless life, that it was natural that they should be afraid of upsetting me now, knowing that all the doctors had advised me to rest.

A day or two later Ogarev showed me a letter from Volkov in which the latter wrote that he simply must have some highly important papers sent to him, and added: "I hope Tata is there with you—she will be of great help to you. Send her to me with the papers. She is the only person I trust now."

"Well, will you take this on?" said Ogarev after a pause. "Otherwise I really do not know how we can do it. They say that it is impossible to send anything by post."

This proposal put me in a quandary. I imagined Natalya's fright and displeasure, for I had heard her once discussing matters with Sasha, and saying: "Let us hope that Bakunin does not use her as a courier. That would be the most dangerous of all, God knows what would happen to her. In her exalted condition she would be ready to go to Russia."

I could see that it was the first step towards making me a courier. I thought, "To go not knowing, who my companions would be, to a rendezvous with an assassin." But this thought too passed through my mind: "He killed a spy though, and that was a good thing. What energy he has, he is a fanatic. He does indeed see nothing except his goal." Besides, I thought he would soon have to go to Russia. I had read some of the leaflets, and I was at a loss to understand how such dreadful things could be printed. I very much wished to discuss this with him. Indeed, there were many things I wanted to understand.

I hesitated and hesitated—then I decided to go. Poor Aga was at once overjoyed and frightened: "Will your health not suffer? You were not feeling very well after your arrival. Are you sure that it will not do you any harm?" I reassured him and then began wondering how I could explain things so that Natalya was as little worried as possible and did not frighten Sasha, and so that Tchorzewski did not think of checking my story.

Although it was repugnant to me to tell Natalya an untruth, I made myself do it and told her that I was going to Berne, and that she was not to worry because I would be staying with Masha.

I could see that the news was extremely unpleasant for her, but she merely said: "You are not a child, and I have no right to interfere in your affairs. But you do realize that you will be causing Sasha great distress—it was travelling he feared most for you. If only you would just take Tchorzewski with you. . ."

"I cannot."

"Well then, do as you think best. You know that I too will be terribly worried. When will you return?"

"The day after tomorrow, and I will write to you."

Tchorzewski was even more horrified, and insisted on accompanying me if only to the station. I did not tell him which train I was travelling on, and so set off on my own with a small bag and a bundle of papers. . .

Natalya stood at the window and worriedly watched me climb into the coach.

"Take care," she shouted after me, "and look after yourself!"

But I thought it all so strange and amusing. I had become a real little conspirator!

I reached N[euchâtel] without the least trouble. There I had to find Mr G[uillaume]. I had never been in N[euchâtel] before; the railway station is outside the town; I did not know the way and I did not wish to ask anyone. I saw that most of the passengers were setting off down a fairly wide road and I followed them. Some of them looked at me in surprise; evidently I stood out as a foreigner. I asked an old woman in a shop where *la rue* [*du*] *S*[*eyon*] was, and I found Mr G[uillaume] with no difficulty.[43] He opened the door to me himself and looked at me suspiciously—might I not be a spy? I asked him if he could tell me where to find Volkov.

"I know him," he replied, "but I do not know where he is at the moment. Do you know him personally?"

Then I remembered the prearranged words and said hastily:

"Of course I know him, and I have come on behalf of *Narodnaya Rasprava*."

He smiled and exclaimed: "Yes, yes, you are the one, then. I know, they have been expecting you for a long time. I was warned two or three weeks ago that you would be passing through. You will have to take the train a little further yet."

"But will I arrive this evening?"

"Of course you will. It will be dark, but do not worry, everything will be arranged, you will be met at the station. But if you would just carry this white handkerchief in your right hand—there, like that—so that they know you are indeed the person they are to accompany. And now allow me to escort you to the station and carry your bag. Did you really come all alone and find me on your own?"

We set off together for the station, but this time by another road, a very secluded way. He remarked that he was doing this as a precaution, since his company could be compromising, and he had many enemies in N[euchâtel].

"Of course I came alone. What is surprising about that? And I found you on my own despite the fact that I have never been here before. Why are you astonished?"

"Truly I would never have guessed that you were a conspirator."

I laughed.

"If I had been instructed to find you in a crowd, it would never have occurred to me that you were the one they were expecting. Are you Russian?"

"Yes, Russian. What is the matter, do you think I am too young?"

"Young, yes. But also—we already have certain ideas about 'Nihilist women', and your appearance, *toute votre apparition, votre extérieur du moins*, does not correspond in the least. One inevitably thinks of a certain carelessness in the dress, hair cropped short, spectacles, and so on. And in addition, I know what our acquaintance and some of his comrades look like. . . Very strange indeed", he added after a minute's silence.

"So you have had occasion to meet Nihilist women? I have much sympathy with them and even consider myself a Nihilist, as I understand the word. But I consider these outward forms and this originality quite superfluous and ridiculous."

We reached the station and found we would have to wait about half an hour. He was amazed that I had not eaten, and insisted that I have something in the buffet. He asked me a few questions, timidly, fearing any indiscretion, and repeated several times:

"How stupid, how annoying it is that neither you nor I was told anything. I can see we have many common acquaintances. For instance, do you know this handwriting?"—I recognized it at once.—"How strange! I know them all, you see, the whole circle. And I played a most active part in the Princess O[bolen-skaya] affair."[44]

"What's to be done! But if you were not told to speak to me, then do not speak. And I must warn you that as far as *your* affairs are concerned, I know very little, to be more precise—nothing."

He asked me also if I needed any money. I refused, of course. The train came in, he saw me to my seat and then went off to send a telegram.

It was already quite dark when I reached the little station at L[ocle]. I held the white handkerchief in my right hand, as I had been told, feeling very foolish. I had hardly given in my ticket and taken two or three steps in the snow along a muddy road, when a tall figure approached me and muttered something. I did not understand anything, but thought that no one would have approached me in this way except the person who had been instructed to do so, and so I followed him. A few minutes later a second man joined us. Wishing to start a conversation somehow, they began apologizing for the road being so bad, for there being so much snow, and so on. Soon we came to a small house and went up a steep wooden staircase to the attic. I was shown into a small, neatly kept room; a little woman with a slight stoop began fussing over me, taking my cloak and asking if there was anything I needed, etc. "*Merci,* I have no need of anything. Where is the young man?'

I was taken into another room, small, low-roofed and lit by a single tallow candle. Volkov was seated at a large desk surrounded by a pile of letters and various papers. He greeted me laconically: "How do you do? Have you brought them? Give them to me!"

"Here they are." And I gave him the papers.

He began reading them at once and it was only after six or seven minutes that he looked up at me and said:

"Surely you must be tired? Give me your hat. I expect you are hungry?"

"I would be glad to have some tea."

I was beginning to answer almost as laconically as he, but without being impolite. The little hunchbacked woman laid the table, brought in coffee, honey, jam, an enormous loaf of bread, etc., all the time scrutinizing me from head to foot. (Then she bustled around over by the bed, changing the linen; I could not help feeling uneasy at the thought of having to sleep with her.) I sat there eating and thinking: "Whatever possessed me to do something like this!"

We began talking, debating and arguing. His attitude to all the printed leaflets was that their contents were designed merely to frighten people. At one o'clock he saw that I was extremely tired and said:

"Why don't you say if you want to sleep? I would have gone. Are you unwell, or something? O[garev] wrote that we were to take care of you, not to irritate you and not to cause you agitation. He is really fond of you."

"Yes, I was feeling a little unwell those last few days in Geneva. I am quite well now, just tired. Where is my room? I was told that it would be inadvisable to go to a hotel—too conspicuous."

"Everything is prepared here. You stay in this room—I will go in that one there. When will you be ready tomorrow? What time, approximately?"

"About nine o'clock. Goodnight!"

"Sleep well!"

I locked myself in with the enormous key and lay down to sleep, thinking of Natalya, Sasha and all my family. How surprised they would be if they knew where I really was!

I awoke very early. The two small windows looked out on to some gardens, a church, two or three houses and a path which disappeared into the snow, and beyond that endless ranges of snow-covered mountains. Evidently we were deep in the country. At precisely nine o'clock Volkov appeared and first of all persuaded me not only not to leave by the first train, but to write to O[garev] that I would be unable to return before the evening of the next day.

"You know yourself that one cannot talk everything over so quickly. And we have a lot to talk over. He explains nothing to me in his letter. And then, you wanted to question me too on various things. Well, write quickly so that he does not become alarmed."

I wrote to [Ogarev] and Nathalie. Then we began once again arguing and debating, and so continued until evening. He informed me that the "Committee" wanted to publish a journal, and to call it *Kolokol* [*The Bell*]. I said that that would be extremely unpleasant, not only for me but for all my family too. I added:

"It must have been your idea and not the Committee's, so you can change it. Your journal will not have anything in common with the old *Bell*, I can see that already—so why take the same title? Only because you hope to attract more readers and have a wider circulation by reminding people of Papasha's name and his journal, and I repeat—it is very unpleasant for us. There are many more [appropriate] titles. Why not call it *The Hammer,* or *The Sword,* or *The Red Cockerel,* anything you like—but not *The Bell.* You know very well that Papasha was not at all sympathetic to all these activities, and. . ."

"Allow me," he broke in. "First of all, don't fly off the handle into a passion and get agitated! I have been ordered not to irritate you, and that is why I am afraid of arguing with you. You will be taken ill, and there will be trouble, and what will Ogarev do to me then?"

And he began trying to prove to me that I was only speaking from the point of view of a *daughter*, without thinking about "the Cause" or about what was necessary or useful to "the Cause". It was useful to the *cause* for the journal to be circulated as quickly as possible. It was obvious that the name of *The Bell* would facilitate this—so they had to call it by that name. It was from this point of view that *everything* should be decided.

"I will never agree with you on that," I said. "You can see that on this point alone my view as a *daughter* does not coincide with yours. It is clear that we shall meet with cases of this kind at every step, and I know that I shall never be able to cultivate such a one-sided view, or make every judgement or decision from the point of view of its usefulness to your 'Cause'."

Volkov: "Do not say '*your* Cause', but '*our* Cause'."

Myself: "I cannot. I cannot and do not wish to consider myself one of *you*. You can see that we do not agree at all."

Volkov: "It only appears so. Think seriously, break free from your various prejudices and sentimental habits, and you will see that the truth is on my side and that you, as an intelligent woman, cannot think otherwise."

It would be impossible to relate everything, and it would take too long to write it all down. We argued about the despotic rules of their society, about their unbelievable intolerance. Then I remarked that, according to him, everything they did was based on mutual trust, whereas my trust in people was formed extremely slowly; I was very suspicious, very cautious. . .

Volkov: "I have already written to you that we have no need of grudging trust."

Myself: "Yes, that was what I also wanted to ask you about. I did not understand that phrase in your letter—'grudging trust only demoralizes and leads to disasters. . .' How can that be? How can one have complete, boundless trust all at once? It is impossible!"

Volkov: "Of course, half-trust is an immoral thing. One should be either a real friend and comrade, so that one conceals absolutely nothing from the other person, so that everything is transparent, every thought, every stirring of the soul—or else an overt enemy, in which case one tries with all one's might to deceive and destroy him. But these half-and-half relationships, what are they? Sometimes you act sincerely to a person as you would to a friend, and at other times you distrust him and betray him as an enemy. So remember, the first rule is to conceal absolutely nothing. The Committee must without fail know all your thoughts, your tastes, and your desires, so that it will not entrust you with tasks or commissions which you would not be willing to execute."

Myself: "For pity's sake! Do you think I would tell all that to strangers—since I do not really know any one of them! One can only place such a trust in a single person, and even then, only after one has known the person for a long time. I repeat it would take me, for example, months or years to cultivate in myself such boundless trust, otherwise it would be just blind faith with no foundation. But in fact that is exactly what you want. It is a sort of religion.

(1) He showed me a piece of paper, hinting that it was an order from the Committee... What *The Bell* (or simply their future journal) should extol. (Marat, Babeuf, etc.) He could see by my endless arguing that I had no sympathy for any of it. But he still did not say what my work would consist of. "Helping Ogarev, seeing that the correspondence is sent off promptly, etc."

(2) He hid a second paper, saying: "To see the second, you must first of all agree with the first." I replied: "That means you will never show it to me, for I will never agree with the first."

But he did show it to me—several signatures, followed by that of B[akunin]. God knows why he showed me the repulsive thing (secret editorial offices, forged money, forged passports, etc.).

(3) He charged me with sorting through O[garev's] desk and tidying all his papers.

I arrived back in Geneva late in the evening and went directly to see Og[arev] to give him the letters and the commissions. There I unexpectedly met Czerniecki; he, thinking that I had come from Berne, began to question me about the Reichels. I felt extremely uncomfortable; it was very unpleasant. I went into another room. Og[arev] came in after me and I gave him a few of the commissions. Suddenly he called Czerniecki and gave him, or explained to him the parts which concerned him and he did this so unsubtly that it was not difficult for Czerniecki to guess that I had not been at the Reichels. Sure enough, soon after that he wrote to Sasha that I had become a *"Carbonarka"*.

I was greatly surprised when, a few days later, I saw Volkov again. I had come to see Og[arev], and there he was. He said that some confusion had arisen and he had had to come there. I declared that I still did not understand what work there could possibly be for me here.

"You will see—we shall discuss it, we'll have a talk." On the pretext that he had no time and that it was awkward for him to talk during the day, he began to spend the evenings with me. Gradually it became clear that I would at first have to deal with the correspondence of booksellers, keep the account-books, send off packets, etc., in short, organize a "Bureau" and keep everything in order.

"But none of that is the real work," he added. "It's all unimportant. It can be done by someone else. The main thing is that you should unite the whole of *émigré* society, rally them all together and steer them in a particular direction."

Myself: "For pity's sake, what could *I* do? I cannot even imagine how to begin such a task."

Volkov: "Well, I will explain to you. When we can no longer influence people by argument and conversation we have to resort to other means. For instance—make all the members of a particular circle quarrel among themselves, all the *émigrés* here, for example, and then work on each one of them separately, talk with them."

Here he launched into details and developed a whole plan of action, "to control everything", which so outraged me that I exclaimed:

NATALIE HERZEN

"... I am sending you my photograph, taken here in Rome. Many people think that I am very like Napoleon I, but that's nothing new ... What is your opinion? Everyone here likes it very much."

ALEXANDER HERZEN

"... Everything that Herzen thought was courageous enough to think—and as a theorist he is unsurpassed—we practical workers, who are humbler, less gifted and of lesser repute, want to do."

(BAKUNIN)

"How he suffered! And how deceptive was his vivacity, his outward gaiety. Those who knew him but little thought him the gayest and most carefree man in the world ..."

(NATALIE HERZEN)

MARIA REICHEL

"Be **very** *cautious with all the Russians who have recently arrived. Remember, a new type of man* **à la** *Nechayev is forming among them, a kind of* **Revolutionary Jesuit** *who is ready to commit any vileness in order to achieve his goal,* **i.e.** *revolution in Russia. To this end, and in the most shameless fashion, he feels free to* **lie,** *to read other people's letters, to steal documents, keys, etc. In Russia they force people to make donations of enormous sums by* **threatening** *to denounce them to the Third Section. Those are* **facts,** *Masha. It is simply outrageous . . ."*

(NATALIE HERZEN)

NATHALIE TUCHKOVA-OGAREVA

". . . She has still not come to her senses, and never will—her life is over . . ."

(NATALIE HERZEN)

"The evil in her nature flows from two sources: jealousy and lack of restraint. She can love people and do goodness-knows-what to them out of jealousy . . . All the evil came from her extravagant licence . . . Keep this letter a secret."

(ALEXANDER HERZEN)

SERGEI NECHAYEV

*". . . I have here with me now
one of these young fanatics who
know no doubts, who fear
nothing and who realise that
many of them will perish at the
hands of the government but who
nevertheless have decided that
they will not relent until the
people rise. They are magnificent,
these young fanatics. Believers
without God and heroes without
phrases . . ."*

(BAKUNIN)

Reproduced from *The Unmentionable
Nechaev* by Michael Prawdin by kind
permission of Mrs. Michael Prawdin

MICHAEL BAKUNIN

*". . . We were now at Bakunin's
door. We entered the diminutive
room of the mighty agitator . . .
He began telling me that I
simply must make up my mind
which side I wished to be on,
because I ought not to be on
both sides at once, it was not a
good thing.
" 'I understand what is stopping
you. You are thinking: They
are fooling me, I know they are
Jesuits, so why should I believe
them? They are saying one thing
to me now but in reality they
are thinking and wanting
another. Perhaps all they are
really after is my money, and
they want to exploit me? Well,
confess, did that thought not
cross your mind just now?' . . ."*

(NATALIE HERZEN)

DRAWING BY NATALIE HERZEN

" 'Have you mentioned the drawings?' he [Nechayev] muttered as he passed Ogarev . . . 'What drawings?' I asked in surprise . . . I was to draw, first of all, a Russian **Muzhik**, but then it appeared it would be better to draw a group of **Muzhiks**. [Nechayev] paid no attention to my remark that all my drawings would be clumsy, unauthentic, and lifeless, because I had never set eyes on a Russian peasant, and I did not know how to draw figures. I only drew heads—which was quite another matter . . ."

FROM NATALIE HERZEN MANUSCRIPTS

"But all you are after is a cunning *intrigante*—the whole thing is repulsive to me! If that is the kind of work you are offering me, then no, thank you!"

He smiled ironically and said:

"Please do not be upset, you have been ordered not to get upset—and what a thing to get upset about! What's an *'intrigante'*?—just a meaningless word!"

Myself: "Well, to me it is *not* a meaningless word. And if you call *that* work, you can be sure that I shall not help you—so there!"

Gradually I also came to notice that my laconic replies to all his questions about various persons were not satisfying him. I told him frankly that I certainly did not intend to communicate to him everything I knew and heard.

"What do you mean?" he said with some displeasure. "What kind of trust is that? I told you that we have no need of grudging trust."

Myself: "And I told you that trust is not so easily acquired, and one cannot force oneself all of a sudden and say: have trust in a particular person."

Volkov: "No, you must have complete, boundless trust—without that we can do nothing. You must make everyone have the same trust in you too, make them tell you everything, so that you know all. . ."

Myself: "So that I can pass it on to you?"

Volkov: "And then you will tell me what you have heard and found out."

Myself: "I understand. In other words, you are proposing that I should be a spy," I said, and the blood rushed to my head.

Again he smiled ironically and said:

"Why use such grand words? You will prove nothing that way."

At the end of every conversation I was more and more convinced that their methods were so repugnant that I could have nothing in common with them. He was continually trying to prove that these methods were essential. Soon B[akunin] arrived and assisted him so well in this that they almost succeeded in driving me completely out of my mind.

o

"What!" he said to me. "Our enemies are ten thousand times stronger than we are, and shrink from no means, and are we to think we can fight them without resorting to the same means? It is madness. Unthinkable! Sending men to their death for nothing! What is our aim? To change the present vile order! Well, the first step towards that is to overthrow the Russian government, and to do that we should use every possible means —or else spit on the whole thing and sit with our arms folded."

A rumour began to circulate that we were petitioning over our Kostroma estate,[45] and that we wished to return to Russia. All three of them launched into the most violent invective against us. Under their influence Og[arev] began inveighing against Sasha and Vogt and saying that they were trying to persuade me to go to Russia and to behave dishonourably. I was, of course, amazed and began defending them, stating that naturally we had ascertained whether we could go back "simply", without behaving dishonourably—that went without saying; we had never even thought of writing or signing a petition.

"We know," began Bakunin, "the very fact that one of you is going there is proof that you, that is, the Herzen family, have been reconciled with the government. You will be welcomed with open arms—and how! You will find yourself moving in aristocratic circles. *Vous verrez comme on vous fêtera!* Your brother will be offered a Chair on the spot—*il se fera une magnifique carrière—mais il souillera par cela le nom de son père!*"

I was on the point of becoming angry, but then I saw how ridiculous it was that a man could be carried away by idle fantasies, or play a part in order to work on my imagination, and finally I said:

"Why are you saying all this? Sasha is not even thinking of going to Russia and looking for a Chair.[46] I repeat, none of us will stoop to anything dishonourable to obtain that estate in Russia. But if Vogt and Scheller are going to put in a claim under Swiss law and are successful, then naturally we shall not say no. But I must admit, I see no reason why we should give away presents to the Russian government. Everything you said is completely irrelevant as far as we are concerned."

Nevertheless, Volkov said to me in a whisper:

"We must talk some more about this without fail this evening. But it's inconvenient here. Let us go to the old man [Bakunin]. Do you understand me?"

Myself: "Of course I understand. But why is it awkward here? You have only to go into another room if you do not wish to talk in Ogarev's presence."

Volkov: "I said it was no good, and that means no. Are you afraid or something? It won't be long—only half an hour."

Myself: "Why should I be afraid? I merely think it is unnecessary; all the same, let us go. But mind you do not keep me later than ten o'clock. I do not wish to alarm them all at home every time."

Volkov: "Afraid, are you?" he said ironically. "Will N. A[lexeevna] scold you?"

Myself: "I am not afraid of anyone! I myself do not want to return home late when it is not necessary."

Volkov: "You will always be a pampered little miss! And you will never shake off your prejudices."

We were by then on the way to Bakunin's place, and Volkov, really agitated (or trying to appear indignant), said, apparently mad with rage:

"Do you not see what they are doing to you? Are you a child who does not understand, or are you made of wood, that you can look on so calmly, so indifferently, while dishonourable deeds are committed all round you?"

Myself: "I do not understand you! Why are you angry, why are you abusing me? Who is committing dishonourable deeds?"

Volkov: "Will you not understand that they are selling you," he said in a furious whisper. "Those people who call themselves your close friends. Selling you to the Russian government."

For a whole minute I thought he had gone mad and I did not reply, particularly since we were now at B[akunin's] door.

We entered the diminutive room of the mighty agitator. Volkov sat down a little apart with a ferocious expression. His Tyrolean hat tipped to one side and an enormous scarf carelessly flung around his neck, his whole figure had the air of a bandit, and his expression was striking in its energy, malice, and cruelty. B[akunin] began explaining to me that I must not be surprised that one could not say everything in Og[arev's] presence. Surely I could see for myself that it was simply dangerous, that he might give something away when he was in a state of intoxication.

Then he began repeating what he had already said to me in the morning, wishing to prove to me that Natalya, Sasha and company were bourgeois parasites who thought only of money and dreamed only of increasing their fortune, and that Natalya was staying by me only because it was to her *advantage*, and that was why she pretended to be attached to me. At this I protested violently, remarking that he had no right to speak of her in that way. And then I listened in amazement to a tirade from him. Some of the remarks he made I found so insulting that I did not even take the trouble to reply to them. He repeated that if we returned to Russia and the Kostroma estate was given back to us it would be a disgrace to our generation, so humiliating, so shameful, etc.

(At this point Volkov joined in, looking at me almost savagely: "It goes without saying that if you *do* go to Russia our people will be obliged to get rid of you somehow!" I looked curiously at this strange being without showing the slightest fear or agitation, and waited to see how it would end. B[akunin] glanced at him reproachfully and said: "Now, what's all this? Threatening, are you? What kind of an idea is that? Well, he really is in a rage—just look at him.")

Then he began telling me that I simply must make up my mind which side I wished to be on, because I ought not to be on both sides at once, it was not a good thing.

"I understand what is stopping you. You are thinking: 'They are fooling me, I know they are Jesuits, so why should I believe them? They are saying one thing to me now but in reality they are thinking and wanting another. Perhaps all they are really after is my money, and they want to exploit me?' Well, confess, did that thought not cross your mind just now?"

Myself: "It has crossed my mind more than once. But the main thing which makes me hesitate is not that, but the fact that I can see no work for myself, and also that I still have doubts about whether you are following the right course at all. *Chi va piano va sano. . .*"

Bakunin launched into a lengthy dissertation which ended thus:

"Will you not understand that all around you, in your private life, nothing is done 'simply', nothing said 'simply'. There you have your real Jesuits, not here among us. You ask what you can do. That will become apparent with time. And meanwhile . . . but it's impossible to talk openly and simply with you, or I would say in words of one syllable—leave yourself the *'stricte nécessaire'* to live on and give the rest to the common cause. But one cannot say that to you now," he continued after a pause, seeing that I was not replying.

("Although there will be nothing you can do. Struggle as much as you like, but sooner or later we'll have your money. . . The social revolution is inevitable . . . and very near. . ." "You may be sure," I said, "that when that day comes I shall not weep—and I will not wait for them to take everything away from me, I will give it away myself." He gave an ironic smile, glanced at Volkov and said: "Well, we shall soon see whether you are sincere or not.")

"Unfortunately you grew up among people who respected gold and money above all. Your father had this weakness and he left it to you, his children, as a legacy. You poor children of Herzen, I pity you. What a life yours is, colourless, passionless. Nothing has ever aroused your enthusiasm. You have always been sensible, afraid of doing something silly, and so you have never done *anything*. He who does nothing never makes a mistake, but he never does anything worthwhile either. Do you really want to be governess to N. A[lexeevna]'s daughter, or nanny to your brother's children? That is beneath you. You need wider horizons. Here is some work ready and waiting for you. Do you seriously think that we want to rob you? Judge for yourself! Did you know that we have a huge capital over there in Russia—millions! As if we wanted your kopecks! They are just a drop in the ocean!" (Contradictions at every point.)

"No, you can be useful to us through your influence on Og[arev], who really is becoming a physical wreck. If you are with him he will almost certainly drink less. Do not leave him, at least. I say this out of a feeling of, well, reverence for the poor old man—I feel terribly sorry for him." (But as he said this I could not help thinking that he was in reality trying to find a way of preventing me from going too far away, because as long as I was with Og[arev] they would certainly manage to squeeze as much as they liked out of me.)

As he was taking his leave, he said:

"Remember, Tata, that we do not want to interfere in your dealings with Og[arev]. Do as you see fit with him, help him as much as you wish. We do not wish to know anything about it, and will never accept anything from you."

I made no reply, but inwardly I was greatly amused at hearing these generous words, since I was perfectly well aware that if I was helping O[garev] it was because they were putting him to expense—the money was coming from the same source, so why this comedy? And I recalled the crude hint he had addressed to me a few days earlier. He had said to me in Og[arev]'s presence and simply *de but en blanc*: "I hope that the children of Herzen will be ashamed to leave Og[arev] without means." I felt the blood rush to my head. What an unimaginable indelicacy!

I still could not make the decision, and I did not clearly understand what exactly they wanted of me.

"You simply must take a decisive step," Volkov kept saying to me, "to prove that you are not lacking in character."

When I asked him what he meant by a decisive step, he replied:

"Well, you must know that yourself by now. Prove that you really are dissatisfied with the existing order, if everything you have said is not empty words. Shake off all your prejudices, protest against the present order, otherwise you will be merely criticizing and continuing to live the same life. We have no need of your criticisms, but if you want some serious work, liberate yourself from all the people around you, all those N.A.s, those Pan Tchorz[ewskis], and so on."

Myself: "So what you mean by a decisive step is just that I should live alone, or at least not with N.A.?"

V[olkov]: "No, not just that, although that, of course, would be a start. It would prove that you are independent."

I tried to show him that it would be all very well if N[atalya] oppressed me, but since she allowed me complete freedom, and did not pry into their affairs, it was decidedly unnecessary.

"You will see," he went on, "that very soon there will be nothing you have in common with her, so why live together then? It would be much better, and you would be much freer, living separately."

Myself: "We shall see. I am fond of them and I want to live with them. If it turns out that we no longer have anything in common, then let *them* leave; I do not want to desert them. In any case, where I live is none of your concern, and I know that at the moment I am perfectly free."

B[akunin] supported me here and said that I should not listen to V[olkov], that he did not recognize any kind of affection; he did not believe that people who lived together became so accustomed to each other that it was hard for them to part; everything that was not "the Cause" was in his opinion triviality, sentimentalism, etc. . . . . There were certain things on which they did not agree. For example, Volkov said to me that in order to help them and really become a "strong woman", I would have to abandon absolutely everything else and work exclusively for *their cause*. "And then you will learn what real life is," he said with pride, "real friendship and complete trust. We live with all our pores, and I have the same trust in my comrades as I have in myself," etc.

They began having arguments about the purpose of the journal and what its "colour" should be. Ogarev and Bakunin tried unsuccessfully to convince Volkov that it was essential that *The Bell* should be *"red"*. Volkov insisted that they take to his fancy: he tried to prove, for his part, that they should publish a "multi-coloured" or a "colourless" paper so that everyone would be intrigued and people of all shades of political opinion could be equally represented in it—of course, for the purpose of expressing their discontent with or their hatred for the Russian government.

I did not like the sound of all this in the least, and I had a feeling that the result would be utter nonsense and trash—and all under the name of *The Bell*!

The old men, as he called O[garev] and B[akunin], argued and argued, and once Ogarev almost came to blows with Volkov over the "colour" of *The Bell*. Volkov insisted that there should not be a word about socialism in the journal, nor any sharply expressed opinions. Ogarev did not like this, he wanted to write freely, and began speaking very rudely and curtly to Volkov. Bakunin cursed them both, until they were ashamed of themselves, and then himself began attempting to persuade Ogarev to try out Volkov's fancy and see what came of it. The old men yielded before the young tyrant.

When the time came to decide details of printing and format, Volkov suddenly declared to me that "the Committee" considered it unseemly and entirely inappropriate to display the names of Bakunin and Ogarev.

"What shall we do, then, whom shall we choose for editor?"

"Take one of the *émigrés*," I said, guessing that he already had a plan prepared in his mind. "There are plenty of them, Zhukovsky, for example, Mechnikov, etc., or Kasatkina, if you prefer a woman."

"No, none of them are any good. I say, why don't *you* be editor?" he exclaimed all of a sudden, as though struck by a brilliant new idea, whereas it was perfectly apparent to me that he had thought up this cunning remark earlier, but did not know how to make it in such a way that I could not possibly reject the proposition. That is why he was not very pleased when I replied: "Not for anything in the world!"

A stream of questions followed: "What? Why? That means that you do not wish to do anything for 'the Cause', you want to be a parasite forever, a pampered little miss." Seeing that insolence and taunts had no effect, he began begging and persuading me in honeyed tones that I, "as an intelligent woman", *could not* refuse, that I must be only too well aware of the desperate situation I would be putting him in, and that the whole Cause would grind to a halt on account of it. It was all in vain. This time I did not give way. I repeated that I really could not be the editor; I was inexperienced and had little knowledge, and did not want to play the part of a puppet. They only wanted my name, and I would not give them my name, especially for God knows what "multi-coloured" journal, in which Papasha was very likely even going to be attacked.

For a few days we had the most terrible arguments about it, which at times drove me to despair. He would not leave me alone, and when I walked away he would say: "So, the matter is settled. We shall not speak of it any more. You are the editor."

And I would repeat: "Yes, we ought to have finished speaking about it a long time ago. You can see I am unshakeable and I will not be the editor of your journal. I will not even give you my address to send letters."

He raged and raged and was finally compelled to give up. Then he had the idea of saying that *The Bell* was published by certain representatives of the Russian Cause.

On Sunday, 3 April the first issue of *The Bell* was due to appear.[47] Ogarev wrote a note asking me to come and assist him for the first time—the Committee had not yet sent anyone—by writing out addresses, sticking labels, etc. I went there in the morning. Mary [Sutherland] told me that on the previous day, late in the evening, another "boy" had suddenly appeared and spent the night there. A fine specimen of contemporary Russian youth! Small, thin and slightly stooped despite his young face; judging by the total absence of moustache and beard, he was about twenty. His hair—thin, dry, and dark—had not seen a comb for so long that it stuck out in all directions in separate wisps and knots.

By the strange, hesitant gaze of his small dark eyes it was easy to see that he was very short-sighted. Under his long, black, tattered frock-coat he wore a red cotton shirt; his neck was adorned with a narrow black tie, knotted crookedly; there was no sign of any linen. As I opened the door he was pacing up and down the room with long strides, and evidently giving a report to Volkov. Seeing that they were discussing very serious matters, I withdrew immediately. He soon left, but returned two or three hours later when I was sitting in Henry [Sutherland]'s room wrapping up the journal. Volkov showed him in in silence; he began helping me, also in silence. To my question "Who is this boy?" Volkov gave the laconic reply, "One of ours, a very good man, and he's not a boy either—he's older than me." I concluded then he did not wish to explain to me who his comrade was, and asked no more questions, nor did I speak to the boy. After a long silence Volkov turned to him and addressed him as Serebrennikov.[48] There began a conversation from which I understood that this Serebrennikov had been living in the house of someone from *Narodnoe Delo*[49] for several months past, enjoying their complete trust, and feigning absolute solidarity with them, while at the same time, here, he mocked them and called them scum who did not want to do anything. He told us he had made one of them drink so that he would show him various files, cupboards, etc. I recalled Volkov once boasting that "one of *ours*," as he expressed it, had been living in the *Narodnoe Delo* circle for several months, and that they believed he was one of their own men. At that time I had said to him that in my opinion it was a most repulsive game. Now I had discovered, or guessed, that it was this young Serebrennikov he had been talking about, and consequently the boy made an extremely disagreeable impression on me. At the time I saw him, *i.e.*, in early April, the *Narodnoe Delo* organization thought he had gone away long ago; and so he was hiding from them. Volkov told me that he had only just arrived, that he had been travelling for three or four days without resting or taking time to wash himself or comb his hair, and that he would be continuing on his way somewhere else the same evening. Serebrennikov himself told me that he had made a speech in French at the grave of Serno-Solovevich.[50]

Once, at the end of March, Volkov sprang a surprise on me, and it was indeed an unexpected one. It occurred to him to announce to me, or at least to suggest, that he found me attractive. He discoursed at length and so obscurely on the subject of trust and friendly relations in general that I understood absolutely nothing, but towards the end it was impossible not to understand, and his question was so unexpected that I was quite confused and even frightened—of what, I did not know myself. Suddenly I remembered the whole business with Penisi. For a long time I made no reply, hoping that I had misunderstood him or that he had not expressed his meaning properly. Yes, I really wished that it were so, because I foresaw that all this would lead to the most tiresome, disagreeable, embarrassing and stupid relations.

However, after a long silence, he repeated his question, and added:

"I understand, it is probably the ring that is preventing you from replying."

There was no reason to doubt or hesitate any longer, and I answered him:

"You are putting me in an extremely embarrassing and disagreeable position. You yourself must have noticed that there is absolutely nothing, as far as I am concerned."

"It is my fault, I was mistaken, let us speak no more of it."

"Naturally, that would be best."

I would never have thought that this crude, half-savage ruffian could have written or offered a single word about love. And because of my scepticism I did not believe him, but instead began searching to discover what he hoped to gain from such an attempt, and what he could possibly expect if he were successful. It was only long afterwards that I began to experience some doubt, that is, to suspect the possibility of there being perhaps a small grain of sincerity in his words, after he had repeated the same thing several times, even in writing, and complained that all his words were having no effect on me and he was literally burning with shame. . .

Why it was that I did not have the wit to abandon everything and go away, in spite of his pleading, and his reproaching me for not wanting to do anything, I cannot understand now. But at that time, when I still believed that they really did have a "Cause", and that I really could be of some help to Aga, and to others too, who were—as they put it—in danger, all V[olkov]'s sallies, however repugnant to me, could not destroy my desire to prove that I was ready and willing to work to the best of my abilities. Moreover, in my mind I was unbearably confused about everything, and this tormented me terribly. I wanted at all costs to reach the truth, to achieve a clear understanding. On all sides I heard conflicting rumours, and to examine and make sense of them in that atmosphere of mystery was impossible. There was only one thing to do: decide to ignore Volkov's uncivilized, crude and insolent behaviour, continue my observations, and hope that time would make everything clearer. And so it did. . .

There were times when I was in despair, when I even wrote to him that I did not believe in anything, and that their theories, systems, and methods were so repugnant to me. Nevertheless, he sometimes succeeded in awakening—for a moment or two—my trust in what he called "the Cause". Once again I would be caught up in it, and in that nebulous state I could not summon up the strength to refuse to render him and Ogarev small services when I received notes of this kind: "We are swamped with work. Help us just for these few days. You know I am completely alone and that bad news is coming in from all sides—and you leave us at such a time." Ogarev wrote and spoke in similar tones; he refused to accept my pleading and my explanations, but repeated: "Yes, we. . . Have patience just a little longer, Tata, you know that in a few days one of 'theirs' will be arriving. It's not nice of you to abandon us like this."

At last I realized that I was being tricked: as long as I gave in to them, they would never let me go. It was essential that Volkov should move.

4. A Revolution Without Heroes

81. Sergey Nechayev: Catechism of the Revolutionist (1869)

I

General Principles of the Organization

(1.) The structure of the organization is based on individual trust.

(2.) The organizer (himself a member) selects five or six persons from amongst his acquaintances and, having held a separate discussion with and secured the consent of each, assembles them together and lays the foundation of a closed cell.

(3.) The mechanism of the organization is concealed from idle eyes, and therefore the whole range of contacts and all the activities of the cell are kept secret from everybody, with the exception of its members and the central cell, to whom the organizer submits a full report on specified dates.

(4.) Members undertake specialized duties in accordance with a definite plan drawn up on the basis of a knowledge of the locality, social class or milieu in which the preparatory work is to be carried out.

(5.) A member of the organization immediately forms in his turn a second-degree cell around himself, in relation to which the previously formed cell assumes the role of a central cell, which all the members of the organization (or, in relation to the second-degree cells, the organizers) supply with the sum total of information obtained through their own cells; this is submitted to the next cell upwards.

(6.) The principle of non-operation by direct methods with regard to all those persons who can be operated upon with equal success indirectly, that is, through other people, must be observed with the utmost scrupulousness.

(7.) The organization's general principle is not to attempt to convince, that is, not to cultivate but to consolidate those forces which are already in evidence, to eliminate all discussions which bear no relation to its aim.

(8.) Members do not ask the organizer questions whose purpose is unconnected with the business of subordinate cells.

(9.) The total frankness of members with the organizer is the basis for the successful progress of the cause.

(10.) Upon the formation of second-category cells, previously organized cells become centres in relation to them, and are supplied with the society's regulations and a definite programme of its activities in the location in which it is situated.

General Principles of the Network of Sections

(1.) The purpose of the sections is to achieve the independence and autonomy of the organization's work and their use as an extra guarantee of the security of the common cause.

(2.) These sections consist initially of two or three persons authorized by the network and with the committee's approval. On the basis of the organization's general principles, they select a group from only those cells which, in the committee's opinion, fulfil their requirements. Contact with the network is maintained through the organizers.

(3.) Persons selected from the cells to membership of a section pledge themselves at the first meeting: *a)* to act concertedly, collectively, in total subordination to the voice of the majority, and to leave the section solely for the purpose of entry into even more intimate ranks, on the instructions of the committee; *b)* at the same time they pledge themselves, in all their relationships with the outside world, to bear in mind only the good of the society.

(4.) Persons are selected to membership of a section only one at a time. When the number reaches six, the section is divided into groups, on the instructions of the committee.

(5.) A person is jointly elected to take charge of clerical work, the compilation of reports, the reception and dispatch of committee members and other agents having a relation to

the section as a whole. The same person takes custody of documents and property, and keeps addresses.

(6.) The other members undertake to carry out preparatory work in a particular class or milieu, and select for themselves assistants from amongst persons organized according to the general principles.

(7.) All the persons organized in accordance with the general principles are regarded as and used as a means of or implements for performing the undertakings and achieving the aim of the society. Therefore in any business to be executed by the section, the overall nature of the plan for this business or undertaking must be known only to the section; the persons executing the business must not under any circumstances know its true nature but merely those details, those parts of the business which it has fallen to their lot to perform. In order to arouse their enthusiasm it is vital to represent the nature of the business in a false light.

(8.) Members inform the committee of the plan for an undertaking conceived by them, and only with the committee's consent do they set about implementing it.

(9.) A plan proposed by the committee is implemented immediately. To prevent the committee from making demands in excess of the section's power, a record as strict and accurate as possible is maintained of the state of the section, through its channels of contact with the committee.

(10.) A section may send its members to inspect subordinate cells and dispatch them to fresh places in order to found new organizations.

(11.) The question of financial resources is of prime importance:

a) a direct levy upon members and sympathizers, made on a committee form, with the amount of the donation set out in words;

b) an indirect levy, on plausible pretexts, upon persons of all estates, albeit non-sympathizers;

c) arrangement of concerts, evenings, nominally for different purposes;

d) various enterprises with regard to private individuals;

the section is forbidden to use any other more ambitious methods, which are beyond its powers, and only upon the instructions of the committee should the section promote the implementation of any such plan;

e) one-third of the entire receipts is to go to the committee.

(12.) Amongst the conditions necessary for a section to commence its activities are:

a) the formation of dens;

b) infiltration of its clever and practical men into the milieu of peddlers, bakers, etc.;

c) knowledge of the town gossips, prostitutes, and other private [means] of gathering and dissemination of rumours;

d) knowledge of the police and the world of old clerks;

e) establishment of relations with the so-called criminal elements of society;

f) influence over high-ranking persons through their womenfolk;

g) continual propaganda by all possible means.

This copy is not to be circulated but kept in the section.

II

Principles by which the Revolutionary Must Be Guided

THE ATTITUDE OF THE REVOLUTIONARY TOWARDS HIMSELF

(1.) The revolutionary is a dedicated man. He has no interests of his own, no affairs, no feelings, no attachments, no belongings, not even a name. Everything in him is absorbed by a single exclusive interest, a single thought, a single passion—the revolution.

(2.) In the very depths of his being, not only in words but also in deeds, he has broken every tie with the civil order and the entire cultured world, with all its laws, proprieties, social conventions and its ethical rules. He is an implacable enemy of this world, and if he continues to live in it, that is only to destroy it more effectively.

(3.) The revolutionary despises all doctrinairism and has rejected the mundane sciences, leaving them to future generations. He knows of only one science, the science of destruction.

To this end, and this end alone, he will study mechanics, physics, chemistry, and perhaps medicine. To this end he will study day and night the living science: people, their characters and circumstances and all the features of the present social order at all possible levels. His sole and constant object is the immediate destruction of this vile order.

(4.) He despises public opinion. He despises and abhors the existing social ethic in all its manifestations and expressions. For him, everything is moral which assists the triumph of revolution. Immoral and criminal is everything which stands in its way.

(5.) The revolutionary is a dedicated man, merciless towards the state and towards the whole of educated and privileged society in general; and he must expect no mercy from them either. Between him and them there exists, declared or undeclared, an unceasing and irreconcilable war for life and death. He must discipline himself to endure torture.

(6.) Hard towards himself, he must be hard towards others also. All the tender and effeminate emotions of kinship, friendship, love, gratitude and even honour must be stifled in him by a cold and single-minded passion for the revolutionary cause. There exists for him only one delight, one consolation, one reward and one gratification—the success of the revolution. Night and day he must have but one thought, one aim— merciless destruction. In cold-blooded and tireless pursuit of this aim, he must be prepared both to die himself and to destroy with his own hands everything that stands in the way of its achievement.

(7.) The nature of the true revolutionary has no place for any romanticism, any sentimentality, rapture or enthusiasm. It has no place either for personal hatred or vengeance. The revolutionary passion, which in him becomes a habitual state of mind, must at every moment be combined with cold calculation. Always and everywhere he must be not what the promptings of his personal inclinations would have him be, but what the general interest of the revolution prescribes.

P

THE ATTITUDE OF THE REVOLUTIONARY TOWARDS HIS COMRADES IN REVOLUTION

(8.) The revolutionary considers his friend and holds dear only a person who has shown himself in practice to be as much a revolutionary as he himself. The extent of his friendship, devotion and other obligations towards his comrade is determined only by their degree of usefulness in the practical work of total revolutionary destruction.

(9.) The need for solidarity among revolutionaries is self-evident. In it lies the whole strength of revolutionary work. Revolutionary comrades who possess the same degree of revolutionary understanding and passion should, as far as possible, discuss all important matters together and come to unanimous decisions. But in implementing a plan decided upon in this manner, each man should as far as possible rely on himself. In performing a series of destructive actions each man must act for himself and have recourse to the advice and help of his comrades only if this is necessary for the success (of the plan).

(10.) Each comrade should have under him several revolutionaries of the second or third category, that is, comrades who are not completely initiated. He should regard them as portions of a common fund of revolutionary capital, placed at his disposal. He should expend his portion of the capital economically, always attempting to derive the utmost possible benefit from it. Himself he should regard as capital consecrated to the triumph of the revolutionary cause; but as capital which he may not dispose of independently without the consent of the entire company of the fully initiated comrades.

(11.) When a comrade gets into trouble, the revolutionary, in deciding whether he should be rescued or not, must think not in terms of his personal feelings but only of the good of the revolutionary cause. Therefore he must balance, on the one hand, the usefulness of the comrade, and on the other, the amount of revolutionary energy that would necessarily be expended on his deliverance, and must settle for whichever is the weightier consideration.

THE ATTITUDE OF THE REVOLUTIONARY TOWARDS SOCIETY

(12.) The admission of a new member, who has proved himself not by words but by deeds, may be decided upon only by unanimous agreement.

(13.) The revolutionary enters into the world of the state, of class and of so-called culture, and lives in it only because he has faith in its speedy and total destruction. He is not a revolutionary if he feels pity for anything in this world. If he is able to, he must face the annihilation of a situation, of a relationship or of any person who is a part of this world—everything and everyone must be equally odious to him. All the worse for him if he has family, friends and loved ones in this world; he is no revolutionary if they can stay his hand.

(14.) Aiming at merciless destruction the revolutionary can and sometimes even must live within society while pretending to be quite other than what he is. The revolutionary must penetrate everywhere, among all the lowest and the middle classes, into the houses of commerce, the church, the mansions of the rich, the world of the bureaucracy, the military and of literature, the Third Section [the Secret Police] and even the Winter Palace.

(15.) All of this foul society must be split up into several categories: the first category comprises those to be condemned immediately to death. The society should compile a list of these condemned persons in order of the relative harm they may do to the successful progress of the revolutionary cause, and thus in order of their removal.

(16.) In compiling these lists and deciding the order referred to above, the guiding principle must not be the individual acts of villainy committed by the person, nor even by the hatred he provokes among the society or the people. This villainy and hatred, however, may to a certain extent be useful, since they help to incite popular rebellion. The guiding principle must be the measure of service the person's death will necessarily render to the revolutionary cause. Therefore, in the first instance all those must be annihilated who are especially harmful to the revolutionary organization, and whose sudden

and violent deaths will also inspire the greatest fear in the government and, by depriving it of its cleverest and most energetic figures, will shatter its strength.

(17.) The second category must consist of those who are granted temporary respite to live, solely in order that their bestial behaviour shall drive the people to inevitable revolt.

(18.) To the third category belong a multitude of high-ranking cattle, or personages distinguished neither for any particular intelligence nor for energy, but who, because of their position, enjoy wealth, connections, influence and power. They must be exploited in every possible fashion and way; they must be enmeshed and confused, and, when we have found out as much as we can about their dirty secrets, we must make them our slaves. Their power, influence, connections, riches and energy thus become an inexhaustible treasure-house and an effective aid to our various enterprises.

(19.) The fourth category consists of politically ambitious persons and liberals of various hues. With them we can conspire according to their own programmes, pretending that we are blindly following them, while in fact we are taking control of them, rooting out all their secrets and compromising them to the utmost, so that they are irreversibly implicated and can be employed to create disorder in the state.

(20.) The fifth category is composed of doctrinaires, conspirators, revolutionaries, all those who are given to idle peroration, whether before audiences or on paper. They must be continually incited and forced into making violent declarations of practical intent, as a result of which the majority of them will vanish without a trace and real revolutionary gain will accrue from a few.

(21.) The sixth, and an important category is that of women. They should be divided into three main types: first, those frivolous, thoughtless, and vapid women who we may use as we use the third and fourth categories of men; second, women who are ardent, gifted, and devoted, but do not belong to us because they have not yet achieved a real, passionless, and practical revolutionary understanding: these must be used like the men of the fifth category; and, finally there are the women

who are with us completely, that is, who have been fully initiated and have accepted our programme in its entirety. We should regard these women as the most valuable of our treasures, whose assistance we cannot do without.

The Attitude of our Society towards the People

(22.) Our society has only one aim—the total emancipation and happiness of the people, that is, the common labourers. But, convinced that their emancipation and the achievement of this happiness can be realized only by means of an all-destroying popular revolution, our society will employ all its power and all its resources in order to promote an intensification and an increase in those calamities and evils which must finally exhaust the patience of the people and drive it to a popular uprising.

(23.) By "popular revolution" our society does not mean a regulated movement on the classical Western model—a movement which has always been restrained by the notion of property and the traditional social order of so-called civilization and morality, which has until now always confined itself to the overthrow of one political structure merely to substitute another, and has striven thus to create the so-called revolutionary state. The only revolution that can save the people is one that eradicates the entire state system and exterminates all state traditions of the regime and classes in Russia.

(24.) Therefore our society does not intend to impose on the people any organization from above. Any future organization will undoubtedly take shape through the movement and life of our people, but that is a task for future generations. Our task is terrible, total, universal, merciless destruction.

(25.) Therefore, in drawing closer to the people, we must ally ourselves above all with those elements of the popular life which, ever since the very foundation of the state power of Muscovy, have never ceased to protest, not only in words but in deeds, against everything directly or indirectly connected with the state: against the nobility, against the bureaucracy,

against the priests, against the world of the [merchant] guilds, and against the tight-fisted peasant profiteer. But [we] shall ally ourselves with the intrepid world of brigands, who are the only true revolutionaries in Russia.

(26.) To knit this world into a single invincible and all-destroying force—this is the purpose of our entire organization, our conspiracy, and our task.

82. *Nechayev's Views on Action and Revolution*[1]

To us an idea is of value only insofar as it can serve the great cause of radical and universal destruction. But in none of the books we read today is there a single such idea. He who initiates himself in the revolutionary cause through books will never be anything but a revolutionary sluggard. An idea able to serve the people's revolution can only be worked out in revolutionary action, and must be the result of a series of practical trials and manifestations, all having one and the same unswerving aim— merciless destruction by any means. Everything that does not follow this course we regard as alien and hostile. We will not let ourselves be seduced by any of the revolutionary phrase-mongering practised nowadays so lavishly by doctrinaire champions of paper revolution. We have lost all faith in the word; for us the word is of significance only when the deed is sensed behind it and follows immediately upon it. But far from everything that is nowadays called a deed *is* a deed. For example, a modest and excessively cautious organization of secret societies which show no outward, practical sign of activity at all is in our opinion nothing more than a ridiculous, abominable, childish game. We term real manifestations only a series of actions which destroy something absolutely: a person, a thing, or an attitude which is an obstacle to the liberation of the people.

With no thought for our lives, and undaunted by any threats, dangers or difficulties, we must by means of a succession of individual acts and sacrifices which follow a strictly ordered and agreed plan, by means of a series of bold, nay, audacious ventures, burst into the life of the people, and when we have inspired them to faith in us and in themselves, must unite them and stir them to the solemn accomplishment of their own task. . .

Of the leaflets that have recently appeared abroad we recommend almost unconditionally the appeal by Bakunin to classless student youth. It is a serious-minded work, although it says far from everything; which is probably attributable to the author's circumstances and position.[2]

Bakunin rightly tries to persuade us to abandon our academies, universities and schools and go to the people. This idea is correct but far from a new one. The question is, *how do we go to the people, and what are we to do among the people?* Bakunin does not say a word about this, and it is this which is the main problem with all honest revolutionaries in Russia who, not satisfied with words, demand deeds, and need advice that is not vague but precise and definite.

Therefore we recommend far more wholeheartedly leaflets in which this practical problem is raised more directly and a solution put forward which is more sincere and more business-like, leaflets such as: "The Formulation of Revolutionary Questions", "Principles of Revolution", the "Proclamation to the Students" by Nechayev. . .[3]

We have only a single, negative, immutable plan—merciless destruction.

We refuse outright to suggest models for living conditions in the future, for that would be incompatible with our activity; and therefore we consider any exclusively theoretical mental work futile.

We regard the task of destruction as one so immense and difficult that we devote all our energies to it and refuse to labour under the delusion that we have sufficient strength and skill to construct.

And so we take it upon ourselves exclusively to destroy the existing social structure; construction is not our business but the business of others to follow us.

We intend to demolish the decayed building of society in which the majority of the inhabitants suffer in order that impure joys and corrupt delights be afforded to the fortunate few. Let the new building be erected by new carpenters whom the people will send forth from their midst when we have given them the opportunity to breathe deeply and freely, their bosoms rid of the state's oppressive yoke.

Concentrating all our energies upon destruction, we have neither doubts nor disillusions; ceaselessly, and always cold-bloodedly, we pursue our sole, our life's aim.

Our recent predecessors[4] did not understand this [although] they had all the facilities to begin the fight and conditions were favourable for a general upheaval. (The time of the declaration of the fake emancipation of the serfs; the time when the inhabitants of the Winter Palace trembled for fear of the consequences of the deceitful trick they had played upon the people.)

They (our predecessors) sat idly by and shunned the populace, which had risen in places in rebellion, instead of plunging into these local revolts and uniting them into a single, terrible, all-destroying popular uprising.

They (our predecessors) were assiduously occupied with implementing irreproachably in their imagination plans for the future life of the people, and missed their chance of liberating the people from conventions of state and class.

And for that reason our recent predecessors achieved nothing positive.

The Karakozov affair[5] we must regard as the prologue!

Yes, this was the prologue! Let us try to ensure, friends, that the drama itself commences as soon as possible! . . .

Let us now, having cast aside all abstract arguments, come face to face with our real task.

Since the final solution of our vital problem (that is, the definitive destruction of the state system) can be reached only through common action, by an uprising of the entire popular force, we, *i.e.* that section of educated youth which has sprung from the people and has felt the full extent of the pain suffered by the people, must now, in view of the imminence of a general popular uprising, devote the whole of our attention and energies to the annihilation of all the patently obvious obstacles which might particularly hamper [this] uprising and impede its progress.

The principal factors which constitute this hindrance are:

(1.) Persons occupying senior government posts and at the centre of control over the armed forces, who carry out their duties as superintendents with particular zeal.

(2.) People of great economic strength and means who use that strength exclusively in their own interests or those of their class, or to assist the state.

(3.) People hired to discourse and to write, that is, publicists bribed by the government, and littérateurs who hope by way of flattery and denunciation to procure hand-outs from the powers-that-be.

Persons in the first category must be exterminated absolutely, without any argument.

Persons in the second category must be dispossessed of their economic strength and means, which are to be used in the cause of popular liberation; and, should dispossession be impossible, this strength and means must be destroyed.

Persons of the third type are to be silenced in one way or another (even if this means depriving them of their tongue).

Now let us be more precise and come closer to the substance, and most important, the first stage of our task.

Having the intent and aim of exterminating the Tsar along with all his family, his goods and chattels and all the so-called royal prayers, in order to eradicate the figure of the sovereign in general, we shall, however, refrain for the time being from laying a finger on [the Tsar] Alexander Nikolaevich, and this is why.

Above the head of this drab, weak-minded despot who rules through the wit and will of his concubines and favourite pet monsters, the clouds of popular indignation and hatred are even now gathering. Deceived, robbed, and starved, the people are beginning to open their eyes; and soon they will see clearly the cause of all their intolerable torments. Lashed with the birch-rods of the liberal rural arbitrator, with the bullets of the soldier-suppressor, they have experienced acutely the vile deception of the Tsar, the so-called "Emancipation of 19

February". Vague longings and resentment turn to intelligent hatred which accumulates rapidly in the peasant's breast. When nine years of his newly-devised slavery have passed, in 1870, the anniversaries of Razin and Pugachev, this intelligent hatred will burst forth in a divine thunderbolt that will strike the aristocracy as it wallows in its own depravity and foulness. Let him live, this hangman of ours, this destroyer and tormentor of the people who has dared to call himself their liberator—let him live until the time, until the moment when the popular storm breaks, when the working people, themselves tortured by him, will rise from their long, agonizing slumbers and solemnly pass their sentence on him, when the free peasant will tear asunder the chains of slavery and smash with his own hands that head with its loathsome crown, on the day of the *people's justice*.

Yes, we shall let the Tsar live until the coming of the days of the peasant's judgement. His reign has cost the people too dearly, and we are not the only ones to lay claim to the right to punish him; it is the right of the entire Russian working people, emaciated, plundered, desecrated and deceived by him; and these working people have paid for this right in the streams of their honest peasant blood that flowed in the Bezdna slaughter when Apraksin massacred the defenceless crowds that surrounded Anton Petrov,[6] in the butcheries of the hungry in the northern provinces, and in a thousand massacres on a less vast scale, perpetrated during the last five years, in which crowds of villagers who had gathered to discuss the "Emancipation of 19 February" were thrown into dungeons without interrogation or inquiries.

No, we will not touch the Tsar unless we are forced prematurely to do so by some stupid and senseless measure or fact in which *his* initiative is apparent. We will save *him* for a solemn, agonizing punishment to be executed in the presence of the whole of the liberated working people, poised upon the ruins of the state.

But for the moment we will immediately set about exterminating his Arakcheevs,[7] that is, those monsters in glittering uniforms spattered with the people's blood, who are regarded as the pillars of the state; those who have been and are fond of slaughtering peasant folk who rise in rebellion; those administrative leeches who suck away ceaselessly at the aching, yearning breast of the people, who have displayed and will display particular zeal in devising ways and means of squeezing the last drops of sap out of the people, in dulling the people's incipient understanding. And above all, all those who prove the greatest obstacle to our rapprochement with the people and our preparatory work.

It goes without saying that employees of the Third Section and the police as a whole who are known to be particularly active and talented sleuths are to be punished in the most agonizing way and given first priority.

Before a national popular uprising can begin we shall have to exterminate a whole horde of robbers of the public purse, base adulators of the Tsar, and tyrannizers of the people. We must cleanse thought of its foul excrescences, and purge contemporary Russian science and literature of its venality and mediocrity which are embodied in the vast numbers of publicists, pen-pushers and pseudo-scholars who are in the pay of the Third Section or who aspire to deserve such pay. We shall have to rid ourselves in one way or another of heretics, informers and traitors who sully the flag of truth with which they drape themselves by setting themselves up as its votaries.[8] This is the basis of a true movement with the aim of preparing favourable conditions for a general popular uprising, in the near future, against the state and the class system.

83. *Natalie Herzen to Maria Reichel*

6 JUNE 1870

Campagne Baumgartner
St-Jean-la-Tour
Genève

FORGIVE ME, forgive me, my dear Masha, I am ashamed and embarrassed at not having replied to you for so long, I cannot explain all the reasons why. Let me say, to cut a long story short, that all this time I have been in such an anxious frame of mind that I have hardly written a word of sense to anyone. Bakunin knows all about it, and perhaps he has told you a thing or two if you have been inquiring after me.

There are times now when I am amazed that I did not fall ill a second time! They pulled the wool over my eyes and told me all sorts of fairy-tales. And I partly believed them, because I could not conceive that talent for lying could be developed to such perfection. Well, I was carried away, though only for a very short time, not by a person but a certain *cause*—but I soon realized that I had almost fallen into the mire.

It is all too long to describe in a letter. Maybe you have heard something of it from other people; perhaps you have even spoken to Bakunin. Well, when we see each other you can ask me about everything.

Now I should very much like to hear *from you*, how the Nechayev business and especially the affair of Serebrennikov[9] is regarded in Berne (he is a compatriot of yours, a Siberian, a former peasant from Irkutsk), *i.e.* your opinion and the opinion of the various Vogts. Bakunin wrote that their advice was to make as much fuss as possible about it, circulate leaflets and articles, and, most importantly, to appeal about the trial, and that they have set to work on it with great ardour. Is that all true? Please do not be surprised, my dear, that I am cross-questioning you. But, *entre nous soit dit*, I know from experience that Bakunin is quite liable to alter the facts so as to present the affair in the most advantageous light.

I had more than once been on the point of coming to see you, Masha, ever since our arrival in Geneva, not simply to visit you but to escape from Geneva, to get away once and for all from all those stupid affairs in which I had become embroiled, or rather, in which they had embroiled me (as they have many other people, by exploiting their honesty and their excessive kindness of heart). There were times when my head was spinning and I thought, "I'll go this minute to my dear kind Masha and rest a little there." Nathalie helped me and tried also to persuade me to go, but all at once all the circumstances altered and I freed myself without going away. I was left merely with a violent hatred of those people who advocate the Jesuit line: *"The end justifies all the means,"* and prove or *demonstrate* in practice that this is their firm conviction.

We have been here on the St-Jean hill, that is, a quarter of an hour from the town centre, since 1 May. We have taken a second-floor [apartment], unfurnished—proof that we intend to stay for some time. The view from our windows is wonderful, and everyone admires it. And indeed it really is one of the finest spots in Geneva. We can see the Arve and the Rhone beyond the dense foliage of our big garden, the iron bridge, the whole of Geneva, and the tip of the lake beyond it; in the distance there are mountain ranges one after another rising into the clouds. All this panorama is so changeable in different lights that it is hard to drag oneself away from the window, it is so fine.

On 1 June I took charge of little Sasha,[10] who is seven. Somehow there have been many complaints about him at school, but then they have treated him badly too, and punished him senselessly; so I have decided to try and see if I can improve his nature. Sasha (my brother) has agreed, but he adds that "all the same he would prefer Masha to take charge of him because she is more democratic in all her ways." It is extremely unlikely, though, that he will develop or fall into "aristocratic habits" in our household—we do everything very simply and everybody helps with the housework and tidies his own room, and Shushka himself (for so I will call him in order not to confuse you) helps. He is an exceedingly affectionate child, and I am almost certain that he will fit in very well with us here. His room is next to my own, and I see to his toilet in the mornings and evenings, and in the daytime too, when he dirties himself. He wakes me at five o'clock, and I am very pleased at this, *autant de gagné sur les heures de sommeil*, and the day is never too long for me. I tell him about you and your children and say that when he is a very good boy we shall go and visit you in Berne during the holidays. At the moment he is going to the junior school near our house, where they are preparing him, with our assistance at home, for a *collège industriel*, where he can start in two years' time.

You probably know already that Sasha has a third son, *Alexey*. He was born on 18 May, that is, on Volodya's birthday. Teresina is feeding him herself and is suffering no discomfort; all of them are well.

Olga and Malwida are still in Paris, but will go shortly to Ems, more for Malwida's treatment than to see "our Emperor". When they have spent some time taking the waters they will come and see us in Geneva, and from here continue on their way to Italy. Liza is working well and preparing for an *école secondaire*.

When do Sasha's holidays begin, I mean, your Alex's? When will he be in Lausanne? It would be a shame if he were to be so near Geneva and not visit us. I insist that he calls to see us. I will send him 50 francs in a day or two; if he is thinking of going on some excursion they will be useful, or he can spend them on books for himself.

And now, my dear Masha, I bid you farewell, embrace and kiss you heartily, and never again will I leave you for so long without news. Kiss Reichel and the children for me too. Give my regards to the Vogts.

TATA HERZEN

On the subject of Tatyana Petrovna Passek: I did not reply because her proposals are not suitable at all. But if you write, give them our best wishes and thank them. Is there any news of poor Egor Ivanovich?

84. *M. Bakunin to Sergey Nechayev*

2 JUNE 1870   *Locarno*[11]

DEAR FRIEND,

I now address you and, through you, your and our Committee. I trust that you have now reached a safe place where, free from petty squabbles and cares, you can quietly consider your own and our common situation, the situation of our common cause.

Let us begin by admitting that our first campaign which started in 1869 is lost and we are beaten. Beaten because of two main causes; first—the people, who we had every *right* to hope would rise, did not rise. It appears that its cup of suffering, the measure of its patience, has not yet overflowed. Apparently no self-confidence, no faith in its rights and its power, has yet kindled within it, and there were not enough men acting in common and dispersed throughout Russia capable of arousing this confidence. Second cause: our organization was found wanting both in quality and quantity of its members and in its structure. That is why we were defeated and lost much strength and many valuable people.

This is an undisputable fact which we ought to realize without equivocation in order to make it a point of departure for further deliberations and deeds.

You, and doubtless your friends as well, had realized it long before you spoke to me about it. In fact one could say that you never spoke to me about it and I had to guess it for myself from many obvious contradictions in your talk and finally to convince myself by reference to the general state of affairs which spoke so clearly that it was impossible to hide it even from uninitiated friends. You more than half realized it when you visited me in Locarno. But nevertheless you spoke to me with complete assurance and in the most positive manner about the imminence of the inevitable revolt. You deceived me, while I, suspecting, or feeling instinctively the presence of *deceit,* consciously and systematically refused to believe it. You continued to speak and act as if you told me nothing but the truth. Had you shown me the real state of affairs during your stay in Locarno, as regards both the people and the organization, I would have written my appeal to the officers in the same spirit but in different words. This would have been better for me, for you and, most important, for the cause. I would not have spoken to them about the impending rising.

I am not angry with you and I do not reproach you, knowing that if you lie or hide the truth, you do it without self-interest and only because you consider it useful to the cause. I, *and all of us*, love you sincerely and have a great respect for you because we have never met a man more unselfish and devoted to the cause than you are.

But neither love nor respect can prevent me telling you frankly that the system of deceit, which is increasingly becoming your sole system, your main weapon and means, is fatal to the cause itself.

But before trying, and I hope succeeding, in proving this to you, I must say a few words about my attitude to you and to your Committee and will try to explain why, in spite of all forebodings and rational or instinctive doubts which increasingly forewarned me about the truth of your words, up to my last visit to Geneva[12] I spoke and acted as if I believed them unreservedly.

It might be said that I have been separated from Russia for *thirty years*. From 1840 to 1851 I was abroad, first with a passport, then as an *émigré*. In 1851, after a two-year imprisonment in Saxon and Austrian fortresses I was extradited to the Russian government which held me prisoner for another six years, first in the Alexeev ravelin of the Peter and Paul Fortress, then in Schlüsselburg. In 1857 I was sent to Siberia and spent two years in western and two in eastern Siberia. In 1861 I fled from Siberia and since then, obviously, I have not returned to Russia. Therefore in the last thirty years I have only lived four years (nine years ago) from 1857 to 1861 in freedom in Russia, *i.e.* in Siberia. This of course gave me the opportunity of getting to know the Russian people better, the peasants, the petty bourgeoisie, the merchants (specifically Siberian merchants), but not the revolutionary youth. In my time there were no other political exiles in Siberia, except a few Decembrists and Poles. True, I knew *also* the four *Petrashevtsy*: Petrashevsky himself, Lvov and Tol,[13] but these people represented only a sort of transition from the Decembrists to the real youth—they were doctrinaire, bookish socialists, Fourierists and pedagogues. I do not know the real youth in whom I believe, this classless class, this hopeless phalanx of the people's revolution about whom I have written several times and only now gradually begin to learn.

The majority of Russians who came to London to do homage to Alexander Herzen were either respectable people, or writers or liberally and democratically inclined officers. The first serious Russian revolutionary was Potebnya;[14] the second was you. I shall not speak about Utin and the other Geneva emigrants. Thus, before I met you, the real Russian revolutionary youth remained for me *terra incognita*.

I did not need much time to understand your earnestness and to believe you. I was convinced and still remain convinced that even if you were few, you represent a serious undertaking, the only serious revolutionary movement in Russia. Having been convinced of this, I said to myself that my duty lay in helping you with all my power and means and in allying myself as much as possible with your Russian cause. This decision was all the easier for me because your programme, at least during the last year, not only resembled but was identical with my programme, worked out on the basis of the total experience of a rather long political life. Let us define in a few lines this programme on the basis of which we were completely united last year and from which you seem now to be departing to a considerable extent, but to which I, on my side, have remained faithful to a degree which would oblige me to break all *intimate political relations* with you, if your convictions and your, or your friends', departure from it were completely final.

The programme can be clearly expressed in a few words: total destruction of the framework of state and law and of the whole of the so-called bourgeois civilization by a spontaneous people's revolution invisibly led, not by an official dictatorship, but by a nameless and collective one, composed of those in favour of total people's liberation from all oppression, firmly united in a secret society and always and everywhere acting in support of a common aim and in accordance with a common programme.

Such was the ideal and such was the plan on the basis of which I joined you and gave you my hand in order to realize it. You know yourself how faithful I remained to the promise of the union which I recognized. You know how much faith I had in you, having once convinced myself of your earnestness and of the similarity in our revolutionary programmes. I did not ask who your friends were, nor how many.[15] I did not check your strength; I took your word.

Q

Did I believe out of weakness, out of blindness, or because of stupidity? You know yourself that this is not so. You know very well that I was never given to blind faith. That even last year when we talked alone together, and once at Ogarev's and in his presence, I told you clearly that we ought not to believe you as you were quite capable of lying when you thought that a lie might be useful to the cause. We thus had no other guarantee of the truth of your words but your obvious sincerity and undoubted devotion to the cause. This was an important guarantee which, however, did not save you from mistakes and us from blunders if we follow you blindly.

Despite this conviction of which I spoke to you several times, I stayed in contact with you and helped you everywhere and as much as I could. Do you want to know why I did it?

Firstly, because, up to your departure from Geneva for Russia, our programmes were truly identical. I was convinced of this not only by our daily conversations, but by the fact that all my writings, conceived and printed while you were here, evoked in you a sympathetic response precisely on the points which most clearly expressed our common programme and because your writings, printed last year, bore the same character.

Secondly, because acknowledging your real and indefatigable strength, devotion, passion and power of thought, I considered you, and still consider you, capable of uniting around yourself real forces, not for your own sake but for the cause. I said to myself and to Ogarev that if they are not yet united, they will necessarily be so shortly.

Thirdly, because of all the Russian people whom I knew I considered you the most capable of carrying out this enterprise and I said to myself and to Ogarev that there was no point in waiting for another man, that we were both old and unlikely to meet another man more dedicated and more able than you. That is why, if we want to be allied with the Russian cause, we must be allied with you and with no one else. We do not know your Committee, or your Society, and can form an opinion about them only through you. If you are in earnest, why should your present and future friends not be in earnest too? Your earnestness was for me a guarantee that, on the one hand you would not admit worthless people to your company and, on the other, that you will not remain alone and will attempt to create a collective force.

You have, it is true, a weak point which astounded me from the first days of our acquaintance and to which, I confess, I did not attach sufficient importance. This is your inexperience, your ignorance of life and people and, associated with this, a fanaticism bordering on mysticism. Your ignorance of the social conditions, customs, morals, ideas and usual feelings of the so-called educated world renders you even now incapable of successful action in this environment even with a view to its destruction. You do not know as yet how to acquire influence and power within it, which is bound to lead to inevitable blunders every time the needs of the cause bring you in contact with it. This was clearly demonstrated in your ill-fated attempt to publish *Kolokol (The Bell)* in impossible conditions. But we shall talk about *Kolokol* later.[16] This ignorance of men leads to inevitable blunders. You demand too much and expect too much from people, giving them tasks beyond their strength in the belief that all people must be filled with the same passion which animates you. At the same time you do not believe in them, and consequently you do not take into consideration the passion which is aroused within them, their orientation, their independently honest devotion to your aim. You try to subdue them, frighten them, to tie them down by external controls which mostly prove to be inadequate, so that once they get into your hands they can never tear themselves free. And at the same time they do escape, and will continue to escape as long as you do not change your behaviour towards them, while you do not look within them for the main reason for joining you. Do you remember how cross you were when I called you an *Abrek*[17] and your catechism a catechism of *Abreks*? You said that all men should be such, that a complete renunciation of self, of all personal wishes, pleasures, feelings, affections and ties, should be a normal, natural, everyday condition of everybody without exception. You wished, and still wish, to make your own selfless cruelty, your own truly extreme fanaticism, into a rule of common life.[18] You wish for an absurdity, an impossibility, a total negation of nature, man, and society. This wish is fatal because it forces you to spend your strength in vain, always shooting to miss. No man, however strong he is, and no society, however perfect its discipline and however powerful its organization, can conquer nature. Only religious fanatics and ascetics could try to conquer it—that is why I was not very surprised, or surprised for long, when I recognized in you a certain mystical, pantheistic idealism. In connection with your characteristic orientation this seemed to me completely obvious, but completely absurd. Yes, dear friend, you are not a materialist like us sinners, but an idealist, a prophet like a monk of the Revolution,[19] your hero should not be Babeuf, not even Marat, but some sort of Savonarola. According to your way of thinking, you are nearer to the Jesuits than to us. You are a fanatic. This is your enormous and peculiar strength. But at the same time this is your blindness, and blindness is a great and fatal weakness; blind energy errs and stumbles, and the more powerful it is, the more inevitable and serious are the blunders. You suffer from an enormous lack of the critical sense without which it is impossible to evaluate people and situations, and to reconcile means with ends.

All this I understood and realized last year. But for me all this was balanced in your favour by two considerations. Firstly, I recognized (and still recognize) in you a great and, one might say, perfectly pure force, free of any admixture of self-love or vanity, such as I had never met in any Russian. Secondly, I told and still tell myself that you are still young and whole-hearted, and being without personal egoistical whims and self-delusions you cannot long remain on the wrong path and under a delusion which is fatal to the cause. I am still convinced of this.

Finally, I clearly saw and felt that you were far from having full confidence in me and in many respects attempted to use me as a means to immediate aims which were unknown to me. But this did not bother me at all.

Firstly, I liked your silence about the people involved in your organization, and the conviction that in such movements even the most trusted people should know only as much as is *practically* necessary for the success of their particular enterprise. You will do me the justice of admitting that I never asked you indiscreet questions. Even if you had, contrary to your duty, given me some names, I should not have known the people to whom these names belonged.[20] I would have had to judge them on your word, and I believed and believe in you. Composed of people like you who have earned your total trust, the Committee, should, I think, be equally trusted by us.

The question is: Did your organization really exist, or were you only going to create it somehow or other? If it did exist, was it large, did it at least represent an embryo of power, or did this all exist only as a hope? Did our holy of holies, the Committee itself, exist in the shape you described and with the undoubted unity of forces for life or death—or were you only going to create it? In a word, were you the only representative of a quite respectable individual power, or of a collective power already in existence? And if the society and the Central Committee really existed, and assuming the participation in it (particularly in the Committee) of only true, firm, fanatically devoted and selfless people like you, still another question arises: Was, and is, there in it sufficient common sense and knowledge, sufficient theoretical training and ability to understand the conditions and relationships of the Russian people and classes to make the revolutionary Committee effective to cover the whole of Russian life and penetrate all social strata with a really powerful organization? The sincerity of the cause depends on the fervent energy of the participants, its success on their common sense and knowledge.

In order to discover this both as regards actual and potential development, *i.e.* in the spirit of your movement, I asked you many questions and I must confess that your replies did not satisfy me in the least. However much you wriggled and dodged, you told me, in spite of yourself, that your society was still numerically insignificant and lacked funds. It had as yet very little common sense, knowledge and skill. But the Committee is created by you and certainly from people like you, among whom you are one of the best and most determined. You are the creator and, up to now, leader of the society. All this, dear friend, I understood and learned last year. But this did not in any way prevent me from joining you, recognizing in you an intelligent and passionately devoted activist of a sort which is rare, and being certain that you had managed to find at least a few people like you and unite with them. Also I was, and still am, certain that with experience and sincere and tireless aspiration you would soon achieve that knowledge, wisdom and skill without which no success is possible. And as I did not, and do not now, suppose that there can exist in Russia in addition to your group another group as much in earnest as yours, I decided, in spite of everything, to remain united with you.

I did not hold it against you that you always tried to exaggerate your strength to me. This is an objective, often useful and sometimes bold gesture of all conspirators. It is true that I saw your attempts to deceive me as a proof of your as yet insufficient knowledge of people. It seemed to me that from our talks you ought to have understood that in order to attract me there was no need to furnish proof of an already existing and organized power, but only proof of an unbending and reasonable determination to create such a power. I also understood that you were appearing before me as if you were an envoy of an existing and fairly powerful organization. Thus, it seemed to you, you put yourself into a position to present your conditions as emanating from great power, while you actually appeared before me as a person who was in the process of collecting strength. You should have talked to me as an equal, person to person, and submit for my [approval] your programme and [plan] of action.[21]

But this did not enter into your calculations. You were too fanatically devoted to your plan and your programme to subject them to criticism by anyone. And secondly you did not have enough faith in my devotion to the cause, in my understanding of it, to show me the cause as it really was. You were sceptical about all *émigrés*, and you were right. About me you were probably less sceptical than about others, because I gave you too many proofs of my readiness to serve the cause without any personal demands or vainglorious calculations. But you still considered me as an invalid whose counsels and knowledge might sometimes be useful, but no more; whose participation in your fervent efforts would have been superfluous and even harmful. I saw this very well but it did not offend me. You knew this could not prompt me to break with you. It was not my business to prove to you that I was not such a hopelessly unfit case for an ardent, a real movement as you thought. I left it (and leave it) to time and your own experience to convince you of the contrary.

At the same time there existed, and still exists, a special circumstance which forced and forces me to be particularly careful in relation to all Russian affairs and people. This is my total lack of funds. I have struggled with poverty all my life, and every time I have managed to undertake and do something more or less useful, I had to do it not with my own, but with other people's money. For a long time it has drawn down on me a whole cloud of slander and reproach, particularly from Russian blackguards.

These fellows have totally besmirched my reputation and thus paralysed my activities to a considerable extent. I needed all the genuine passion and sincere determination which I recognize in myself, from experience and not boastfully, to prevent me from breaking and discontinuing my activities. You also know how untrue and ignoble are the rumours about my personal luxury, about my attempts to make a fortune at the expense of others and by duping them. In spite of this, the Russian *émigré* blackguards, Utin and Co, dare to call me a swindler and a self-seeking exploiter, me, who ever since I can remember have never lived or wanted to live for my own pleasure and have always striven for the liberation of others. Do not take this as boasting—I tell *it to you* and to friends. I feel that it is necessary and right to say it to you once and for all.

It is clear that in order to devote myself fully to the service of the cause, I must have the means to live. I am getting old. Eight years of imprisonment have led to a chronic illness and my impaired health demands certain care and certain conditions so that I can usefully serve the cause. I also have a wife and children whom I cannot condemn to death by starvation.

I try to reduce expenses to the minimum, but I still cannot exist without a certain monthly sum. Where can I get this sum if I give all my labour to the common cause?

There is another consideration. Having founded some years ago the secret International Revolutionary Union, I cannot and will not abandon it in order to devote myself entirely to the Russian cause. And besides, in my opinion, the international and the Russian cause are one and the same. Up to now the international cause did not provide me with the means of existence, but only involved me in expense. This, in a few words, is the key to my situation. You will understand that this poverty on the one hand, and ignoble slander spread about me by the Russian *émigrés* on the other, hamper me in relation to all new people and to all my activities. You see how many reasons there were not to foist myself upon you, not to demand your trust to a greater extent than you deemed useful; to wait until you and your friends should finally be convinced of the possibility, the usefulness, and the necessity of trust.

At the same time I saw and felt very keenly that in approaching me not as an equal, not as a trusting person or a trustworthy one, you considered me, according to your system and obeying so to say the logic of necessity, a three-quarters blind but experienced instrument for the cause and used my name and my activity as a means. Thus, in fact, lacking the power which you pretended to have, you used my name in order to create power in Russia. So that many people do in fact think that I stand at the head of a secret society about which, as you are aware, I know nothing.

Should I have allowed my name to be used as a means of propaganda and in order to attract people into an organization whose plans and immediate aims were three-quarters unknown to me? Without hesitation I reply in the affirmative, yes, I could and should. Here are my reasons:

Firstly, I was always convinced that the Russian Revolutionary Committee could and should act only within Russia, and it is an absurdity to lead the Russian revolution from abroad.

If you and your friends remained abroad for a long time, I should have proclaimed you incapable of remaining members of the Committee. If you become *émigrés*, you will have, as I have had, to accept orders, as far as any Russian movement is concerned, from the undisputed leadership of a new Committee in Russia recognized by you on the basis of mutually discussed programmes and plans; while you yourself would have to create a Russian Committee Abroad for independent management of all Russian relations, activities, individuals and groups abroad, in full agreement with the views of the Russian Committee, but with suitable autonomy in the choice of men and methods of action and, most important, in complete agreement with the International Union. In such a case I would demand, as my duty and right, full membership of this Russian Committee Abroad, which I did, by the way, in my last letter to the Committee and to you,[22] recognizing the fact that the Russian Committee must be within Russia itself. Obviously I did not wish, nor was I able, to return to Russia, and so do not desire to be a member of that. I got to know its programme and the general aims of its activity through you. I was in full agreement with you and expressed my readiness and my firm resolution to help and serve it by all means available to me. Since *you* considered my name useful for attracting new people into *your* organization, I gave you my name. I knew that it would be used for the cause and our common programme and that your character was a guarantee of this, and was not afraid that, as a consequence of mistakes and blunders, I might be generally condemned—I am used to insults.

However, you remember that last summer we agreed that all Russian efforts and persons abroad should be known to me, and nothing that was done or undertaken abroad should be done without my knowledge and consent. This was an essential condition. Firstly, because I know the world abroad much better than any of you and, secondly, because a blind and dependent solidarity with you in actions and publications abroad might conflict with my duties and rights as a member of the International Union. This condition, as we shall see, was not carried out by you and if *it is not going to be* carried out *completely*, I shall be forced to break off all intimate political relations with you.[23]

To begin with, my views are different in that they do not acknowledge the usefulness, or even the possibility, of any revolution except a spontaneous or a people's social revolution. I am deeply convinced that any other revolution is dishonest, harmful, and spells death to liberty and the people. It dooms them to new penury and new slavery. But the main point is that any other revolution has now become impossible and unattainable. Centralization and civilization; railways, the telegraph, new arms and new military organization; in general the techniques of administration, *i.e.*, the science of systematic enslavement and exploitation of the masses of the people; and the science and suppression of people's and all other riots, carefully worked out, tested by experiment and perfected in the last seventy-five years of contemporary history—all this has at present armed the state with such enormous power that all contrived secret conspiracies and non-popular attempts, sudden attacks, surprises and coups—are bound to be shattered against it. It can only be conquered by a spontaneous people's revolution.

Thus the sole aim of a secret society must be, not the creation of an artificial power outside the people, but the rousing, uniting and organizing of the spontaneous power of the people; therefore, the only possible, the only real revolutionary army is not outside the people, it is the people itself. It is impossible to arouse the people artificially. People's revolutions are born from the course of events, or from historical currents which, continuously and usually slowly, flow underground and unseen within the popular strata, increasingly embracing, penetrating, and undermining them, until they emerge from the ground and their turbulent waters break all barriers and destroy everything that impedes their course.

Such a revolution cannot be artificially induced. It is even impossible to hasten it, although I have no doubt that an efficient and intelligent organization can facilitate the explosion. There are historical periods when revolutions are simply impossible; there are other periods when they are inevitable. In which of the two periods are we today? I am deeply convinced that we are in a period of a general, inevitable popular revolution. I will refrain from proving the truth of this conviction because this will lead me too far. Furthermore, it is unnecessary for me to prove it as I address a man and people who, I think, fully share this conviction. I maintain that a popular social revolution is inevitable everywhere within Europe as a whole. Will it catch fire soon and where first? In Russia, or in France, or elsewhere in the West? Nobody can foretell. Perhaps it will blaze up in a year's time, or even earlier, or perhaps in ten or twenty years. This does not matter, and the people who intend to serve it honestly, do not serve for their own pleasure. All secret societies who wish to be really useful to it must, first of all, renounce all nervousness, all impatience. They must not sleep; on the contrary, they must be as ready as possible every minute of the time, alert and always capable of seizing every opportunity. But, at the same time, they must be harnessed and organized, not with a view to an imminent rising, but aiming at long and patient underground work, taking as an example your friends the Jesuit Fathers.

I will confine my considerations to Russia. When will the Russian revolution break out? We do not know. Many, and I a sinner among them, expected a people's rising in 1870, but the people did not awake. Must we conclude that the Russian people can do without the revolution, that it will pass them by? No, this conclusion is impossible; it would be nonsense. Whoever knows the desperate, indeed critical condition of our people economically and politically and, on the other hand, the absolute incapacity of our government and our state not only to alter it, but to ameliorate it at all, an incapacity stemming not from one or another characteristic of the individuals in our government, but from the very essence of any government structure and our government in particular, must conclude that the Russian people's revolution is inevitable. It is not only negatively but positively inevitable, because our people, in spite of its ignorance, has historically arrived at an ideal which it strives, consciously or not, to achieve. This ideal is the common ownership of land with freedom from state oppression and all extortion. The people tried to achieve this under the False Dimitris, under Stenka Razin, and under Pugachev, and still tries by means of continual riots which are, however, scattered and therefore always suppressed.

I have merely pointed out the two main features of the Russian people's ideal and do not claim to describe it fully in a few words. One does not know what else exists in the intellectual aspirations of the Russian people and what will emerge in the light of day with the first revolution. At the moment it suffices for me to prove that our land is not a blank page on which any secret society can write whatever it wishes—for instance, say, your Communist Programme. It has worked out, partly consciously, probably three-quarters unconsciously, its own programme which the secret society must get to know or guess and to which it would have to adapt itself if it wants to succeed.

It is an indisputable and well-known fact that under Stenka Razin and also under Pugachev, every time the people's rising succeeded for a while, the people did one thing only: they took all the land into common ownership, sent the landowning gentry and the Tsar's government officials, sometimes the clergy as well, to the devil and organized its own free commune. This means that our people holds in its memory and as its ideal one precious element which the Western people do not possess, that is, *a free economic community*. In our people's life and thought there are two principles, two facts on which we can build: frequent riots and a free economic community. There is a third principle, a third fact, this is the Cossacks and the world of brigands and thieves which includes both protest against oppression by the state and by the patriarchal society and incorporates, so to say, the first two features.

Frequent riots, although they are always provoked by accidental circumstances, nevertheless stem from general causes and express the deep and general dissatisfaction of the people. They constitute, in a way, an everyday and customary phenomenon of the Russian people's life. There is no village in Russia which is not deeply discontented with its condition, which does not experience poverty, overcrowding, oppression, and which does not hide, in the depth of its collective heart, the desire to seize all the land belonging to the landlords and then that of the richer peasants *(kulaks)*, and the conviction that this is its indubitable right. There is no village which, with skill, cannot be induced to revolt. If the villages do not revolt more often, this is due to fear or to a realization of their weakness. This awareness comes from the disunity of peasant communes, from the lack of real solidarity among them. If each village knew that when it rises all others will rise, one could say for certain that there is no village in Russia which would not revolt. Hence it follows that the first duty, purpose and aim of a secret organization is to awaken in all peasant communities a realization of their inevitable solidarity and thus to arouse the Russian people to a consciousness of their power—in other words, to merge the multitude of private peasant revolts into one general all-people's revolt.

One of the main means for the achievement of this aim, I am deeply convinced, must and should be our free Cossacks, our innumerable saintly and not so saintly tramps *(brodiagi)*, pilgrims, members of *"beguny"* sects,[24] thieves, and brigands— this whole wide and numerous underground world which from time immemorial has protested against the state and statism and against the Teutonic civilization of the whip. This was expressed in the anonymous broadsheet *Statement of the Revolutionary Question* which provoked a howl of indignation from all our vainglorious chatterers who take their doctrinaire Byzantine words for deeds.[25] This, however, is quite correct and is confirmed by all our history. The world of Cossacks, thieves, brigands and tramps played the role of a catalyst and unifier of separate revolts under Stenka Razin and under Pugachev. The tramping fraternity are the best and truest conductors of people's revolution, promoters of general popular unrest, this precursor of popular revolt. Who does not know that tramps, given the opportunity, easily turn into thieves and brigands? In fact, who among us in Russia is not a brigand and a thief? Is it perhaps the government? Or our official and private speculators and fixers? Or our landowners and our merchants? For myself, I cannot tolerate either brigandage or thieving, nor any other anti-human violence. But I confess, if I had to choose between the brigandage and thieving of those occupying the throne and enjoying all privileges, and popular thieving and brigandage, I would, without hesitation, take the side of the latter. I find it natural, necessary, and even, in some sense, legal. I must confess that the popular world of brigands is far from beautiful from the truly human point of view. But what is beautiful in Russia? Can anything be dirtier than our respectably official or civilized bourgeois and decent world, which hides under its smooth Western form the most horrible depravity of thought, feelings, relationships and deeds, or at best a joyless and inescapable emptiness! On the other hand, the people's depravity is natural, forceful and vital. By sacrifice over many centuries the people have earned the right to it. It is a mighty protest against the root cause of all depravity and against the state and, therefore, contains the seeds of the future. That is why I am on the side of popular brigandage and see in it one of the most essential tools for the future people's revolution in Russia.

I understand that this could enrage our scrupulous or even unscrupulous idealists—idealists of all colours from Utin to Lopatin, who imagine that they can force on the people their ideas, their will, and their mode of action through an artificial secret organization. I do not believe in this possibility and am convinced that as soon as the All-Russian state is destroyed, from wherever this destruction comes, the people will rise not for Utin's, or Lopatin's, or even for *your* ideal, but for *their own*, that no artificial conspiratorial force will be capable of containing or even altering its *native* movement—as no dam can contain a turbulent ocean. You, my friends, will be sent flying like chips of wood, if you cannot swim with the popular current. I am certain that with the first big popular revolt, the world of tramps, thieves and brigands, which is firmly imbedded in our life and constitutes one of its essential manifestations, will be on the move and will move powerfully and not weakly.

Be it good or bad, it is an indisputable and inevitable fact, and whoever really wishes for a Russian popular revolution, wants to serve it, help it, organize it, not on paper only but in deed, must know this. Moreover, he must take this fact into account and not try to avoid it; he must establish conscious and practical relations with it and be able to use it as a powerful instrument for the triumph of the revolution. It is no use being too scrupulous about it. He who wishes to retain his ideal and virginal purity should stay in the study, dream, think, write discourses or poetry. He who wants to be a real revolutionary in Russia must take off his gloves; no gloves will save him from the deep and all-embracing Russian mud. The Russian world, both privileged state and popular, is a terrible world. A Russian revolution will certainly be a terrible revolution. Whoever is frightened of horrors or dirt should turn away from this world and this revolution. He who wants to serve the latter must know what he is facing, must strengthen his nerves, and be prepared for anything.

It is not easy to use the world of brigandage as a weapon of the people's revolution, as a catalyst of separate popular revolts; I recognize the necessity, but, at the same time, am fully conscious of my incapacity for this task. In order to undertake it and bring it to a conclusion, one must be equipped with strong nerves, the strength of a giant, passionate conviction, and iron will. You might find such people in your ranks. But people of our generation and with our upbringing are incapable of it. To join the brigands does not mean becoming wholly one of them, sharing with them all their unquiet passions, misfortunes, frequently ignoble aims, feelings and actions; but it does mean giving them new souls and arousing within them a new, truly popular aim. These wild and cruelly coarse people have a fresh, strong, untried and unused nature which is open to lively propaganda, obviously only if the propaganda is lively and not doctrinaire and is capable of reaching them. I could say much more on this subject should our correspondence continue.

Another precious element in the future life of the Russian people is, as mentioned before, the free economic commune, a truly precious element which does not exist in the West. The Western social revolution will have to create this necessary and basic embryo of all future organization, and its creation will give a lot of trouble to the West. Here it is created already. Should revolution occur in Russia, should the state with all its officials fall into ruin, the Russian peasantry would organize itself without any trouble the same day. But Russia is faced with a difficulty of another kind which does not exist in the West. Our communes are terribly scattered, hardly know each other and are often at enmity with each other, according to the old Russian custom. Lately, *thanks to the government's financial measures*, they are becoming used to being joined into rural districts *(Volosti)* so that a rural district is progressively acquiring some popular awareness and content, but that is all. Rural districts do not know and do not want to know anything about each other. In order to achieve revolutionary success, to organize future popular liberty, it is essential that rural districts should, of *their own popular volition*, join into larger districts *(Uezdy)* and these into regions *(Oblasti)*. Regions should set up a free Russian Federation.

To awaken in our communes the consciousness of this necessity, for the sake of their own liberty and advantage, is again the task of the secret organization, since nobody else will want to take on this job which is totally contrary to the interests of the state and all privileged classes. This is no place to describe at length how to approach it, and how and what to do to awaken in the communes this saving consciousness, the only one promising salvation.

There, dear friend, are the main lines of a whole programme for the Russian popular revolution which is deeply imprinted on the people's instinct, on the whole situation of our people. He who wants to be at the head of a popular movement must adopt it as a whole and execute it. He who tries to foist *his own* programme on the people will be left holding the baby.

As a result of its ignorance and disunity, the people are unable to formulate the programme, to systematize it and to unite for its sake. Therefore they need helpers. Where can one find these helpers? This is the most difficult question in any revolution. In the West as a whole, up to now, the helpers of the revolution came from the privileged classes, and nearly always became its exploiters. In this respect also, Russia is more fortunate than the West. There is in Russia an enormous number of people who are educated, intelligent, and deprived at the same time of any position and career and without a solution to their problem. At least three-quarters of young persons studying at the present time find themselves in this position, theological students, children of peasants and petty bourgeoisie, children of junior officials and ruined gentry . . . but need one speak about this, you know this world better than I do. If one considers the people as a revolutionary army, here is our General Staff, here is the precious material for a secret organization.

But this world must be really organized and *moralized* while your system depraves it and prepares within it traitors to the system and exploiters of the people. You must remember that there is very little true morality within this world with the exception of a small number of strong and highly moral characters which have emerged, by Darwinian selection, from sordid oppression and inexpressible poverty. They are virtuous, *i.e.* they love the people and stand for justice against any injustice, for all oppressed against all oppressors, only because of their situation, not consciously or deliberately. Choose a hundred people by lot out of this world and put them in a situation which would enable them to exploit and oppress the people—one can be sure that they will exploit and oppress it. It follows that there is little original virtue in them. One must use their poverty-stricken condition which makes them virtuous in spite of themselves and, by constant propaganda and the power of organization, arouse this virtue, educate it, confirm it in them and make it passionately conscious. Whereas you do the opposite: following the Jesuit system you systematically kill all personal human feeling in them, all feeling of personal fairness—as if feeling and fairness could be impersonal —educate them in lying, suspicion, spying and denunciation, relying much more on the external hobbles with which you have bound them, than on their inner courage. It follows that should circumstances change, should they realize that the terror of the state is stronger than the fear which you inspire,

257

they would (educated by you) become excellent state servants and spies. The fact is now indisputable, my dear friend, that the overwhelming majority of your comrades who have fallen into the hands of the police have betrayed everything and everybody without any special efforts by the government and without torture. This sad fact should open your eyes and make you change the system if you are at all capable of amendment.

How can this world be made more moral? By arousing in it frankly and consciously, by strengthening within its reason and heart one all-embracing passion for the liberation of the people and all mankind. This is the new and only religion which has the power to move souls and create a collective force of salvation. From now on this must be the exclusive content of our propaganda. Its immediate aim is the creation of a secret organization, an organization which should, at one and the same time, create a popular auxiliary force and become a practical school of moral education for all its members.

Let us first of all define more exactly the aim, meaning, and purpose of this organization. As I have mentioned several times above, according to my system it would not constitute a revolutionary army—we should have only one revolutionary army: the people—the organization should only be the staff of this army, an organizer of the people's power, not its own, a middle-man between popular instinct and revolutionary thought. A revolutionary idea is revolutionary, vital, real and true only because it expresses and only as far as it represents popular instincts which are the result of history. To strive to foist on the people *your own* thoughts—foreign to its instinct —implies a wish to make it subservient to a new state. Therefore, an organization sincerely wishing only for a liberation of people's life, must adopt a programme which should express popular demands as fully as possible. It seems to me that the programme delineated in the first number of *The People's Cause (Narodnoe Delo)* fully answers this purpose. It does not foist upon the people any new regulations, orders, styles of life, but merely unleashes its will and gives wide scope to its self-determination and its economic and social organization, which must be created by itself from below and not from above. The organization must accept in all sincerity the idea that it is a servant and a helper, but never a commander of the people, never under any pretext its manager, not even under the pretext of the people's welfare.

The organization is faced with an enormous task: not only to prepare the success of the people's revolution through propaganda and the unification of popular power; not only to destroy totally, by the power of this revolution, the whole existing economic, social, and political order; but, in addition, having survived the success of the revolution, to make impossible after the popular victory the establishment of any state power over the people—even the most revolutionary, even your power—because any power, whatever it called itself, would inevitably subject the people to old slavery in a new form. Therefore our organization must be strong and vital to survive the first victory of the people and—this is not at all a simple matter—the organization must be so deeply imbued with its principles that one could hope that even in the midst of revolution it will not change its thoughts, or character or direction.

Which, then, should be this direction? What would be the main purpose and task of the organization? *To help the people to achieve self-determination on a basis of complete and comprehensive human liberty, without the slightest interference from even temporary or transitional power,* i.e. *without any mediation of the state.*

We are bitter foes of all *official power,* even if it were ultra-revolutionary power. We are enemies of all publicly acknowledged dictatorship; we are social-revolutionary anarchists. But you will ask, if we are anarchists, by what right do we wish to and by what method can we influence the people? Rejecting any power, by what power or rather by what force shall we direct the people's revolution? *An invisible force—recognized by no one, imposed by no one—through which the collective dictatorship of our organization will be all the mightier, the more it remains invisible and unacknowledged, the more it remains without any official legality and significance.*

Imagine yourself in the midst of a successful spontaneous revolution in Russia. The state and with it all socio-political order is in ruins. The people has risen, has taken all it needed and has chased away all its oppressors. Neither law nor power exist any longer. The stormy ocean has burst all dams. This far from homogeneous, on the contrary extremely varied mass, the Russian people, covers the illimitable space of the Russian Empire. It has begun to live and act for itself as it really is, and no longer as it was ordered to be, everywhere in its own way— general anarchy. The enormous quantity of mud which has accumulated within the people is stirred and rises to the surface. In various places emerge a large number of new, brave, clever, unscrupulous and ambitious people who, of course, attempt each in his own way to obtain the people's trust and to direct it to his own advantage. These people come into collision, fight and destroy each other. It seems this is a terrible and hopeless anarchy.

But imagine, in the midst of this general anarchy, a secret organization which has scattered its members in small groups over the whole territory of the Empire but, is nevertheless, firmly united: inspired by a common ideal and a common aim which are applied everywhere, of course modified according to prevailing conditions: an organization which acts everywhere according to a common plan. These small groups, unknown by anybody as such, have no officially recognized power but they are strong in their ideal, which expresses the very essence of the people's instincts, desires and demands, strong also in their clearly realized purpose among a mass of people struggling without purpose or plan. Finally, they are strong in their solidarity which ties all the obscure groups into one organic whole, in the intelligence and energy of their members who have managed to create around themselves a circle of people more or less devoted to the same ideal and naturally subject to their influence—these groups will be able to lead the popular movement without seeking for themselves privileges, honours or power, in defiance of all ambitious persons who are divided and fighting among themselves and to lead it to the greatest possible realization of the socio-economic ideal and to the organization of fullest liberty for the people. This is what I call *the collective dictatorship* of the secret organization.

This dictatorship is free from all self-interest, vanity, and ambition for it is anonymous, invisible, and does not give advantage or honour or official recognition of power to a member of the group or to the groups themselves. It does not threaten the liberty of the people because it is free from all official character. It is not placed above the people like state power because its whole aim, defined by its programme, consists of the fullest realization of the liberty of the people.

This dictatorship is not contrary to the free development and self-determination of the people, or its organization from below according to its own customs and instincts for it acts on the people only by the natural personal influence of its members who are not invested with any power and are scattered like an invisible net in all regions, districts, and rural communities and, each one in his own place and in agreement with others, trying to direct the spontaneous revolutionary movement of the people towards a general plan which has been fully agreed and defined beforehand. This plan for the organization of the people's liberty must firstly be firmly and clearly delineated as regards its main principles and aims in order to exclude any possibility of misunderstanding and deviation by its members who will be called upon to help in its realization. Secondly, it must be sufficiently wide and human to embrace and take in all the inescapable changes which arise from differing circumstances, all varied movements arising from the variety of national life.

Thus the problem is at present how to organize from elements which we know and to which we have access this secret collective dictatorship and strength—which could, firstly, disseminate at present a wide popular propaganda, a propaganda which would *really* penetrate among the people, and by the power of this propaganda and by *organization within the people itself* unite the divided strength of the people into a mighty force which could break the state—and, secondly, which is capable of remaining in being in the midst of revolution itself without breaking apart or altering its direction on the morrow of the people's liberation.

This organization, particularly its basic nucleus, must be composed of persons who are most determined, *most intelligent and as far as possible knowledgeable,* i.e. *intelligent by experience,* who are passionately and undeviatingly devoted, who have, as far as possible, renounced all personal interests and have renounced once and for all, for life, or for death itself, all that attracts people, all material comforts and delights, all satisfaction of ambition, status, and fame. They must be totally and wholly absorbed by one passion, the people's liberation. They must be persons who would renounce personal historical importance while they are alive and even a name in history after their death.

Such complete self-denial is only possible in the presence of passion. It cannot be arrived at by a consciousness of absolute duty, but even less by a system of external control, of restriction and compulsion. Passion alone can bring about this miracle within a man, this strength without effort. Where does passion come from, and how does it arise in a man? It comes from life and arises through an interaction of life and thought; negatively, as a protest hating all that exists and oppresses; positively, in the society of people of the same mind and with the same feelings, as a collective creation of a new ideal. Nevertheless, one must point out that this passion is only real and salutary when both sides, the positive and the negative, are closely connected in it. Hate, the negative side alone, does not create anything, does not even create the power necessary for destruction and thus destroys nothing. The positive side alone will not destroy anything since the creation of the new is impossible without the destruction of the old, and will not create anything, remaining always a doctrinaire dream or a dreaming doctrine.

Deep passion which cannot be uprooted or shaken is, therefore, the foundation of everything. Without it, even if he is the wisest of men, if he is the most honest of men, he would not have the strength to carry on to the end the fight against the terrible socio-political power which oppresses us all. He would not have the strength to withstand all the difficulties, possibilities, and (most of all) the disappointments which await him and which he will meet without fail in this unequal and daily struggle. A passionless man would not have the strength, faith, or initiative; he would not have the courage; and this business cannot be carried out without courage. But passion alone is not enough. Passion engenders energy, but energy without sensible guidance is fruitless and absurd. Allied to passion there must be reason, cold, calculating, real and practical, but also based on theory, educated by knowledge and experience, wide-ranging but not overlooking details, capable of understanding and discerning people, capable of grasping the realities, relationships and conditions of social life in all strata of society and in all their manifestations, in their true aspect and sense and not arbitrarily and in a dream, as is often done by my friend, namely, you. Finally, it is necessary to know well both Russia and Europe and the real social and political situation in both. Thus passion, while always remaining the basic element, must be led by reason and knowledge, must not rush aimlessly about but, without losing its inward fire, its fervent inexorability, must become cold and thereby much stronger.

Here is the ideal of the conspirator destined to be a member of the nucleus of the secret organization.

You will ask, where are we to find these people, are there many of them in Russia, or even in the whole of Europe? The point is that according to my system not many are needed. Remember that you do not have to create an army but a revolutionary staff. You might find possibly ten such people who are nearly ready, perhaps fifty or sixty capable of becoming such men and preparing themselves for this role—this is more than enough. I am deeply convinced that you yourself, in spite of all blunders, regrettable and harmful mistakes, in spite of a series of disgusting petty and stupid deceits, into which you were drawn only by a false system, not by ambition, vanity, or self-interest, as many, too many people begin to believe, you with whom I would be obliged to break and have resolved to do so if you do not renounce this system—you belong to the number of these rare people. *This is the only reason for my love for you, my faith in you in spite of everything, and my patience with you, a patience which, however, is now exhausted.* In addition to all your terrible shortcomings and abortive thinking, I recognized and continue to recognize in you an intelligent, strong and energetic man, capable of cold calculation and, be it from inexperience, ignorance, and frequently from false argument, capable also of complete self-denial. A man passionately and wholly devoted and consecrated to the cause of popular liberation.

Renounce your system and you will become a valuable man; if, however, you do not wish to renounce it, you will certainly become a harmful militant, highly destructive not to the state but to the cause of liberty. But I very much hope that the latest events in Russia and abroad have opened your eyes and that you will want and understand the necessity of joining hands with us on a basis of sincerity. In that case, I repeat, we shall acknowledge you as a valuable man and will gladly recognize you as our leader for all Russian activities. But if you are as I described, then surely there will be found in Russia at least ten people like you. If they have not yet been found, look for them and set up a new society with them on the following principles and mutual conditions:

1. To adopt fully, wholly and passionately the above-mentioned programme in *The People's Cause (Narodnoe Delo)*, with additions and clarifications which seem necessary to you.

2. Equality among all members and their unconditional and absolute solidarity—one for all and all for one—with the obligation for each and everyone to help each other, support and save each other to the uttermost, in as much as it is possible without danger of annihilation to the society itself.

3. Complete frankness among members and proscription of any Jesuitical methods in their relationship, of all ignoble distrust, all perfidious control, of spying and mutual accusations, the absence and a positive strict prohibition of all tattling behind members' backs. When a member has to say anything against another member, this must be done at a general meeting and in his presence. *General fraternal control* of each other, a control which should not be captious or petty and above all not malicious. This type of control must take the place of your system of Jesuitical control and must become a moral education, a support for the moral strength of each member. It must be the basis of *mutual fraternal trust* on which rests all the internal and, therefore, external power of the society.

4. All weak-nerved, cowardly, ambitious and self-seeking people are excluded from the society. They can be used as weapons by the society without their knowledge, but on no account must they belong to its nucleus.

5. In joining the society, every member condemns himself for ever to be socially unknown and insignificant. All his energy and all his intel-

ligence belong to the society and must be directed not to the creation of
personal social strength, but to the collective strength of the organization. Each must be convinced that personal influence is powerless and
fruitless and that only collective strength can overcome the common
enemy and achieve the common positive aim. Therefore collective
passion must gradually be substituted for personal passions within each
member.

6. Everyone's personal intelligence vanishes like a river in the sea in
the collective intelligence and all members obey unconditionally the
decisions of the latter.

7. All members are equal; they know all their comrades and discuss
and decide with them all the most important and essential questions
bearing on the programme of the society and the progress of the cause.
The decision of the general meeting is absolute law.

8. In principle each member has the right to know everything. But
idle curiosity is forbidden in the society as is aimless talk about the
business and aims of the secret society. Knowing the general programme and the general direction of affairs, no member asks or tries
to find out details which are not needed for better execution of that part
of the enterprise with which he is entrusted and, if it is not necessary in
practice, will not talk with any of his comrades about it.

9. The society chooses an Executive Committee from among their
number consisting of three or five members who should organize the
branches of the society and manage its activities in all the regions of the
Empire on the basis of the programme and general plan of action
adopted by the decision of the society as a whole.

10. This Committee is elected for an indefinite term. If the society—I
shall call it the People's Fraternity—if the People's Fraternity is satisfied
with the actions of the Committee, it will be left as such; and while it
remains a Committee each member of the People's Fraternity and each
regional group have to obey it unconditionally, except for such cases
where the orders of the Committee contradict either the general programme of the principal rules, or the general revolutionary plan of
action, which are known to everybody as all the Brothers have participated equally in the discussion of them.

11. In such a case members of the group must halt the execution of
the Committee's orders and call the Committee to judgement before
the general meeting of the People's Fraternity. If the general meeting is
discontented with the Committee, it can always substitute another one
for it.

12. Any member and any group is subject to judgement by the general
meeting of the People's Fraternity.

13. Since each Brother knows everything and knows even the per-
sonnel of the Committee, the acceptance of a new member among them
must be conducted with extreme caution, difficulties and obstacles.

One bad choice can ruin everything. No new Brother can be accepted without the consent of all or at the very least three-quarters of all the members of the People's Fraternity.

14. The Committee divides the members of the Fraternity among the Regions and constitutes Regional groups of leaderships from them. This leadership could consist of one Brother alone, if there are too few members.

15. Regional leadership is charged with organizing the second tier of the society—the *Regional Fraternity*, on the basis of the same programme, the same rules, and the same revolutionary plan.

16. All members of the *Regional Fraternity* know each other, but do not know of the existence of the *People's Fraternity*. They only know that there exists a *Central Committee* which hands down to them their orders for execution through *Regional Committee* which has been set up by it, *i.e.* by the *Central Committee*.

17. As far as possible the Regional Committee is composed exclusively of People's Brothers appointed and replaced by the Central Committee, with at least one People's Brother. In such a case this Brother, with the consent of the C.C., will appoint the two best members of the Regional Fraternity to act jointly with himself as a Regional Committee; but these will not have equal membership rights in so far as only the People's Brother will be in contact with the C.C. whose orders he will pass on to his comrades of the Regional Committee.

18. People's Brothers or Brothers in the regions will seek out from among members of the Regional Fraternity people capable and worthy of being admitted to the People's Fraternity, and will introduce them through the C.C. to the general meeting of the People's Fraternity.

19. Each Regional Committee will set up *District* Committees from members of *Regional Fraternity* and will appoint and replace them.

20. District Committees can, if necessary and only with the consent of the Regional Committee, set up a third tier of the organization— *District Fraternity* with a programme and regulations as near as possible to the general programme and regulations of the People's Fraternity. The programme and regulations of the District Fraternity will not come into force until they are discussed and passed by the general meeting of the Regional Fraternity and have been confirmed by the Regional Committee.

21. Jesuitical control and a system of entanglement by police methods and lies are totally excluded from all three tiers of the secret organization, likewise from the District, Regional, and People's Fraternities. The strength of the whole society, as well as the morality, loyalty, energy and dedication of each member, is based exclusively and totally on the shared truth, sincerity and trust, and on the open fraternal control of all over each one.

Here you have the main outline of a plan for the society such as I conceive it to be. Obviously this plan must be developed, supplemented, and sometimes altered according to circumstances and the character of the environment and should be defined much more clearly. But I am convinced that its essence must remain, if you wish to create a real collective power which is capable of serving the cause of people's liberation and not initiate a new exploitation of the people.

The system of entanglement and of Jesuitical lies is totally excluded from this plan as being harmful, divisive, and corrupting principle and means. But parliamentary chatter and ambitious fussiness are also excluded. Strong discipline of all members in their relations with the Committees and all individual Committees in their relation with the C.C. are retained. The right of judgement and control over members belongs to Fraternities and not to Committees. New executive power is in the hands of the Committees. The right of judgement over Committees, including the Central, is the province of the People's Fraternity alone.

According to my plan the People's Fraternity will never consist of more than fifty to seventy members. At first it will probably consist of ten men or even less and will grow slowly, accepting one man after another, submitting each one to the strictest and most thorough study and, if possible, accepting him only with the unanimous consent of all members of the People's Fraternity, but in any case not less than three-quarters of the Fraternity. It is impossible that in the course of two or three years thirty or forty men cannot be found who would be capable of being People's Brothers.

Imagine the People's Fraternity for the whole of Russia consisting of forty, at most of seventy members. In addition there would be some hundreds of members belonging to the second tier of the organization. Regional Brothers—and you have covered the whole of Russia with a mighty net. Your staff is set up. One has, as mentioned, assured within it—in addition to strict caution and the exclusion of all chatter, all ambitious and idle parliamentary debate—sincerity and mutual trust, real solidarity, as the only moralizing unifying elements.

The whole society constitute's one body and a firmly united whole, led by the C.C. and engaged in unceasing underground struggle against the government and against other societies either inimical to it or even those acting independently of it. Where there is war, there is politics, and there inescapably arises the necessity for violence, cunning, and deceit.

Societies[26] whose aims are near to ours must be forced to merge with our society or, at least, must be subordinated to it without their knowledge, while harmful people must be removed from them. Societies which are inimical or positively harmful must be dissolved, and finally the government must be destroyed. All this cannot be achieved only be propagating the truth; cunning, diplomacy, deceit are necessary. Jesuit methods or even entanglement can be used for this—entanglement is a necessary and marvellous means for demoralizing and destroying the enemy, though *certainly not*[27] a useful means of obtaining and attracting a new friend.

Thus this simple law must be the basis of our activity: truth, honesty, mutual trust between all Brothers and towards any man who is capable of becoming and whom you would wish to become a Brother—lies, cunning, entanglement, and, if necessary, violence towards enemies. In this way you will moralize, strengthen, and unite your own people and destroy the strength of others.

You, my dear friend—and this is a terrible mistake—have become fascinated by the system of Loyola and Machiavelli, the first of whom intended to enslave the whole of mankind, and the second to create a powerful state (whether monarchist or republican is of no importance, it would equally lead to the enslavement of the people). Having fallen in love with police and Jesuitical principles and methods, you intended to base on them your own organization, your secret collective power, so to say, the heart and soul of your whole society. You therefore treat your friends as you treat your enemies, with cunning and lies, try to divide them, even to foment quarrels, so that they should not be able to unite against your tutelage. You look for strength not in their unity but in their disunity and do not trust them at all. You try to collect damning facts or letters (which frequently you have read without having the right to do so, and which are even stolen), and try to entangle them in every way, so that they should be your slaves. At the same time you do it so clumsily, so awkwardly and carelessly, so rashly and in-considerately, that all your deceits, perfidies, and cunning are exposed very quickly. You have fallen so much in love with Jesuit methods that you have forgotten everything else. You have even forgotten the aim which led you to them, the passionate desire for the people's liberation. You have fallen so much in love with Jesuit methods that you are prepared to preach their necessity to anybody, even to Zhukovsky. You even wanted to write about them, to fill *Kolokol (The Bell)* with these theories—reminding one of Suvorov's saying, "Thank goodness, he is not cunning whom everybody knows to be cunning." Briefly, you are playing with Jesuit methods as a child plays with a doll or Utin at Revolution.

Now let us have a look at what you have achieved and have had time to do in Geneva thanks to your Jesuit system. You were given the Bakhmetev fund. This is the only real result which you have achieved. But Ogarev gave it to you and I warmly advised that you should be given it, not because you played the Jesuit with us, but because we felt and recognized in you, in addition to your far-from-clever Jesuitism, a man who is deeply, warmly, and earnestly devoted to the Russian cause. But you know—this is a bitter confession for me—I almost repent that I advised Ogarev to give you the fund. Not because I could think that you might use it dishonestly or for your own advantage—saints preserve me from such an ignoble and simply inept thought! I am prepared to answer with my life that you will never use one penny more than necessary for yourself. No, I begin to repent because, observing your actions, I have stopped believing in your political wisdom, in the earnestness and the reality of your Committee and your whole society. The sum is not large, but it is the only one and it will disappear in vain, uselessly, and wantonly in mad and impossible activities.

You could have done a lot of useful things in Geneva with this modest sum in your hands and with the help of a few people who met you with complete sincerity and expressed their readiness to serve the common cause without demands or claims, without vanity or ambition. You could have set up a serious organ with an avowed social-revolutionary programme and, attached to it, a foreign bureau for the management of Russian activities outside Russia and in a certain, though not absolute but positive [. . .]²⁸ to it. Your Committee, *i.e.* you, invited me to Geneva for this purpose for the first time. What did I find in Geneva? First of all, a mangled programme for *Kolokol* on which the Committee and you made simply absurd and impossible demands. Do you know, I simply cannot forgive my weakness in yielding to you on this question—I have to answer for this poor *Kolokol* and for solidarity with you to all my international friends, thanks on the one hand to Utin and on the other to Zhukovsky, the first of whom slanders me and you maliciously, and the second good-humouredly.

By the way, about Zhukovsky. You demonstrated with regard to him your complete ignorance and your incomprehension of people, your inability to attract them in a straightforward, honest, firm way to your cause. Knowing him intimately, I have described his character to you in detail, his abilities and ineptitudes, so that it should not have been difficult for you to establish serious relations with him. I described him to you as a very kind and able man, far from stupid, although without any intellectual initiative, accepting all ideas at second hand and capable of popularizing them or chattering about them fairly eloquently, not so much on paper as in conversation. As a man of artistic sensibility fairly firmly committed to a certain orientation, but without much character, in the sense that he does not like danger, he bows before strong contradiction and easily succumbs to all sorts of influences. In a word, he is a man very capable of being a conductor of propaganda, but completely incapable of being a member of a secret society. You ought to have believed me, but did not do so; and instead of attracting Zhukovsky to our cause, alienated him from you and from me. You tried to enlist and ensnare him, and having ensnared him, to make him your slave. To do this you started to scold and ridicule me;

but Zhukovsky has an instinct for honesty which rebelled. He told me everything that you told him about me, told it with indignation and scorn and had I been a vainer and weaker man this would have been enough for me to break my connection with you. You will remember that I contented myself with faithfully repeating to you Zhukovsky's words without comment. You did not reply, and I did not think it necessary to continue this discussion. Then you started to explain to Zhukovsky your favourite state-communist and police-Jesuit theories, and this finally estranged him from you. Finally, there was this unfortunate gossip by Henry,[29] and Zhukovsky became your bitter and irreconcilable foe, not only your foe but almost mine as well. And he might have been useful in spite of all his weaknesses.

I must also confess, dear friend, that your system of black-mailing, entangling and scaring Tata was extremely repugnant to me and I told you about this several times. The result was that you instilled in her a deep suspicion towards all of us and a conviction that you and I intended to exploit [her] financial resources and to exploit them, of course, for ourselves and not for the cause. Tata is a truly honest and truthful person in-capable, it seems to me, of giving herself completely to anyone or anything, therefore a dilettante if not by nature then by perception, an intellectual and moral dilettante, whose word, however, one can trust and who is capable of being, if not our friend, at least a true well-wisher. She should have been treated in a straightforward and honest manner, without resorting to the tricks which you think are your strength, but which in fact show your weakness. While I considered it possible and useful to speak to her directly and openly to try to influence her free convictions, I did so. I did not wish to go any further with you in this matter as I found it repugnant. As soon as I heard from you that Natalya Alexeevna had slandered me, maintaining that I had designs on Tata's pocket and saw that Tata herself was doubtful, not knowing whether this was true, I withdrew from her decisively.

By the way, you insisted several times that you heard from Tata herself that Natalya Alexeevna and Tchorzewski claim everywhere, shout and write to everybody, that I want to exploit Tata's financial resources. Natalya Alexeevna and Tchorzewski, on the contrary, maintain that they have never written and said it, and Tata herself confirmed this. During your last visit to Geneva you told me that you heard from Serebrennikov (Semen) that Zhukovsky had told him that I exploit Tata. I asked Serebrennikov and found out that Zhukovsky said that not about me, but about you. You also told me that Zhukovsky's wife tried to persuade you to join Utin, assuring you that an alliance with me was useless, impossible, and harmful. She maintains the contrary: she did not speak about me to you; she did not invite you to join Utin with whom she herself had more or less broken, and that you, not she, proposed that you find funds to achieve this alliance and she was waiting to receive these funds from you.

You see how many unnecessary, stupid lies there are, and how easily they are revealed. Yes, I must confess that my first visit to Geneva[30] had already disappointed me and undermined my faith in the possibility of a firm alliance and common action with you. In addition, not a sensible word was said between us about the business for which I was summoned and solely for which I came to Geneva. Several times I started a discussion about the foreign bureau; you avoided it, awaiting some sort of final answer from the Committee, which never arrived. Finally, I left, having sent through you a letter to the Committee in which I demanded a clear definition and explanation of the business for which I was summoned, firmly intending not to return to Geneva unless I had received a satisfactory reply.

In May you again started asking me to come to Geneva. I refused several times; finally I came. The last trip confirmed all doubts and completely shook my faith in the honesty and truthfulness of your word. Your conversations with Lopatin in my presence on the evening of my arrival: his direct and sharp accusations, which he made to your face with a conviction which did not permit any doubt as to the veracity of his words—words which showed your statements to be lies. His direct contradiction of all details in the story written by you about your escape.[31] His direct accusations against your dearest friends, accusations of ignoble, even stupid treachery before the commission of inquiry, accusations which were not unsupported but based on their written evidence which (according to him and confirmed by you later) he had a chance to read. In particular, the contempt expressed by him about the completely unnecessary denunciation by Pryzhov,[32] of whom you spoke as being one of your best and firmest friends. Finally, his direct and definite denial of the existence of your Committee which was expressed in the following words:

> N[echayev] can tell the story to you who live outside Russia. However, he will not repeat all this in my presence, knowing full well that I am familiar with all the groups, all the people and all attitudes and facts in Russia. You see that he confirms by his silence the truth of all I say both about his escape, the circumstances of which, as he is aware, are only too well known to me, down to the smallest detail, and I know also about his friends and imaginary Committee.

And in fact you remained silent and did not attempt to defend yourself, or any of your friends, or even the reality of the existence of your Committee.

He triumphed; you retreated before him. I cannot express to you, my dear friend, how hurt I was both for your sake and for mine. I could not doubt the truth of Lopatin's words any longer. It followed that you systematically lied to us, that your whole enterprise was riddled with rotten lies and was founded on sand. It meant that your Committee consisted of you accounting for at least three-quarters of it, with a following of two, three, or four people who are subordinate to you, or at least under your predominant influence. It meant that the cause to which you had entirely dedicated your life had burst, dissipated in a puff of smoke, as a result of false and stupid orientation, as a result of your Jesuitical system which had corrupted you and, even more, your friends. I loved you deeply and still love you, Nechayev. I firmly, too firmly, believed in you and to see you in such a position, so humiliated in front of the chatterer Lopatin, was inexpressibly bitter to me.

s

I was also hurt on my own account. Carried away by my faith in you, I gave you my name and publicly espoused your cause. I tried as much as I could to strengthen Ogarev's sympathy towards you and his faith in your cause. I continually advised him to give up to you all the money. I attracted Ozerov to you and spared no efforts in order to persuade Tata to join us, *i.e.* you, and to devote herself wholly to your cause. Finally, against my better judgement, I persuaded Ogarev to agree to publish *Kolokol* according to the wild and impossible programme invented by you. Briefly, having complete faith in you, while you systematically duped me, I turned out to be a complete fool. This is painful and shameful for a man of my experience and my age. Worse than this, I spoilt my situation with regard to the Russian and the International causes.

When Lopatin left, I asked you: Is it possible that he told the truth, that everything you told me was a lie? You evaded an answer. It was late and I left. All the conversations and discussions with Lopatin the following day finally convinced me that Lopatin told the truth. You were silent. I awaited the result of your last talk with Lopatin; you did not tell me about it, but I found it out from Lopatin's letter which Ozerov will read to you.[33]

What I found out was enough to induce me to take measures against further exploitation of myself and my friends by you. Accordingly I wrote you an ultimatum which I hastily read to you at the Turks[34] and which you appeared to accept.

Since then I have not seen you.

The day before yesterday I finally received a letter from Lopatin from which I gathered two rather sad facts: firstly you (I do not wish to use any adjectives) you lied when you reported to me your talk with Lopatin. Everything you told me about his alleged words was a complete lie. He did not tell you that I gave him letters from Lyubavin: "The old man could not hold out, he is in our hands now and cannot do anything against us, and we can now all . . .", to which you were supposed to have replied: "If Bakunin was so weak as to give you Lyubavin's letters, we have other letters, etc."[35] You lied, you slandered Lopatin, and you deliberately duped me. Lopatin is surprised that I believed you, and in a polite form deduces from this fact a conclusion less than flattering to my mental capacities. He is right. In this case I showed myself a complete fool. He would not have judged me quite so severely had he known how deeply, how passionately, how tenderly I loved you and believed in you! You were able, and found it useful, to kill this belief in me—so much the worse for you. How could I think that a man who was intelligent and devoted to the cause, as you still remain in my eyes in spite of all that has happened—how could I imagine that you would tell such barefaced and stupid lies[36] to me of whose devotion you could have no doubts? Why did you not realize that your impudent lies would be discovered and that I would demand, would have to demand, an explanation from Lopatin, the more so because my ultimatum contained a clearly expressed demand that the Lyubavin affair must be completely clarified? *Another fact*: Lyubavin did not get my reply to his rude letter, therefore he did not receive my receipt which I enclosed with this reply. When I showed you my reply and receipt, you asked me to wait and not send them. I did not agree, and you offered to post them but did not do so.

This is enough, Nechayev—our old relationship and our mutual obligations are at an end. You yourself have destroyed them. If you thought and still think that you have bound me, entangled me morally and materially, you are completely mistaken. Nothing on earth can bind me against my conscience, against my honour, against my will, against my revolutionary convictions and duty.

It is true that thanks to you my financial position is now very difficult. I have no means of existence, and my only source of income, translating Marx and the hope of other literary work connected with it, has now dried up. I am aground and do not know how I shall manage to get off, but that is the least of my troubles.

It is true that I have compromised friends and was compromised in front of them. It is true that I am being slandered in connection with the fund, in connection with Tata, and finally in connection with all the recent events in Russia.

But all this will not deter me. In case of dire necessity I am prepared for a public admission and confession of my stupidity, of which of course I shall be very much ashamed, but which will reflect even more upon you—but I shall not remain your unwilling ally.

Thus I give notice to you that all my horrid relationships with you and with your cause are at an end. *But in breaking them off I offer you new relations on a different basis.*

Lopatin, who does not know you as well as I do, would have been surprised at my suggestion after all that has happened between us. You will not be surprised, nor will my close friends.

There is no doubt that you have perpetrated many stupidities and many dirty tricks, positively harmful and destructive to the cause. But it is also clear to me that all your inept actions and terrible blunders were not caused by your self-interest, greed, vanity, or ambition, but only by your misunderstanding of the situation. You are a passionately dedicated man; there are few like you. This is your strength, your valour and your justification. You and your Committee, if the latter really exists, are full of energy and are prepared to execute without fuss anything you consider useful for the cause—this is valuable. But neither your Committee nor you possess any common sense—this is now obvious. You have taken to the Jesuit system like children, and seeing in it your whole strength, success, and salvation have forgotten the very essence and aim of the society: liberation of the people not only from the government but from you, from yourselves. Having adopted this system you have carried it to a monstrously stupid extreme, have corrupted yourselves by it and have disgraced the society throughout the world by your only too obvious guile and incredible stupidities—like your stern letters to Lyubavin and to Natalya Alexeevna[37] which were matched by your polite patience towards Utin; like your attempts to ingratiate yourself with him while he slandered all of us loudly and impudently; like your stupid communist programme and a whole series of shameless deceits. All this proves an absence of common sense, an ignorance of people, relationships, and things. It follows that one cannot rely on your common sense, at least at present, in spite of the fact that you are an extremely intelligent man, capable of further development. This, however, gives hope for the future; at present you are as clumsy and inept as a boy.

Having finally convinced myself of this, my position is now as follows:

I do not believe your words, your unsupported assurances and promises which are not confirmed by facts, knowing that you would not hesitate to lie if this seemed to you to be useful to the cause. Nor do I believe in the justice or wisdom of what you imagine to be useful, because you and your Committee have given me too many proofs of your positive lack of sense. But denying your veracity and your wisdom, I do not deny your energy and your undoubted devotion to the cause, and believe that there are few people in Russia equal to you in either. This, I repeat again, was the chief, indeed the only basis of my love for you and my faith in you and I am convinced it still remains a guarantee that you alone of all the Russians I know are capable of serving the revolutionary cause in Russia and destined to do so but only if you want and are able to alter the whole system of your activities in Russia and abroad. However, if you do not wish to change it, you will inevitably become a man highly harmful to the cause as a result of those very qualities which are your strength.

As a consequence of these considerations and in spite of all that has happened between us, I would wish not only to remain allied with you, but to make this union even closer and firmer, on condition that you will change the system entirely and will make mutual trust, sincerity and truth the foundation of our future relations. Otherwise the break between us is inevitable.

Now here are my personal and general conditions. I will enumerate the personal ones first:

1. You must shield and clear me entirely in the Lyubavin affair by writing a collective letter to Ogarev, Tata, Ozerov and S. Serebrennikov in which you will announce, as is indeed the truth, that I did not know

anything about the letter of the Committee and that it has been written without my knowledge and consent.

2. That you have read my reply to Lyubavin with the enclosed receipt for 300 rubles and having undertaken to send it, have either posted it or not.

3. That I have never directly or indirectly interfered in the disposal of the Bakhmetev fund. That you have received the whole of the monies at various times: first from the hands of Herzen[38] and Ogarev and the remaining, larger part from the hands of Ogarev who, after the death of Herzen, was the only one who had the right to dispose of it, and that you received this fund in the name of the Committee whose manager you were.

4. If you have not yet given Ogarev the receipt for this fund, then you must do so.

5. You have to return as soon as possible the note from Danielson through us and through Lopatin. If you have not got it (though I am sure you have) you must in the same letter undertake to deliver it in the shortest possible time.

6. You will abandon purposeless or, worse, positively harmful attempts for a *rapprochement* with Utin, who most vilely slanders both of us and all that is ours in Russia, and on the contrary will undertake, having chosen the right time and occasion in order not to harm the cause, to conduct open war against him.

These are my personal conditions; a refusal of one of them, in particular of the first five and the first half of the sixth (*i.e.* breaking off all ties with Utin) will be sufficient reason for me to break all relations with you. All this has to be done by you generously, frankly, honestly without any misunderstandings, reservations, hints and equivocations. It is time we put our cards on the table.

Here are the general conditions:

1. Without naming the names, which we do not need, you will show us the actual state of your organization and cause in Russia, of your hopes, your propaganda, your movements, without exaggeration and deceit.

2. You will eradicate from your organization any use of police and Jesuitical systems, confining their application to the government and inimical parties and only when it is really necessary in practice and in accordance with common sense.

3. You will drop the absurd idea that revolution can be made outside the people and without its participation, and will adopt as a basis of your organization the spontaneous people's revolution in which the people will be the army and the organization only its staff.

4. You will adopt as a basis of the organization the social-revolutionary programme expounded in the first number of *The People's Cause* [*Narodnoe Delo*], the plan of organization and revolutionary propaganda expounded by me in my letter, with such additions and alterations as we shall together find necessary at a general meeting.

5. All that has been agreed in our common discussion and unanimous decisions will be proposed by you to all your friends in Russia and abroad. Should they reject our decisions, you will have to decide for yourself whether you wish to follow them or us, to break your ties with them or with us.

6. If they accept the programme, organizational plan, the rules of the society, the plan for propaganda and for revolutionary action worked out by us, you will, in your own and their name, give us your hand and your word of honour that from now on this programme, this plan of organization, propaganda and action, will be absolute law and the indispensable basis of the whole society in Russia.

7. We shall believe you and will make a new firm bond with you—Ogarev, Ozerov, S. Serebrennikov and I, possibly Tata, if she should so wish and if you and all the others agree. We shall in truth be People's Brothers who live and act abroad. Therefore, without ever showing any undue curiosity, we shall have the right to know and will indeed know actively and in the necessary detail the situation of conspiratorial affairs and immediate aims in Russia.

8. Then we, all the above-mentioned, will set up a bureau abroad to deal with all Russian affairs abroad, without exception, taking into consideration the lines of Russian policy, but choosing freely methods, people and means.

9. In addition, *Kolokol* will be published with a clear revolutionary, socialist programme, if this is necessary and if money for it is available.

Here are my conditions, Nechayev. If you have been inspired by good sense and sober judgement and if love of the cause is really stronger in you than all other considerations, you will accept them.

And if you do not accept, my decision is inflexible. I shall have to break all ties with you. I will act independently, taking nothing into consideration except my own conscience, understanding, and duty.

M. BAKUNIN

85. M. Bakunin to N. Ogarev, V. Ozerov, S. Serebrennikov and Natalie Herzen

9 JUNE 1870   *Locarno*

HERE, MY FRIENDS, is at last the end of my enormous letter to the Baron. Please read it all attentively. You will find in it many longueurs and repetitions, but I hope that you will agree with its contents and, most important, with its conclusion. If you do agree, will you signify it at the end of the letter by your signature—there is enough space left for all remarks—and try to convey it as soon as possible and, if possible, in person and by hand through Ozerov to the Baron. I have not re-read it and wrote without reflection straight from my head and heart.

The letter is so long, so unbearably long, that I am afraid to ask Tata or friend Sasha, and if not them then Serebrennikov, to copy it from the beginning and keep the copy—nevertheless this is essential for me and for us all.

I hope you will be pleased with my reply to Lopatin which I shall send you tomorrow together with Lopatin's letter (which must be read by Serebrennikov and kept in your hands as neutrals and witnesses; it must also be read to the Baron but not given to him).

Our friend, the Baron, has completely drowned himself in lies and this must be ended. It was with good reason that for several years, from 1863 to 1867, I kept myself apart from Russians and Russian affairs. As soon as I touched them I got into a muck heap, but now I want to keep up with them. It is necessary to unravel the whole thing patiently and put it on a sound basis. If you want to help me, I hope that together we will succeed.

The main thing for the moment is to save our erring and confused friend. In spite of all he remains a valuable man, and there are few valuable men in the world.

Therefore, let us save him together. We will not let Lopatins, Zhukovskys and Utins [. . .] him finally into the mud. First of all it is necessary that he should help us himself—and all our efforts must now be directed to this end.

Yours M. BAKUNIN

86. M. Bakunin to N. Ogarev, N. Herzen, V. Ozerov and S. Serebrennikov

10 JUNE 1870 *Locarno*

WELL, MY DEAR FRIENDS, here is my reply to Lopatin with a receipt for Lyubavin enclosed.[39] I am sending you also Lopatin's letter to me, which you simply must read, but on no account let it fall into the hands of Baron Neville[40]—keep it in your possession as a document which you might need.

Please send my reply on to Lopatin at once, but first make a copy of it to read to the Baron and also to keep in your possession as a document. Whom should I ask to undertake the laborious task of copying it, if not Serebrennikov, who will apparently now be left with no occupation? For myself, I am swamped by various writings and compositions which I shall never have time to complete.

In my reply to Lopatin I have tried as far as possible not to condemn the Baron. A difficult, almost impossible task. Having once convinced myself of his falsehood, I had to call it barefaced lying and so to express my suspicion—not to say my certainty—that he had withheld my letter to Lyubavin.

What can one expect? Our friend, under the spell of this accursed Jesuitical system, has taken to lying and scheming to the point of folly. I say again, we must all of us make every effort to dissuade him from this course which will mean the ruin of himself and the cause.

I repeat for the hundredth time—he is an invaluable person, the most energetic and committed of all the Russians of our acquaintance. He is extremely obstinate, true, but very clever with it, though hardly wise; therefore, by preserving all his valiant features, above all his iron energy, ruthless even to himself, his utter self-abnegation and his passionate and total devotion to the cause—he can change all that is bad in himself.

But it is imperative that he make up his mind to cure himself this very moment, for it will be impossible for us to remain behind him any longer if he does not change his course and his system, and we shall be obliged to break our links with him not only for our honour's sake but for the sake of the cause itself.

His first act as a conspirator and revolutionary ended in what was for him a terrible and shameful fiasco. To persist with a lie which has [already] proved fatal would be unforgivably stupid on his part, and for us to continue to follow him in a direction which we have acknowledged as mistaken and base would be more than stupid.

Ogarev, I absolutely insist that you give me, without delay, through our friends and natural intermediaries, Tata, Ozerov and Serebrennikov, a written affidavit that the entire fund was given over to Nechayev by you and that I had no concern whatsoever in its administration. It is unnecessary to draw up any accounts for this purpose, after all. We shall compile detailed accounts later and demand receipts from Nechayev then. For the moment we can sign a declaration of this kind, worded briefly but clearly and firmly, in order to avert the possibility of any misunderstanding. And your statement can, I believe, be signed by Tata in all good faith, since she was in fact a witness of that transfer, at which I really was not present and the details of which are unknown to me. *I urgently demand such a statement of you, demand it in the name of justice and friendship, and you have not the right to refuse it to me.*[41] It might prove essential to me in view of the malicious and filthy slanders being propagated by Mr Utin, who, I happen to know, is assembling a collection of facts against me to send to Marx. Ozerov writes to me that what is stopping you is a fear of doing damage to the *cause*, that is, something of the nature of a *raison d'État*. But that is unlike you, my dear Ogarev. Such a Jesuitical consideration, a consideration of state, is entirely out of keeping with your character, your spirit and your habits—truth and justice above all, such has always been your motto. Can it be that you too want to become, and can become, a Jesuit in your old age? All this is nonsense, and, moreover, has absolutely nothing to do with *the cause*. It is time we understood, after all, that Nechayev, in spite of all those precious qualities which earned him your and my trust, is, nevertheless, not himself the cause made flesh. The cause is one thing, and he is another, and to identify him with the cause means to abase and to annihilate the cause. First of all we must explain this to [Nechayev] himself, so that he ceases to think of himself as the Louis XIV of revolution: *"L'État (the cause) c'est moi."* Facts of the most tangible kind have proved to us that his dictatorship, the dictatorship of his Committee (which comes to the same thing, because 3/4 or 9/10 of the Committee consists indubitably of himself), that this dictatorship has had disastrous consequences both in Russia and abroad, and therefore the time has come to put an end to it. To continue believing in it and blindly following it would be more than folly on our part—it would be a crime. We know little about the facts in Russia, but what we do know, and what we know as a certainty, weighed against and compared with his own stories, is very bad. On the other hand, we have a full and detailed knowledge of the facts of what is happening abroad, and these facts are sufficient to convince us that [. . .]⁴² the Committee, that is, Nechayev, is filled with energy, passionate activity, devotion to the cause. But he also displays an enormous, staggering lack of wisdom and inward integrity. He has based his entire organization on systematic deceit and the entanglement of people. That is bad, and bad too is the fact that with all his ardent desire to dupe each and everyone, he has not even discovered how to conceal his deception. All his ruses are transparently thin and have been the ruses of either a child or an ostrich hiding its head behind a tree but unable to hide its huge body. This incapacity of Nechayev's for skilful deception cheers me. It means, on the one hand, that falsehood has not yet succeeded in permeating him entirely, in becoming second nature to him, and therefore it will not be difficult for him to rid himself of it. But, on the other hand, taking into account his natural intelligence, this lack of skill bears witness to a dire insufficiency of experience, practical reason, understanding and knowledge of people and things; and what dictator can there be without reason? Can the cause succeed without reason?

We love him, we believe in him, and we are expecting of him activity in the future which will be of great benefit to the people, and this is precisely why we have to halt him on his false and fatal path—but we shall not manage to halt him by force of words or reasoning. Words and reason have no effect upon natures like that of Nechayev, which respect only facts; facts alone can act upon them. That is to say, we have to halt Nechayev by force of the facts. If we were to set about protesting against him by using reasoning and words alone while continuing in fact to follow him blindly, he would listen half-distractedly and half-ironically to us, and continue to ruin the cause and exploit us in the most unscrupulous manner. But if we tell him the truth, all of us together, not individually, and declare that we shall go no further with him along this path, but will separate from him if he will not desist from it, he will have second thoughts and probably give way—and if he does not, then let us have nothing more to do with him! But he will be obliged to yield. We have given him so much proof both of our devotion to the cause and our friendship with him that he cannot doubt the sincerity of our actions and our words. Moreover, he has not many friends left either abroad or in Russia itself. He has been abandoned by everybody, and all respectable people like Lopatin, and all the not-so-respectable ones, such as Utin and *compagnie*, are slinging mud at him.

At this moment, the most critical in his life and the most decisive for all his future activity, the friendly voice of a whole group of honest people willing to support him if he agrees to abandon an obviously pernicious system, but at the same time [. . .][43] to abandon him if, in his *vanity*, obduracy and wilfulness, he wishes to persist in it—such a voice can save him.

He has now to perform one final act of self-determination, gain one final victory over himself, over his *vanity* which appears to be greater than we had imagined. The total shipwreck which has overtaken him both in Russia and abroad must open his eyes. He must acknowledge and have the strength and nobility to admit to us that he was mistaken in his choice of system, persons, and means, and that it behoves him now to change his course and embark upon a new task, on a new basis, using only that portion of the old material which will truly suit his purpose on that new course.

If he proves capable of performing a feat of this nature and achieving such a difficult victory over his pride (which is all the greater for being concealed), over his wilfulness, then he will indeed be a fine man, and we shall be able to go along with him and perhaps even follow him with full confidence. If he is incapable of doing so, or unwilling to do so, then we shall have no alternative but to break with him for the sake of our conscience, our convictions, and the good of the cause itself. Such, for the present, at least, is my immutable resolve.

In what way can the declaration I require of you, my dear Aga—and which I consider I have the right to require of you —harm the cause? In the first place, it will remain a secret, as a document in the possession of our friends, who, it goes without saying, will not divulge its existence. It will be made public only in case of extreme necessity.

And besides that, you must demand—we all must demand— of Nechayev that he give you and all of us a written statement to the effect that he received, first, one part of the Bakhmetev fund from Herzen and yourself, and then the whole of the remainder from you alone, since you had the sole right to dispose of the entire Bakhmetev fund, and that he alone, with or without the Committee's knowledge (we cannot know which), was in charge of the fund and spent it as he saw fit. Not to demand this of him would be a weakness on our part, sheer ignominy, not service to the cause. The affair is clear and demands clarity: the Committee, whether real or imaginary, does not and never did conceal its existence. It has proclaimed itself in preposterous letters to Lyubavin and Natalya Alexeevna, and even in printed form in the *People's Vengeance*.

We—that is, you and I—can be rebuked for having recognized this Committee: I, in print; you, in fact, by handing over the fund. But there can be no doubt that we recognized it as the sole representative of the serious revolutionary cause in Russia. It was on that basis that you gave the fund to Nechayev, as a representative of the Committee, and it was in that capacity that Nechayev took it from you. Consequently there is nothing to hide from the public—everything was done properly.

But do you know what I am beginning to fear? If Nechayev does not want to, or thinks it inconvenient to give you a receipt for the fund, that will be not so much for fear of the public as through misgivings at the thought of his own friends, the members of the so-called Committee, whom perhaps he is deceiving in exactly the same way as he has been deceiving us. He might have told them that he received from you only a part of the fund, or that the fund was administered not at his sole discretion but in conjunction with you and me, or any other lie he thought it necessary to tell, not for his own personal gain, of course, but for the good of the cause. I have a mass of evidence that he has employed his Jesuitical lying absolutely everywhere, including even amongst his own Committee-members. Trusting and believing in no one, he has come to the point where he considers himself the sole and exclusive revolutionary, and with an obduracy comparable to Elpidin's,[44] believes he has the right to dupe each and every man in the name of the revolution. I fervently hope that my fears prove unfounded, but I am very much afraid that they are justified. In any case it is obvious to me that only fear of his friends, not of the revolutionary public or of his enemies, can stop him from giving you this receipt.

That is why you and all of us must persistently and unanimously demand it of him for the salvation of the cause.

M. Bakunin to N. Ogarev, N. Herzen, V. Ozerov and S. Serebrennikov

I end this letter by expressing my hope that after you have read to the last word my long letter to Nechayev, you will agree with its conclusions and on that basis will consent, together with myself, to make a determined joint attempt to save Nechayev from his disastrous falsehood and the common cause from defeat.

Your M. BAKUNIN

87. Michael Bakunin to Nikolay Ogarev

14 JUNE 1870   *Locarno*

MY DEAR AGA,
I have not replied to your brief note written in French and sent unsigned to me through our one-eyed friend.[45] Nor have I answered your inquiry whether I would like to take a flat and buy our one-eyed friend's furniture cheaply. I did not answer because I thought that the two enormous packets you would be getting at the same time (both of them insured and containing letters to Neville and yourself jointly) ought to prove an adequate reply.

I hope you are persuaded upon reading all my letters that I *had* to put all the clearly defined conditions listed in them to Neville—and that, having decided to put them to him, I do not intend to, cannot and must not go back on them a single step. Now whether he will agree to accept them or not will, I think, depend in the main on whether or not you agree, and consider it right, useful, and necessary to give me your friendly support. I have said all I was able, all I could, to persuade him and persuade you. So now I have only to wait for his and your reply. If both are satisfactory, if you can rise above all the quibbles and misunderstandings in which he used to entangle us all, you will be giving me an assurance that it will be possible to continue with the cause on a basis firmer and more genuine than it has so far been—in fact, on the basis and on the conditions I have suggested to you both—then I shall go, but not otherwise.

What will I do in Geneva? And also, how can I pay my way to you? I am now reduced to the extremity of ruin and desperation. There are debts, and I haven't a kopeck, I simply have nothing to live on. And what am I to do? It has become impossible for me to engage in any transactions as a result of the unfortunate affair of L[yubavin]. I have no other Russian acquaintances. In a word, things are very bad. I have made my last effort to arouse my dear brothers. Will they wake up? I don't know. I shall await their reply.

Things are bad here, but in Geneva they would be twice as bad. Travelling expenses and [the cost of] living are twice as high, as in fact are all the expenses that setting up the smallest, even the most meagre household, of necessity entails. How can I think of buying the furniture of our one-eyed friend, even at a quarter of the price!

And anyway, have I not told you several times both verbally and in writing that for various reasons of importance to myself and Antosya, even were I to come to Geneva I would certainly be obliged to make my home outside the town.

But, my dear friend, what is the point of talking about this? It is most likely that I shall stay here. Our Boy is obstinate, and I, having once taken a decision and made it known, am not accustomed to change it. Ergo, a rupture with him, at least, my rupture seems inevitable. If we were all of the same opinion and all acted in unison, inseparably and amicably bound [to one another], we should probably succeed in overcoming his obstinacy, or in the last resort, we should leave him aside and get a real cause off to a real start. But does there exist in our midst such a unity of thought, feelings and will? I doubt it.

In any case I will wait here for your replies to my many and interminable letters and I will not stir from this spot until I am completely convinced that I am being summoned to a real cause with all the true conditions of a cause, and not to some new word-game.

Write quickly.

Your M.B.

88. *Natalie Herzen to Maria Reichel*

16 JUNE 1870   *Campagne Baumgartner*
                                                    St-Jean-la-Tour
                                                    Genève

I SHALL make no attempt to explain anything to you by letter, my dear Masha. I'll explain all and tell you everything when we see each other, and that will be, if not in July (since that is inconvenient for you) then in August. For the moment let Shushka profit a little longer from school, since the holidays haven't started yet. I am very pleased with him; at times I am amazed how quickly he is improving. He is a real little mischief, but that is only natural at his age, isn't it? He is a clever boy and not averse to studying.

Zhukovsky has just been to see us. Recently he sent the Vogt brothers several copies of articles in French, Serebrennikov's leaflets, and a letter in which he asks them to express somehow their *disagreement* with the actions taken by the government here in the case of Serebrennikov. Could they not write a short collective letter and gather a few signatures for that letter or protest? Please be so good as to pass that on to them on Zhukovsky's behalf, Masha dear. Karl Vogt and all the radicals here greatly approve of Serebrennikov's appealing against the Swiss government. The trial begins next Saturday.

Why do you wish to deprive me of the pleasure of spoiling your Sasha, if it can be called spoiling? If he really does not need anything then tell him from me to go on some nice excursion somewhere and have a good time—and drop in to see us *en passant*.

Farewell for the time being, I embrace and kiss you heartily. I send you all my regards, and Adolf Vogt *et famille* too.

TATA H[erzen]

T

89. *Natalie Herzen to Michael Bakunin*[46]

16 JUNE 1870   *Campagne Baumgartner*
                                          St-Jean-la-Tour
                                          Genève

I HOPE you will not reproach me, Mikhail Alexandrovich, for having shown a distrust of your *protégé* and all his affairs? You ought to think it natural that everything concerning your affairs was *obscure* for me, that I vacillated for so long, striving to discover the truth and attain a clear understanding, and, having satisfied myself that that was well-nigh impossible, decided to withdraw and to have nothing to do with these *obscure* Russian affairs—despite the interminable talking and arguing, and despite all the efforts of yourself, Ogarev and Nechayev to convince me that I would come to grief if I *refused* to participate in them!

I could not conceive of anyone's really being attracted to that repulsive Jesuitical system, being loyal to it to such a shockingly inhuman degree as is Nechayev. For with him, consistency has reached the point of a monstrosity!

How can you still envisage the possibility of working with him after all that has passed between you, after all that you say yourself in your letter to him? On what will you base your trust? And if you have none, how will you work with him? How do you know that, even if Nechayev accepts your conditions and goes as far as to put his acceptance in writing (using his real name or some invented one)—[how do you know] that he will not secretly be tricking you precisely as he has been doing ever since you have known each other? For myself that would be absolutely impossible. Although he never hypnotized me, as you seem to think, he did something worse. He poisoned and paralysed me by developing in me a mistrust so great that it will be a long time before I manage to rid myself of it.

Now I cannot and do not wish to participate in any Russian affairs whatsoever. Call me a sceptic, Mikhail Alexandrovich— perhaps you are right. [But] on this occasion my scepticism has saved me from God knows what toils and troubles.

Natalie Herzen to Michael Bakunin

Do you really want your letter to N[echayev] to be kept a secret? Will you let me read just a few extracts to two or three people who still believe that you and N[echayev] are synonymous?[47] It seems to me that this could only do you good, and not harm. Kindly let me know what you think of the idea.[48]

When do you intend to come to Geneva?

Give my regards to your wife, and kiss the children, with whom I hope I shall sometime become acquainted.

I press your hand
N. HERZEN
Dispatched 21 *June* [18]70, *Tuesday*

90. Michael Bakunin to N. Ogarev and friends

SUNDAY, 19 JUNE [1870]   [*Locarno*]

MY DEAR ONES. I have just received a dispatch from Barni[49] informing me that the whole family is expecting me and that I will soon receive a new dispatch, this time actually summoning me to Geneva. Do not forget, my friends, that I have no money. I shall have to pay 400 francs here and 150 francs travel costs for the family. Where do I get them, and where am I to go? I have no flat, you see. The whole idea is rotten, falls apart at the seams. It means going once more on my own, only to return again for the family—that is, spending more than 100 francs on a single journey there and back! Think it over carefully: if it is really necessary that I should be with you, I shall of course come, borrow money and come. *But, but* make sure it is not in vain. I await your prompt reply.

Your M.B.

Also, Neville writes telling me to expect a letter from him—and he wishes to arrange a meeting with me. What am I to do? I received your tea, Aga.

91. Collective Message to Ogarev, Tata, Ozerov and Serebrennikov, and if [. . .] has been co-opted to your council, then to [. . .] also.[50]

20 JUNE 1870   *Locarno*

FRIENDS: judging by the letters I have received from various quarters, it seems to me that your council has begun to take too unfavourable a view of our friend the Baron. I use the word friend not ironically, but in all seriousness, because I, at least, have not ceased to regard him as the most valuable man amongst us all to the Russian cause, and the purest, or (to use Serebrennikov's expression) the most *saintly* person in the sense of his total dedication to the cause and his utter self-denial, and further, as one endowed with an energy, constancy of will and tireless industry the like of which we have never encountered before. I do not think that any one of you would go as far with his criticism as to deny that he possesses these qualities. It is impossible to deny them, for they stare one in the face. The Baron, then, is a jewel, and one doesn't throw away jewels. Our efforts should, it seems to me, be directed towards preserving him for the cause, and, since we are ourselves dedicated to the cause and wish to serve the cause, towards preserving our links with him.

In this passionately devoted jewel of a man there are many and considerable faults, and they should not surprise one: the stronger and more passionate the nature, the more striking appear its faults. A person who is virtuous in the sense that he has no faults is merely a nonentity. The relatively virtuous are shallow, sleek and smiling people, like Lopatin and Zhukovsky. Our friend the Baron is not the slightest bit virtuous or sleek; on the contrary, he is rough-hewn in the extreme, and not easy to get on with. However, he has one great advantage: he dedicates himself and gives himself utterly, while the others dabble in dilettante fashion. He wears workman's overalls, the others white gloves; he acts while the others wag their tongues; he is, the others are not. He can be caught and held firmly in a corner, while the others are so sleek that they are certain to slip out of your [hands]. But the others are extremely pleasant people while he is utterly unpleasant. Despite this, I prefer the Baron to all the others and love and respect him more than the others.

However, I was the first to raise the banner of revolt against his dictatorship.[51] Not because his dictatorship was an insult to my pride: in my view, the man who best understands the job, who does more and is utterly dedicated, is—so long as he understands, dedicates himself and acts—a dictator by right, that is, a guide, stimulus, encouragement and inspiration to all the others, and all the others naturally follow him. I have rebelled against the Baron's dictatorship because it has become permeated by the false system of Jesuitical devices and lies which our friend the Baron has lately come to regard more or less as the best means of achieving his aim. I shall not repeat the facts; you all know them by now. I had to rebel because I am convinced, as you are, that such a system would be the death of the cause itself.

But let us be fair here also. Why did the Baron choose this system? Was it as the result of some vice ingrained in his being— egoism, vanity, ambition, the thirst for glory, covetousness, the hunger for power? No, anyone who has the slightest knowledge of the Baron will swear with me, not that there is not in him the smallest grain of any of these vices, for in my view, every man, and particularly a passionate-natured man, contains the grains of all kinds of vices, but that his life has been such that most of them have not been able to develop, and that in him all other passions have been stifled by a higher passion, the passion for revolution or liberation of the people. He is a fanatic of the first order, and he has all the qualities as well as the failings of a fanatic. Such people are frequently capable of terrible blunders and dangerous errors. The errors of nice people are usually just as [. . .]⁵² or as smooth and incon- spicuous as their virtue. With the fanatic, however, everything is on a large scale, and if he errs, then he errs on a large scale. Get Ogarev to tell you the story of how our mutual friend, the late Belinsky, suddenly became a frenzied admirer and advo- cate of Tsarist power, to the consternation of all his friends. Those are the sort of paroxysms of absurdity that sincere and passionate natures can sometimes reach in their development. And the Baron is very young yet, and his development still has far to go.

At the heart of his entire moral and intellectual being—and I say and maintain this with all certainty and reason, since I spent a total of four months last year living with him, so to speak, in the same room, and passing almost every night in conversations about all sorts of questions; I have a detailed knowledge of the story of his childhood and early youth. And so I repeat, at the heart of his entire being and all his aspirations there lies a passionate love for the people, an indignation for the people and a long-standing hatred for everything that oppresses them, and, consequently, for the government and the state above all. I have yet to meet another revolutionary as sincere and consistent as he. The Baron is intelligent, very intelligent. But his intelligence is as untamed as his passion, his nature, and he has developed in a far from balanced way, although he does appear to have reached a considerable level of development.

But everything in him—mind, heart, and will—and with heart and will he is generously endowed—everything is subordinated to a ruling passion, [the passion] for destroying the existing order of things. Consequently his first thought was of necessity to create an organization or a collective power capable of carrying out this great work of destruction—to hatch a conspiracy.

Those who in their time have occupied themselves with hatching conspiracies will know what terrible disillusionment can be encountered along the road—the eternal disproportion between the grandeur of the goal and the wretchedness of the means, the insufficiency and ignorance of people—a hundred failures for one successful choice, one earnest man to a hundred garrulous and barren minds. And then also there is the perpetual play of vanities, ambitions great and small, grudges, misunderstandings, evasions, gossip, intrigue—and all this in the face of a gigantic, superbly organized, oppressive and punitive power which one wishes to destroy. A hundred times a week one makes a gesture of one's despair and weariness. It is all very well and relatively easy to hatch a conspiracy at a time when, and in a country where, the entire people or at least a section of the society, a whole class, is obsessed with one and the same violent passion, as, for example, in Poland at the beginning of the 1860s. But in a country where there is little or no uniting passion, or where, instead of the passion of the heart there exists and operates the passion of the head, where the inclination is more to argument than to action, where Byzantine benediction still continues its corrupting influence, and where, on the other hand, scientific criticism, having successfully destroyed the old morality, has not yet succeeded in creating a new morality, where the scientific negation of free will means for the majority of the youth an indulgent and objective contemplation of their own depravities and has as its natural consequence the dissolution and emaciation of the character, the absence of any passionate concentration of the will—in a word, in Russia—the formation of a secret society, serious, effective, deserving of the name and capable of real action, becomes inconceivably difficult.

Having tried, honestly but vainly, all honourable means— propaganda of principles, passionate persuasion—a man, and a young man in particular, striving passionately to create at all costs a powerful and secret collective force, and convinced that only the activity of such a force can liberate the people, comes naturally to the following conclusion, the following thought: "Our youth is too corrupt and flaccid to be trusted to form an organization by force of persuasion alone—but since an organization is essential, and since our young people are incapable of uniting and unwilling to unite freely, they must be united involuntarily and unawares—and in order that this organization, half-founded on coercion and deceit, should not crumble, they must be confounded and compromised to such an extent that it becomes impossible for them to withdraw."

This is the first natural step towards the Jesuit system. It is a desperate step. At first sight the system is repellent to a strong, passionate, *upright* and fervently *sincere* nature like that of our Baron. But at the stage of intellectual and [. . .][53] development he had reached at that moment he could see no other way out. He had either to abandon the cause entirely or adopt the Jesuit system. Abandon the cause he could not, and so he adopted the system. And having once adopted it, albeit with a heavy heart, he took the system to its ultimate, ugly extreme, with his characteristic passionate, pitiless impetuosity, sparing neither self nor others, sacrificing with savage passion both himself and other people for the cause, or what seemed to him the cause.

I referred to the Baron as an *upright* and *profoundly earnest* man. Do not be surprised at this, my dear friends. This man is filled with love, and indeed cannot be otherwise. A person with no love could not act with such utter self-abnegation, such a total disregard not only for his own comfort, profit, personal desires, aspirations and emotions, but even for his reputation and name. For he is willing to condemn himself to dishonour, general contempt and even to utter oblivion for the sake of the liberation of the people. It is here that his *profound, highly courageous, and virginally pure integrity* lies, and it is with the power of this purity and integrity that he crushes us all: whether we like it or not, if we want to be honest with ourselves we have to bow to him. He is a deeply loving man who becomes passionately attached to people, and is ready to give away everything to his friends, and cannot in any respect be ranked with those cold minds and natures which, to achieve their ends, toy with people like [. . .]⁵⁴. He is not a vain egoist or an intriguer, my dear friends, because he does not pursue *his own* aims, and not only would he not sacrifice a single man for *his own* gain, *his own* glory or the satisfaction of *his own* ambition; he would sooner sacrifice himself for every man. This man has a tender heart.

How could he have gone as far in his actions as brazen lying, incessant intrigue, ruthless exploitation and compromise of his best friends? What about the system? Do not forget the system. Once persuaded, albeit mistakenly, of the necessity of using Jesuitical rules and methods *within* the organization—and notice that I am not talking about their external use, which, even in my view, is frequently necessary, since in the fight against organized despotism that which cannot be taken by force must be taken by stratagem, but of course by real stratagem, and one which does not have writ large upon its forehead: I am a stratagem—once persuaded of the necessity of adopting the Jesuit system, he gave himself up to it *as one duty bound*, all the more passionately since it was repugnant to his own nature. Ruthless both towards himself and to others, and with the austerity of a religious ascetic or fanatic, he began to destroy in himself and in others any manifestations of personal feelings, personal rectitude and all personal obligations and relationships in general, regarding them as criminal weaknesses, that is [weaknesses] which hampered the cause. The more he sensed in himself inclinations to passionate personal affection, the more fanatically he hounded them down both in himself and in other people. He made himself and all his friends undergo a systematic course of re-education having as its sole aim the systematic annihilation—in himself and others—of all that is personally and socially (not secretly, but publicly and socially) sacred and dear to every man. His idea and aim are clear. He saw and was too violently aware, on the one hand, of the immensity of the state's power which had to be destroyed. He saw with despair, on the other hand, the historical backwardness, the apathy, the inarticulateness, the infinite patience and the sluggishness of our Orthodox people, who could, if they realized and so desired, sink this entire ship of state with one wave of their mighty hand, but who appear still to be sleeping the sleep of the dead. And thirdly, and lastly, he saw the flaccidity of our youth, which is wasting all its energy in interminable and aimless argument and chatter. Such was his vision of Russian reality. How was he to topple it? Where was that Archimedean fulcrum point at which the cause might place a lever to raise this world and turn it upside-down? The fulcrum is the general wretchedness of Russia; the lever is youth. But this youth, in its present condition, is far from being a lever, but rather a corrupt and inane herd of jabbering doctrinaires. Consequently, the first task must be to transform it, and change its manners and morals.

What corrupts it most of all? The influence of the social milieu. In other words, youth must be uprooted from this milieu. It is tied to it by two threads: firstly, career; and secondly, family bonds, romantic attachment and vain social relationships. Therefore these threads should be broken, and the possibility of a career or any [other] outlet crushed. Young people must be compromised to the utmost and their return to society made impossible, and similarly, all family ties must be shattered, together with all attachments of the heart and vain relations with society, and in this manner a phalanx of unsparing outlaws created with a single passion in common: *the passion to destroy the state and society.* You must admit that this fantasy is not the product of a petty mind or a paltry soul, and that it has, alas!—a great deal of validity and truth.

Society—and I am not talking of the people—our society, that is, the society of the more or less privileged classes which are inseparably linked with the state and exist only through the medium of it, has no other means of reforming [itself] than to destroy itself once and for all. He who does not beguile himself with selfish dreams and illusions, with splendid but sterile aspirations, and idle chatter, but who truly desires the triumph of the Russian revolution, that is, the liberation of the people, must wish for the radical destruction of this society. But shall I be in a condition to give myself wholly and sincerely to the service of this destructive cause while there still exist so much as the traces of bonds of covetousness, vainglory, ambition, and habitual, family and other emotional ties between myself and this society? No, I shall not. Must these bonds, then, be destroyed? Yes, they must. And if you have not the strength to destroy them, do not become involved in the revolutionary cause!

The Baron's mistake has, *in my view,* consisted not in his wanting definitively to tear youth away from society and set it at loggerheads with society—this, in my opinion, is a necessity arising from the totality of the present situation in Russia—but in his impatient desire to assemble in the shortest possible time as great a force as he could. Unable, of course, to find in this era of depravity the hundreds of people who might be equal to his programme, he collected people indiscriminately and, because of the absence of any real inner bond between them, was forced to bind them by means of deceit, compromise, and coercion, and finally reached the point where *he was obliged to introduce the Jesuit system into his organization.* By so doing, he corrupted it. He did not understand that, having destroyed all the social, family, and emotional ties of the members of his organization, he had to create for them a new tie, within the organization itself, not a negative but a positive one of passionate, fraternal solidarity, based on a common purpose, on reciprocal truth and trust, and on the strictest guarantees of mutual assistance.

The absence of this kind of positive tie had the most grievous consequences at the very first reverse; the thunder rumbled and the whole organization crumbled. And further, the arrested members of the organization, corrupted by the Jesuit doctrine, began shamelessly denouncing and betraying one another.

Our poor Baron thus suffered a total shipwreck. But instead of changing his system, he has adhered obstinately to it and, like Doctor Sangrado in the novel *Gil Blas*, who treated all his patients by means of hot water and blood-letting, and when they died maintained that their deaths were due solely to the fact that they had not drunk enough hot water or been sufficiently bled, so does our Baron, instead of abandoning the Jesuit system, wish to persuade himself that the whole of his misfortunes stem from his having insufficiently incorporated the system into the flesh and blood of his organization. This obstinacy, this obdurate blindness is disastrous, beyond doubt. But are we to be angry with the Baron for this? Can we even be surprised that he does not give in to us so easily?

My dear friends, were he to make an easy concession to us, that would be a proof of his light-headedness, proof that he did not seriously or passionately believe in the system he had used to create his organization. When natures as whole-hearted, strong, and passionate as that of our Baron err, they become so deeply entrenched in their error that to abandon it is far more difficult for them than it is for other, nicer and more pleasant people, that is, for idle talkers and sterile minds.

For the Baron, abandonment is hard, but not impossible. And since he is a valuable man, and is both finer and purer, more devoted, more active, and more useful than all of us together, we must leave aside all the petty and vain currents of our souls, all our personal feelings and resentments—I say this to you, Tata, in particular—and join forces in order to help him extricate himself from this bog and to give him an opportunity, on the basis of mutual truth, trust, and total candour, to enter our ranks, to be at the head of our ranks—

for he will still be the most tirelessly and relentlessly active one of us all.

To this end we must:

firstly, being agreed amongst ourselves, without any pride or feeling of personal resentment towards him, firmly, precisely, and clearly lay before him our conditions;

and *secondly,* we must, with his assistance, of course, make every effort to defend him against[55] the malicious and slanderous gossip of well- and ill-meaning idlers, redeem his honour, and as far as possible clear his name.

I have written frankly about everything to you, my dear friends, because I am convinced of the necessity of acting upon him jointly and in concert for his own personal salvation. I have spoken frankly, relying upon your integrity and honour, your respect for the cause, and in the assurance that all that has been said in our intimate circle will remain *strictly and absolutely* between ourselves, and that none of us will be so pettily selfish, so frivolously unscrupulous, so foolish or weak-minded as to broadcast in public outside our circle—thus playing into the hands of those sharks who hover around us and devour scandal and slander with such malice and eagerness— [will not disclose] even the smallest part of what has been or is being uttered in our midst. If it were otherwise, I would never forgive myself for this letter and would regard it as an act of betrayal and a crime against the Russian cause.

Concerning the terms of our agreement and the methods by which we must act upon the Baron: this, my friends, we shall discuss in person. Tomorrow I am leaving here and shall be with you in a few days' time. I beg you not to inform anyone of my impending arrival.

Your M. BAKUNIN

92. *Michael Bakunin to Natalie Herzen*

28 JUNE 1870[56]   [*Saint-Maurice*]

NATALYA ALEXANDROVNA,

Serebrennikov, with whom I have spent the entire evening, is asleep, and before following his example I want to say a few words to you. From what Serebrennikov has told me I am convinced that you are terribly incensed by Barsov [Nechayev], whom you considered until recently the finest of all of us. I know little of your personal relationship with him, but let us assume even that he has offended you personally in some way. That still does not give you the right to betray us. Remember the day when in the presence of all of us you gave him and us your hand in the common cause. Since that time you have been entrusted with many confidences and have come to know certain people who belong to our camp, our cause. However great and even legitimate your anger with Barsov may now be, you have not the right now to break your word. It would be treachery against your conscience and your honour. I cannot write to you in detail at present, but I implore you not to say or do anything that might damage Barsov and the work he is accomplishing, perhaps not always in the correct manner, but always with boundless dedication and self-forgetfulness. Whatever his errors, he remains nevertheless, in my opinion and I hope in yours, the finest and, where the cause is concerned though not where people are concerned, the most honourable of us all.

Tomorrow I shall send you a detailed letter through Serebrennikov. And now I beg you once more, do not commit a crime against your conscience and honour.

Your M. B[AKUNIN]

This letter will, I trust, remain between ourselves, and you will not, I hope, show it to Natalya Alexeevna, whom none of you had any right to involve in our affairs.

93. Natalie Herzen: Diary

3 JULY 1870

TODAY I had my first meeting with Bakunin after all these annoyances and letters. He was very eager to see me. What interests and worries them most of all is that I know young Vladimir Serebrennikov. In effect, that was all B[akunin] wished to know from me—*what* had I said to the *Narodnoe Delo* people? I repeated that to Utin I had said nothing, and Olga Stepanovna[57] I had warned to be very careful. I was afraid for her, knowing that she was about to go to Russia. I imagined that this Vladimir Serebrennikov, since he enjoyed her complete trust, might keep in his possession, or hand over to *Narodnaya Rasprava*, some of her papers or secrets and make use of them while she was in Russia. They stop at nothing and are ready to have her imprisoned, or otherwise torture her to squeeze all her money out of her. From Bakunin I learned that Nechayev told him that they would not let go of me for anything, adding: "Only think of it, three hundred thousand francs!" And also, that I was very difficult to *please*, but someone could possibly be *sent* especially, to make me fall in love with one of "*theirs*".

I finally said that in the meantime I would say nothing and I did not want to get mixed up in anything, but that I did not consider myself in any way bound to keep any promises whatsoever, since I had right from the beginning been most shamefully deceived. They had shown me a marvellously constructed machine, given me the handle, and asked me to help them turn it, saying that it would produce cheap bread or flour for the People. But after some time I found that they had tricked me, and that I was helping to manufacture a kind of poisonous paste which caused suffering to the friendly, the indifferent, and the hostile alike. Was I bound to continue the work I had begun, to help them and keep all this a secret? Not in the least! I had been tricked, and there was nothing binding me. . .

Bakunin agreed, merely remarking that I "had perhaps spoken prematurely to Olga Stepanovna," and asking me to say nothing more about Vladimir Serebrennikov for the moment. He said that I was perfectly free to tell Natalya of the circumstances surrounding my journey to Locle, and that Nechayev had played a much greater part in all this than he, Bakunin. Also, that the letters I had been receiving in Paris were from Nechayev and not Bakunin. I should tell Natalya all this now so that she should know the facts before receiving her explanation from Bakunin.

7 JULY 1870

It appears that all is indeed over between Bakunin, Ogarev, and Nechayev. The latter, too, is here in Geneva once again. Apparently they have had terrible arguments in recent days. On the morning of Tuesday, 5th, Semen Serebrennikov brought me a note from Ogarev asking me to come at once to see him. Fortunately I had a headache and refused; besides, I somehow guessed that Nechayev was there. After lunch Bystrov arrived with a warning that Nechayev intended to come and see me. Upon learning that I would not be there, he apparently became angry and demanded that they all accompany him to my house immediately. The others refused. They argued without a break until evening. At about seven o'clock that evening Vladimir Serebrennikov appeared with a note from Nechayev himself saying that *"an explanation was imperative."*[*][58] Vladimir Serebrennikov refused to believe that I was not at home; but I had just gone out with Sasha Reichel. At ten o'clock in the evening Bystrov came in haste with a message from Bakunin, who feared for me, and advised me to go away for a few days, leaving the remaining funds with Ogarev. Bystrov stayed for a little while, intending to help if the need arose, that is, if Nechayev, Vladimir Serebrennikov, and Charles tried to enter by force. But no one came. However, Vladimir Serebrennikov turned up again yesterday and demanded to see me without fail. Erminia told him that I had gone away for a few days. Very likely he did not believe her, for he left a note asking me—or ordering me[59]—to be in between six o'clock and half-past-six.

I did not intend to receive him. I stayed at home the whole day, but none of them arrived. Instead, Ogarev came. He

---

* Nechayev's note, preserved in Natalie's papers at the Bibliothèque Nationale, reads:

"You have done certain things, and therefore an explanation with you is imperative. Call at Ogarev's for a short while and do not oblige us to come to you. Do not delay, I am only here *en passant*.

"Write your answer on the back of this note and return it to the messenger. You will not, of course, blab about the content of this note or who it is from."

The note is undated and seems to be the last letter of Nechayev to Tata.

arrived at one o'clock despite the terrible heat—*33 degrees* Centigrade. The poor old man was afraid for me. He feared that Nechayev might treat me roughly. Poor Aga! How many times must he be disappointed in his "children"? He took the funds from me—that is, the 740 francs 50, which remained— and gave me a receipt in case Nechayev or Vladimir Serebrennikov should demand the money.[60] Then he went off with Semen Serebrennikov to give it to the banker Reverdin.

Why should I see Nechayev again? What does he want of me? God knows. Very likely he will start assuring me again that he has always been sincere and frank with me! Or perhaps he will simply demand the rest of the money from me, or else some of Bakunin's letters, or his own, or possibly try to frighten me from speaking about Vladimir Serebrennikov to Olga Stepanovna or to anyone of the *Narodnoe Delo*!

But even so, after all this, there is still one question I have not settled in my mind: Is he a fanatic or an unscrupulous crook? Was he sincere when he tried to convince people of the necessity for his Polish-Jesuitic system of deceit and mystification, or that[61] all [are] the ignoble instruments of the Russian government?

5. *Ignoble Crooks or Sincere Fanatics?*

94. Michael Bakunin to Alfred Talandier[1]

24 JULY 1870   *Neuchâtel*

MY DEAR FRIEND,

I have just learned that N[echayev] went to see you and you hastened to tell him the address of our friends (M[roczkowski] and his wife). From this I conclude that the two letters in which O[garev] and I warned and implored you to have nothing to do with him arrived too late; and I say without the least exaggeration that I consider the consequences of this tardiness a real misfortune. It may seem strange to you that we are advising you to avoid a man to whom we have given letters recommending him to you, and couched in the most complimentary terms. But those letters date from the month of May, and since then we have been forcibly persuaded of the existence of facts so grave as to have obliged us to break off all our relations with N[echayev] and at the risk of your thinking us inconsistent and rash we thought it our sacred duty to forewarn and forearm you against him. Now I shall attempt to explain to you in a few words the reasons for this change.

It remains perfectly true that N[echayev] is the man most persecuted by the Russian government and that the latter has covered the entire continent of Europe with a swarm of spies to search for him in every country, and that it has called for his extradition from both Germany and Switzerland. It is also true that N[echayev] is one of the most active and energetic men I have ever encountered. When it comes to serving what he calls the cause, he hesitates and stops at nothing and acts as ruthlessly with regard to himself as to everyone else. That

U

305

is the main quality that attracted me to him and made me seek an alliance with him for so long. There are some who claim that he is simply an adventurer; that is a lie! He is a dedicated fanatic, but at the same time a very dangerous fanatic, alliance with whom could not be otherwise than fatal for everybody, and here is why:

He had at first been a member of an underground Committee which really did exist in Russia. This Committee no longer exists, all its members have been arrested. N[echayev] alone remains, and alone constitutes today what he calls the Committee. As the Russian organization, in Russia, has been decimated, he is striving to create a new one abroad. All this would be perfectly natural, legitimate, and extremely useful; but the way in which he goes about it is loathsome. Deeply affected by the catastrophe which has just destroyed the secret organization in Russia, he has gradually become convinced that to found a serious and indestructible society one must base it on the politics of Machiavelli and adopt in its entirety the Jesuit system, whose body is violence from first to last, whose soul falsehood.

Truth, mutual trust, serious and strict solidarity exist only amongst a dozen or so individuals who form the *sanctus sanctorum* of the society. All the others must serve as blind tools, exploitable material in the hands of these dozen men with real solidarity. It is allowed and even ordered to trick them, compromise them, rob them and even destroy them if need be; they are fodder for conspiracy. For example: you have received N[echayev] thanks to our letter of recommendation, you have trusted in him absolutely, you have recommended him to your friends, M. and Mme M[roczkowski] among others. There he is, with a foothold in your world, and what will he do? He will first of all spin you a pack of lies to increase your sympathy and trust, but he won't be satisfied with that. The sympathies of lukewarm people who are devoted only in part to the revolutionary cause and who, besides this cause, have other human interests such as love, friendship, the family, social relationships—these sympathies he does not consider sufficiently justifiable, and in the name of the cause he has to take possession of your whole being without your knowledge. To this end he will spy on you and try to gain possession of all your secrets; and in order to do that he will, if he finds himself alone in your room in your absence, open all your drawers, read all your correspondence and, when he finds an interesting letter, that is, one that is compromising in any respect whatever for yourself or one of your friends, he will steal it and keep it carefully as a document against you or your friend. He has done this with O[garev], with myself, with Tata and other friends—and when we have accused him in company he has had the audacity to say to us: "Ah yes, that's our system—we regard as enemies, and we are duty bound to deceive and compromise everyone who is not *completely* with us", that is, everyone who is not convinced of the beauty of the system and who has not promised to apply it himself. If you introduce him to a friend, his first task will be to sow discord, gossip, intrigue between you—in a word, to set you at loggerheads. If your friend has a wife, a daughter, he will try to seduce her, to give her a child to tear her away from the official morality and plunge her forcibly into revolutionary protest against society. They regard any personal attachment, any friendship, any *intimacy* as an evil which it is their duty to destroy, because all of it constitutes a power which, existing as it does independently of the secret organization, diminishes the unique power of the latter.

Don't accuse me of exaggeration—all of this has been amply developed and proved for me. This poor N[echayev] is still so naive, such a child, despite his systematic perversity, that seeing himself exposed he thought he could convert me—he even begged me to be so good as to develop this theory in a Russian journal which he had suggested that I found. He has betrayed the trust of all of us, stolen our letters, compromised us terribly, in short he has behaved like a despicable wretch. His fanaticism is his sole excuse! He is dreadfully ambitious, unbeknown to himself, because he has ended up by completely identifying the revolutionary cause with his own person. But he isn't an egoist in the ordinary sense of the word, because he takes terrible personal risks and leads a martyr's life of privation and unparalleled toil. He is a fanatic, and it is his fanaticism that makes him an absolute Jesuit—at times he is simply a fool. Most of his lies are too obvious. He plays at Jesuitism as other people play at revolution. But despite this relative naiveté of his, he is extremely dangerous because he *daily* commits acts, breaches of trust, betrayals, from which it is far more difficult to protect oneself for one would never suspect them. With all that, N[echayev] is a force because he has immense energy.

It was with great sorrow that I broke with him, because the service of our cause demands a great deal of energy, and one rarely comes across it developed to such a degree. But having exhausted all methods of persuading myself, I had to break with him and, having once broken, I had to fight him to the bitter end. His latest plan was nothing less than to form a band of thieves and brigands in Switzerland, with the aim, naturally, of building up revolutionary capital. I saved him by having him leave Switzerland, because he would certainly have been discovered, and his band, within a few weeks. He would have been ruined, and would have ruined all of us with him. His comrade and companion S[allier, *i.e.* Vladimir Serebrennikov] is a downright rogue, a brazen-faced liar without the excuse, the saving grace of fanaticism. There have taken place before my very eyes numerous thefts of documents and letters, all of them his doing. And these are the people whom M[roczkowski] thought it his duty, despite Z[hukovsky]'s warning, to introduce to Dupont and Bradlaugh.[2] The evil is done, it must be put right as far as possible *without any fuss or scandal*.

1. For the sake of your inner peace, family tranquillity and out of personal regard for you, I implore you to close your door against them. Do it *without explaining*, just cut them off. There are many reasons why we do not wish them to know *at this moment* that we are at war with them on all fronts. They must be led to suspect that the warnings against them have come from the enemy camp—which, incidentally, is perfectly true, for I know that urgent letters have been written against them to the General Council in London.[3] Do not therefore give us away prematurely to them. They have stolen documents from us which we must first of all retrieve.

2. Persuade M[roczkowski] that [consideration for] the

welfare of all his family demands that he break absolutely with them. That he protect N. from them.[4] Their system, their amusement is to seduce and corrupt young girls, for that way they gain a hold over the entire family. I am distressed that they have learned of M[roczkowski]'s address, for *they would be capable of denouncing him.* Have they not dared to admit openly to me and in the presence of a witness that to denounce a member, a devoted or semi-devoted follower to the secret police is one of the methods they regard as quite legitimate and useful at times? To gain possession of a person's, a family's secrets, in order to have complete control over them—that is their chief method. I am so afraid of their knowing M[roczkowski]'s address that I advise, I implore him and his family to take new lodgings so that they cannot be discovered. If after this M[roczkowski] continues, infatuated with *his own judgement,* to have contact with these gentlemen, may the fatal and inevitable consequences of this blind conceit be on his own head.

3. You and M[roczkowski] must warn all the friends to whom you might have introduced these gentlemen to be on their guard and to show them no trust or assistance. N[echayev] is more obstinate than a gambler and will fatally destroy himself—the other one is a lost man. Our friends must not have any share in their shameful ruin. It is all very sad and humiliating for us who recommended them to you, but truth is still the best way out and the best remedy for all one's mistakes.

95. Michael Bakunin to Valerian Mroczkowski

Pour Valérien
24 JULY 1870   *Neuchâtel*

DEAR FRIEND,

For God's sake don't make a fool of yourself, that is, don't be too clever, but take our advice and believe us absolutely—every word of my letter to Talandier, which you are to read, is the truth. It is a matter of our salvation, all of us; you will realize this when you take the trouble to examine the meaning of every word of that letter.

It would be splendid of you and you would be doing our sacred common cause an enormous service if you were to succeed in stealing from Nechayev all the papers he stole and all his own papers. But I am afraid you will have become quite rusty and lost all of your former agility, and so I implore you, for your own sake to break off all relations with Nechayev and his little companion Vladimir S. (Sallier), and if possible to avoid them completely. As the princess [Obolenskaya, Mroczkowski's wife] belongs to Utin's enemy camp, ask her on my behalf to write nothing of this matter to Utin.

Your M. B[AKUNIN]

96. *Michael Bakunin to Nikolay Ogarev*

28 JULY 1870   *Locarno*

WELL, MY OLD FRIEND. Here I am again in my peaceful Locarno and I will not move out of it until a real cause beckons me. I found all my family in good health and I am glad to be with them. Did you know that Nechayev found his way over to Talandier after all and that despite all our warnings our friend received him and introduced him to Mroczkowski, who lost no time in introducing him to that iconoclast Bradlaugh and the Frenchman Dupont, who is a member of the General Council of the International Workers' Association. I wrote urgent letters from Neuchâtel to Talandier and Mroczkowski, telling them the whole truth, and I hope they will make some attempt to rectify their mistake. They write that Nechayev wishes to continue in London with the publication of *The Bell* which he could not go on doing in Geneva, you see, after the appearance of Semen S.'s brochure. Question Zhukovsky— he will tell you everything in detail.

I received the tea. Many thanks from me to Mary and Henry. I have set about working in earnest. And what about you, my old friend, what are you doing, how are you getting on? And what of your [work on the] Russian commune? If you learn or read anything of interest, particularly in the Russian journals,

send it to me. And send me the Russian paper when you have
read it—I will return it promptly.

Farewell. Your M. B[akunin]

97. Sergey Nechayev to Bakunin and Ogarev

[END OF JULY 1870]

WHY, WHEN we parted and you kissed me like Judases, did you
not tell me you were going to write to your acquaintances?
Your last letter to Talandier, and the warning to Guillaume
about the danger of participating in a cause of which you have
always been the theoretical instigators, are acts of the most
dishonourable and despicable kind, committed out of petty
spite. With total disregard of common sense and the interests
of the cause you are bent on wallowing in the mire—well, then,
wallow!

Farewell
[S. NECHAYEV]

98. Michael Bakunin to Nikolay Ogarev

2 AUGUST 1870   *Locarno*

HERE IS a note from "our Boy" for you too, Aga my friend. I
received it yesterday evening and am sending it to you today
so that you may take soonest consolation from it as I did myself.
Well, we were indeed fools, and how Herzen would have
laughed at us if he were alive, and how rightly he would have
inveighed against us! Well, there is nothing for it but to
swallow the bitter pill and be wiser in future.

Let Ozerov read the note and give it to Tata to keep. She
is our archivist. I do not intend to reply. I think that you will
not reply either. *Give the attached letter to Tata*, whose address I
do not know exactly. And I beg you not to forget and lose it.

I am hard at work and waiting to see who will beat whom.[5]
When something big happens please telegraph me. Do you see

311

Tata, Ozerov, and Zhukovsky often? Give me news of them. I have written to them all, but have so far received no reply from any of them.

Your M. B.[AUKUNIN]

99. *Michael Bakunin to Natalie Herzen*

2 AUGUST 1870   *Locarno*

DEAR TATA,

I was very sad myself to have left Geneva without seeing you and saying farewell. But what was I to do? I could not overcome the revulsion aroused in me by the very thought of your old friend and namesake—and, most of all, I was in a hurry: poor Antonia summoned me, she was completely alone, and I rushed to her assistance. And so I had to leave without bidding you farewell.

Here is Semen Serebrennikov's address for you:

Suisse, Herrn S. Serebrennikoff
Öttingen 360. Bei Frau Bölsterli
Zürich.

I am extremely anxious about him. I wrote to him the day after my return here, and I still have not had any reply. I know that he and an old friend, whom he was to have met in Zurich, were going to go on a trip to the mountains, and look what I discovered in the day-before-yesterday's *Bund*: "A young Russian student of the Zurich Polytechnical School fell into a gorge while climbing Mount Pilatus near Lucerne and suffered injuries which proved fatal." I at once wrote to Zurich to ascertain the whereabouts of Serebrennikov. I hope he was not the victim of this unfortunate accident. That would be a great misfortune. I have rarely encountered a Russian youth more likeable and more deserving of respect and trust than he is. If you know anything of him, I beg you to write to me.

You ask me if I have heard anything of our amiable "Baron" (Nechayev)[6] and his comrades. I am sending a note of his to

312

Ogarev by this very post; I received it yesterday evening. Read it and keep it as a document, numbered along with the other documents. You are our archivist, after all! Give it to Ozerov and Zhukovsky to read, but on condition that they say nothing of it.

How do you like the note? Our fanatic, with his more or less sincere monomania, surpasses even Robert Macaire,[7] and I am beginning to doubt the sincerity even of his mania. And all we, and myself most of all, can do is to sprinkle ashes upon our heads and cry out in our grief: we have been utter fools! We have learned our lesson for the future. It is a shame that old age is approaching and we have few years left in which to profit by the lesson. I have asked Mroczkowski, to whom he has introduced himself, to give me as detailed information as he can concerning his address, his new contacts, and all his latest tricks. I will let you know what I learn.

Would it be indiscreet of me to trouble you with the following request? News of military operations reaches you immediately by telegraph, and us only two days later. Every time something important happens, say, for example, the French invade Germany and give the Germans a thrashing, or the Germans invade France and the French get a thrashing, or the French fleet routs the Prussian and lands on the German beaches, or if any other power—Russia, Austria, Denmark, Italy, or England—enters the war, in a word, if anything major occurs in any respect whatsoever, telegraph me at the following address: Locarno, Signora Teresa Pedrazzini, and make it as precise and detailed as possible. If you do this I shall be extremely grateful to you.

Farewell, I press your hand

M. BAKUNIN

Antosya sends her kind regards.

I am writing to you via Ogarev on this occasion, because I forgot to make a note of your address and I am afraid I might be mistaken. Send me your exact address.

100. German Lopatin to Natalie Herzen

1 AUGUST [1870]   *London*

HERE, IN brief, is the information I have obtained about the Ivanov affair.

I already knew that I[vanov] was killed not as a spy but as a man who had changed his opinions and deviated from certain paragraphs of the statutes of the "Committee"; but of *what* those deviations consisted I did not know. This is what people who took part in the murder, and some other people, say: Ivanov was well off (perhaps even rich), and had supplied Nechayev with money on more than one occasion. Towards the end he began to have doubts that the money was being put to the right use. One day he said to N[echayev]: "This is the last time I'm giving you any money. You know I am ready to give all I have to the 'cause', but here I must lay down two conditions: (1.) that the person to whom I am to give the money inspires me with more confidence than you do; (2.) that I have some kind of guarantee that the person himself knows where the money is going and is not merely a blind tool in someone else's hands." They say N[echayev] did not take the money but went to Uspensky,[8] Pryzhov and the others, and told them that words like these were a breach of discipline, a failure to observe the paragraph of the statutes which declared that "the property of members is at the disposal of the 'Committee' "; such things, [he said,] must be nipped in the bud . . . and so on.

And so I[vanov] was killed as a consequence: (1.) of N[echayev]'s wounded pride (ambition, if you like); and (2.) of his violation of the paragraph in the statutes according to which the "Committee" has unlimited powers to dispose of its members' property. In my opinion these facts are extremely regrettable.

To continue: I knew that Uspensky had lured I[vanov] into the wood on some false pretext, and I had always wondered why, since he was walking right beside him, he did not shoot him in the temple. Why did he need five men? But now I hear in letters that the participants, by their own account, lost their heads to such a degree that they forgot they had weapons on them and began striking I[vanov] with stones and their own fists and strangling him with their own hands. Altogether it was a most brutal murder. I[vanov] was already dead when N[echayev] remembered about his revolver, and to make quite sure he shot the corpse through the head. If I am not mistaken, though, I have already related this last fact to you, and described how, in the darkness, N[echayev] mistook U[spensky] for I[vanov] and pounced upon him; and how I[vanov] broke into a run, and the "Committee" after him . . . and so on, right to the end of the whole tragi-comic scene.

Elsewhere in the letter my correspondent tells me the story of the origins of the "Committee" and its development. But since the whole thing turns on names and surnames I cannot enlarge upon it. And anyway almost all the persons are unknown to you, so it cannot be of any particular interest to you.

You may make whatever use you see fit of the information I have imparted to you. But bear in mind one thing only, which is, that *I trust* the persons who have given me all this information. But, in case of mistrust or doubt *on the part of anyone whatsoever*, in case the need should arise for any *explanations*, I warn you in advance that I absolutely refuse to reveal the names of those persons or to provide any proof whatsoever of the truthfulness of my words and my account. I do not consider it either my right or my duty to do so. You can trust me or not—take your choice: it is all the same to me.

It is curious too how the case was started. When the investigator saw that the corpse had not been robbed, he did not know what to think. He questioned I[vanov]'s landlady as to who his last visitor had been, and, more for form's sake, conducted a search of Uspensky's house. He found nothing. As he was about to leave the apartment, one of the gendarmes (an officer or a soldier, I do not know which) noticed a scrap of paper sticking out of the sofa. They pulled the sofa to pieces and discovered inside it a lithograph press, and various other odds-and-ends, among them a list of about four hundred persons. (Don't imagine they were all members of the society! No! but they used to include in their lists the names of everyone whom they had heard might be of use to them in some enterprise: and against the names they noted various qualities, etc. Incidentally, I happen to know that myself and my brother had the additional honour of being included in this list. Though Bakunin can supply far more information on that score than I can, since he personally has seen, if not all, then at least some of those lists.) Note the technique of the affair: a man who has resolved to commit a murder and must be expecting an inquiry and other eventualities still keeps a printing press, various lists, etc. in his apartment! Cunning, don't you think?!

Nechayev tells a slightly different version of the beginning of the case and cloaks it far more thickly in mystery. . . But I have already had the pleasure of assuring him that it began in precisely this way.

Excuse my writing on scraps of paper: I do not feel like making a special trip out of the house.

Lopatin

This is my address:

Mr W. Hollington, for Mr G.L.
10 Thornhill Street, Caledonian Road,
London N., England.

I am sending you my address in case of need. You will be doing me a great favour if you inform Ozerov of it (thus sparing me the unnecessary expenditure of three pence).

101. Michael Bakunin to Nikolay Ogarev

11 AUGUST [1870]   *Locarno*

MY DEAR AGA,

I received your letter. Amidst [these] events you secretly think only about our proposed journal and your article. A fine philosopher you are. It's all very well for you—you are *only* a Russian, whereas I am an internationalist, and consequently [these] events have stirred me to a veritable delirium.

I have spent three days writing precisely twenty-three long letters, and this short one is the twenty-fourth. I have worked out a whole scheme; O[zer]ov will pass it on to you, or better, he will read you a letter I have written to a certain Frenchman.[9] And you are to be a good friend and give the attached letter at once to O[zer]ov—and ask Mary to call in at the *épicerie*, give my address, and tell the *épicier* to send me immediately, *contre remboursement,* two pounds of tea at five francs.

Instead of your sending the *Supplément du Journal de Genève,* telegraph me whenever something of great importance happens —only don't beat about the bush, but call things by their proper names, precisely and clearly; all the telegrams I have had from you are exactly like the riddles of the sphinx.

Your M. B[AKUNIN]

102. Michael Bakunin to Valerian Mroczkowski

Pour Valérien
19 AUGUST 1870   *Locarno*

MY DEAR FRIENDS,

Five days have passed already since I got your letter, and I have been intending every day to reply to you, and have been unable, overloaded as I am with correspondence concerning current events—and current events have now assumed and are daily assuming a more and more important and decisive character. War is bringing with it chaos of an entirely different kind, our all-embracing chaos. You understand how many things there are [to be done]. It is very possible, and even likely, that I shall go away from here soon—alone, naturally— Antosya and the children I shall leave here, and myself go to Geneva and beyond. But write to me here at Locarno in any case, in that way I shall certainly receive your letters, if a few days late. I turn now to a much-needed explanation.

Thank you, my friends, for not being too angry with me for my bold expressions. By way of apology for them I shall say two things. First, that I learned of your cold relations with

Talandier only from your letter which I found here upon my return from Geneva, in other words, after I had written my letter to Talandier. Second, I used them precisely in order to astonish you and *save you* from continuing your acquaintance with Nechayev. I was afraid you would not believe me and was horrified at the thought of the *fatal consequences* it might and sooner or later *would certainly have* for you. And so, my friend Mruk, it was not a *dictatorial gesture*, and not foolish irritability at the very thought of your being able, your daring to ignore my autocratic instruction, but simply a sincerely felt fear for you that provoked me to those expressions, for which I heartily beg your forgiveness.

All that I wrote to you concerning Nechayev was not an exaggeration but an understatement of the truth. Yes, he did betray us, he was *continually betraying us at the very time* when we were giving him everything and defending him with might and main. Yes, he has been stealing our letters ever since last year. Yes, he has compromised us by acting in our name without our knowledge or consent. Yes, he has always lied shamelessly to us. I have caught him at all this with O[zer]ov, with Ogarev, with Tata (Mlle) Herzen—and, driven by my evidence to realize the impossibility of denying it, do you know how he answered me?

"We are very grateful for all you have done for us, but since you never wanted to devote yourself to us utterly, saying that you had international obligations, we wished to insure ourselves against you just in case. To that end I felt I had the right to steal your letters, and felt myself duty bound to sow discord in your ranks, because it was not to our advantage that there should be such a strong bond apart from us, other than us."

Who are they, this "we"? There used to be quite a few of them. But since their rout they are left with only Nechayev and S. [Vladimir Serebrennikov] and two other friends abroad. His failures in Russia have driven Nechayev to insanity. He has begun committing folly after folly. All his wiles and deceptions have anyhow been so transparent that they have turned against himself. He has made himself ridiculous with his lying. His Jesuitical system has finally corrupted and crazed him. I always defended him, and I am even now willing still to stand up for him as against Zh[ukovsky], because Nechayev does at least act, and act not for himself, foolish and pernicious though his actions are, while the prodigal Zh[ukovsky] rattles and drones on more long-windedly than ever, opening open doors with a heroic flourish.

But our link with Nechayev has become impossible—he has betrayed our solidarity utterly. Imagine, he even tried to involve me in quarrels with Guillaume and my other friends in the mountains. Having lost his ground in Russia he was trying to make ground for himself here, and stupidly—with the abstraction of idealism—without any knowledge of the milieu and the people. Well, would you say that any solidarity is possible with a man when you know that every word he utters is a lie, and any trust you place in him ends in betrayal? And it had all reached of late such vile dimensions *à la* Robert Macaire, and towards the end it was all being done with such cynicism that I was simply at a loss. I would have exposed it all much sooner if I had not been living most of the time in Locarno, far away from him. And as for his latest enterprise in Switzerland,[10] you are very much mistaken, my dear Mruk, if you imagine that by thwarting it I would be setting myself at variance with the principles and plans I myself defended at one time against Monchal. I have in no respect renounced them, and I shall soon prove this extensively in practice. But the thing is that it should all be carried out, *firstly*, with strictest solidarity; and *secondly*, with a knowledge of the place, the circumstances, and the people, and with extreme cleverness. Nechayev though, wished to start on it without our knowing, having secretly induced our people, Henry, for example, [to participate] in it, and moreover, in such a stupid fashion that he would have brought shame upon the entire cause and ruined us all in the process. That is why I frustrated him. And as for his sham avowal to you that I allegedly wanted a dictatorship— spit in his face, Mruk, it's an impudent lie. If I needed witnesses to convince you, I would cite the evidence of O[zer]ov, Ogarev, and many other people, and you would see that what I wanted was not dictatorship for myself but the liberation of myself and

319

my friends from the wilful tyranny of his dictatorship, from his exploitation.

I think I have said enough to show you the true essence of the affair. Nechayev is a ruined man and henceforth one can say with certainty that he will not do anything substantial; but he is capable of playing dirty tricks. It's a pity I was not able to send you the copy of my long letter to him written from Locarno. The copy is being kept by friends in Geneva. It would explain everything to you in detail. But I hope that now you will understand; and where you do not understand, that you will trust me.

You write to me of the reactionary activities of Marx and company. I beg you, my friend, tell me in detail everything you know on this subject. It is important and may be very useful to me. Farewell, write promptly. These are hectic times. Perhaps we shall even meet soon in France. I embrace you and all yours.

M. B[akunin]

103. *Natalie Herzen to Maria Reichel*

2 OCTOBER 1870
Campagne Baumgartner
St-Jean-[la-Tour]
Genève

UPON HIS departure Bakunin left me the original of his will, Masha my dear, and asked me to send it on to you—you know what to do with it.

You must have heard how he incited the people of Lyons to revolt and how he (that is, he and half a dozen ultra-radicals) succeeded in gaining control of the Hôtel de Ville for seven hours! But their jubilation was premature—the people grew distrustful and began saying that God-knows-who-they-were, they might be "Prussian spies". In the present situation that was no joke, and they were obliged to make a speedy escape. They say Bakunin is in Marseilles now and wants to do a *repeat performance*. But the question is, what good will come of it? Every day gives one cause to wonder at the ignorance and indifference of the French.

Olga and Malwida departed a few days ago. I keep wondering when we shall see each other again, and whether we shall ever see each other any more; partings, departures and suchlike always distress me and make me uneasy. They must be in Florence by now.

I have put Papasha's letters in order but have not copied them out yet. I should be very grateful to you if you would let me keep them just a little while longer. Ogarev has asked me to sort out his own collection of letters from Papa also; he *needs* them, and as soon as possible, and therefore I should like to finish his and then complete yours afterwards. Will you allow me?

I am a little angry with you, dear kind Masha, because you sent the money back to me. You might at least have given the children some present from me, and then let me send you something, if only a packet of tea, and not worry about the bill as long as the tea is to your taste. And if it is not, then I'll try and find another sort, just tell me *what kind* of tea you like.

Farewell for now. How are you all keeping? I embrace and kiss all of you heartily.

Your TATA

Have you had any letters from Stankev[ich] and Egor Ivan[ovich] in Russia? You will receive the *Anthology of Posthumous Articles* shortly. Warm regards to the Vogts.

104. *Natalie Herzen to Maria Reichel*

8 OCTOBER 1870 *Campagne Baumgartner*
St-Jean-la-Tour
Genève

I AM sending you the *Anthology* which has just come out, and [your] 20 francs for your tea—I don't want them and if you send them to me ten times I'll send them back ten times to you. Mme Sally is a different matter. You will receive the tea in the next few days, ten pounds for her and ten for you. Next, I have a request to make of Alex or yourself, if it is not too much

W

trouble, Masha dear. When you have a moment to spare, call in, please, at the shop opposite Adolf Vogt's and buy me *two more little bears* made in nielloed silver, the *bigger* ones; I think the storekeeper said they cost *7 francs* but then he let me have them for 6. And see that they have nice snouts, you know, *bien ciselés*. Have them sent to me by post and I will send you fifteen francs to pay with; if there is a franc or two left over, please give the money to Sasha for him to buy you some pies (*you are to tell him so*).

What makes you say that Mme Bakunin is *en détresse*? Do you mean financially or morally? That is to say, is she worrying over Bakunin? If it is a case of the former, we ought to try somehow to help her, although that would be difficult for us now. If I am not mistaken, she has been receiving money from someone; but it is hard to find out about it all.

I have been visiting the Vogts despite the inclement weather, and there I saw a crowd of children of all ages, and invited them all to our house on Monday. Vogt was suffering from a severe migraine, but that did not prevent him from very firmly expressing his opinion of Bakunin and the mad *rouges* in France. Indeed, they are doing more damage now, I think, that they have scared the bourgeoisie, who, without them, would perhaps have stayed and defended their country. Yes, the situation is terrible, and it is impossible to see a way out, the destruction of both countries, [. . .]¹¹ Prussia will not be destroyed, but she will lose the best part of her population, which is even worse. Those poor *Sharloki!*¹² Karl Vogt is predicting dreadful reaction and militarism in the "German Empire".

Olga and Malwida are now in Florence and our house is as quiet as before. Nathalie (let this be *entre nous* for the moment) is dreaming of Russia, and I think about it more and more, but—but Nechayev and Compagnie have distinguished themselves by publishing an issue of the journal *Obshchina* [*The Commune*] in which they demand money from Ogarev and Bakunin, and want them to send it via *myself* since I am *in charge of their funds*. It is nothing but a charming little joke, a way of taking their vengeance on me for my having seen through them and recoiled in horror. Perhaps it will pass unnoticed in Russia, and I hope no one will believe it. People know what masterly liars they are. I embrace you all and kiss you warmly. Write sometime to

your TATA

I have Papasha's letters under lock and key.

105. Michael Bakunin to Nikolay Ogarev

2 NOVEMBER 1872   *Locarno*

So THEN, my old friend, the unheard-of has come to pass. The Republic has delivered up the wretched Nechayev.[13] What is saddest of all is that our government will doubtless resume the Nechayev trial and there will be new victims. Some kind of inner voice, though, tells me that Nechayev, who is irretrievably lost and certainly knows he is lost, will summon up on this occasion from the depths of his confused, sullied, but far from despicable being, all his primordial energy and prowess. He will perish a hero, and this time will betray nothing and no one. Such is my belief. We shall soon see if I am right.

I don't know about you, but I feel dreadfully sorry for him. No one has done me, and deliberately done me, so much harm as he, but still I feel sorry for him. He was a man of rare energy, and when you and I met him he was ablaze with a bright flame of love for our poor, oppressed people, was suffering real anguish at the historical misfortunes of our people. Then his slovenliness was still only outward; inwardly he was not dirty. His [love of] playing the general and the petty tyrant, and his methods of so-called Machiavellism and Jesuitism finally, thanks to his ignorance, plunged him wretchedly into the mire. Towards the end he became an utter fool.

Imagine, as early as two or three weeks before his arrest, we warned him through some acquaintances—not directly, because neither I nor any of my friends wished to meet him— to get out of Zurich as quickly as he could and that the police were looking for him. He wouldn't believe us, and said: "It's the Bakuninites trying to drive me away from Zurich," adding:

323

"Things are different now from what they were in 1870—now I've got my own people, friends in the Federal Council in Berne—they would warn me if I was threatened by such a danger." Well, he's had it now.

Now, my old friend, I have a request to make of you. You know that Marx, Utin and their company of German Yids have set in motion the most ferocious, slanderous campaign against me. I have to prove that I am not a thief. Therefore I am sending you a draft statement which I would like you to sign. Because you are a classicist, a stylist, you may disapprove of my turn of phrase. I do not defend it, alter it as much as you like, in accordance with your fastidious taste. But I doubt if you will want or find it necessary to alter any of the actual content of the statement I am furnishing you with—because that content, as you know yourself, is in strict conformity with the purest truth—and truth may not be altered.

I do not feel it necessary to call upon you in the name of our old friendship to write and sign such a statement. Your sense of justice will be sufficient for that—let us save our friendship for other, more pleasant things.

Your M. BAKUNIN

My address is still the same: Canton de Tessin. Locarno, Monsieur M. Bakounine.

Draft Statement[14]

I HEREBY declare that I did myself, in person and directly hand over to Nechayev the so-called Bakhmetev fund to be passed on to the Russian Committee, which, as Nechayev assured me, existed in Russia and of which Nechayev was, in his own words and by virtue of the documents he showed me, merely a secret agent abroad.

Bakunin did not have any right whatever to the administration of the Bakhmetev fund. That right belonged exclusively to Herzen and myself and, after Herzen's death, to myself alone. Therefore Bakunin was not present when the fund was handed over to Nechayev, an action performed by myself alone in the presence of Natalya Alexandrovna Herzen. In this I made a great mistake. Believing almost unconditionally in Nechayev's revolutionary honour, I did not ask him for a receipt. Later, when, on the strength of facts which shattered my good opinion of Nechayev, I requested a receipt from him, in the presence of Bakunin, O[zer]ov, R[os]s[15] and Semen Serebrennikov, Nechayev, whilst fully admitting that he had received the Bakhmetev fund from me, refused, however, to give me a receipt to that effect, on the grounds that the Russian Committee was not in the habit of giving receipts. This was extremely dishonourable on Nechayev's part and finally convinced me of his moral bankruptcy.

Bakunin's part in this matter was as follows. Upon the death of Herzen he set about persuading me to hand over the entire Bakhmetev fund to Nechayev as agent of the Russian Committee and sole representative of the Russian revolutionary cause. This was anyway not a very difficult task, since both I and Bakunin had an identical belief in both the existence and the serious character of this Committee and both regarded Nechayev as its chief representative abroad.

This testimony, which fully accords with the truth, I sign with my own name.   *N. Og[arev]*
Witnesses to signature:
 Zaitsev *O[zer]ov* and *Jacobi* (if he wishes)

106. *A View of Nechayev's Writings in Prison*

(a police report submitted to the Tsar)[16]

THE PAPERS examined by me may be divided, according to their content, into four categories.

To the *first* category I have assigned two letters to His Imperial Majesty and the initial draft of one of them. These have already been communicated to His Majesty. Having considered them carefully in relation to the other papers, one might say that the first letter is, as it stands, not a statement of the author's political convictions, but an account of the immediate political aims pursued by the author, and in this latter sense it is fairly sincere.

To the *second* category I have assigned several publicistic articles which contain partly an apology for the activities of the author as chief instigator of a certain kind of political propaganda amongst students, and partly his own personal thoughts and impressions. Your Excellency will be able to form a more correct opinion of this section on the basis of a few extracts. Of relevance here are the letters from London concerning the aims of modern democracy; political reflections; impressions of prison life ("A Living Grave"); and the most remarkable of all the articles I examined—one on the nature of the youth movement at the end of the 1860s.

The *third* category includes the following works of literary fiction:

(1) fragments of a rather bulky novel entitled "Georgette" and set in the time of the fall of the Second Empire in France;

(2) fragments from another novel dealing with life in the student milieu and among *émigrés* and Russian travellers abroad, entitled: "Whose is the Future", "On the Waters", and, also of particular interest, *"Une Vieille Connaissance"*;

(3) fragments entitled "Recollections of Paris", which describe scenes from the fall of the Second Empire;

(4) rough sketches apparently also related to the novel "Georgette": "In the Realm of the Bourgeoisie"—concerning the fall of the Paris Commune, and "In the Grand Circle and the Garret"—which describes the preparations for putting the International into action;

(5) a lengthy but utterly drab extract from a novel "With the Lipovans";[17] and

(6) a short fragment "Milovzorov's School", in which an old-style grammar school run by a sexton is presented in a vile light. More interesting than the other novels in this category is "Georgette", and the fragments "Whose is the Future" and "On the Waters".

"Georgette" is the story of a French girl of modest means who, despite a convent education, becomes, through the influence of her old republican father and the young man with whom she has fallen in love, a republican of the reddest hue. Her beloved turns out to be one of the ringleaders of the International and commands the love of one of the great ladies of the Second Empire, herself a highly depraved woman. The leader of the International, after Georgette refuses to become his mistress until a Republic is proclaimed, enters into a liaison with the great lady, and during the siege of Paris divides his time between her and Georgette. On the day of MacMahon's capture of Paris he is killed on the barricades, while Georgette, after going through all kinds of sufferings and humiliations, dies at Versailles. Prominent on this canvas are the rather numerous erotic scenes upon which the author dwells with especial love, their physiological source evidently being his youth and solitary confinement. Apart from this, there are many exalted socialistic and humanitarian tirades. The idea that people who love one another should not waste their energies on the gratification of their feelings while they are needed to help solve social problems is developed with great fervour and at great length both in this novel and in the fragment "Whose is the Future". But in the latter work, the heroine finally decides that indulgence in the delights of eroticism will not enfeeble the energetic man, and sets off to visit him in his bedroom. In both novels, women of higher social standing are portrayed as monsters of depravity. The picture he [Nechayev] paints in his fragment "On the Waters" descends to cynicism of the foulest order. But then, cynicism and deliberate crudeness are notable features of the language too of these "fighters for new ideas". If, in the articles I have assigned to the second category, the author occasionally displays an undeniable respect for erudition and the power of thought, his works of fiction are striking for the total absence in them of any moral sentiment.

The *fourth* category includes a good half of the papers examined, and I venture to describe them as trash of no interest to anyone other than their author. They are: various excerpts from and sketches of novels, copied extracts from works of poetry and prose in the German, French, and English languages, vocabularies, excerpts from and résumés of various books and newspaper articles [Nechayev had] read, a translation of Macaulay's articles "William Pitt" and "Atterbury", odd jottings, and so on. Naturally all this gives some indication of the author's opinions and inclinations, but we have a much more detailed and more accurate knowledge of these from other sources.

In general, one cannot call the author an ordinary individual. The extreme scantiness of his elementary education is everywhere apparent, but we can discern an amazing persistence and strength of will in the mass of knowledge he has since acquired. This knowledge, this concentration of his energies, has developed in him to the extreme all the virtues of the self-taught man: energy, the habit of self-reliance, utter mastery of the knowledge at his disposal, and a fascination exercised over those who, proceeding from an identical standpoint, have been unable to achieve as much as he has. But at the same time he has developed all the shortcomings of the self-taught man: a contempt for all he doesn't know, the absence of any critical approach to the knowledge he possesses; envy, and the most ruthless hatred of everyone who has come easily by what he has had to struggle for; lack of a sense of moderation; inability to distinguish the sophism from the correct deduction; deliberate disregard for what does not fit in with his desired theories; suspicion, scorn, hatred and enmity towards all who are, by their wealth, social position, or even education, his superiors. Even a devotion to the same aims as those pursued by the author does not save such persons. Doubts are cast upon its sincerity and, where this is impossible, it is labelled as dull-witted or amateurish; and suspicion and scorn are poured upon its adherents. Only the author and the persons in his own circle, [persons] of the same origin and mode of thought as himself, are acknowleged as servants of the people, and repositories of the popular sympathy and trust. Everything else originating from the people is declared to be hostile to the people, and the era of fruitful, peaceful and many-sided development is to commence only with its annihilation.

Especially typical is the author's attitude to the idea of a violent upheaval. He repeatedly rejects it as an event that does not create anything lasting—on the contrary, it engenders reaction. But he does not acknowledge any sincerity in the turning of the upper classes towards service of the people, considering them an obstacle to be removed at all costs. He admits that [violent] upheavals are nevertheless inevitable, and that the harmonious development of the community is a task for the future. At the same time he believes that hatred is one of the most essential strengths of the public leader. I do not think it possible to see in all this an unconscious contradiction; it is rather the mask of moderation with which the author has not managed to come to terms.

Very often, people in the author's position earn, by the dignity of their conduct, the respect of those who are inimical to their activities and mode of thought. The personality of the author, insofar as it is reflected in his papers, inspires no such feeling of respect. The papers were not written with the intention of public circulation; and yet the author depicts himself as one enmeshed in privations which he has [in fact] never suffered, while there is no trace of any sincerity or explanation of his motives for particular actions. For example, he gives as an explanation of his behaviour at the trial his respect for the dignity of Switzerland, etc. Recognition of the victors' right to self-defence,[18] so frequently found among the Decembrists, is totally lacking in the author. A tendency to revel in the contemplation of the force of his own loathing for all well-to-do people, the deliberate development in himself of instincts whose soundness and legitimacy he has not verified, [instincts] that drive him to an almost blind hostility to the existing order—these are all features of one who is a revolutionary not by conviction but rather by temperament, as the author—not without a certain amount of satisfaction—admits to seeing himself. Perhaps the author is indebted to them for some of the influence he exerts over people who are even less cultured and less accustomed to take a critical view of their own opinions. But of course, these features would not increase the respect of an impartial person for the author—even the respect that one cannot deny a talented enemy.

III

MEMORIES IN EXILE

"His bedroom was the same as before, just as he had left it; not a book had been moved, yet it did not seem to be his . . . He looked for his old school notebooks in a drawer, a diary he had kept for years, some letters. He was amazed that he had written them—he had no recollection of them, everything referred to strange forgotten incidents. . ."

DINO BUZZATI, *The Tartar Steppe*

6. The Aftermath of Ideology

107. Natalie Herzen to Maria Reichel

24 January 1871
St-Jean-la-Tour
Genève

MERCI, MY DEAR, good, kind Masha, for remembering me on the 21st and writing to me. I for my part was thinking of you at that time more than you suppose, perhaps because ever since the 14th (exactly a year since Papasha fell ill) I have been continuing to copy out Papasha's letters to you. How he loved and respected you, dear Masha! Those letters are a treasure-house; for there can scarcely be anyone to whom he wrote at greater length with greater frankness than to yourself, especially at the most painful moments of his life. To Ogarev he wrote frequently, when they were separated; but those separations did not last long; his letters to Ogarev are more like business communications, with the exception of a dozen or so. He left everything that was on his mind until their meetings, and sorted things out, *viva voce*.

How he suffered! And how deceptive was his vivacity, his outward gaiety. Those who knew him but little thought him the gayest and most carefree man in the world in his private life.

I think I wrote to you of how I spent 25 December of 1870, of how, when I learned that the workers were organizing a "Children's Party" at the *Internationale*, I decided to present them with a Christmas tree, decorated. The children, that is Liza and Shushka, and myself, spent the whole week working on it, making paper flowers, gold chains, tinsel, and so on. The members of the women's section staged a *tableau vivant*—in

333

a word, the party was a great success, and I spent my birthday in the company of three hundred children. It was nice to gaze at their cheerful little faces. I couldn't have chosen a better way of spending the day; to stay at home would have been too dismal. I welcomed the New Year gloomily. There was no consolation either in memories or in the present. Ogarev's situation, or his state, both disturbs and pains me; but I will tell you all about that *viva voce*, because I shall certainly be paying you a visit before the spring.

We are thinking ever more and more about Russia, and unless something unexpected happens I hope to be in Florence at the end of April, and in May or June on my way to Petersburg with Nathalie and Liza. Whether we shall stay there I do not know; I think it unlikely. Did you hear that they have begun arresting people again in Petersburg? The Engelhardts, husband and wife, are in jail, and a young girl *chemist*, Volkova, too (a remarkable woman by all accounts), and masses of students. We do not know the reason here. Perhaps I too will find myself spending a little time in jail; but let us hope for the best. Forgive me for writing so badly and confusedly, but I have such a terrible headache that I shall have to end here— and it hasn't ached for a long time.

I give Sasha a special kiss; his letter made me very happy; for I confess I was afraid he would grow into a *blind* German patriot, but I see I was mistaken and that he is capable of regarding his compatriots with a critical eye; tell him that I am very happy indeed to see that. And really, how can one retain one's composure when one reads the details of the merciless brutality and the senseless plundering, the *pillage* of these Germans, who pride themselves on being the most cultured of peoples. Obviously, cerebral development has little effect upon the heart.

How is old "mémé"? Was she very grieved by the death of poor Martin? Perhaps I ought to send her something? She is probably living in great poverty, and we ought to make the most of our Paris house before the Prussians destroy it completely, and give things to everybody who has suffered in this senseless war.

Farewell, then, I am going to lie down for a while. I embrace you and all yours. Goodbye, my dear, old friend.

TATA

Nathalie and Liza send their regards to you all.
I know nothing of Bakunin and have not heard anything.

108. *Natalie Herzen to Maria Reichel*

7 FEBRUARY 1871   *St-Jean-la-Tour*
                                                         Genève

I KNOW, my dear Masha, that you are not advising me to turn into a "niggardly bourgeois"! And I know it's silly to spend money, throw it around and give it to people who are not really in extremity; it is madness and even a sin. Of course money is power, tremendous power! And if I have come to possess the tiniest fraction of this power, I want to use it as sensibly as I can.

We have enough unfortunate instances before our very eyes— Ogarev, for example. What has become of his fortune? After all, it was ten times greater than ours. Did he do anything useful at all with his wealth? Absolutely nothing. He gave away huge sums to scoundrels who drank, caroused, and gambled them away, while he himself was left virtually penniless. The money, that is the 20,000 roubles, are out of the question. Where could we get such an amount? At the most favourable times our joint income amounts to perhaps 48 or 50,000 francs a year. In 1870 we received only 9,000 francs apiece, because there were various unaccustomed expenses and debts. This year we shall as likely as not receive less rather than more, as a result of the war—the Paris house is yielding nothing. I do not use it all on myself, of course; you know I dress comparatively simply and am not fastidious or anything like that. A part goes for Shushka, and as for my savings, I know just how to use them, after all, we are surrounded by people who are in somewhat greater need than Egor Ivanovich! So please write to him and say that, although we are not ruined, we do not have such

335

[large] amounts at our disposal. Tell him what you know about us; and next week I myself will write to him *without mentioning his request*. It is so disagreeable; I cannot accustom myself to refuse, and yet I have to. I think, therefore, that it is better not to tell him that you have shown me *the whole of his letter*. What do you think? How am I to write to him? Send me his address, please.

None of us has any thought of taking *Russian citizenship*, of that there can be no question. If I go to Russia it will be as a *citoyenne Fribourgeoise*, and so I shall have no right to the estate, and moreover the date is long past. They have been asking the heirs to come forward for ten years, but when we learned of that it was too late. But if Egor Ivanovich can secure it, all the better, for it will be *more innocuous*, of course, in his hands, than in the hands of the Russian government.

Shushka is unwell again; he is such a sickly child; he would do better to live in the South. There is an *ambulance française* just down the street, I will go after dinner and see if I can be of any use.

I kiss you all. Farewell.

TATA H[ERZEN]

Poor France . . . what has happened to your Sasha? Judging by his last letter but one, his reasoning is not that of a blind patriot. I thank him for his letter, I have no time to answer it, and in any case I shall soon be able to argue with him *viva voce*.

109. *Natalie Herzen to Maria Reichel*

6 MARCH 1871 *St-Jean-la-Tour*
Genève

YES, MASHA my dear, the situation of poor Egor Ivanovich is an unenviable one, but we must try and do something for him. How can we be sure, though, that if we do send him some [money] it will not be used again by some Z[. . .]d's or other, or similar friends? I have just written to Sasha and sent on Tatyana Petrovna's[1] letter to him (to read and return) and I have suggested that he write to her himself asking her to send the 3,500 francs which she owes us to Egor Ivanovich; if not all at once then, say, in lots of 200 roubles every three or six months. Let us wait and see what will be Sasha's reply.

Tatyana Petrovna borrowed the money from Papasha seven or eight years ago. She came specially from Paris to us at Torquay—[in] Devonshire. Since that time her sons have come into some legacies or other, and they must be fairly wealthy. If Sasha is unwilling then I will send the poor old man as much as I can afford out of my own savings—but I should like to be sure that Egor Ivanovich will use the money on himself.

Masha, my dear, you once promised me to make one or two inquiries about the school at Hofwyl. Can you tell me something about it or obtain for me a *prospectus* or syllabus through the acquaintance of whom you wrote?

Farewell and goodbye, dear Masha of ours, I hope to be with you by April. I shall be coming with Shushka because I want to show him to Adolf Vogt; the doctor here has discovered that he has a very weak *chest*, and this frightens and alarms me somewhat; I should like to know Adolf Vogt's opinion and whether he thinks it essential to take Shushka to the *South*.

Tessié is alive and well; his daughter is now Mme Berthe Armangout; she and her husband are in Florence. Jules Armangout or Armangod (I am not sure) has been all this time in Paris with old Tessié, and Mme Tessié and her daughter have been in Bordeaux.

I embrace you and all of you, and kiss you warmly. Once more, farewell.

TATA H[ERZEN]

110. *Natalie Herzen to Maria Reichel*

St-Jean-la-Tour
Genève

WELL, HOW is your tummy, Masha my dear? Let me know if you have recovered, or are you still troubled?

We arrived in Geneva at eleven o'clock and everyone at home had already gone to bed. Poor Pan Tchorzewski had been three days in a row to meet us at the railway station, but on Sunday, of all days, he wasn't there.

Imagine, Masha, our tradesman has no more buckwheat left! It really is a nuisance! But he has promised to get some, and when he does I will send you some immediately.

Toots misses you very much and still keeps on saying: "*Je regrette bien Berne, et les bois, et surtout Alexandre et Ernest et Max et Mascha et Mr Reichel, enfin tout—tout—tout.*" But he evidently has a particular *foible* for Sasha—he is determined to write to him. As for me, I forgot after all to note down the name of that codliver oil that Adolf Vogt was talking about. Send it to me, please, with your new address too.

I am sending you the latest photograph of myself—*nobody* here likes it *at all*, so I have very few copies of it.

We have begun packing—phew, what a tedious business. There has still been no reply from the Embassy.

I read in the papers here that amongst the insurgents taken prisoner by the Versaillais are the Reclus brothers, our good friends, and exceedingly noble, honourable, and cultured persons. Elisée Reclus is considerably well known for his scholarly works. The fact that they took part in the uprising reinforces my faith in the Paris movement and makes me wonder yet again if the Versaillais are not deliberately exaggerating the *horrific stories* that are being told about the Paris Terror. The Reclus brothers are by no means *ultra-rouge*. They know Bakunin but are not in sympathy with his *actions*. Surely they are not going to shoot them too?

Man is indeed the most brutal and vicious of beasts.

We shall almost certainly see each other again before our journey to Russia, but meanwhile I embrace and kiss you from the bottom of my heart, my dear kind Masha. Nathalie and Liza send you all "flirtatious glances".

TATA H[ERZEN]

18 APRIL
We seem to have only one volume of *Dead Souls*, which I am sending you; Sasha will send you the other.

111. *Natalie Herzen to Maria Reichel*

9 JULY 1871

Pension Sutterlin
80 Quai du Léman
Pâquis
Genève

YES, SOMEHOW we have not written to each other for a very long time, Masha dear, probably because our personal lives have been jogging along their usual course, just like old times, and then, too, there have been such dreadful happenings as to make one's hair stand on end, in public life, that is.

In my opinion it was preposterous of the "Commune" to destroy the Tuileries, and as for the other horrors of which there has been so much scandalous talk, one should not form a hasty judgement. God knows what tales people are telling about this wretched "Commune". I am personally acquainted with several of its members and know that they would never permit any *excès*. Everything people are saying about *petroleuses* and *petroleurs* is pure invention too; they destroyed the houses which prevented them from defending themselves. But all the *anti-socialists* and bourgeois find it profitable to blacken the movement and try to prove that the members of the "Commune" are nothing better than a gang of robbers and *échappés de bagne*, and it appears that your Sasha too is disposed to regard them in the same light, is he not?

But what makes one's hair stand on end is the conduct of the Versaillais now. We know for a certainty here that they are mercilessly shooting men, women and even *children*—this I know from the tales of *eye-witnesses*. And then their official journal (of the Versaillais, that is) announces that: "such-and-such a man or woman has been executed"—while I know *for sure* that those people are alive and well and have managed to flee. So what does that prove?—that they have been executing *innocent people* in their places.

This letter has remained unfinished for more than ten days, Masha dear. I was daily expecting Sasha—he was to have come at the beginning of July—but yesterday I received a dispatch in which he said that he would not be arriving until the end of this month because his children had fallen ill, though it appears to be nothing serious. Sasha is going to Paris to arrange and complete the division (of the inheritance) since Olga has come of age according to the Fribourg laws (she is almost twenty-one). Sasha is going to [. . .][2] too in order to legalize Toots, and he will probably come and stay with you for a day or two.

Olga and Malwida are in Ems, and will go from there to Schwalbach—the doctors say that Olga is short of blood, and are sending her there. It's terrible, to be running to the *"waters"* and taking cures at her age. From there they are to go south to the Tirol and I am to join them there. What we shall do after that I do not know; Sasha and I want to hold a family "consultation". At first we all hoped still that we should be allowed into Russia, in spite of the refusal. But after the Paris Commune business it is out of the question. There will be a period of reaction in Russia too; everyone is telling us so, even those who believed most strongly in the possibility of our returning. Yesterday we received the Russian papers with a complete account of the Nechayev trial.[3] Knowing how interested you are in it, I will send it to you as soon as everyone here has read it. He is a crafty fellow indeed, and played an important part in the murder of Ivanov, as you will see.

Farewell for today. I embrace and kiss you warmly, and Reichel and the children also. Write and tell me how you are. Why did Sasha-Gottekind not go with the other pupils? Give my regards to all the Adolf-Vogts.

TATA H[ERZEN]

Compliments from Nathalie, Lisa et Toots.[4]

21 JULY 1871

112. *Natalie Herzen to Maria Reichel*

UNDATED[5]   *Geneva*

YOUR SASHA is here with us, Masha my dear, and is in good health and spirits. I think he is developing very well. If only you could hear our interminable arguments and philosophical conversations—it's simply marvellous! How is poor Ernest—will he be laid up a long while yet? Was he amused by the book or was it too childish for him?

Be *very* cautious with all the Russians who have recently arrived. Remember, a new type of man *à la* Nechayev is forming among them, a kind of *revolutionary Jesuit* who is ready to commit any vileness in order to achieve his goal, *i.e.* revolution in Russia. To this end, and in the most shameless fashion, he feels free to *lie*, to read other people's letters, to steal documents, keys, etc. In Russia they force people to make donations of enormous sums by *threatening* to denounce them to the Third Section. Those are *facts*, Masha. It is simply outrageous.

I embrace and kiss you, Reichel, Ernest, and Max.

TATA H[ERZEN]

Zhukovsky would like to know *what* Gustav Vogt has published about the Serebrennikov Case, and in which newspapers.

113. Natalie Herzen to Nikolay Ogarev

20 OCTOBER 1875　　　　　　　　　　　　　*No. 76 Rue d'Assas*
　　　　　　　　　　　　　　　　　　　　　　　Paris

I FEEL very guilty towards you, my dear kind Aga. I haven't written to you for God knows how long. Somehow I haven't been able to bring myself to write at all, my spirits have not been very high, and all my friends have had almost no news from me for the whole of the summer. I have spent all my time either in or around Paris; three or four weeks with Olga in Maisons-Laffitte, then back to Paris for about the same length of time, either alone or with Bébé (that is, Olga's little son).

Did you know that I have a flat near Olga? It is a very nice and pleasant arrangement; we are together, and yet we each of us have our own corner. I was hoping that Liza would be coming, but at the moment she is still in Nice with Nathalie, and will in all probability spend the whole winter there. Sasha has started thinking of moving to Switzerland. Everything in Italy is becoming so expensive that he cannot conceive of bringing up the children there, and moreover, he wants to be closer to Toots but without taking charge of him entirely. I do not think anyone would advise him to take Toots into his house now; Volodya is already seven, he and Lelya *commencent à donner du fil à retordre*, while Toots continues to get up to all kinds of tricks, and doesn't learn a thing, so that dear patient Masha (Mme Reichel) has no idea what to do with him. I would willingly take him into my own home, but I fear that "more harm than good would come of it", since I am insufficiently strict; and also, Switzerland would be far better than Paris for a boy of his age, while I have no intention of moving from here in the near future. I shall travel in the summer, but my *pied à terre* will be in Paris, around Olga's nest at 76 Rue d'Assas.

Luginin is here with his wife. We see one another quite often, and I am very glad they have decided to spend all their winters in Paris; in summer they will be in the country near Kiev. Do you ever see Lavrov? If so, then please thank him on my behalf for the journal (nos. 18 and 19 of *Vpered* [*Forward*]) he sent me with the beginning of the article on Papasha.

So they are continuing still to make arrests in Russia. Now it is the professors' turn; did you see it in the papers the other day?

Did you hear that Doctor Botkin has gone mad? His wife died, and he torments himself with the thought that he gave her the wrong treatment and failed to understand what her illness was.

Well, I have run out of space. Farewell, I kiss you affectionately and with all my heart, my dear Aga. Do not be angry with me, and write and tell me what you are doing, how you are getting on, and whom you are seeing.

Tata H[erzen]

114. Natalie Herzen to Nikolay Ogarev

5 December 1875

No. 76 Rue d'Assas
Paris

Yes, my dear Aga, I had thought about your birthday even before receiving your letter, and was about to hug and kiss you—at least, on paper.

The first days of December are filled with memories for us: the birthdays of Lelya-boy and Lelya-girl, your birthday, Papasha's name-day (today, 5 December) which we always used to celebrate so gaily; then on 14 December the Russians will meet at our place; the 25th is my birthday, and then there is the New Year, and so on. Olga's boy will be two on the 24th. But the time of family celebrations is seemingly over for us, at any rate for myself. However, my life here is a very agreeable one, and I shall very likely take up permanent residence here, that is, I shall not leave Paris until Olga moves, and that will in all probability never happen, since Gabriel [Olga Monod's husband] *prend plus et plus racine ici*; the various schools, societies, journals and publications to which he contributes make his moving inconceivable except as a last resort, that is, in case of a *coup d'État*, for instance the return of the Bonapartes.

Liza is still in Nice with Nathalie.[6] It appears that neither of them is enjoying herself very much there, but they cannot think of anything; they don't know where to go or what to do. I feel sorry for both of them, but I do not know what I could do for them or how to help them arrange their life more reasonably.

It is cold and snowing here; my hands are so frozen that I can barely hold the pen—hence my terrible writing. Farewell, my dear, 62-year-old Aga, I hug you warmly and kiss you with all my heart.

TATA

Compliments to Mary.[7]

115. *Natalie Herzen to Nikolay Ogarev*

SUNDAY, 8 OCTOBER 1876
Villa Herzen
Via Bolognese
Florence

I AM so ashamed, my dear good Aga, at not having written to you with news for so long, that I will make no attempt to excuse myself; instead I will begin at once telling you what we are all doing. You know that I spent July and August in Bayreuth with Malwida, Olga, Gabriel and Bébé. Well, we had a very

343

good time there, in a pleasant flat with a big garden; towards the end we were joined by cousin Meshchersky (he was at your place in Geneva, remember?). We went to all the rehearsals and performances of Wagner's opera *Der Ring des Nibelungen*, which has several parts (1) *Rheingold*, (2) *Walküre*, (3) *Siegfried*, and lastly (4) *Götterdämmerung*. You have probably read the various critics and studied the subject more than I have, so I will not go into details, but merely say, in a few words, that the whole made a great impression upon me, that I very much enjoyed the music and am very pleased to have been in Bayreuth.

Olga and I parted at the end of August; she left for the waters at Schwalbach, with Gabriel, Malwida and Bébé, while I went south to Sasha, and have now been five weeks with them in their *dacha*. The children are growing and developing; Volodya and Alexey (or Alessino, as he is called here) are starting to read and write. They are being brought up very simply and reasonably, and the result is exceedingly satisfactory: they are lively, intelligent, and get up to tricks, which is natural for children of their age, but they are rarely, almost never, wilfully naughty. The latest child—a girl—was born in August; they have called her "Nella"—God knows why.

Precisely one week ago Toots arrived here from Switzerland. I had not seen him for about two years and found him little altered—he has grown slightly but his features have remained the same. He will be staying in the family now and going to the Domangé school with Volodya; the others are continuing at the Kindergarten for the time being. So we now have nine children in the house—and Meshchersky too, who is more pranksome than the others. He came to us for two days from Livorno and, while playing with the children, sprained something in his knee, and so awkwardly at that, that he had to spend two weeks lying in bed, and even now he still cannot walk easily.

I shall very likely stay in Florence for all of October, and then return to my little Parisian "home" at 76 Rue d'Assas. So then, send your answer meanwhile to me here at the *dacha* and tell me what you are doing, how your poor hand is, and your legs, and your health in general.

The Ozerovs are here in Florence, and Mme Kasatkina also, who is now Madame Celloni—her husband is a young Italian doctor, and good-looking. Her daughters are being brought up and educated by Ozerov *père*.

They say Nathalie is in Russia,[8] but I do not know for certain; for some reason she hasn't written for a long time.

Farewell, my dear Aga, all of us hug and kiss you and beg you not to leave us for long without news.

TATA H[ERZEN]

Compliments to Mary.[9]

116. *Natalie Herzen to Nikolay Ogarev*

10 FEBRUARY 1877   *No. 76 Rue d'Assas*
                                                          Paris

I FEEL guilty towards you, my dear Aga, for having left you once again without news for so long. But perhaps it may console you to know that you are not the only one to complain —all my friends and acquaintances [are doing the same]; I am rebuked on all sides and told that I am an exceedingly bad correspondent. I do not know myself how it happens or why I do not have time to do one half of what I should like to. We are leading a quiet, regular existence, in which *family life* plays a considerable role, and this shortens the day a great deal. I calculate that I have eleven or even twelve children, because I love my nephews and nieces as though they were my own children, and care for them even from afar—I correspond with them, and try to influence Toots and the rest of them by my advice so as to lighten as far as possible the task of Teresina and Sasha. I even look upon Olga just a little bit as my own child. She is getting better, thanks to a well-ordered, normal life; she rises early, goes to bed early, and twice a day takes a walk in the Luxembourg gardens and does gymnastics. After coming home we read together. We spend much time together and are becoming closer and closer to one another. After dinner we all play with the children and, after bidding them good night, the

345

three of us—myself, Olga and Gavryusha [Gabriel Monod] read until nine o'clock—a journal, an article or a newspaper, or the novel of Turgenev's which is being printed in French translation at the moment in the supplement to the journal *Temps*. I have not seen Turgenev since I received your last letter but one. But I shall certainly call and see him next week and try to obtain his novel for you.

Merci for your verses, my dear Aga. Take Mary's advice, write down your dreams and do not forget to send me a copy; it gives me great pleasure.

The young S. I. Taneev, Rubinstein's favourite pupil, visits us from time to time and plays the fortepiano for hours on end—he knows everything by heart. It is wonderfully agreeable. His family has been acquainted with Egor Ivanovich Herzen (our old uncle in Moscow, Papasha's brother, you remember?) ever since the turn of the century. He himself has often visited my uncle, and tells many sad tales of the poor old man, who is now totally blind and so poor that he sometimes has nothing to keep himself warm with.

What news of Henry? How are things with you, Aga? Is your hand giving you more peace now?

Farewell, do not leave us long without news. I embrace and kiss you affectionately.

TATA H[ERZEN]

Compliments to Mary.[10]

117. *Natalie Herzen to Nikolay Ogarev*

MONDAY, 14 MAY 1877

No. 76 Rue d'Assas
Paris

THIS TIME I am guilty of being late with the money; forgive me, Aga my dear. Gavryusha gave it to me several days ago now, as I intended long since to write to you. Although Olga and the children are still in Le Havre, we have had quite a lot of trouble here.

We have probably already told you about Gavryusha's brother, a lad of about twenty-two, Avgust Eduardovich by name. He limps heavily, and at times his leg hurts and gives him a great deal of pain. Well, he had an attack here in Paris at the beginning of April. His father came to order some special kind of mechanism for his leg, then his mother arrived. The invalid was transferred to our flat, where he still lies to this day. The old lady is still here also and time flies seemingly even more quickly than usual. We are on excellent terms with Gavryusha's mother and father—in fact, with all the members of his family; they are all such simple, good people, one can get along splendidly with them despite differences of opinion on many subjects.

Yesterday evening I was at Turgenev's—no, the day before. He had fixed that day for his departure, but suddenly fell ill with gout, and is lying in bed with it even now, poor man. But he is still amazingly handsome and attractive in spite of it.

Of course I followed the trial of the people accused of social-revolutionary propaganda, but nevertheless I would very much like to read the pamphlet you mentioned, published, I think, under the editorship of *Vpered* [*Forward*]—please send it, don't forget. How sorry I feel for all these young people! So much self-sacrifice, so much strength expended to no purpose! One cannot but admire their courage, especially that of the women, but at the same time I have to admit that they act like madmen and their aim is beyond my comprehension.

Thank you very much for your latest verses, my dear Aga; send me everything you write or compose. I embrace and kiss you affectionately, with all my heart. Write and tell me when you receive the money.

TATA H[ERZEN]

Tatyana Alexeevna Astrakova[11] often inquires about you, and sends her regards to her *amico*, as she calls you.

118. Natalie Herzen to Maria Reichel

13 MAY 1879   *76 Rue d'Assas*
                                                              Paris
MY DEAR MASHA,

Rumours are going around here that a certain girl student tried to poison herself in Berne, but was saved, and people are collecting money to pay her debts and make it possible for her to return to Russia. Do you know her, or know of the story? After hearing of all that is happening in Russia I am absolutely at a loss to know whom to believe. If a wretched woman comes along, a compatriot of mine, and says that she is starving to death, how am I to know that the money I give her will not be spent on some silly and ultra-pernicious leaflet instead of on food? Leo Berline has already written to Meshchersky about this student, but I should like to hear from *you* if you are personally acquainted with her and if she is worthy of our interest. I want to be *certain* that the money (assuming that we manage to collect any) will not be used for some political folly, and on that score I still have my doubts.

Olga, Gabriel, and the children are still in Le Havre. They are all thriving. I paid them a visit and returned here on Friday with Isabelle (Gabriel's sister) who will be staying here until the end of the month. She has remembered Alex on more than one occasion, and asks you to give him her very best regards. If he should ever be in Le Havre he will be welcomed with open arms.

It has almost definitely been decided that Olga and Gabriel will spend two months in Switzerland this summer, August and September, that is. I intend to go to Florence in September, but will make a stop in Switzerland on the way, and hope to cover you all with kisses then. Where will you be, in Berne itself or in the Oberland?

How are you all keeping? How is Reichel's health and your own, Masha, my dear? I don't think I need to ask after your little lads; they are so healthy. I was overjoyed at the news that Alex is in Berne again. But what of Ernest? Isn't he thinking of coming to Paris? Do you remember how we talked of his coming to complete his education, his studies and so on in Paris, and after him, Max Adolfovich?

Is there any news amongst our Berne acquaintances?

Everything is fine with Sasha in Florence too. Next Saturday they are having a big celebration; Teresina and all the children are celebrating together on 18 May, since they were almost all born in May. Volodya is ten already!

Farewell, my dear sweet Masha, I embrace you and yours with all my heart.

TATA

Give my regards to the Vogts.
Meshchersky sends you all his warmest regards.

7. The Ideology of an Aftermath

119. N. Tuchkova-Ogareva: Memoirs (1894)

. . . . HAVING BADE Victor Hugo goodbye on the eve of our departure, we set off for Geneva again. This time there were various troubles in store for Herzen there: Bakunin and Nechayev were with Ogarev and were trying to persuade the latter to join forces with them in demanding the Bakhmetev money, or the *fund*, from Herzen. These persistent requests annoyed and worried Herzen. In addition he was distressed that Ogarev could so easily have succumbed to the will of these gentlemen.

Gathering almost daily at Ogarev's they talked and talked and never could reach an agreement. When he told me about those discussions at cross purposes Alexander Ivanovich said sadly: "When I object to the senseless use of this money for the imaginary salvation of some persons or other in Russia—and it seems to me that it will, on the contrary, bring only worse ruin upon the persons in Russia, because these gentlemen are dreadfully imprudent—well, when I protest against all this, Ogarev answers: 'But look, Alexander, we have put our joint signatures to the receipt for the money, and I am of the opinion that it can be used to advantage as Bakunin and Nechayev describe.' What can I say to that? It's the truth, after all, and I am entirely to blame for not having wanted to accept the money on my own."

Thinking over all the aforementioned I chanced upon a happy thought, of which I at once informed Herzen. He approved of it and acted upon my advice. It was as follows: that the fund should be divided between Ogarev and Herzen, with 10,000 francs to each, and that amounts should be paid out of Ogarev's part whenever it was at his request, but the other half should be used at the discretion of Herzen and Herzen only.

Herzen wished to use this money to expand the activities of the Russian press so that new Russian *émigrés* could make use of it in due course, and at the same time he wanted to give some work to Czerniecki, who was incapable of doing any other kind of job. Czerniecki was in danger of dying of starvation, and Alexander Ivanovich, himself a humane and a sick man, was greatly troubled by this. But my idea was only half realized. Ogarev quickly used up all his part, and he began pressing Herzen once again to give him more money for some emergency or other. But Alexander Ivanovich did not give him any of his own half: it was still intact when he died. Subsequently, after the death of his father, Alexander Alexandrovich said to me:

"We are honest people, Nathalie, and I would like to keep this money in our hands. Is there much of it left? You know more about these things than I do."

"Ten thousand francs," I replied.

"Tell me your view," he said.

"Your father wanted to use this money to expand the Russian press, but since you will not be engaging in Russian propaganda activities, I think it would be better to give the money over to Ogarev and Bakunin; then you will bear no personal responsibility for it", I said.

Alexander Alexandrovich went to Geneva and handed over the money, as I have already written. Shortly afterwards poor Czerniecki fell gravely ill and was no longer able to work; he had developed cancer of the stomach. Natalya Alexandrovna alone (Herzen's daughter) supported him to the end.

To return to my account of Herzen's stay in Geneva. On the day after the agreement concerning the fund had been concluded with Ogarev, Nechayev was to come to Herzen to collect the cheque. I was in Herzen's study, where he was occupied, when Nechayev presented himself. He was a young man of medium build, with small features, short dark hair and a low forehead. As he entered, his small, black, fiery eyes were fixed upon Herzen. He was very reserved and spoke little. According to Herzen, he bowed stiffly and then somewhat awkwardly and unwillingly held out his hand to Alexander Ivanovich.

Few people aroused as much antipathy in Herzen as did Nechayev. Alexander Ivanovich felt there was something grim and savage in his look. Perhaps he was influenced by the story of the murder of Ivanov at the Petrovsky Academy, which was being much talked about at the time.[1]

After spending some time in Geneva we travelled to Paris; Herzen's French friends and Vyrubov were very eager for him to settle down in Paris with all his family. Since he did not dabble in foreign propaganda, why should Napoleon harass him, particularly as at that time (the end of 1869) the ground was somehow beginning to give way beneath the audacious usurper's feet? I recall various events which had struck us at the time of our last visit to Paris: the story of the murder of V. Noir by Pierre Bonaparte, which had caused a great sensation and provoked a demonstration at V. Noir's funeral.[2] I recall too a fact no less striking: Napoleon was presiding over the Chamber of Deputies and, glancing at Henri Rochefort, gave an almost imperceptible smile. Rochefort took offence and said in a loud voice: "Why is that man smiling as he looks at me? What does he find so ludicrous about me? In my opinion the man who places a piece of raw meat on his hat during the hunt so that the eagle will hover over him is far more ludicrous." Napoleon was displeased at his election and so his smile had been an expression of his annoyance and contempt for the choice, but Rochefort's response was undoubtedly heard by many people and did Napoleon great harm. Mockery can kill, especially in France.

On this occasion we found Sergey Petrovich Botkin and his family in Paris, which made Herzen very happy. Sergey Petrovich hoped then that Herzen's organic strength would overcome the diabetes; the reverse happened. But doctors cannot foresee the fatal contingencies that can sometimes have such a decisive influence on [the course of] an illness.

We stayed at the Grand Hôtel, on the fourth floor. Sergey Petrovich was kind and considerate as always. There was such light and goodness in his wonderful smile that I found him handsome; I was pleasantly struck in particular when he would let his gaze dwell upon Herzen, filled with such unfeigned love and delight. Herzen too was very glad to see him; he even felt better in the presence of Sergey Petrovich because the latter had a reassuring effect on him.

We were sitting at home in our small drawing-room and talking almost gaily of how we should probably be able to settle down here. There would be suitable and even interesting society for Natasha; regarding education, there was no doubt that we would find all we desired here. . . Suddenly a letter was delivered to Herzen from his son, saying that Natasha had been taken very ill, and asking his father to come immediately to Florence.

Knowing his daughter's strong constitution, Herzen was puzzled and sent a telegram inquiring what the nature of the illness was. After a short time he received a reply, silently handed me the telegram, and then said: "I would sooner learn that she has departed this life." The telegram bore the words: *"Dérangement des facultés intellectuelles."* The dreadful imprudence of this message almost paralysed him. He sat there in a kind of numbness, pale, and made no effort to collect his thoughts. Obviously we could not let him go alone, and he said himself: "It would be better if we all went together."

I quickly packed the most necessary things and, after paying our hotel bill, and having no time to bid farewell to anyone in Paris, we went on the offchance to the southern railway terminal—trains left frequently from there. As it happened, we had not to wait but to hurry. Herzen bought the tickets, I registered the suitcases, and my daughter (who was then ten) purchased some victuals in the buffet for the journey and managed to pay for them herself. We travelled non-stop. It was very tiring for us all, but especially for the child. As if she understood the important reason for our haste, my daughter did not complain, and longed impatiently to arrive so she could see Natasha. Herzen was silent almost the whole way; his inward anxiety and impatience were visible on his haggard face. At last we reached Genoa; from there Herzen continued the journey alone, having requested me to wait in Genoa for news from him. If the patient was in any condition to travel, Herzen would bring her here and we would go back together to Paris; if the doctor ordered her to remain a little longer in Florence, Herzen would inform us and we too would set off for Florence. The next day we presented our card at the post office and were given a letter and a telegram. The telegram merely said that we were to expect a letter, but the letter told us to come immediately to Florence. We did so. When our train pulled into the station at Florence we saw Alexander Ivanovich and his son who had come to meet us. They hired a carriage and drove us straight to the *dacha* which Alexander Alexandrovich had purchased. There we saw first of all Alexander Alexandrovich's wife and their firstborn, a delightful child for whom Herzen was full of admiration. Then we went to visit the patient—she was overjoyed to see us, but Herzen decided that it would be more convenient for the patient and for all of us to live in the town now, and so the next day we moved with the patient to the Hôtel de France, where Herzen had already taken several rooms prior to our arrival. We spent approximately two weeks in this hotel. Again I had to part with my daughter: I put her for the moment with Meysenbug and Olga, and myself stayed with Natasha. There was no one in the family except myself to attend to her. Meysenbug made no attempt to look after the invalid, and I did not wish to entrust the sick girl to strangers. True, before my arrival, a friend, Miss Raymond (a Negress), had been engaged [to nurse the invalid], on the advice of the doctor, but despite all her experience she merely irritated the patient. What was needed here was not experience but love.[3]

However, my care was rewarded with success: the invalid began to improve. Little by little she recovered her sleep and her appetite, but I searched in vain for any expression of joy on Herzen's sombre face: he was shattered and had not the strength either to believe in or hope for his beloved daughter's recovery. He lived in a kind of morbid expectancy. The doctor allowed the invalid to leave Florence and travel with us to Paris, where there were medical facilities on an even larger scale than in Florence. My daughter and Natasha went with us. Alexander Alexandrovich accompanied us to the station alone. For some reason Olga and Meysenbug did not say goodbye to us.

This time there was no hurry. On the contrary, we journeyed very slowly. We made several rest-stops along the way. We spent a day in Genoa;[4] I remember that Herzen wrote to Florence then and said to me: "What should I say to Olga and Malwida? Should I summon them to Paris or leave them in Italy? They are so unwilling to go away from here!" But I advised him to summon them because I could see the sick girl still needed me, and Herzen, shaken and distraught as he was, was in no state to look after my own daughter. Nor could he spend time with the invalid: her shattered nerves could not bear the sound of her father's sonorous voice.[5]

We stopped also in Nice for a day or two,[6] then rested in Lyons, and finally came to Paris where we lodged at the Pension Rovigo. But as it turned out, the pension was unsuitable for the sick girl and so Herzen, in the course of his daily strolls about the town, searched for a spacious flat which would accommodate us all in comfort. Soon after our arrival Olga and Malwida appeared,[7] though actually with great reluctance. They were sorry to exchange Florence for Paris. Then we moved to a large flat in the Rue de Rivoli—Pavillon Rohan, No. 172 —to that terrible, fateful house where he who, forgetful of himself, had lived and thought for his country, for mankind, for his family, after an illness lasting only some five days[8] suddenly departed from us for ever.

I fear I shall not manage to describe everything that I would like to convey. I feel the approach of old age, and I am often possessed by a kind of apathy, an inertia . . . therefore I have resolved to note down, albeit in fragments, what comes to mind.

After Herzen's death I had quite made up my mind to remain in Paris for the education of my daughter, on the advice of Vyrubov. The change in my plans perhaps paved the way in the future for those fateful circumstances which were subsequently to strike me a terrible blow [Liza's suicide], a blow which put an end to my life as an individual. For after that, what remained was not life but service: service to near ones and distant ones, service to convictions and recollections. But first I must say what induced me to go back on my intention of setting up my residence in Paris.

Shortly after the demise of A. I. Herzen his elder daughter Natasha went with Tchorzewski to Geneva for a meeting with N. P. Ogarev. There at the time were Bakunin, Nechayev and many other less noteworthy of their revolutionary accomplices. Bakunin and Ogarev knew of Natasha's recent illness, which had hardly begun to pass and during which she had had visions of the most dramatic scenes of revolution.[9] At the time of her illness her sufferings had been so intense, so vivid, that I myself had suffered a great deal [merely] in watching her. Nevertheless these gentlemen had made the strange and ill-considered decision to draw her into the revolutionary network of their party. Seeing in the sick girl the rich heiress to a part of Herzen's fortune, Bakunin did not hesitate to sacrifice her for the *cause*, forgetting that it was precisely this kind of revolutionary situation that could put her in danger of a relapse. Bakunin did this not out of any personal greed for money; he attached no importance to it. But he loved the revolutionary cause as an occupation, an activity more essential to his restless nature than his daily bread.

Natasha returned to us in Paris, uncommunicative and full of mystery, and informed us that she was intending to settle near Ogarev in Geneva. Her brother, A.A., and I were struck not only by her determination but also by her enigmatic air and her pensiveness. With tears in his eyes A.A. begged me to go with her to Geneva and not leave her under the exclusive influence of the revolutionaries. But his pleadings were unnecessary: I loved Natasha. Having cared for her through two illnesses which had, according to knowledgeable persons, been probably not unconnected, I was glad that fate had given me the opportunity to prove, in memory of Herzen, that I loved his Natasha no less than my own daughter. A.A. and Malwida von Meysenbug suggested that we should put Natasha in an institution; to look after her seemed inconceivable to them. But I, myself a stranger, refused to have her handed over to the care of strangers: "As long as I am still on my feet I will not abandon her." My care was rewarded with success; she soon began to recuperate; but her loving father departed from us without seeing her well. My awareness of this has been one of the most painful emotions I have ever experienced.

Upon our arrival in Geneva we lodged at first in a small pension. The company at this pension was of the most uninteresting kind, and the food seemed to be there merely for appearances' sake—there was nothing nutritious about it. On that score I recall our laughing once while at the table d'hôte when some young man, probably a *commis-voyageur,* passed me a dish with pompous gravity, saying: *"Permettez-moi, madame, de vous offrir ces ossements",* since there was no meat but simply bones.

But to return to my story. Every morning Natasha went off to Ogarev's and sat at a desk there. She had been given the responsibility of secretary to the society, and for some time she did not realize that they were playing at secrecy as children play with dolls. Occasionally she would be going away with a terrible migraine and I would try to dissuade her from doing so, but she would answer that she was not allowed to miss a single day. It sometimes happened that, once there, she would feel even worse and be obliged to abandon her work, lie down on the sofa and spend the night at Ogarev's, while I waited for her with extreme anxiety. Once, an hour or two after her leaving, a note was delivered to me in which she said that she was going away to Berne for a couple of days to visit Maria Kasparovna Reichel, an old friend of Herzen's and his family. On the third day she came back and admitted to me that she had not been to Maria Kasparovna's at all, but that Nechayev had sent her with a commission to some gentleman who lived in the mountains.[10] She had had to make the difficult journey alone with a guide and pass the night in some deserted place in the house of a deaf and unwelcoming old woman. She had been given a little room in the attic; the door would not close and was continually banging in the strong wind. Natasha had moved a heavy chest of drawers over to the door and then gone to bed, but was quite unable to sleep. My heart sank as I listened to her story. I was afraid that all these agitations and fears might have affected her nervous nature, shattered as it was by her illness. Fortunately there were none of the consequences I had expected—evidently she was on the mend. I tried to prove to her in our conversations that it was all a game, that there had probably been no need to send her into the mountains. The commission had been invented in order to test her courage and obedience, and also to excite her interest. In his correspondence with his sister Alexander Alexandrovich also sought to weaken Bakunin's influence, by saying that he had considered the activities of his father and Ogarev as serious-minded propaganda—but these revolutionaries did not have any aim, they were simply playing at revolution.

We were engaged at that time in printing a posthumous edition of Herzen's writings. For some reason Nechayev and company discovered that this volume was to include an article on the Nihilists,[11] and so I received by post from Germany a document headed *"The People's Vengeance"*. This missive had evidently been written in Geneva;[12] it contained an instruction forbidding us to print the works of the thoughtless but talented parasite,[13] Herzen, and saying that if I and his family did not heed this warning drastic measures would be taken against us. I sent the original of this document to the editors of *Russkaya Starina* during the lifetime of M. I. Semevsky.

Of course we continued the printing, if anything with increased zeal. Informed by me of this mysterious message, Alexander Alexandrovich Herzen wrote and asked me to go and seek the advice of Karl Vogt and give him the original manuscript for safe keeping, since I had an accurate copy. I had been an occasional visitor to the Vogt household, I knew Vogt's charming wife, and I went to see them as Alexander Alexandrovich had advised; but this time, after I had sat a little while with Mme Vogt, I told her that I had to discuss a serious matter with her husband. She went upstairs to him and returned shortly to fetch me, saying that Karl Vogt had asked me to come up because he was lying down with a terrible migraine. He too was prone to this disease, as was the entire Herzen family.

When I entered Vogt was lying in his dressing-gown on his bed; his face expressed his unbearable suffering, and I tried to give a concise account of my business. I told him briefly of the threats from the Nihilists. He became highly indignant and was of the same opinion as we—that these threats could only lend more energy to our efforts to publish the posthumous anthology, and he readily took the original manuscript into his keeping. Since I did not know what was meant by *drastic measures*,[14] I thought they might wish to seize the manuscript by force, and so I entrusted it to Vogt.

Natasha was improving. Since her illness she had regarded the revolutionaries with more equanimity and begun to go less often to Ogarev, and to see Bakunin and his followers less frequently. As a consequence of this we moved from the pension to somewhere farther away and settled in a small house which had apparently been built for its tenants with an eye to beauty rather than durability. The house was situated in a big garden; in the same garden stood a large house which was occupied by the landlord and his household.

A few words should be said on the subject of the landlord, for he was, in his own way, a curiosity. I have forgotten his name, but I have not forgotten his obnoxious looks. He was the embodiment of the bourgeois and had earned the reputation of being a dreadful reactionary: of medium height and remarkably lean, he was rather like a spider or a skeleton and held himself so unnaturally erect that he looked as if he had swallowed a yardstick and from that moment lost all his elasticity and flexibility of limb. His voice was clipped and its sound more reminiscent of some bird of prey than the human voice. His head was always tilted proudly back; he wore a hat (a *cheminée*), and I often marvelled that it did not fall off his tilting head. The sight of his property would cause him to fly into raptures of tender emotion. He cherished all that belonged to him, and therefore passionately loved the apartment we had taken. At least once a week and sometimes even more frequently he would call on us and lovingly inspect all the rooms on various pretexts, but actually because he did not trust us. He wanted to see how we were treating his property and made us feel that it was all his and that we were there only to ensure that the property brought in an income. Sometimes these visitations were very amusing, but for the most part they were a nuisance, because each of us had her own affairs to attend to, and we had to follow him around the rooms and sometimes even sit with him in the drawing-room.

I was occupied at the time with the publication of the posthumous anthology and, apart from that, with a translation into French of the "Letters from France and Italy"; and Natasha had taken charge of the education of her brother's eldest son, who was called Toots; the same child who is occasionally mentioned in Herzen's letters to Ogarev and whose mother ended her brief days in so tragic a manner, by throwing herself into the river at the exact spot where the waters of the dark-blue Rhone and the white Arvier meet.[15] It is a very strange sight. The two rivers flow side by side for a long stretch, each preserving its own colour, and only farther down do they merge completely. The Rhone has deep grottoes, and into one of them the body of the wretched Charlotta was washed. When she had arrived from England with little Toots she had been accommodated in Ogarev's house, but soon Mary had begun to be jealous of the partiality shown to her by Ogarev and her own son Henry. Charlotta loved Ogarev like a father. When she found herself hearing obscure reproaches from Ogarev she realized that Mary had been casting slurs upon her for his benefit; she had cried bitterly on that last day and asked Mary to give her some vodka. Mary did so, and that evening Charlotta vanished—which gave the virtuous Mary occasion to spread abroad the rumour that Charlotta had abandoned her child to Mary's care and eloped with a new lover. But the Rhone took its vengeance upon Mary and acquitted its unhappy victim. Four years later it cast up out of the grotto on to the surface of the waters the body of Charlotta. The police recalled the disappearance of the young Englishwoman from Lancy and requested Mary to take a look at her victim: one leg was still booted, and there was a bunch of keys in her pocket. Mary identified the keys and the remains of the deceased. Surely she must have felt some pangs in her heart for her unworthy slander.[16]

Little Toots was very gifted, but unbelievably obstinate and capricious. There were frequent amusing scenes between the patient aunt and the obstinate nephew. Once he absolutely refused to go to school, and when his aunt said that they would stop sending him, he announced that he would go immediately, and started screaming through the house. Neither Natasha nor myself could calm him. I left them, and then suddenly I had the brilliant idea of calming him by cunning. After waiting a little while, I went back in to Natasha and told her, in Toot's presence, that the landlord had sent word to us that he was being so disturbed by the dreadful screaming that he had asked us to lock the screamer in the cellar. The ruse could not have succeeded better: not only did Toots believe it, but Natasha too.

"Is it really true?" she questioned me in English.

"Of course not, it's all nonsense," I replied in a serious voice so as not to undeceive Toots by my laughter.

The landlord was so odd that one could believe anything.

In Geneva we became acquainted with a fellow-countryman (one of the Nihilists). He had left Russia several years ago and had been in America too. We liked him because he was more open and unpretentious than the [other] Nihilists. He told us his name was Serebrennikov, but that was quite possibly an assumed name. Many of the *émigrés* lived under assumed names.

The police were already searching for Nechayev then, and it was while Nechayev was out walking with Serebrennikov that the police swooped upon them. Nechayev, however, succeeded in escaping; but Serebrennikov was seized and taken off to prison. In the prison Serebrennikov was interrogated and his testimony recorded. Some Russian general or other was summoned by telegram from St Petersburg, came and read Serebrennikov's testimony and went to have a look at him in the prison. At the time of his arrest Serebrennikov had been living at Ogarev's. A few days after his arrest a policeman called on Ogarev saying that Serebrennikov had asked for his travelling bag with his documents; Ogarev, not suspecting that it was a police trap, handed over Serebrennikov's papers. The latter was in despair when he learned of this, because amongst those papers there were letters and names, and they could prejudice many people.

At that time the Russian *émigrés*, women included, were much given to discussing the murder of Ivanov by Nechayev. From Nechayev himself no one ever heard a word; he was obstinately silent. The *émigrés* were split into two factions. One of these was of the opinion that a petition should be sent to the Swiss government trying to prevail upon it not to extradite Nechayev and declaring that the entire Russian *émigré* community was in sympathy with Nechayev. The other, on the contrary, refused to admit to any solidarity with him and maintained that since they had heard nothing from Nechayev himself they were unable to form a true idea of the affair or come to any conclusion, and Natasha and myself were of this mind.

On this account it was decided to call a meeting of all the Russian *émigrés* to hear their views. We thought that there would be much talk and no meeting. But one day Nikolay Ivanovich Zhukovsky, who was giving my daughter Russian language lessons at the time, informed us that the meeting of *émigrés* would certainly be held in the next few days, and that we too would be summoned to it. We were not a little surprised at this, for we were well aware of how the Nihilists regarded our family. They called us aristocrats, parasites, and so on. However, we were soon presented with a formal invitation, and we decided to go out of curiosity, without attaching any importance to this assemblage. My daughter, then twelve years old, insisted on accompanying us, but fortunately I succeeded in dissuading her. She had to get up early and the meeting had been arranged for ten o'clock in the evening and might last until after midnight; we lived at some distance and would have to go on foot since there would be no carriages at such a late hour in Geneva. I often recalled this meeting in later life and I was glad that my daughter had not been with us.

In the evening of the appointed day we both set off to find the café where the conference of *émigrés* was to take place. There was a large hall on the *rez-de-chaussée*: a table covered with an oil-cloth stretched the entire length of the room, and chairs had been placed around it. The room was already filled with many of our compatriots, both familiar and unfamiliar. Two or three hanging lamps brightly illuminated the whole room and its occupants. At last Ogarev appeared and the conference began. I think the chairman was Mechnikov. I could tell at once by Ogarev's face that he was not entirely sober; all were seated, and Ogarev who was beside me rested his elbow on my chair and dozed. He tried to listen attentively to what was being said, but could not, and merely said from time to time, apropos and malapropos: "Have pity on him, gentlemen, intercede for him" (that is, for Nechayev). Nechayev was pacing up and down the room, never approaching the table or joining in the talk; but his presence probably caused many of them great embarrassment. When all had seated themselves and fallen silent, the chairman gave a résumé of the purpose of the meeting and the questions he would put to the *émigrés*.

"It would be desirable to know if many people present at this gathering consider themselves in sympathy with Nechayev. Will those who do not, please raise their hands?"

I raised my hand, and so did Natasha and many others. Then there began a discussion as to whether it was necessary to request the Swiss government not to extradite Russian political offenders. At this point the discussion became more noisy, and it was difficult to distinguish what was being said. Some suggested that there was no need to talk of this because it had not happened and never would happen. Others spoke of the unhappy position of Serebrennikov. How was one to prove that he was not Nechayev? The witnesses summoned from Russia were feeling homesick and beginning to have their doubts: might he not be Nechayev himself? And Serebrennikov's papers were in the hands of Russian spies. What was to be done to obtain Serebrennikov's release? Something must be thought of quickly; every hour was precious, he might be extradited at any moment.

They talked and talked and came to no decision.

At the stroke of midnight Mary came to fetch Ogarev. Regretfully she was not at all that mild little woman described so charmingly by T. P. Passek, who did not know her in the slightest. Her face *(couprosie)*[17] showed that she had often had a drop too much. By her awkward gait and jerky movements I guessed that she was drunk, and tried to move my chair away from Ogarev who noticed nothing, smiled benevolently, and drew his chair nearer again. I was glad when everyone rose and began making ready to leave. Only Ogarev still remained seated. Suddenly, pushing her way unceremoniously through the crowd, Mary came up to us and started to utter insolent remarks in English, shaking her fists.

"Gentlemen", I cried in a fright, "What am I to do? I don't know how to fight."

Then Nechayev and some others seized Mary and escorted her away. Someone came up to Ogarev and offered to see him home. Natasha and I were overjoyed at our unexpected deliverance but frightened for Ogarev. Having handed Mary over to someone else, Nechayev again approached us and we both with one voice began begging him not to leave Ogarev alone with that dreadful woman.

"Of course not," he answered, "I have given orders for him to be protected, but what's to be done? He often catches it, and who's to blame? Why did he become involved with a woman like that?"

He could not see my face, for my veil was lowered. He did not know what pain he had caused me or what a reproach he was flinging at me.

When we took our leave I held out my hand to him in farewell and thanked him warmly for having saved me from being insulted. We set off home. Nechayev walked with us, saying that since it was so late he would accompany us. Next day Natasha once again went to Ogarev; she was occupied with the fate of poor Serebrennikov.

When we were alone together in the evenings she would question me about my impressions of the meeting of the *émigrés*. She was generally fonder of questioning than of speaking her own mind. I answered that that meeting had not even been worth meeting for.

"What solidarity can one feel," I said, "with a man who does not have sufficient respect for the *émigrés* to explain the Ivanov affair to them? Now Serebrennikov I do feel sorry for. He must be rescued, and I have been thinking it over. Karl

Vogt is a member of the Grand Conseil. He is highly respected and people would believe him—but how can Vogt be made to believe us?"

"What do you mean, believe what?" asked Natasha.

"Why, that Serebrennikov is not Nechayev, of course. He will think that we want to save Nechayev."

A few days went by after this conversation.

"Nechayev is having great difficulty in concealing himself, they are searching everywhere for him," Natasha said to me suddenly, late one evening.

"What can we do?" I replied. "He ought to go away. . . It's late, time to go to bed."

"No, let's stay up a little longer," she insisted. "Tell me, what would you do if Nechayev were to come and ask you to hide him?" And she glanced at me with that sweet smile of hers. "Tell me, eh?"

"I don't know—anyway, where could we hide anyone here, with our landlord as well? You know my views on Nechayev. Forget about him! Let's go to bed."

"But supposing he were to come and beg you to hide him for just two or three days?" Natasha continued to question me. "Would you really refuse, Nathalie, if he had no roof over his head?"

"I have no love for him and no respect for him, and he will not come here," I replied sharply.

Suddenly there was a ring at the bell.

"How late it is," I said. "No matter who it is, the girl is asleep."

"Wait, I'll go and see," said Natasha, "—and what if it's he?"

She returned a few minutes later and said to me in a whisper: "It *is* he, you know!"

"What, really?" I exclaimed in consternation.

"Surely you aren't going to send him away?" she said softly.

"No, we can't do that, but how disagreeable I find all this!" I said.

I went out into the hall and caught sight of Nechayev. He bowed, held out his hand to me, and said:

"Allow me to stay with you for two or three days, no more."

"Very well," I said, "but it is impossible to conceal yourself for very long here."

He came in, unnoticed by the servants since they were all asleep.

Next to Natasha's room there was a narrow, unoccupied room. Here we placed a mattress, a pillow and linen; he made himself a bed on the floor. In Natasha's room we moved her heavy dressing-table up against the door which led between the two rooms; apart from this door each room had a door opening onto a small corridor. I attached a handbell to one of the legs of the dressing-table and said to Natasha that if anyone moved the table the bell would ring and I would come at once. I highly disapproved of Natasha's and Nechayev's being in such close proximity, but there was no other accommodation. We dispersed very late and, tired as we were, slept soundly. But a few days later I was woken early in the morning by the sound of a bell and I rushed in to Natasha.

"The bell rang!" I said in a fright.

"But it was in the pension across the road, and you've woken me up," said the sleepy Natasha.

"I'm so sorry. . ." I was very frightened.

The only person we had occasion to tell of the presence of a stranger in the house was my daughter; the domestics did not know of it and never went into the empty room, the windows of which were curtained over. On various pretexts my daughter would keep some food, ostensibly for herself, and take it up to Nechayev. He spent the daytime in Natasha's room and was constantly visited by some Italian revolutionary, Zamperini, who was always promising to bring Nechayev a workingman's shirt and basket, but in fact would come and talk and nothing more.

A week had already passed since Nechayev had come and accommodated himself with us; I was extremely eager that he should leave, but he was continually postponing [his departure].

Serebrennikov's position was becoming very dangerous, and therefore I decided to go and see Karl Vogt. This time I found him well. He was sitting on his own in the drawing-room.

Having exchanged greetings with him I said:

"I have come, Monsieur Vogt, to beg a great favour of you—you are our only hope."

"What, are the Nihilists threatening you again?" he inquired.

"No, it is something else," I replied. "You have heard about the arrest of our compatriot Serebrennikov, and perhaps you have heard too of Ogarev's mistake in handing over Serebrennikov's travelling bag to a policeman. If Serebrennikov is extradited things will be very bad both for him and for many other people, because those papers included letters and names. . ."

"Yes, yes," he said, "I have heard something about it."

"I should like you to give your word of honour to the Grand Conseil that Serebrennikov is not Nechayev—they will believe you."

"I understand," he said, with a barely perceptible smile; "you wish to save Nechayev and that's why you say that it is not he."

"No, he really is not Nechayev, I assure you," I rejoined.

"But what proof have you that he is not?" inquired Vogt.

"I cannot give you any proof, but I can only give you my word of honour that he is not," was my reply.

"But if he were Nechayev you would probably not hesitate either to say that he was not, in order to get him released."

"That is true. Although I am not a friend of his I would have to try and save him even then. What good can it do Switzerland to brand herself with such a shameful stigma as the extradition of a political offender?"

"Where is Nechayev, then?" asked Karl Vogt.

"He is in hiding," I answered. "I give you my word that he is at large—I know it for certain, but there can be no question of proving it."

Vogt was silent and sat lost in thought; then he suddenly looked up, turned to me and, with remarkable perspicacity, exclaimed: "He's hiding in your house!"

"You have guessed right—I am not afraid to admit it to you."

"He is your enemy, and Herzen's too, and yet you expose yourself [to danger] in order to save him," he said, with an expression I had never seen on his face.

"Well, it can't be helped, it's the truth," I said, getting up. "Now you will believe me and tell them that Serebrennikov is not Nechayev."

"Yes, I will do it," he agreed, and, taking my hand, he pressed it warmly. And so we parted.

When Natasha and I saw each other that evening I told her of my conversation with Vogt and of his promise. Natasha was very glad that the Serebrennikov affair was taking such a happy turn. A few days later we learned that Serebrennikov had been released thanks to Vogt's intervention.

A day or two after my visit to Karl Vogt our landlord took it into his head to inspect our apartment. I thought with horror of Nechayev and set off to tour the rooms with the landlord. We went everywhere, even into the kitchen, and then he came into the corridor beside Natasha's room, while I stood with my back to the door of the empty room, having no intention of letting him in there, but wondering how [I could prevent him]? I had to think of something quickly. . .

The landlord kept me outside that door for a long, long time as he related to me his plans for converting the house. I don't remember what I managed to say to him, for I was almost feverish. At last, to my great joy and surprise, he bowed, turned on his heels and went away. I went over to the window and nervously followed him with my gaze, fearing that he might turn and come back, as he sometimes did. Finally, frightened and out of sorts, I went in to Natasha. Natasha glanced at me and laughed:

"What's the matter with you, you look awful?"

"I feel awful! I have just spent some very unpleasant moments outside Nechayev's door. What if the landlord had opened it! He would have seen a young man, a bed on the floor, and the curtains drawn. For one thing, what would he have thought of us? Fine ladies we are and in mourning! Then he would have asked to see Nechayev's passport, made a fuss, and handed him over to the police, and the lord-knows-what consequences there might have been. No, it's time he left our house and Geneva—he's been with us ten days now already."

At that moment Nechayev entered.

"It seems to me," I said, "that it will be awkward for you to remain in our house any longer. Our landlord is a terrible reactionary—he could have handed you over [to the authorities] today, and that is no trifling matter."

"But Zamperini keeps promising to bring me a worker's tunic and a basket, and I'll go out without anyone noticing" Nechayev replied to me.

"A fine revolutionary he is if he hasn't managed to get hold of such trivialities in ten days! And where do you have to go?" I inquired. "Probably you want to cross the lake and go ashore in Savoy?"

"Yes, of course," Nechayev said. "I must go into retreat if only for a little while."

"If you like, I will drive you out somewhere tomorrow?" I said promptly.

Nechayev gave a distrusting smile and Natasha glanced at me curiously.

"It's very simple," I said. "You'll see. Be ready at twelve o'clock tomorrow."

In the morning I ordered a carriage with a pair of good horses for twelve o'clock. And at twelve o'clock a carriage with a beautiful pair of bays was standing at our porch. The wife of our landlord was walking with her children across the garden on her way into the house for lunch. Noticing the carriage outside our house she came over and said good-day to me, and inquired who had come to visit us or who was driving out. We always went on foot.

"I am going for a drive," I answered her calmly. "The doctor has ordered us to drive somewhere a little farther out of town, for my daughter's health—so I have hired a carriage."

Her curiosity satisfied, she took her leave of me and went on her way, while I went in to Nechayev.

"You are ready, and the carriage has arrived—let's go," I said hastily.

He held out his hand to Natasha, said farewell to her, and followed me out.

The maid-servant, who had taken Nechayev for one of the Russians who used to frequent our house, paid no attention to him, particularly as it was all being done openly, in broad daylight and without any secrecy. The three of us went outside. I sat next to Nechayev [in the carriage] and my daughter went in front, and we sped quickly away from Geneva to some little place—I no longer remember where—about three hours' drive from Geneva. When we had left the city behind I gave a sigh of relief, even though I had been sure that the police would never imagine that Nechayev would drive out of Geneva at mid-day in such a fine carriage with such swift horses. I found the thought of more or less assured success a pleasant one, but I also experienced the awful sensation that gamblers must feel.

In about three hours we came to the spot we had chosen. As usual the coachman took us to the only tavern, where there was nothing edible to be had but the view over the lake was magnificent. In the little garden which surrounded the inn there were beds of flowers and arbours with tables; during holidays there were probably many visitors here who, having had their hours of boating on the lake, would come and taste the unpretentious Swiss dishes and sip the local wine. And so we seated ourselves in one of the arbours, asked for something to eat, and were served with cheese and sour-sweet white wine.

"You didn't believe me," I said to Nechayev with an exultant air, "but I was more prompt in arranging your removal than that Zamperini of yours."

I was pleased and laughed heartily.

"We didn't know you," Nechayev rejoined. "I am very sorry that I judged you without knowing you."

But Nechayev could not relax. He was evidently in a hurry: he had almost made his escape, that was why he was terrified, and he was eager to get across to the other side. When he took his leave he told me that he would never forget what I had done for him, and thanked my daughter too for her concern for him and for having known how to keep a secret despite her tender years. He got into a boat and waved his handkerchief to us for a long time—and crossed safely to Savoy.

Why did he not go off to America, as Natasha and myself frequently advised him to do during his sojourn in our house? At that time I had occasional heated arguments with him, saying that I did not understand the Nihilists, that we should work for reforms and popular education in our country, while they were after goodness-knows-what and would never achieve anything.

On one occasion he and Natasha were sitting alone together in her room. Nechayev noticed that she was staring fixedly at his hands, and asked her why. At first she was unwilling to say what was in her mind, but he insisted.

"There is something odd about your fingers, they look as if they have been bitten—I was thinking that it was Ivanov . . ." she said.

Nechayev did not let her finish.

"What nonsense!" he said, and started to pace up and down the room; and then he changed the subject.

Nechayev subsequently returned to Geneva and was arrested by the police. It happened while I and my daughter were in the mountains; Tchorzewski was there too, and we were expecting Natasha Herzen. Suddenly I received a telegram to say that the chief of police wished to see me. I had caught a cold and was unwell at the time, and Tchorzewski advised me to reply that I could not receive him on account of my illness; but it occurred to me that I might try to arouse his humanity and pride in his country. I answered that I was ill but able to receive him.

He came, and we spent more than an hour together.

After the usual formalities of greeting, he said to me:

"You knew Nechayev—I should like to satisfy myself that it is he we have arrested," and he placed [before me] photographs showing various views of the same face.

"It was a few years ago that I saw Nechayev, and only briefly—you see, he was not one of Herzen's followers—I should be afraid of making a mistake, there is such an amazing likeness, [but] such a vital question cannot be decided on likeness alone—and if one were mistaken, how disastrous the consequences would be! I have been wanting to see you too, to beg you to save not only him who is at your mercy but also the honour of your country. Surely she is not going to brand herself with such an indelible scar as that of the extradition of a political offender?"

"But our government," said the chief of police, "regards Nechayev purely as a criminal offender."

"But still, the affair is implicitly a political one," I rejoined. "And is Switzerland, the land of freedom, really going to stoop so low as to extradite the accused man?"

"Probably. The Russian government has promised ours not to judge Nechayev as a political offender," he answered.

I smiled: so the wolf was promising to protect the sheep!

"Please," I continued, with fervour, "if the honour of your country is dear to you, give your prisoner the opportunity to slip away, to escape to America if you like, they haven't started extraditing people there yet. Think well—nothing will wash this stain away, it will go down in history—have pity on free Helvetia, she knows not what she is doing, she is in a bourgeois fever!"

He rose, and we parted, neither of us having achieved our desired aim. How could he, senior police officer though he was, understand the pain I felt at the possibility of the degradation of a country once proud of its freedom and its ability to remain independent amidst the powerful states?

Staroe Aksheno
20 OCTOBER 1894

120. *Natalie Herzen: Reminiscences (1931)*

AFTER MY father's death on 21 January 1870 I thought only of Ogarev, of the shock he was feeling, and I insisted upon being allowed to go to Geneva to ascertain in what measure I could console him.

Upon arriving in Geneva I found Ogarev better than I had expected. He was engrossed in the intrigues of Bakunin and

Nechayev, but he had some concern for me, tried to set me at ease, and said that I might be able to continue the work of my father. "How?" I asked Ogarev in surprise. "I don't myself know as yet," he answered. "We must have a look and see what you can do. For the moment, help me to sort out these papers: they are in such a mess, and you know how tired I get sorting them. Tatyana Petrovna Passek has already been rummaging in these drawers and left the papers in the most dreadful disorder."

He could not have found anything better for me, and at the beginning I occupied myself exclusively with it, observing all the while what was happening about us. I did not know then that Nechayev, unbeknown to Ogarev, had already ransacked his papers.

Bakunin visited us daily. Seated at the end of the table in the dining-cum-sitting room, he rolled himself cigarettes by the dozen.

Often young people would arrive. Bakunin would greet them with: "Hello, brother, and who are you? Where from? Well, come in and sit down, tell us. . ." With his hail-fellow-well-met manner Bakunin immediately won the heart and the confidence of every new arrival.

Later on Nechayev would come and stay for hour after hour arguing with Bakunin and Ogarev and pacing up and down the entire length of the room. From time to time Bakunin would say to me: "Yes, yes, you must follow in your father's footsteps and work for Russia."

"I don't know what I could do for this cause."

"Well, we shall see. In the meantime Nechayev will give you some work."

Nechayev, with his customary abruptness, said: "The work's in the next room. Come, and I'll show you."

I followed him into the small, adjacent room. There I saw piles of packets, wrapped books, and sealed envelopes. "There, begin with this—write all the addresses on them."

That took me several days. Once, while I was writing, Nechayev entered and asked meaningfully: "Can you draw?" I replied "Yes", and continued to write. "Can you draw me a *muzhik*?" With some surprise I answered, "Yes, I can draw one from a model: I have never set eyes on a *muzhik* in my life. And you are very vague. What size of drawing do you need, and what has the *muzhik* to be doing?"

"Well I never, so many questions! Look, like this, on paper this size, at the top, a *muzhik* in a circle the size of a five-franc piece."

"What, are you perhaps thinking of printing banknotes?"

"What nonsense are you talking?" And he spat to one side. Suddenly he stopped and asked: "Could you draw a torch and an axe?"

"What do you want to make with this emblem?" I exclaimed. "Leaflets or banknotes?"

"What rubbish!" And he left the room.

Bakunin tried every day to show me that I must be with them, if only to continue my father's work. I always made the same reply: "I need to have a clear idea of the ends and the means."

Ogarev too attempted to persuade me. He was the only one whom I trusted. I remembered my father's negative attitude to Bakunin's mode of operation. This memory reinforced my distrust, and I was on my guard despite my love and respect for Ogarev, who had evidently, to my great sorrow, fallen under the influence of Bakunin and Nechayev. I was constantly seeking an answer to the question of what I could do. Bakunin hinted at things that filled me with revulsion. For example: a beautiful, young lady can always be useful. I was speechless with amazement. "It's very simple. There are so many rich men, young and old, and it's easy to turn their heads and make them give money to the cause."

When he noticed my indignation he at once changed the subject. Seeing that he was making no progress he tried to act upon my imagination. One day he told me that he must have a serious talk with me, without Ogarev knowing, and that he wished to make an appointment to see me in a certain house, in a particular street, with which I was unfamiliar and which I do not remember. Late that evening, in the dark, I searched for that street in the Saint-Pierre district, and went up to the floor he had indicated in a house that was completely unknown to me. I was led into a room, where I found Bakunin waiting for me.[18] Soon Nechayev appeared and began immediately to pace the room from end to end. Both of them set about exhorting, nay, coercing, me to join them. They tried to prove to me how easily I might help them, if only by providing money. I might authorize them to put my name to the title-page of *The Bell* which they desired to publish as a continuation of the old one.

"Never," I said. "Never, because your *Bell* will have nothing in common with the old one."

Infuriated by my reply, both of them called me a pampered little miss, and a good-for-nothing. In his words and gestures Nechayev overstepped all bounds. Bakunin tried to pacify him [by saying]. "Now, now, calm down, you little tiger."

It was by then very late, and I announced that I wished to leave. Nechayev vanished, but Bakunin offered to see me home, and accompanied me right to the door of our lodging.

A little while later, the Russian government requested that the Swiss authorities extradite Nechayev as a common criminal. Nechayev went into hiding and changed his name as a precaution. I had lost contact with him when one day Ogarev invited me to his house to discuss a [certain] matter. I set off at once to see him.

"This is what it's all about," he said. "This manuscript—it's very important—it must be delivered to Nechayev, who is hiding under the guise of an Englishman. I was asked if I knew of anyone on whom I could rely absolutely. I replied that I could answer only for you. So then, will you undertake to deliver this manuscript?"

"Where do I have to go?"

Ogarev replied: "I don't know exactly. First you will have to go to Neuchâtel. They'll tell you there, at Guillaume's printing-works, where to go. But you have to know the password before they will tell you." (I think it was the names of three flowers, gentian, rhododendron, and edelweiss.)[19]

I was uneasy at this strange commission and my ignorance of the aim of the journey, but to please Ogarev and set his mind at rest I agreed.

"Under what name am I to seek Nechayev?"

"You will be told that in Neuchâtel."

"So all I have to do is deliver the manuscript?"

"No, no. You see these paragraphs? You are to say to Nechayev that I will never, never consent to subscribe to their programme unless those paragraphs are struck out. Never," Ogarev reiterated, with a forcefulness unusual for him.[20]

I skimmed through those paragraphs, rejoiced with all my heart at Ogarev's indignation, and set off reassured and certain that I should return the same day.

I did not feel well when I arrived at Neuchâtel, a town with which I was totally unfamiliar. At times I had the impression I was being followed, and I hardly had the courage to ask my way, although it was necessary. At last I came to some kind of passageway which I was told was the entrance to Guillaume's printing-works. There was a worker standing at the door, whom I asked how I could find Mr Guillaume. "I'll call him for you."

A lean, wooden-faced gentleman wearing spectacles came out. Stiffly he asked me: "What can I do for you?"

"The address of Mr X, to whom I have to give a manuscript."

"Mr X, Mr X . . . I don't know him." I was utterly taken aback and repeated: "I was told you would give me his address." Guillaume reiterated sternly and immovably: "I don't know him." Wretchedly agitated, I exclaimed after a few minutes: "Oh, Mr Guillaume, there was a pre-arranged phrase I was supposed to say to you, but I have forgotten it. Wait, wait, it was something to do with flowers, I believe it began with gentian. . ." He smiled and named the remaining two flowers.

Melting slightly, he called to me: "Come in, come in. Do you know that you have not yet reached your destination?"

"I do not know where I have to go, but I must return to Geneva by this evening".[21]

"Geneva? But that is impossible! There are no night trains going there."

Somewhat upset, I repeated, "But I have to be back in Geneva, I have to. . ."

"Impossible. It will be evening by the time you reach the place you have to go to, and there will be no more trains after that." (At that time there were no night trains at all in the whole of Switzerland.)

I was utterly distracted and wondered what I should do.

After a moment's thought Guillaume said: "I will telegraph Locle, which is where you are to go. It will be night by the time you arrive there. I will ask my friends to give you shelter, because you cannot stay in a hotel. Your appearance would arouse curiosity and the whole village would learn of your arrival, and that is precisely what we must avoid for the sake of X's safety. We have arranged for you to be met at the station, and you for your part are to hold a handkerchief in your left hand. . ."

My anxiety mounted, and I sighed, feeling sick at heart. Finally I asked: "When does my train leave?"

"You still have a little time," said Mr Guillaume, "and I will escort you to the station."

When we came to the station he asked me: "Have you eaten?"

"No," I replied.

"You cannot travel like that. Allow me to buy you a meal."

I declined. He insisted, saying: "But it's cold, have some soup, at least." I gave in and agreed to soup. While I was eating, Guillaume pulled a letter out of his pocket and, without opening it, showed it to me and asked: "Do you know this handwriting?"

"Of course," I replied. "It's Bakunin's."

"And this?" I recognized it, and several more which he showed me. "Amazing," he muttered, as though to himself. "You Russians are amazing." I looked at him questioningly. "Yes, you are so young, and already a conspirator."

"Ogarev has asked me to take this manuscript to Mr X, and that is what I am doing. Nothing more."

"But still, all the same. . ."

My train pulled in. Guillaume reminded me to hold the handkerchief in my left hand and trust the persons to whom he was recommending me. I got into the carriage. Passengers came in and got out one after another. And finally I was alone in the train. It was dark when I arrived at Locle. I stepped out of the train. The station was no more than a hut. And there was nobody waiting for me, apart from the ticket-collector. I was obliged to hand in my ticket and go outside into the street, where I saw only a snow-covered field stretching before me. I was still pondering what I should do, when two figures appeared from behind the hut, one of them tall, the other slightly shorter. They came up to me and said something I did not understand, but I replied agitatedly: "Yes, yes." "Come with us, then." And I followed them, speechless, along a path which crossed the snow-field.

My companions stopped outside the first house in the village. It was smaller and lower than all the other houses. They knocked. The door opened and we all three of us found ourselves in a pitch dark, narrow passage. They whistled, and a voice answered them from upstairs. They mumbled something, and left. I remained pressed against the wall, not daring to move, in case I slipped and fell down the stairs. After a moment, which seemed to me a very long one, I saw a light at the top of a spiral staircase; there stood a little hunchback with a candle. He motioned to me with his finger to come up. I followed him and he led me into a tiny, charmingly furnished sitting-room. The hunchback signalled to me to sit down on a small settee, and vanished.

I did not know what lay in store for me; time seemed to pass very slowly. At last the door opened and a dwarf-woman appeared, also humpbacked. She inquired what she could do for me. "I wish to see Mr X."

"One minute," she replied, and disappeared.

Outside was the blackness of night, and I wondered what would become of me. After some considerable time the little dwarf re-appeared, motioned to me to follow her, and we left the room by a different stairway from the one I had used to enter it. She opened a door and I saw a rather large, low-ceilinged room such as one usually finds in a chalet. Nechayev was pacing up and down the room, as was his custom.

"Ah, it's you," he said curtly upon catching sight of me.

"Take off your hat and sit down. Well, what've you brought?"

"A manuscript from Ogarev," I replied. "He charged me to point out to you two paragraphs of which he does not approve and which he cannot endorse."

"What foolish tales are these! We cannot do without them."

"Ogarev was quite categorical, and I am convinced that he will not sign the manuscript in its present form."

Nechayev paced back and forth across the room several times, cursing, then halted in front of me and said sharply: "But what about you? You have such influence over Ogarev, why don't you persuade him?"

Amazed and indignant, I retorted: "That I would never do! I agreed entirely with Ogarev and will support him."

"Pampered little miss! Your sort are quite impossible!"

Ceasing to stride up and down, he asked me: "You must be hungry?" It was already eleven p.m. Nechayev went out for a moment, and a little later the dwarf-woman appeared with a tray of tea and all the requisite accompaniments.

I was not averse to drinking something hot. But Nechayev gave me no peace, and continued to develop his arguments until midnight.

I had grown quite weak, and he must have noticed this, for he asked: "You probably need to rest?"

"Yes, but where?"

"Here." And he indicated a large wooden bed with eider-down, sheets and pillows in red-and-white checkerwork material to match the curtains over the low windows which were set into almost all the walls (as they usually are in chalets).

"But isn't that *your* bed? Where do you mean to sleep?"

"Don't worry about me. Our brother knows how to take care of himself. I'll find a chair in the kitchen, or make myself comfortable on the table, or under it."

I protested, but to no avail. The dwarf-woman came in, made my bed, and disappeared. Once alone in that big room I examined the locks and discovered that the key was missing and there was no bolt. With profound misgivings I made ready to lie down without undressing, when I noticed two enormous hooks, one on each side of the door. I realized that there must be something that fitted into them, set about searching for it, and found a huge iron bar under the bed. I managed to drag it out and fix it in the hooks. Only then did I feel at ease. I undressed, went to bed, and slept very well.

Next morning the dwarf-woman brought me my breakfast, beautifully served. Nechayev, too, appeared, and at once began discoursing on the subject of the two paragraphs. I was no longer listening to him, because my sole desire was to leave this place as soon as I could. I asked at what time the train went.

"Oh, you still have plenty of time to spare, there's no train until half past ten." At ten o'clock I was ready and about to depart. Nechayev kept saying: "It's too soon yet, too soon! We're only two steps away from the station—I'll see you there."

"That would be risky: someone might see you with a stranger; and I decidedly do not wish you to accompany me."

"I'll only go a little way with you, not right to the station."

He took me by a roundabout way, as a result of which we missed the train.[22] I was furious and declared I would remain at the station until the next train because I wanted to be back in Geneva that evening at all costs.

"That is impossible," Nechayev replied. "There is only one train this afternoon and it does not connect with the Geneva train."

My exasperation knew no bounds, but there was nothing for it but to return to the little hunchback and the little dwarf-woman and spend another twenty-four hours listening to the speeches of Nechayev, who became more and more incensed as he tried to convince me that Ogarev must sign the manuscript, and that they would be powerless to achieve anything if the two disputed paragraphs were omitted. And my reply to him was that they were advocating hypocrisy and Jesuitism, and I could only rejoice at Ogarev's refusal to sign.

And so it continued all day and all evening right until the moment of my departure in the morning of the next day. It was a most painful day for me, for I was tormented the whole time by the thought of Natalya Alexeevna (Ogareva)'s concern at my mysterious disappearance, which I would not be able to explain even when I returned. How should I answer all the questions that would be flung at me, when I had been charged not to speak of all I had done?

Such were my agonizing thoughts until the very moment of my arrival home.

What a comfort it was when Natalya Alexeevna, upon seeing me, came to meet me with open arms, overjoyed, and exclaimed: "At last I see you alive and well!"

Sparing my feelings, she did not ask any questions, but described the anxiety she and Tchorzewski (a friend of Herzen and his family) had lived through. Alarmed at my absence, Natalya Alexeevna had asked Tchorzewski's advice. The latter had advised her to wait until the next day, but when I did not appear next day either, he became worried and suggested: "Let's go to Karl Vogt and ask his opinion before going to the police." Karl Vogt reassured them and advised them not to involve the police in this affair, saying: "Calm down. Tata is a woman of sense, she'll come back!" So they decided to wait, and I did come back.

I lost sight of Nechayev, but I did know that the police were on his trail and that he was in hiding, changing his name and place of residence. We too had moved from the lodging-house where we had been living to a small house at Saint-Jean-la-Tour. By "we" I mean Natalya Alexeevna, her daughter Liza, my nephew Alexander (whom I had taken into my charge at the time), our Italian maid, the faithful and devoted Erminia Jardel,[23] and myself.

One evening there was a ring at the door. I went to open it and to my amazement found myself face to face with Nechayev.

"What are you doing here?" I said. "You know the police are after you?"

Nechayev was unperturbed. "Yes, I know. That's why I've come to you to ask for shelter for one night."

"I am not alone. I must tell Natalya Alexeevna about this." And I ran off to tell her.

"You know how I feel about Nechayev" (she could not stand him).

"So, then, do we refuse?"

"In the circumstances we cannot refuse. Bring him in."[24]

Nechayev came in and shook hands with Natalya Alexeevna. She and I exchanged glances and wondered what to do, and how to accommodate him so that nobody would notice, particularly our landlord, who lived in the large house next door, and whose windows looked out on to our yard. Next to my room there was another small room which served as a storeroom for the furniture we did not need. We began by stacking mattresses up against the windows through which the landlord might direct his inquisitive gaze. After this we somehow fixed a bed for Nechayev. We took it in turns to bring him his food in this room. We were assisted by the faithful Erminia, to whom we were obliged to reveal the secret. A true Italian, she felt as much at home in this atmosphere of secrecy as a fish in water. We prepared Nechayev's food in the dining-room and Erminia herself washed the dishes and plates and put them back in their places in such a way that the cook never suspected that there was an extra person in the house.

Twenty-four hours passed. Nechayev was still with us and did not show any signs of departing, so after a few days we reminded him that it was really dangerous for him to remain here in Switzerland. "Yes," he replied. "Yes, but Zamperini (an Italian conspirator and the only person to come and see Nechayev while he was at our house) keeps promising to bring me a shirt and a work-bag, but he never brings them. . ."

"I'll see you across the frontier myself," said Natalya Alexeevna, and left the room.

Once we were alone, Nechayev said to me: "I have to make a very important journey."

"It's very dangerous for you to go out. You cannot do it."

"I've thought it all out. The best thing would be for me to put on women's clothing and go to the rendezvous late in the evening, when it is dark. Give me a dress at once and tell me what movements I must avoid making. I have been advised to pay attention to my gestures; they are very abrupt and might easily betray me."

"That is true. To start with, sit down."

I gave him the strangest directions on how to introduce just a little harmony into his movements. He then said to me: "I am counting on you to come with me and keep a watch on my movements."

"I cannot go out so late without telling Natalya Alexeevna."

"Why in the world not? Are you under age?"

I went and told Natalya Alexeevna, who objected.

"What kind of an idea is this? I absolutely refuse to let you go out alone. Go and tell him that I am coming with you." Nechayev was appalled at the proposition.

After much hesitation it was decided that I could go if the trusty Erminia came with us. Eager to be rid of Nechayev as soon as possible, Natalya Alexeevna brought him the necessary clothing.

The dressing completed, we set off at ten o'clock in the direction of Lausanne. Walking on either side of Nechayev, we would tell him to take smaller steps whenever we saw any figure approaching.

Soon we found ourselves alone on the road. The hour was late and we passed through village after village without meeting a soul. "Where are we going, then?" I asked Nechayev.

"We're nearly there."

We had turned off towards a villa hidden by shrubbery from the road.

"Here we are," Nechayev said, pushing open a small gate.

We found ourselves descending a few steps to enter the house, which was below road level. The garden extended down to the shores of a lake.

Nechayev brought us into a passage and said: "Wait here. My business will only take me a few minutes, and then I shall be back."

He disappeared into an adjacent room. Erminia sighed: "When shall we ever get home? It's getting close to midnight already."

I could hear conversation in the room next door, but could not understand the subject of the discussion, although I could identify the voices. To my utter amazement I recognized the voice of Bakunin. Is it possible? I asked myself. Or am I mistaken? The conversation was becoming more animated all the time, and Erminia's sighs had reached a crescendo.

At last Nechayev appeared and said simply: "We can go now."

We set off. I had no idea where we had been, and it was not until several years later that I was told that the villa had been inhabited by a company of Turks in the old days.

We walked in silence, which was broken only by the moans of poor Erminia. I felt as though my feet were on fire, and when we arrived home at three o'clock, and I took off my shoes, I found that my feet had been rubbed raw.

Natalya Alexeevna had waited up for us, naturally. She was glad to see me safe and sound, but she had had enough of Nechayev.

Next day she informed Nechayev of her plan. "When all's said and done, the only important thing is that you get across the frontier," she said. "You don't need Zamperini for that. I'll do it all. Be ready by tomorrow midday."

At midday on the following day a pair-horse carriage stopped outside our porch. Natalya Alexeevna and her small daughter were ready. They asked Nechayev to follow them down. Nechayev pressed my hand in farewell, got into the carriage, and the three of them set off at a trot for Ferney (Voltaire's estate).

Upon her return Natalya Alexeevna told me that everything had gone without a hitch, and the enterprise had been a total success.

Nechayev vanished from our sight, and our life returned to its usual routine, while the *émigrés* were immersed in their quarrels.

Imagine my surprise when, one morning, Nechayev reappeared at our door. Really frightened, I said to him: "What are you doing? You know the police are searching for you now?"

"Oh, don't worry!"

"I'm worried for you, not myself."

"I shan't stay with you; all I want is a few moments' *tête-à-tête* with you."

I invited him in, and this is what he said to me:

"You know the students and *émigrés* are organizing an extraordinary meeting at which they will discuss our affairs. I have come to ask you to go to that meeting."

I had not the slightest desire to do this, and I declined. But he insisted. And I ended by consenting.

"Promise me you will go. It's very important to me."

I gave him my word to get rid of him, and I would have kept it had not an unforeseen circumstance persuaded me to change my mind.

Soon after lunch the maid came to say that some gentleman wished to speak with me. I went to the drawing-room, where I found a young man, tall and thickset, with a small, blonde moustache, and wearing spectacles. His face was somehow familiar, but I could not remember his name.

"You probably do not recognize me," he said, making his bow. "I am German Lopatin, I used to visit your father in London."

"I remember you well," I interrupted him. "I saw you at my father's in London."

"I am a great admirer of your father, and that is why I have taken the liberty of presenting myself to you and asking you to give me your attention for a few minutes. It is a very serious matter, and I must speak with you alone. Here in the drawing-room we might be interrupted."

I led him into my room and said that I was ready to listen to him. He came to the point immediately: "You know there is to be a meeting this evening of Russian youth and *émigrés* to discuss the Nechayev business? Do you intend to go to it?"

"Yes, I have just now promised to do so."

He leapt up in great agitation and said: "No, no, it's impossible. The daughter of Alexander Ivanovich Herzen must not lend her presence to such a gathering."

Struck by the force and animation of his speech, I said: "But why? What are you talking about?"

"Do you know who Nechayev is? Do you know what role he played in the affair of Ivanov?"

"No," I replied, greatly surprised. . .[25] Upon which he related to me the tragedy of that unfortunate student, a tragedy in which Nechayev had played the chief role. It had been he who had lured Ivanov into an ambush, and then finished him off after a terrible struggle.

"Have you noticed the scars on his thumb?"

"Yes, I have seen them and even asked what they were, what they meant."[26]

"He could not answer you, because they were the traces of the bites his wretched victim inflicted upon him. Do you understand—you must not go to this meeting! The idea of your participation would be unendurable to those who love and honour the memory of your father. They must do all they can to keep you from going."

I was overwhelmed and dispirited by this revelation. I could only express my gratitude to Lopatin for his intervention. His entire being was inspired with sentiments of sincerity and justice, and I did not doubt the truth of his story for a moment.

Lopatin rose and said, as he pressed my hand: "So you will not be going to the meeting? Can I be sure of it?"

"Yes," I replied,[27] and thanked him once again. He took his leave. From that moment I always regarded Lopatin as my saviour, and always said as much when telling of those events.

I only saw Lopatin once more, about twelve years afterwards, at a Russian party in the *Salle des Mille Colonnes* in Paris. I recognized him immediately in spite of his large white beard.

Nechayev I never saw again, and, of course, had no further dealings with him.[28]

NATALIE HERZEN

Notes

Introduction

1. Herzen to Ogarev, 3 August 1868, in *Sobranie Sochineniy v tridtsati tomakh* (cited thereafter as: *Sobranie*), vol. XXIX/2 (Moscow, 1964), p. 428; see also *Literaturnoe nasledstvo*, vol. 61 (Moscow, 1953), p. 428.
2. A. I. Gertsen, *Polnoe sobranie sochineniy i pisem*, pod red. M. K. Lemke (cited thereafter as: Lemke), vol. VIII (Petrograd, 1917), p. 323.
3. A. A. Serno-Solovevich, *Nashi domashnie dela.* . . (Vevey, 1867); see also *Literaturnoe nasledstvo*, vols. 41–2 (Moscow, 1941), pp. 24 ff.; B. P. Kozmin, "Gertsen, Ogarev i 'molodaya emigratsiya' ", in *Iz istorii revolyutsionnoy mysli v Rossii* (Moscow, 1961), pp. 545–7; E. Lampert, *Studies in Rebellion* (London: Routledge & Kegan Paul, 1957), p. 258.
4. Herzen to Sasha Herzen, 28 October 1869, *Sobranie*, vol. XXX/1 (Moscow, 1964), p. 229.
5. Herzen to Ogarev, 3 November 1869; Herzen to Tuchkova-Ogareva and Liza, 3 November 1869 (below, documents nos. 40, 41); Herzen to Ivan Turgenev, 3 December 1869; *Sobranie*, vol. XXX/1 (Moscow, 1964), p. 273.
6. Herzen to Ogarev, 19 November 1869, *Sobranie*, vol. XXX/1, p. 257.
7. Herzen, "Iz dnevnika", 3 December 1869, Lemke, vol. XXI (Moscow-Petrograd, 1923), p. 531.
8. Herzen to Tuchkova-Ogareva and Liza, 3 November 1869 (below, document no. 41); see also Herzen's comments in his Diary, 2 December 1869, Lemke, vol. XXI, p. 531.
9. Herzen to Sasha Herzen, 31 July 1869 (below, document no. 34).
10. Herzen to Ogarev, 15 April 1868; Herzen to Ogarev and Tchorzewski, 7 June 1868; Herzen to Sasha Herzen, 22 November 1868; *Sobranie*, vol. XXIX/1, pp. 310, 361, vol. XXIX/2, p. 493.
11. Bakunin to Ogarev, 22 February 1870 (below, document no. 59); Herzen to Tuchkova-Ogareva and Liza, 9 February 1867; Herzen to Ogarev, 13 February 1867: *Sobranie*, vol. XXIX/1, pp. 30, 33.
12. Herzen, "Iz dnevnika", 2 December 1869, Lemke, vol. XXI, p. 531; Herzen to Sasha Herzen, 27 May 1868, 1 April 1869, 31 July 1869; Herzen to Ogarev, 28 June 1868: *Sobranie*, vol. XXIX/1, pp. 348, 380; vol. XXX/1, pp. 73, 155, and below, document no. 34.
13. Herzen to Ogarev, letters of 4, 8, 13–14 and 16 November 1869; and to Sasha Herzen, 29 November 1869: *Sobranie*, vol. XXX/1, pp. 238, 248–9, 252, 266, and below, documents nos. 42, 43, 44.

14. Herzen to Sasha Herzen, 4 December 1869; see also Herzen to Ogarev, letters of 16, 18 and 20 November 1869; and to Ivan Turgenev, 18 November 1869: *Sobranie*, vol. XXX/1, pp. 274, 252, 254, 258, 255.
15. Natalie to Herzen, 24 September 1869 (below, document no. 36); see also Herzen to Ogarev, 13–14 November 1869 (below, document no. 43).
16. Natalie to Herzen, 2 October 1869 (below, document no. 37).
17. Natalie to Herzen, 2 October 1869 (below, document no. 37).
18. Herzen to Sasha Herzen, 19 July 1869, *Sobranie*, vol. XXX/1, p. 150.
19. Herzen to Sasha Herzen, 28 October 1869, *Sobranie*, vol. XXX/1, p. 229.
20. Herzen to Natalie, 1–2 May 1868, *Sobranie*, vol. XXIX/1, p. 328.
21. Natalie is referring to Herzen's letter to Malwida von Meysenbug and Olga Herzen, 27 September 1869, *Sobranie*, vol. XXX/1, p. 212.
22. Natalie to Herzen, 6 October 1869 (below, document no. 38).
23. Natalie to Tuchkova-Ogareva, 12 October 1869 (below, document no. 39).
24. See Herzen to Natalie and Malwida, 20 October 1869, *Sobranie*, vol. XXX/1, p. 221.
25. See Herzen to Ogarev, 10 and 16 November 1869, *Sobranie*, vol. XXX/1, pp. 242, 252.
26. Notwithstanding the fact that Natalie too appears to have been disturbed by the prospect of such expenses. More generally, her attitude in financial matters was, to say the least, extremely cautious; see, for example, her letters to Maria Reichel, 8 October 1870, 7 February 1871 and 6 March 1871 (below, documents nos. 103, 108, 109).
27. Maria Reichel to Herzen, [1866], Bibliothèque Nationale (cited thereafter as: *BN*) (Paris), MSS., Slave 109, f. 39. As regards Meshchersky, Herzen later changed his mind; Natalie seems to have hesitated also because of the prince's modest income (see Natalie to Herzen, 25 May 1869, below, document no. 31).
28. These doubts existed also with regard to Penisi (see Natalie's Diary, below, document no. 35). They were further strengthened by an additional detail, as Natalie wrote concisely (in English) in her notebook: "The fortune promised him by his family, as soon as he would be married" (*BN*, MSS., Slave 110, f. [106]). She apparently suspected that Penisi wanted to marry her in order to get this fortune.
29. Natalie, Diary (below, document no. 80, pp. 218–19); Natalie to Nechayev, 13, 20 and 31 March 1870 (below, documents nos. 62, 65, 69, 70); Nechayev to Natalie, undated (below, document no. 73).
30. Natalie, Diary (below, document no. 80, pp. 212–14).
31. Bakunin to Guillaume, 13 April 1869; quoted from Yu. Steklov, *M. A. Bakunin, ego zhizn i deyatelnost*, vol. III (Moscow-Leningrad, 1927), p. 435.
32. Natalie, Diary (below, document no. 93).
33. Below, document no. 84.

34. F. Venturi, *Roots of Revolution. A History of the Populist and Socialist Movements in Nineteenth-Century Russia* (New York: Alfred A. Knopf, 1960), p. 773, n. 28.
35. Bakunin to Nechayev, 2 June 1870 (below, document no. 84, pp. 273, 275).
36. A. Camus, *The Rebel* (London: Penguin Books, 1969), p. 129.
37. Bakunin to Nechayev, 2 June 1870 (below, document no. 84, p. 242).
38. Bakunin to Nechayev, 2 June 1870 (below, document no. 84, pp. 240, 241).
39. Bakunin to Ogarev, 8 February 1870 (below, document no. 51); M. Bakounine, "Aux compagnons de la Fédération des Sections internationales du Jura", in *Archives Bakounine*, A. Lehning ed., vol. II (Leiden, 1965), p. 3.
40. Bakounine, "Aux compagnons . . .", p. 5.
41. See Bakunin to Nechayev, 2 June 1870 (below, document no. 84, pp. 272–7).
42. Bakunin to Ogarev, N. Herzen, Ozerov and S. Serebrennikov, 20 June 1870 (below, document no. 91).
43. V. Zasulich, "Nechayevskoe delo", *Gruppa "Osvobozhdenie Truda"*, *Sbornik*, no. 2 (Moscow, 1924), p. 69.
44. A. Uspenskaya, "Vospominaniya shestidesyatnitsy", *Byloe*, vol. 18 (1922), pp. 40–41. Other members of the People's Vengeance, *e.g.* N. Nikolaev and P. Uspensky shared the same view.
45. V. Zasulich, "Nechayevskoe delo", pp. 52–3. By contrast, Vera Zasulich, born of a gentry family, attributed most of Nechayev's revolting traits to his social origin and deprived youth.
46. See below, document no. 106.
47. Venturi, *Roots*, p. 412.
48. See B. Nikolaevsky, "Pamyati poslednego 'yakobintsa'—semidesyatnika (Gaspar-Mikhail Tursky)", *Katorga i ssylka*, 2(23) (1926), pp. 211–27; Steklov, *M. A. Bakunin*, vol. III, p. 426; Venturi, *Roots*, pp. 383–4, 390.
49. Quoted from Venturi, *Roots*, p. 412.
50. *Narodnaya Rasprava*, no. 1, "Summer 1869".
51. *Nechayev i Nechayevtsy. Sbornik materyalov* (Moscow–Leningrad, 1931), pp. 57, 94, 108, 110.
52. V. Zasulich, "Nechayevskoe delo", p. 31.
53. Quoted from S. G. Svatikov, "Studencheskoe dvizhenie 1869 goda (Bakunin i Nechayev)", *Istorichesky sbornik "Nasha strana"*, vol. I (St Petersburg, 1907), p. 191.
54. Quoted from B. Kozmin, "Istoriya ili fantastika", *Pechat i revolyutsiya*, no. 6 (1926), p. 106.
55. Nechayev asserted that all reflections about a social regime in the future are "a sterile corruption of the mind, an onanism of thought"; such reflections are "criminal because they hinder the pure destruction, obstruct the beginnings of the revolution, and consequently postpone its completion" (*ibid.* p. 106). However, as far as he indulged himself in such "onanism of thought", Nechayev explicitly declared that his views about the social regime in the future are akin to Marx's and Engels's as formulated in the *Communist Manifesto*,

which, by the way, Nechayev was the first to publish in the Russian language (see Venturi, *Roots*, pp. 383–4).

56. Bakunin to Ogarev, N. Herzen, Ozerov and S. Serebrennikov, 20 June 1870 (below, document no. 91, p. 292).
57. *Ibid.*, p. 294.
58. *Ibid.*, p. 295.
59. *Ibid.*, p. 295.
60. *Ibid.*, p. 297.
61. E. H. Carr, *The Romantic Exiles. A Nineteenth-Century Portrait Gallery* (Boston: Beacon Press, 1961), p. 290.
62. A. Camus, *The Rebel*, p. 130.
63. Quoted from Steklov, *M. A. Bakunin*, vol. III, p. 509 (Nechayev wrote this to justify the murder of Ivanov).
64. A. Camus, *The Rebel*, p. 128.
65. See Bakunin to Ogarev, N. Herzen, Ozerov and S. Serebrennikov, 20 June 1870 (below, document no. 91, p. 296; underlined by Bakunin). Whatever one's opinion of Bakunin's view, it must be admitted that it is not identical with Nechayev's.
66. Among authorities in this field, such is, for instance, the view of Yu. Steklov, Franz Mehring, E. H. Carr, B. P. Kozmin.
67. E. H. Carr, *Michael Bakunin* (New York: Random House, 1961), pp. 395–6.
68. See N. Pirumova, "M. Bakunin ili S. Nechayev?", *Prometey*, no. 5, 1968, pp. 168–81.
69. "Programma revolyutsionnykh deystviy", *Istoriko-revolyutsionnaya khrestomatiya*, vol. I (Moscow, 1923), pp. 81–5; Venturi, *Roots*, pp. 361–2, 364. This also indicates that once the members of the group chose the term "catechism" for that document, they had to follow a very definite form of composition in writing it.
70. "Lyudi budushchego i geroi meshchanstva", *Delo*, nos. 4 and 5, 1868. Analogies between this article and the *Catechism* have been pointed out by B. P. Kozmin, *P. N. Tkachev, Revolyutsionnoe dvizhenie 1860–kh godov* (Moscow, 1922), pp. 95, 98. Despite this finding, Kozmin nevertheless contends that the author of the *Catechism* was Bakunin.
71. Bakunin to Nechayev, 2 June 1870 (below, document no. 84, p. 246).
72. *Ibid.*, p. 243; for "Abrek", see below, no. 17, p. 399.
73. *Ibid.*, p. 244.
74. An example to the point is Nechayev's view of the political line of the new *Kolokol*; see below, Natalie's Diary, document no. 80, pp. 215–17.
75. Bakunin to Nechayev, 2 June 1870 (below, document no. 84, p. 241).
76. The "Bakhmetev fund" represented a sum of 20,000 francs donated in 1857 by P. A. Bakhmetev, a young landowner, to Herzen and Ogarev for the purpose of carrying on radical propaganda. Herzen decided to keep the sum intact, and use only the interest, and he invested it in stock through the Rothschild Bank. In July 1869, Herzen yielded to Ogarev's demands that half the fund be given to Nechayev. After Herzen's death, Nechayev received most of the remaining half from Ogarev and Alexander Herzen *fils*. In both cases Ogarev had acted under Bakunin's influence and pressure.
77. Finally, Bakunin had to content himself with two attestations given

by Ogarev and signed by several witnesses; the first is dated 20 June 1870, the second is from 1872.
78. Bakunin to Nechayev, 2 June 1870 (below, document no. 84, pp. 247–8).
79. *Ibid.*, pp. 244, 248.
80. See *Catechism of the Revolutionist*, below, pp. 226, 228.
81. See, for instance, Nechayev to N. Herzen, undated (below, document no. 73, p. 177).
82. N. Herzen, Diary (below, document no. 80, p. 190).
83. Bakunin to Nechayev, 2 June 1870 (below, document no. 84, p. 243).
84. A well-known and respected Russian radical, G. Lopatin arrived in Geneva in May 1870 for the specific purpose of informing Bakunin and his friends about Nechayev's activity. For an account of these conversations see Bakunin to Nechayev, 2 June 1870 (below, document no. 84, pp. 272–5); see also M. Confino, "Autour de 'l'affaire Nechaev'. Lettres inédites de M. Bakunin et de G. Lopatin", *Cahiers du Monde russe et soviétique* (VIII, no. 3, 1967), pp. 452–95.
85. Natalie to Bakunin, 16 June 1870 (below, document no. 89).
86. Bakunin to Nechayev, 2 June 1870 (below, document no. 84, p. 271).
87. Bakunin to Natalie, 28 June 1870 (below, document no. 92).
88. Natalie, Diary (below, document no. 93).
89. Bakunin to Mroczkowski, 24 July 1870 (below, document no. 95).
90. Nechayev to Bakunin and Ogarev, undated (below, document no. 97).
91. Bakunin to Ogarev, 2 November 1872 (below, document no. 105).
92. Natalie to Bakunin, 16 June 1870 (below, document no. 89).
93. Below, document no. 120.

I

Section 1

1. Emily Reeve (?–1865), a friend of Herzen's family and Tata's governess.
2. Karl Alexander Reichel (born 1853), son of Adolf and Maria Reichel.
3. Sergey Lvovich Levitsky (1819–98), Herzen's cousin and the son of L. A. Yakovlev; from the late 1850s worked as photographer in Paris; returned to Russia in 1865.
4. Dell'Ongaro, a friend of the Herzens and a close collaborator of Mazzini in the Italian Risorgimento.
5. Alexey Fedorovich Friken ("Montecchi"), art historian and friend of Herzen's family; lived in Western Europe from 1859 to 1869.
6. Valeriano Tassinari, a cook in Herzen's household in London.
7. The wife of Nikolay Nikolaevich Ghé (1831–94), a Russian painter.
8. "There was no reason to congratulate, just to [?] remind you." (N. Herzen's note.)
9. In Russified English "enjoyirovali". (Translator's note.)
10. Marian Langiewicz (1827–87), a participant in the Polish national movement; joined in Garibaldi's expedition in Southern Italy (1860); took part in the Polish uprising of 1863; on 19 March, after an

unsuccessful battle with a Russian detachment, crossed the Austrian border, where he was arrested and imprisoned till 1865.

11. Mazzini's nickname in Herzen's correspondence.

12. Mikhail Petrovich Botkin (1839–1914), a painter and engraver.

13. Ferdinand Grigorovius (or Gregorovius) (1821–91), German poet and historian, author of *Die Geschichte der Stadt Rom in Mittelalter* (8 volumes; 1859–72).

14. Monstewart Elphinston Grant Duff (1829–1906), writer and M.P.

15. In English in the original.

16. Jean-Pierre Vieusseux (1778–1863), Italian writer and publisher (brother of the former).

17. One illegible word.

18. Probably Jan Stella, *nom de guerre* of Ivan Mikhaylovich Savitsky, a leader of the Polish insurrection of 1863, and Natalie's teacher in mathematics, physics and chemistry.

19. Nikolay Alexandrovich Herzen (1843–51), Natalie's brother.

20. Johanna Kinkel (?–1863), daughter of Johann Gottfried Kinkel (1815–82), German poet and publicist who lived in exile in London.

21. Petr Vladimirovich Dolgorukov (1816–68), historian and publicist; lived in exile from 1859; published *émigré* papers in Paris, Leipzig, Brussels and London; a contributor to *The Bell*.

22. Noël Gueneau de Mussy (1813–85), French physician.

23. A reference to Alexander Herzen's memoirs *My Past and Thoughts*. (Translator's note.)

24. Actually Alexander Herzen's. Liza, Alexey (Lelya-boy) and Elena (Lelya-girl) are the children of Herzen and Nathalie Tuchkova-Ogareva.

25. Mme Salis-Schwabe, a friend of Malwida von Meysenbug and widow of an English industrialist.

26. One illegible word.

27. In English in the original.

28. Elizaveta Vasilievna Kasatkina, the wife of Victor Ivanovich Kasatkin (1831–67), a publicist and political exile.

29. Olga Ivanovna Lion, *née* Kuruta, an acquaintance of Herzen's from the time of his internment in Vladimir; daughter of Ivan Emmanuilovich Kuruta (1780–1853), Governor of that region from 1838 to 1842.

30. An allusion to the death of the twins Lelya-boy and Lelya-girl.

31. Lyudmila Petrovna Shelgunova, *née* Michaelis (1832–1901), writer and translator; wife of Nikolay Vasilievich Shelgunov, himself a radical and publicist (1824–91).

32. In the summer and autumn of 1865 several newspapers in Russia *(Russkiy invalid, Moskovskie Vedomosti, Den)* accused "Herzen's agents" of being responsible for a series of fires that occurred at that time in the country.

33. Pavel Vasilievich Annenkov (1812–87), literary critic and memoirist.

34. From here onwards the original text is in English.

35. Probably V. F. Luginin.

36. A reference to the conflict between Prussia and Austria. A Prussian–Italian alliance was signed on 8 April 1866; Bismarck's army subsequently invaded Holstein on 8 June 1866.

37. On 2 April 1866 a radical student, **D. V. Karakozov** (1840–66), tried unsuccessfully to kill Alexander II.

38. Count **Mikhail Nikolaevich Muravev** (1796–1866), Governor-General of the North-Western provinces in 1863–5; member of the State Council; was in charge of the investigation of the Karakozov plot.

39. On 10 December 1865 the Russian government issued a decree forbidding the Poles to buy landed estates in nine Western *gubernias*. Thereafter, expropriated estates could be bought only by Russian landlords. Referring to this legislation, Ogarev wrote an article "The Sale of Landed Estates in the Western Regions" (*The Bell*, 1 November 1866), advocating that the right to buy these lands be given to Russian peasants (assuming that this would strengthen the peasant commune and contribute to the spread of "Russian Socialism"). Part of the Polish emigration in Switzerland took issue with this article and received the support of Serno-Solovevich.

40. In English in the original text.

41. **Emile Vogt** (1820–83), Swiss lawyer, brother of Karl and Adolphe Vogt.

42. **Jessy Mario**, *née* White (1832–?), English writer and wife of Count Alberto Mario (1825–83), Italian publicist and friend of Garibaldi.

43. In English in the original text.

44. *Le Blocus*, a novel by Erckmann-Chatrian, published in 1867.

45. On 6 June 1867 a Polish *émigré*, A. Berezovsky, attempted unsuccessfully to kill Alexander II, then on a visit in Paris.

46. The shipwreck in which Herzen's mother, Louisa Haag, and his son, Kolya, perished (1851).

47. **Heinrich Panovka** (1807–87), German musician, teacher of Olga and Natalie.

48. Erckmann-Chatrian's novel *L'Histoire d'un paysan de 1789–1815*.

49. One illegible word.

50. A reference to Herzen's article *"Variations psychiatriques sur le thème du docteur Kroupoff "*.

51. In English in the original text.

52. [*Sic.*] Rather whimsical Italian.

53. A pun on a verse of Wilhelm Muller's poem (and Schubert's song) "Winterreise".

54. *Mein Kopf ist schwer* . . .: perhaps a pun on a verse in Goethe's *Faust*.

55. **Tit Leviatansky**, a character in Herzen's article *"Variations psychiatriques sur le thème du docteur Kroupoff "*.

56. Chernyshevsky's trial and "civil execution" on 19 May 1864; he was condemned to fourteen (later reduced to seven) years' forced labour and life-time deportation to Siberia, with permanent loss of rights.

57. **Nadezhda Prokofievna Suslova** (1843–1918), physician, graduated at the University of Zurich in 1867 and was the first Russian woman to receive a university degree.

58. **Grigory Evlampievich Blagosvetlov** (1824–80), publicist and literary critic; editor of the radical journals *Russkoe slovo* (1860–66) and *Delo* (1866–80); from 1857 to 1860 lived abroad and served as teacher to Herzen's children.

59. Ekaterina Volodimirova, sister-in-law of G. G. Ustinov, a Russian landlord.
60. A reference to Charles Mazade's article "Deux années de l'histoire intérieure de la Russie, 1866–1867" (*Revue des Deux Mondes*, 1 April 1868). Herzen took issue with it in his "L'article de M. Charles Mazade", *La Cloche*, no. 8, 15 May 1868.
61. From Mignon's songs in Goethe's novel *Wilhelm Meisters Lehrjahre*.
62. The Russian text repeats *"weht"*; Herzen is punning on the Russian *"veyet"*. (Translator's note.)
63. In English in the original text.
64. Probably V. Hugo's poem "Mentana".
65. Maurice Schiff's book *Leçons sur la physiologie de la digestion faites au Museum d'histoire naturelle de Florence*, 2 vols., Florence–Turin, 1867.
66. A pun: literally translated these names read: Puppy's-son, Nightingale's-son [and the other] Sons of Bitches. (Translator's note.)
67. Herzen is referring to an article published (apparently with the collaboration of A. Serno-Solovevich) in A. Szczesnowicz's journal *Le Peuple polonais* (no. 1, 15 May 1868) and directed against his "Frisant la question polonaise" (*La Cloche*, no. 7, 15 April 1868), which took issue with a pamphlet written by General Mieroslawski.
68. According to M. Mervaud, the correct date should be 11 July 1868 (see *Cahiers du Monde russe et soviétique*, X, nos. 3–4, 1969).
69. The son of Ogarev and Mary Sutherland.
70. Ogarev wrote this "story", entitled "A Day", and sent it to Natalie in February 1869. This certainly gave Tata the idea for the form and genre of her "Photograph (From the Original)" (see following text, no. 28). For more details about other Ogarev writings as a possible source of inspiration, cf. *Literaturnoe nasledstvo*, vol. 63, p. 472.
71. The title-page of the manuscript bears the inscription: "In memory of Villa Filippi, Ruelle Meslanzone, Rue de France, Nice. 6 April 1869 A.D.".
72. Babetta (Babette), a housemaid.
73. A. Herzen's story "Doctor Krupov".
74. Grigory Nikolaevich Vyrubov (1843–1913), studied natural sciences and medicine in Moscow, Berlin and Paris; became closely associated with Littré and the widow of Auguste Comte; from 1867 on was editor of the *Revue de philosophie positive*.
75. Mme Rocca: the landlady.
76. Nikolay Mikhaylovich Satin (1814–73), poet and translator; participated in Ogarev's and Herzen's students circle; married Nathalie's sister, Elena (Lelya) Alexeevna Satina, *née* Tuchkova (1827–71).
77. Nathalie Alexeevna.
78. Natalie Alexandrovna.

Section 2

1. The letter ends here with no signature.
2. In a letter of 13 June 1869, A. Herzen wrote to Olga that he (and not Ogarev) is Liza's father. Letters to Olga on that same topic were sent by Ogarev and Tuchkova-Ogareva as well.

3. The first issue of the weekly *L'Egalité*, published in Geneva, appeared on 23 January 1869; one of its editors was M. Bakunin. Herzen subscribed for Tata and Olga.

4. From 6 to 11 June several clashes between workers and police occurred in Paris.

5. A reference to Herzen's article "To an Old Comrade" *(K staromu tovarishchu)*, in which he took issue with Bakunin's stand and with his appeals for total destruction.

6. Volodya was born on 18 May 1869.

7. Two essays by Herzen. *Mazurka* was published in Russian in *The Bell*, no. 242, 15 June 1867; a translation into French appeared in Geneva in May 1869, dedicated by the author to E. Quinet. *Interrupted Tales (Prervannye rasskazy)* were first published in London in 1854.

8. Goncharov's novel *Obryv* was published in 1869.

9. A reference to Herzen's estate in Kostroma province, sequestered twenty years earlier and to its income, appropriated by the Russian Treasury during all this period.

10. An allusion to Ogarev's collaboration with Bakunin and Nechayev during the latter's first visit to Switzerland.

11. Hugo Schiff.

12. Crossed out by N. Herzen.

13. Probably a reference to Ekaterina Volodimirova and to a somewhat unclear sentimental affair between her and Penisi.

14. One illegible word.

15. A reference to the *première* of Wagner's opera *Das Rheingold* on 22 September 1869 in Munich.

16. "That was *after* I had received your last letter but one, so do not say that I was acting contrary to your advice." (N. Herzen's note.)

17. "Because he will once again abandon all his affairs and go away, and that, of course, will attract attention." (N. Herzen's note.)

18. Tessié du Motay, French chemist, participated in the revolution of 1848, then lived in exile from 1849 to 1852; met the Herzens in Nice and was Sasha's teacher in chemistry.

19. "The creole woman": Mme Raymond, the *garde-malade*. Osip Ivanovich: Mazzini.

20. Louisa Ivanovna Haag: Herzen's mother, who was drowned (with Herzen's son, Kolya) in a shipwreck in the Mediterranean in 1851. Tata is mixing up this event with the death of the twins in Paris in 1864.

21. An allusion to Georg Herwegh's behaviour (or at least to the way the Herzens looked at his behaviour) after his liaison with Natalie, Tata's mother. On this episode, see Herzen's "A Family Drama" in *My Past and Thoughts*, Part V.

22. Jules-Emile-Aristide Rey (1834–1901), French anarchist and close friend of Bakunin.

23. Paul Robin (1837–1912), French scientist; anarchist and member of the Council of the First International; editor of *Egalité*. (He declined Herzen's proposal.)

24. Mauricio Quadrio (1800–76), publicist and one of the leaders of the Italian Risorgimento; close friend of Mazzini.

25. One indecipherable word.
26. Herzen's wife died in 1852, shortly after the Herwegh affair.
27. In English in the original text.
28. During his stay in Vienna in 1838 T. N. Granovsky used to visit the house of Mme A. Walter, the wife of a Viennese banker. She may have heard that A. Stankevich, in his biography of Granovsky (Moscow 1869), relates some critical remarks of the latter about various personalities he met at her house.
29. Sasha's remark on Turgenev's letter to Herzen of 25 November 1869 has been torn off; the context of this sentence remains unclear.
30. From Goethe's poem "Epirrhema".
31. In English in the original text.

II

Section 3

1. The letter is also intended for N. Zhukovsky and V. Ozerov.
2. That is, the news of Nechayev's escape from Russia and arrival in Geneva.
3. "Pogodin's pupil": Nechayev. In August 1865, on his first visit to Moscow Nechayev lived in a sort of *pension* kept by the well-known publicist M. P. Pogodin. At that time Nechayev wanted to become a schoolmaster but failed the examinations.
4. Probably an allusion to Bakunin's wife's pregnancy.
5. In Russian a pun on "Boy" and "boevoy" (militant). (Translator's note.)
6. Antosya: Bakunin's wife.
7. Charles Perron (1837–1909) one of the editors of *L'Egalité*; member of the Geneva section of the First International and of Bakunin's *Alliance*; on Robin see above, II, n. 23.
8. Zoya Sergeevna Obolenskaya, *née* Sumarokova, had left her husband, General A. V. Obolensky, and was living in Switzerland with Valerian Mroczkowski. In July 1869 General Obolensky, with the help of the Swiss authorities, took his two daughters by force from their mother's house to Russia.
9. The Bakhmetev fund.
10. Bakunin refers to the military repression of a peasant rising led by Anton Petrov at Bezdna (Kazan province) in April 1861.
11. Johann Philipp Becker (1809–96), brush-maker; organizer of the sections of the International in Switzerland and Germany; editor of *Der Vorbote* (1866–71); friend and follower of Karl Marx.
12. William Frederic Cowell Stepney (1820–72), English socialist, member of the Reform League; member of the General Council of the International (1867–72) and its Treasurer (1868–70).
13. After Herzen's death, at the beginning of February, Tata (accompanied by Sasha and Tchorzewski) visited Ogarev in Geneva and there met S. Nechayev. On 11 February she left for Paris.

14. *Nom de guerre* of Nechayev in his correspondence with Natalie; hers was Reginald Wilson. (The letters are in Russian.)
15. A reference to the paper *La Marseillaise*; its chief editor was H. de Rochefort.
16. Probably the Russian publisher N. P. Polyakov; the matter referred to is, however, unclear.
17. N. Tuchkova-Ogareva and Liza.
18. See the next document, no. 58.
19. Nechayev and his revolutionary committee in Russia.
20. Bakunin did not yet know that following her discussions with Nechayev, Natalie was already on her way back to Geneva.
21. Natalie Herzen (a Bakunin trick in calling her Ogarev's daughter).
22. Malwida von Meysenbug.
23. Draft.
24. Draft.
25. Crossed out.
26. On this trip of Nechayev with Tuchkova-Ogareva, see her account below, document no. 119, pp. 366–71.
27. Draft.
28. Unfinished sentence. In the margin Natalie has added: ". . . civilized and not [. . .] and do not confuse people's relationships. Stop believing in the power of the 'simpleton'."
29. One word crossed out.
30. A reference to Natalie's visit to Locle when Nechayev was hiding there; on this episode see her account below, document no. 120, pp. 375–81.
31. Draft.
32. The back of the page has "10 and 11 May 1870". However, this can hardly be the date of the letter. This one refers clearly to Nechayev's of 30 May ("What makes you ask if I have taken fright?"); in the following one of Nechayev (dated June 1870), he replies to Natalie's refusal "to participate in any intrigues".
33. *Narodnaya Rasprava*: Nechayev's revolutionary organization.
34. End of manuscript.
35. Actually a little older. Natalie was born on 13 December 1844, and the Herzen family left Russia in January 1847.
36. An allusion to the murder of the student I. Ivanov by Nechayev and his accomplices; for an account of the murder, see document no. 100.
37. This was the legend disseminated by Nechayev himself that he had escaped from the Peter and Paul Fortress.
38. Nechayev had been assuring Natalie, Bakunin, and Ogarev that the revolution would break out in Russia on the anniversary of the liberation of the serfs.
39. Probably Neuchâtel.
40. Probably James Guillaume.
41. The letter is not included in the Diary and is probably lost. It was received by Natalie Herzen between 17 and 20 February.
42. See above, letter no. 58.

43. James Guillaume's address was: *14 rue du Seyon*, as it appears in Nechayev's notebook, confiscated by the police on his arrest, and kept in Zurich's Staatsarchiv, *"P 191 b, Fremdenpolizei, Auslieferung des Sergius Netschajeff 1872/73"*.

44. See above, note 8.

45. On Herzen's Kostroma estate, see above, Section II, note 9.

46. Actually Natalie knew that Sasha, following his father's advice, did think of going to Russia and looking for a chair. To that effect Sasha met with M. A. Gorchakov, counsellor to the Russian Embassy in Berlin (the son of the Russian Foreign Minister). The visa was refused. Herzen kept Ogarev informed of the matter, although the latter disapproved. (All these details are in Herzen's correspondence with Natalie, Sasha and Ogarev from October to November 1868: *Sobranie*, XXIX/2, pp. 469, 472, 473, 476, 483, 495.)

47. Six weekly issues were published from 2 April to 9 May 1870.

48. Vladimir Serebrennikov (not to be confused with Semen Serebrennikov).

49. *The People's Cause*, published by N. Utin and a few followers of Marx and opponents of Bakunin and Nechayev among the Russian colony in Switzerland.

50. Alexander Alexandrovich Serno-Solovevich (1838–69), Russian radical; lived in exile from 1862 on; a leader of the so-called "young emigration"; member of the Geneva group of the First International.

Section 4

1. The following is a selection from Nechayev's articles in *Narodnaya Rasprava* as published in V. Burtsev (ed.), *Za sto let (1800–1896). Sbornik po istorii politicheskikh i obshchestvennykh dvizheniy v Rossii* (London, 1897), pp. 91–6.

2. "We hope that all honest and active members of the Russian emigration (such as Bakunin, the publishers of *The Bell*, and the unknown author of the first issue of *The People's Cause*), having come to form a single, common, harmonious body, will now begin to work in concord for the Russian movement" (Nechayev's note). The author of the article in *The People's Cause (Narodnoe Delo)* referred to was Bakunin.

3. "Which unfortunately displays an exclusively student nature." (Author's note, in which Nechayev is criticizing himself.)

4. An allusion to the preceding "generation" of Russian radicals such as Herzen, Ogarev, and perhaps Bakunin.

5. On the Karakozov affair see above, Section 1, note 37.

6. See above, Section 3, note 10.

7. Count Alexey Andreevich Arakcheev (1769–1834), favourite of Alexander I; War Minister in 1808 and the most influential Russian statesman between 1814 and 1824. His name became the symbol of intolerable despotism.

8. "There is a sense of pressing need in the detailed list of names arranged not in alphabetical order but in order of the degree of their

loathsomeness and perniciousness, with their rank and title and also their place of residence affixed. The list, compiled by well-informed persons, will, of course, be not long in appearing. We shall cite here by way of illustration some of the particularly striking names." [There follows an enumeration of the surnames of some of the persons who were to have been included in this proposed list: Adlerberg, Mezentsev, Trepov, the Shuvalovs, the Timashevs, the Valuevs, the Potapovs, the Obukhovs, the Zelenys, the Tolstoys, the Dolgorukys, the Apraksins, the Katkovs, A. Gradovsky, Ya. Lamansky, the Kraevskys, the Pogodins, the Skaryatins...] (Author's note.)

9. On the false assumption that he was Nechayev, the Swiss police arrested Semen Serebrennikov on 9 May 1870; released on 21 May, he was arrested again two days later.

10. Toots, the first child of Alexander Herzen *fils*, from his liaison with Charlotte Hudson.

11. The next document (no. 85) indicates that Bakunin wrote this letter from 2 to 9 June 1870. The manuscript is a copy mainly in the handwriting of Natalie Herzen and partly in that of S. Serebrennikov. It is the only known copy of this letter of Bakunin to Nechayev.

12. The last visit of Bakunin to Geneva referred to took place in the first half of May 1870. It is then that he met German Lopatin whose revelations about Nechayev's personality and real activity had a decisive effect on Bakunin's attitude towards him. (On Lopatin's role in this matter, see pp. 272–5). After leaving Geneva Bakunin stayed a short while in Berne, and arrived back in Locarno on 28 May 1870.

13. Three names only appear in the original. Mikhail Vasilievich Butashevich-Petrashevsky (1821–66) studied jurisprudence at St Petersburg and organized in 1844 a socialist-oriented circle for discussions and exchange of ideas; arrested on 23 April 1849 and sentenced to exile in Siberia. Fedor Nikolaevich Lvov (1823–85), an officer and scientist, member of the circle, was arrested on 29 April 1849 and sentenced to twelve years' hard labour in Siberia. Felix Gustavovich Tol (1823–67), writer and teacher of literature, was sentenced to two years' hard labour in Siberia. Dostoevsky was arrested and stood trial in connection with the activity of this circle.

14. Andrey Afanasievich Potebnya (1838–63), member of the revolutionary organization among the Russian officers in Poland; participated in the Polish uprising in 1863 and was killed on 4 March 1863.

15. On this statement, see below, note 20.

16. See also Tata's account, above, pp. 215–17.

17. *Abrek*: a Caucasian mountaineer banished from his clan, or having made a vow of deadly (bloody) revenge. In a larger sense: combatant acting with the courage of despair.

18. These convictions of Nechayev are incorporated in the *Catechism of the Revolutionist*, Part II, paragraphs 1, 2, 5, 6, 7.

19. Curiously enough, Albert Camus too—and he could not have known Bakunin's letter—wrote of Nechayev: "He made himself the cruel monk *(moine)* of a desperate revolution..." (*The Rebel*, Part III, section entitled "Three of the Possessed".)

20. Available evidence indicates that Bakunin knew the name of P. Tkachev (see Z. Ralli, in *Minuvshie gody*, 1908, no. 10, p. 157). The present letter shows that he knew also that of Pryzhov.

21. Two illegible words; those in brackets have been added according to the context.

22. This letter is apparently lost. Another reference to it is to be found below, and in Bakunin's letter to Ogarev of 30 May 1870.

23. This page of the manuscript is unfinished. Considering the content of the following paragraph, it would seem that a part of the original text is missing.

24. *Beguny* (or *stranniki*): members of an Orthodox sect formed in the second half of the eighteenth century. They believed that the Antichrist reigns over this earthly world (and particularly in the person of the Russian Tsars); consequently, they considered the laws (as well as the taxes, military service, and "passports") as inadmissible for true believers. Persecuted by the authorities, the members of this sect often looked for safety and salvation in remote and isolated regions of the Empire.

25. Bakunin alludes here to N. Utin and the Marxian group around the *Narodnoe Delo*, which sharply criticized the idea of using the "brigand-revolutionary" in order to spread popular unrest. (The first number of this journal was edited by Bakunin and Zhukovsky; thereafter it passed under the influence of N. Utin and his group.)

26. In the margin of this paragraph, Natalie Herzen has noted: *"N.B."*.

27. "On Bakunin's request Semen Serebrennikov added later, on another copy, the words 'certainly not' which completely change the sense of this sentence. These words do not occur in the original." (Remark by Natalie Herzen.)

28. One (or more) missing words in the copy.

29. Henry Sutherland. (The "unfortunate gossip" referred to remains unclear.)

30. This visit took place from the middle of March to 18 April 1870.

31. A reference to Nechayev's story about his alleged escape from the Peter and Paul Fortress in 1869.

32. Ivan Gavrilovich Pryzhov (1827–85), writer and publicist; author of a *History of Taverns in Russia*. There is no reliable evidence to substantiate this statement of Bakunin; however, Pryzhov seems to have been in a state of nervous exhaustion during the examination and the police may have exploited this fact.

33. A reference to Lopatin's letter to Bakunin, 26 May 1870. For full text in Russian, and a translation in French, see M. Confino, "Autour de 'l'affaire Nechayev'. Lettres inédites de Michel Bakunin et German Lopatin," in *Cahiers du Monde russe et soviétique*, VIII, 1967, no. 3, pp. 460–79.)

34. "At the Turks": a villa where a meeting took place between Bakunin and Nechayev, and which, according to Natalie's memoirs (see document 120), was previously inhabited by "a company of Turks".

35. Succinctly, the "affaire Lyubavin" consisted of the following. Out of financial considerations, Bakunin undertook to translate into Russian

the first volume of Marx's *Capital*. The student Lyubavin acted as a middleman between him and the publisher Polyakov, who gave Bakunin an advance of 300 roubles. In February 1870 Nechayev convinced Bakunin to give up this work in order to devote himself entirely to the "cause"; Nechayev also assured him that he would take care to "settle the matter" with the publisher. On 3 March 1870 Nechayev wrote a threatening letter to Lyubavin, on behalf of *The People's Vengeance*, requiring that Bakunin be freed from all obligations. Karl Marx later used this letter as an incriminating document for the expulsion of Bakunin from the International; there is no evidence, however, that Bakunin knew of the way Nechayev intended to "settle the matter" and of the content of the letter.

36. "The word 'lies' is missing in the original." (Remark by Natalie Herzen.)

37. On the "affaire Lyubavin" see above, note 35. The incident with the "stern letter" to Natalya Alexeevna consisted of the following. After Herzen's death, the members of the family prepared for publication a collection of posthumous articles (see below, Section VII, note 11). These included also several essays of Herzen criticizing the "young emigration". On 7 March, 1870 Nechayev wrote a threatening letter (on behalf of the *Bureau des agents étrangers de la Société révolutionnaire russe Narodnaya Rasprava*) requiring that these articles not be published. Nathalie forwarded the letter to Sasha, who informed Karl Vogt and Ogarev of the threats and the "impudent and stupid letter". The Herzens did not yield and the collection appeared as planned. (For Nathalie's account, see document no. 119.)

38. "Quite wrong." (Natalie Herzen's comment.)

39. For Bakunin's letter to Lopatin, 9 June 1870, see *Cahiers du Monde russe et soviétique*, VIII, 1967, no. 3, pp. 486–91.

40. Baron Neville: Nechayev.

41. Ogarev gave the required statement; it bears the date 20 June 1870 as well as the signatures of Natalie, Tuchkova-Ogareva and Sere-brennikov. The original is to be found in the Bibliothèque Nationale in Paris.

42. One illegible word in the manuscript.

43. Another illegible word.

44. Mikhail Konstantinovich Elpidin (1835–1908), Russian radical; arrested in Kazan in 1863 for revolutionary propaganda; in exile from 1865; founded a printing press in Geneva, and published the *Narodnoe Delo* in 1868–70; became an agent of the Secret Police in the 1880s. The allusion to his "obduracy" remains unclear.

45. An unidentified friend.

46. Draft version.

47. The words "entirely in sympathy with Nechayev" are crossed out; a marginal note written in the hand of N. Herzen reads: "Not your *plans*, of course, but *facts* proving that you were not in sympathy with him on every score."

48. Note by N. Herzen: "about the fund."

49. Jules Barni (1818–78), French philosopher and politician; emigrated to Geneva after the *coup d'État* of Louis Napoleon; one of the organizers of the Congress of "The League of Peace and Liberty" in 1867.
50. Bakunin's title. Two words crossed out by Bakunin remain illegible.
51. At this point there is a note in the handwriting of S. Serebrennikov: "The last, and yet not quite, as this letter shows. S. Serebr."
52. One illegible word.
53. An illegible word.
54. An illegible word.
55. The words "save him from" are crossed out.
56. On the back side of the page, a note in Bakunin's handwriting reads: "*En secret.*"
57. Olga Stepanovna Levasheva, an organizer (with N. Utin) of the Russian section of the International in Geneva; sister of Adelaida Stepanovna, Zhukovsky's wife.
58. This note has been published by Tatyana Bakounine and Jacques Catteau who erroneously date it early in June *(Cahiers du Monde russe et soviétique*, VII, 1966, no. 2, p. 263).
59. This note is to be found in the Bibliothèque Nationale; it reads: "*Je vous prie . . .*" (*BN* MSS Slave, 109, p. 819).
60. The correct amount is 940 francs 50, as stated in the receipt given by Ogarev (*BN* MSS Slave, 109, p. 821).
61. The word "them" has been crossed out and replaced by "that".

Section 5

1. Original in French.
2. Eugène Dupont (1837–81), musical-instrument-maker; took part in the June 1848 uprising in Paris; from 1862 on lived in London; and from 1874 on in the United States; a prominent member of the First International in which he supported Marx. Charles Bradlaugh (1833–91), British journalist and editor of the weekly *National Reformer* (1860); Vice-President of the League for Parliamentary Reform (1865), and M.P. for Northampton (1880).
3. The General Council of the First International.
4. [*Sic*]. (Dragomanov, *Pis'ma* . . . , p. 289; the Russian translation has "M", p. 294.)
5. An allusion to the Franco-Prussian war, which began on 19 July 1870.
6. The name in parentheses appears in the original text.
7. Character in a theatre play, *L'Auberge des Adrets* (staged in 1826 at the *Ambigu*) who became the symbol of a crook and a sharper. He also appears in a series of caricatures by Daumier.
8. Petr Gavrilovich Uspensky (1847–81), the closest associate of Nechayev in the *Narodnaya Rasprava* in Moscow. Participated in the murder of Ivanov and was sentenced to fifteen years' hard labour and life-time deportation to Siberia. His wife, Alexandra Ivanovna (Vera Zasulich's sister), followed him into exile. On 1 January 1881 he was hanged by his cell-mates who suspected him of being a police spy; the charge was groundless.

9. A reference to Bakunin's writing, for eventual publication, *Letter to a Frenchman*. The supposed addressee is Gaspard Blanc.
10. The allusion is to Nechayev's plan to carry out armed robberies in Switzerland as a means of financing revolutionary activities.
11. One illegible word.
12. [*Sic*].
13. Nechayev was arrested in a suburb of Zurich, on 14 August 1872, upon denunciation by a Polish *émigré*, A. Stempkowski. On 26 October 1872 the Regierungsrat decided to extradite Nechayev as a common criminal, and the extradition took place on 28 October.
14. Bakunin's title.
15. Armand Ross (pseudonym): Mikhail Petrovich Sazhin (1845–1934), Russian anarchist and publicist; took part in the Paris Commune; back in Russia participated in the "going to the people" (1874–5), for which he was sentenced to five years' exile in Siberia where he remained till 1900.
16. After his trial (January 1873) Nechayev was imprisoned in the Alexis Ravelin of the Peter and Paul Fortress from 1873 till his death in 1882. Initially he was allowed to read and to write. In 1876 this permission was withdrawn, and his papers were taken and examined in the Third Section. The results of the examination are set forth in a lengthy report presented to the Chief of the Gendarmerie, Potapov, and delivered by him to the Tsar on 24 April 1876. "By order of His Imperial Majesty all manuscripts of the criminal Nechayev are to be destroyed," Potapov wrote on the report. And the Head of the Third Section, A. F. Shults, added a note of his own: "This report to be kept in the dossier; the papers will be burned by myself." The following text, authorship of which is unknown, represents that report in its entirety. The source is E. P. Shchegolev, "S. G. Nechayev v Alexeevskom raveline (1873–82)", *Krasniy Arkhiv*, no. 4, 1923, pp. 259–62.
17. Lipovans *(lipovane)*: the name given to the adherents of a Russian Orthodox dissenting sect (the *bezpopovtsy*) living in Austria and in the Danube region. Nechayev may have met some of them during his passage through Rumania in August 1869, on his way back to Russia.
18. [*Sic*].

III

Section 6

1. Tatyana Petrovna Passek, *née* Kuchina (1810–89), writer and memoirist; Vadim Passek's wife and a relative of Herzen.
2. One illegible word.
3. That is, the trial of Nechayev's accomplices.
4. Thus in the original.
5. Probably end of 1872.
6. On 5 December 1875 Nathalie and Liza had left Nice and were already in Florence. Liza committed suicide a few days later.

7. In English in the original text.
8. In March 1876 Nathalie Tuchkova-Ogareva was given imperial permission to enter Russia, "under the guarantee of her father and strict police supervision, particularly as concerns her connections abroad".
9. In English in the original text.
10. In English in the original text.
11. T. A. Astrakova (1814–92), memoirist and friend of the Herzens.

Section 7

1. This statement is inaccurate. Herzen met Nechayev only once, and this happened six months before the murder of Ivanov (21 November 1869); Nechayev (who arrived again in Switzerland at the beginning of January 1870) never met Herzen after the murder.
2. The funeral and demonstration referred to took place on 12 January 1870. That day Herzen caught a cold which was the beginning of his fatal illness. Tuchkova's chronology of events is somewhat erratic.
3. Tuchkova's account of Tata's illness is clearly one-sided, particularly the role she attributes to herself.
4. Actually eight days (23–30 November 1869), at the Hôtel Feder.
5. No other source confirms this opinion.
6. More exactly, eight days (1–8 December 1869), at the Hôtel d'Europe et d'Amérique.
7. Olga and Malwida joined Herzen and the party in Genoa, on 29 November 1869, on their way to Paris, not after their arrival there.
8. Actually seven days.
9. This detail is not corroborated by other sources.
10. Tata's account in her Diary differs on that point (see above, pp. 201–8), as well as on several other details.
11. A chapter of *My Past and Thoughts* (Part VII) on the "young emigration", published in the *Anthology of Posthumous Articles* (Geneva, 1870), under the title "The Common Fund".
12. It bore the explicit heading: "Geneva, 7 March 1870."
13. No such statement appears in the letter.
14. The expression in the letter is "the sad necessity to use less delicate means".
15. Probably should be Arve.
16. Tuchkova's description of Mary Sutherland's role and personality seems to be clearly biased.
17. Must be *couperose*.
18. Compare with Natalie's account in her Diary, above, pp. 211–15.
19. Cf. Natalie's Diary, above, p. 202.
20. This important detail is not to be found in Natalie's Diary.
21. Cf. Natalie's Diary, above, p. 202.
22. Cf. Natalie's Diary, above, p. 205.
23. Maiden name: Erminia Marietti.
24. Compare with Tuchkova's account, above, pp. 365–70.
25. This conversation with Lopatin appears to have taken place in May 1870. According to her Diary, Tata knew not later than February

1870 the role Nechayev had played in the affair of Ivanov (see above, pp. 190, 200).

26. Compare with Tuchkova's account, above, p. 371.

27. In Tuchkova's account, Natalie Herzen did attend that meeting; see above, pp. 362–3.

28. "Of course . . .": Natalie means that she never saw Nechayev again after she learned from Lopatin, according to her reminiscences, that he was an assassin. But the facts are different, for she knew about it before meeting Lopatin and during the time when she had dealings with Nechayev. This detail is worth pointing out—for, in history, assassins too should have the right to a true and accurate account of their actions.

A Note on Sources

THE ORIGINALS of all the previously unpublished documents included in this collection are deposited in the Bibliothèque Nationale in Paris, Département des Manuscrits, *Slave 108, 109, 110*. Also in the Bibliothèque Nationale are several other documents, which have been published in *Cahiers du Monde russe et soviétique* (Russian text and French translation); three of them, translated into English, appeared also in *Encounter*; full references to these publications are given below.

Most of Natalie Herzen's correspondence in this volume is published here for the first time in any language. This includes all the letters to her father (19 letters), to Maria Reichel (20 letters), to Sergey Nechayev (14 letters), to Nathalie Tuchkova-Ogareva (1 letter), as well as five letters to Nikolay Ogarev (items 113, 114, 115, 116, 117); four other letters to Nikolay Ogarev (items 6, 17, 45, 46) have been published in *Literaturnoe nasledstvo*, vol. 63 (Moscow, 1956).

All eight letters of Alexander Herzen (to various correspondents) appeared in his collected works: *Sobranie sochineniy v tridtsati tomakh. Pis'ma* (Moscow, 1961–5), as well as two letters (items 9, 13) of Natalie Herzen to Sasha Herzen (*Sobranie*, vols. XXVII/2, XXVIII).

N. Ogarev's letters to Natalie Herzen (items 3, 25, 27) have been published by M. Mervaud in *Cahiers du Monde russe et soviétique*, X, 1969, nos. 3–4, pp. 478–523.

S. Nechayev's ten letters to Natalie Herzen have been published by T. Bakounine and J. Catteau in *Cahiers du Monde russe et soviétique*, VII, 1966, no. 2, pp. 249–64.

The following documents have been published by M. Confino in *Cahiers du Monde russe et soviétique* (VII, 1966, no. 4, pp. 581–699; VIII, 1967, no. 1, pp. 56–123; no. 3, pp. 452–95; no. 4, pp. 628–36; X, 1969, no. 1, pp. 52–149): six letters of M. Bakunin (items 84, 85, 86, 91, 92, 99), one letter of German Lopatin (item 100), one letter of S. Nechayev (item 97), one letter of N. Herzen (item 89) as well as her Diary (items 35, 80, 93).

Encounter published for the first time in English Natalie's Diary (May 1970), and (July and August 1972) M. Bakunin's letters to S. Nechayev (item 84) and to N. Ogarev, N. Herzen, S. Serebrennikov and V. Ozerov (item 85).

M. Bakunin's letters to N. Ogarev, A. Talandier and V. Mroczkowski appeared in M. P. Dragomanov, *Pis'ma M. A. Bakunina k A. I. Gertsenu i N. P. Ogarevu* (Geneva, 1896); his letter to "the two Natalies" (item 58) in *Literaturnoe nasledstvo*, vol. 63.

N. Tuchkova-Ogareva's recollections (item 119) are from her *Vospominaniya* (Leningrad, 1929).

Natalie Herzen's reminiscences (item 120) were first published in
Posledniya novosti (Paris), no. 3614, 13 February 1931, and thereafter in
Literaturnoe nasledstvo, vol. 63, where Natalie's "A Photograph (From the
Original)" (item 28) also appeared.

For a few documents, not mentioned here (items 81, 82, 106), references
are given in the Introduction or with the texts.

The original of all the documents is in the Russian language, except for
part of one letter of Natalie to Sasha (item 13, in English), and one letter of
Bakunin to Talandier (item 94, in French).

Glossary of Names, Nicknames,
Noms de Plume *and* Noms de Guerre

THIS GLOSSARY is intended to serve as a guide for identifying the most frequently mentioned people in the texts. Items appear in alphabetical order, not necessarily by family name.

Aga: Nikolay Ogarev.

Antonia (Antosya) Ksaweryevna Bakunin (*née* Kwiatkowska): Michael Bakunin's wife.

Bakunin, Michael (1814–76): Russian anarchist and revolutionary leader.

The Baron: Sergey Nechayev.

Barsov: Sergey Nechayev.

Boy: Sergey Nechayev.

Charlotte Hudson: an English girl with whom Alexander Herzen *fils* had a liaison and a child (Toots); lived at Ogarev's, first in Lancy, then in Geneva. Committed suicide in 1867 in the Geneva lake; the body was found three years later in the Rhône.

Czerniecki, Ludwik (1828–72): Polish *émigré*; manager of the Free Russian Press in London and in Geneva; close friend of the Herzens.

Granovsky, Timofey Nikolaevich (1813–55): professor of history at Moscow University; friend of Alexander Herzen. Served Dostoevsky as one of the types for the portrayal of Stefan Trofimovich in *The Possessed*.

Henry Sutherland (born 1851): the son of Mary Sutherland.

Herzen, Alexander Alexandrovich (Sasha) (1839–1906): Herzen's son; physiologist.

Herzen, Alexander Alexandrovich (Toots): the son of Alexander Herzen *fils* and Charlotte Hudson.

Herzen, Alexander Ivanovich (1812–70): Russian radical; brilliant publicist and memoirist; son of Ivan Yakovlev and Louisa Haag. Lived in exile in Western Europe from 1847.

Herzen, Alexey Alexandrovich (Lelya-boy) (1861–4): son of Herzen and Nathalie Tuchkova-Ogareva.

Herzen, Egor Ivanovich (1803–82): Herzen's brother.

Herzen, Elena Alexandrovna (Lelya-girl) (1861–4): daughter of Herzen and Nathalie Tuchkova-Ogareva.

Herzen, Elizaveta Alexandrovna (Liza) (1858–75): daughter of Herzen and Nathalie Tuchkova-Ogareva. Committed suicide.

Herzen, Natalie Alexandrovna (née Zakharyna) (1817–52): Herzen's cousin and wife.

Herzen, Natalie Alexandrovna (Tata) (1844–1936): Herzen's daughter.

Herzen, Olga Alexandrovna (1850–1953): Herzen's daughter; married Gabriel Monod.

Iskander: Alexander Herzen's *nom de plume*.

Lelya-boy: Alexey Herzen.

Lelya-girl: Elena Herzen.

Levier, Emmanuel: physician in Florence; friend and colleague of Sasha Herzen in Maurice Schiff's laboratory.

Liza: Elizaveta Herzen.

Luginin, Vladimir Fedorovich (1834–1911): Russian radical and *émigré*; later professor of chemistry at Moscow University.

Mamasha: Natalie Herzen (Tata's mother).

Mary Sutherland: a prostitute Ogarev met in London, who thereafter lived with him.

Masha: Maria Reichel.

Mechnikov, Lev Ilych (1838–88): geographer and sociologist; participated in Garibaldi's campaign in 1860; wrote for *The Bell* and edited in Switzerland the journal *Sovremennost (The Present)* (1868). Returned to Russia in 1871.

Meshchersky, Alexander Nikolaevich (prince) (1844–?): formerly a student in geography; lived in Switzerland; a friend of the Herzens.

Meysenbug, Malwida Amalia von (1816–1903): German memoirist and translator; in 1852 emigrated to London; from 1853 Olga Herzen's governess.

Mikhail Alexandrovich: Michael Bakunin.

Monod, Gabriel (1844–1912): French historian; son of a businessman in Le Havre, and descendant of a Swiss protestant family. Married Olga Herzen in 1873.

Mroczkowski, Valerian (Mruk) (1840–89): Polish *émigré*; participated in the Polish uprising of 1863; member of Bakunin's Fraternité and Alliance internationale de la Démocratie socialiste.

Nechayev, Sergey Gennadievich (1847–82): Russian revolutionist; born of a poor family in the village Ivanovo-Voznesensk; failed in his examinations for schoolmaster; tried unsuccessfully to set up revolutionary groups among the students in St Petersburg and Moscow. Organized the murder of the student I. Ivanov. Arrested in Switzerland in 1872 and extradited to Russia as common criminal. Died in the Peter and Paul Fortress. Served as prototype for Verkhovensky in Dostoevsky's novel *The Possessed* (1871–2). Also known as *Neville; Volkov; Barsov; Boy; Baron;* etc.

Neville: S. Nechayev.

Ogarev, Nikolay Platonovich (1813–77): Herzen's lifelong friend; publicist; co-editor of *The Bell*.

Osip Ivanovich: Giuseppe Mazzini.

Ozerov, Vladimir Alexandrovich (1838–*c.*1915): revolutionist and *émigré*; a Russian officer, he participated in the Polish uprising; friend of Bakunin and member of the Geneva section of the First International.

Pan: S. Tchorzewski.

Papasha: Alexander Herzen (Tata's father).

Penisi (Count) (1842–?): a blind Italian nobleman from Sicily; lived in Florence; occupied himself with music and literary work; translated some of Herzen's writings into Italian; a friend of E. Levier.

Reichel, Maria Kasparovna (*née* Ern) (1823–1916): a close friend of the Herzens; lived in Berne; wife of Adolf Reichel (1817–96), German musician and composer.

Sallier: Vladimir Serebrennikov.

Sasha: Alexander Herzen *fils.*

Schiff, Hugo: German physician and acquaintance of the Herzens; lived in Florence with his eldest brother, Maurice Schiff (1825–96), a physiologist, where he served as professor of comparative anatomy in 1865–76.

Serebrennikov, Semen Ivanovich: born in Siberia; from 1864 studied at the Polytechnic Institute in St Petersburg and worked as printer; collaborated with Nechayev in 1868; from 1869 a student in Zurich; arrested in 1874 in Prussia and delivered to the Russian authorities.

Serebrennikov, Vladimir Ivanovich (*c.*1850–?): son of a police officer and student of medicine in St Petersburg; took part in the student movement in 1869, was arrested and succeeded in escaping abroad in November 1869; Nechayev's inseparable comrade in Switzerland and London. Arrested in Russia in May 1873.

Serno-Solovevich, Alexander Alexandrovich (1838–69): Russian revolutionary; an exile from 1862 and one of the leaders of the "young emigration".

Talandier, Alfred Pierre Théodore (1822–90): French lawyer; participated in the 1848 Revolution, then emigrated to England; an acquaintance of Herzen and friend of Bakunin.

Tata: Natalie Herzen.

Tchorzewski, Stanislaw (Pan): an exile from 1845; owned a bookstore and library for Polish *émigrés* in London; worked as Herzen's closest assistant in the publication and diffusion of *The Bell*; in 1865 moved with the Herzens to Geneva and practically became a member of the household.

Teresina Felice (1851–1927): an Italian girl from a modest Florentine family; married Alexander Herzen *fils* in August 1868.

Toots: Alexandre, the son of Alexander Herzen *fils* and Charlotte Hudson.

Tuchkova-Ogareva, Nathalie Alexeevna (1829–1923): Ogarev's second wife; lived with Herzen from 1857 on.

Utin, Nikolay Isaakovich (1841–83): Russian radical and son of a wealthy contractor; emigrated in 1863; editor of *The People's Cause (Narodnoe Delo)*, 1868–70; a founder of the Russian section of the First International; follower of K. Marx. Later on renounced all political activity and was allowed to return to Russia.

Vogt: family name of four brothers, acquaintances of the Herzens and Bakunin: Adolf (1823–1907), physician and professor at Berne University; Gustav (1829–1901), publicist and editor of the *Neue Zürcher Zeitung* and *Les Etats-Unis d'Europe*. Karl (1817–95), political *émigré*, naturalist and philosopher, professor at Geneva University, member of several state councils in Switzerland; Emile (1820–83), lawyer.

Volkov: S. Nechayev.

Zamperini: Italian radical; member of the Geneva section of the First International.

Zhukovsky, Nikolay Ivanovich (1833–95): Russian revolutionist and *émigré* from 1862; edited with Bakunin the first number of *The People's Cause (Narodnoe Delo)*, 1 September 1868; founded with him the Alliance internationale de la Démocratie socialiste; member of the First International.

Contents

Daughter of a Revolutionary

Natalie Herzen and the Bakunin–Nechayev Circle

Preface

Introduction

I

Russian Aristocrats as Professional Exiles

II

Russian Exiles as Professional Revolutionaries